# AIDS, Sex, and Culture

For Philip and Jonah

# AIDS, Sex, and Culture

## Global Politics and Survival in Southern Africa

*Ida Susser*

*with a contribution by Sibongile Mkhize*

**WILEY-BLACKWELL**

A John Wiley & Sons, Ltd., Publication

Blackwell Publishing was acquired by John Wiley & Sons in February 2007. Blackwell's publishing program
has been merged with Wiley's global Scientific, Technical, and Medical business to form Wiley-Blackwell.

*Registered Office*
John Wiley & Sons Ltd, The Atrium, Southern Gate, Chichester, West Sussex, PO19 8SQ, United Kingdom

*Editorial Offices*
350 Main Street, Malden, MA 02148-5020, USA
9600 Garsington Road, Oxford, OX4 2DQ, UK
The Atrium, Southern Gate, Chichester, West Sussex, PO19 8SQ, UK

For details of our global editorial offices, for customer services, and for information about how to apply
for permission to reuse the copyright material in this book please see our website at www.wiley.com/
wiley-blackwell.

*Library of Congress Cataloging-in-Publication Data*

Susser, Ida.
   AIDS, culture, and gender in southern Africa / Ida Susser.
      p. ; cm.
   Includes bibliographical references and index.
   ISBN 978-1-4051-5586-1 (hardcover : alk. paper) – ISBN 978-1-4051-5587-8 (pbk. : alk.
paper)   1. AIDS (Disease)–Social aspects–Africa, Southern.   I. Title.
   [DNLM:   1. Acquired Immunodeficiency Syndrome–prevention & control–Africa South of the
Sahara.   2. Gender Identity–Africa South of the Sahara.   3. Preventive Health Services–Africa South of
the Sahara.   4. Sexual Behavior–Africa South of the Sahara.   5. Socioeconomic Factors–Africa South of
the Sahara.   6. Women's Health–Africa South of the Sahara.  WC 503.6 S9646a 2009]
   RA643.86.A356S87 2009
   362.196′979200968–dc22

                                                                                                    2008037694

A catalogue record for this book is available from the British Library.

Set in 10.5 on 13 pt Minion by SNP Best-set Typesetter Ltd., Hong Kong
Printed in Singapore by C.O.S. Printers Pte Ltd

1   2009

# Contents

# List of Figures

# Preface

## *Southern Africa: A Personal Geography, History, and Politics*

Feminists and anthropologists have long recognized that understanding the author's position is an important aspect in interpreting text. For this reason I have decided to situate myself at the beginning of this book in terms of my own personal history and politics. I believe this is one way in which an author claims neither more credibility nor legitimacy than they are entitled to, but claims anyway the right to speak from whatever background they may have emerged. Those readers who regard this as irrelevant may skip this section.

As neither a South African nor completely an outsider, I have chosen to take advantage of my ambiguous standing and to address crucial and controversial issues from a global and comparative perspective. In both South Africa and the United States, HIV/AIDS, sexuality, women's place, and global corporate investment are highly explosive topics. I argue in this book that growing inequalities have generated sharp divisions buttressed by identity politics.

As a woman born in South Africa, I take the contemporary tragedies of HIV/AIDS as a personal as well as a political concern. However, this stance does not represent any theoretical espousal of the constraints of identity politics. My first book was based on research as somewhat of a foreigner in New York City. Perhaps I had the advantage at that time that the United States still appeared to me as mysterious and exciting. I have never known what country to claim as my own or even any way to describe my accent. As a consequence, a universalistic framework seemed the path of least resistance.

The analysis in this volume is based on fieldwork and the systematic tracing of particular events across space and time. The journey and the perspective taken derive from my own peripatetic experience, stretched across oceans and lacking national allegiance. I have focused on southern Africa but at the same time drawn into the analysis significant events that have taken place in the United States as well as discussions of the transformations in global capital.[1] In addition, I have developed a comparative analysis of the ways in which national policies in South Africa and the US frame women's chances for liberty, equality, and the pursuit of happiness.

Ethnography is a form of science that in many ways relies on the art of creative and synthetic analysis in connecting the uneventful happenings of everyday life to broader themes. In a brilliant article summarizing the work of situational analysis in what came to be known as the Manchester School of anthropology, Jaap Van Velsen (1967) delineated the importance of ethnography in capturing the early signs of social change rather than the statistical rendition of established behavior. Van Velsen was a student of Max Gluckman, a South African-born anthropologist who led the Manchester School and was himself trained by one of the founders of the discipline of anthropology, Bronislaw Malinowski. Van Velsen succeeded Gluckman as director of the Zambian Institute of Social Research and later became Professor of Sociology at the University of Aberystwyth in Wales. As he recognized, the power of ethnography can be its ability to sense trends or transformations as they emerge.[2]

In the past three decades, anthropologists have come to analyze and incorporate more explicitly the idea that ethnography is part humanism and part science.[3] As a science, requiring detailed on-the-ground observations, it is based on humanism in that the observations are mediated by the intuitive researcher. Insights are generated through a form of immersion of the self in the data and a reevaluation of all hints and experiences. Similar to the idea of transference in psychological analysis, ethnography puts the self in the equation. I would argue that the self can be called into question in the process and in many cases is never quite the same afterwards. In fact, that change which takes place in the ethnographer as she or he works in a place or interviews people is perhaps the source of the intuitive understanding of a society or cultural setting. A good ethnographer combines theoretical rigor with the continuing interpretation and rethinking of chance circumstance, everyday dynamics, historical events, and passing conversations. Such observations are not necessarily representative but rather indicative of larger conceptions.

Thus, recent discussions in anthropology suggest that situational analysis be illuminated and rethought with an emphasis on the reflexive. The patterns and features identified or deciphered depend partly on the varied experiences and frameworks of the ethnographer: the self that entered the field and the potential transformations of self by the field. From this point of view, I believe that my own life and the way I encountered southern Africa and the centers of capital in the United States are significant historical factors framing the arguments in this book. In the spirit of collaboration with many other researchers and approaches (Altman 2001; Campbell 2003; Farmer et al. 1993; Nattrass 2007; Parker et al. 2000), I offer this as one perspective in a broader effort to understand the global pandemic of HIV.

As the granddaughter of Jewish immigrants who fled to South Africa to escape the pogroms of eastern Europe in the late nineteenth century, I did not suffer as did black South Africans from the bitter oppressions of segregation, poverty, and the racist violence of a police state. I was reared in the shadow of apartheid and, fortunately, the light of the anti-apartheid movement. My parents, Mervyn Susser and Zena Stein, were led by their experiences fighting against Nazi Germany in World War II to reorient their professional interests from early training in English and history toward medicine and eventually public health.

In 1948, the Nationalist government was elected in South Africa on the platform of apartheid. Nationalist Party policies aimed at the black population echoed those of Hitler's Germany and were explicitly positively compared with National Socialism by the Party leadership. By 1950, when I was born, my parents, along with many of their friends and relatives, were already immersed in the battle against apartheid. Simultaneously, they were taking their final medical school examinations.

Under this oppressive regime, the Communist Party became the only non-racial anti-apartheid group still active. Many people, disillusioned by reports of Stalin's repressive policies and his 1939 pact with Hitler, had abandoned the Communist Party in the 1940s but later joined with the South African Communist Party (SACP) to fight apartheid. In 1952, the Communist Party was banned by the apartheid government but then re-formed underground as the South African Communist Party. Party members formed underground cells, connected only by pairs, four to a cell. As activists were forced into exile, many, including my relatives, left the CP but were unable to discuss the topic because of anti-communist regimes in the United States, Australia, and many of the other countries to which they fled. Secrecy was so great that my mother and her brother did not tell each other until 50 years later that each of them had joined in the early 1950s and operated from different cells.

In my early years, we lived in Johannesburg. With my parents' full-time commitment to medicine and politics, our family life resembled that portrayed in Shawn Slovo's film *A World Apart*. In fact, Shawn is the oldest daughter of Joe Slovo and Ruth First and we are only a few months separated in age – my mother claims that the pregnancy clothes were handed from Ruth to Myrtle Berman to her as each of them became pregnant with their first child. This ritual was repeated consecutively with the second and third children. In between, the clothes were dry cleaned at the Immaculate Cleaners, a business Monty Berman inherited from his father. (The Bermans were both anti-apartheid activists and, later, exiles with their children in London.)

Most of the politically active families I knew involved active mothers as well as active fathers. The mothers were heroic intellectuals, activists, and strong role models for their daughters. However, as documented by one such historic mother, Hilda Bernstein, in *Rivonia's Children: Three Families and the Cost of Conscience in White South Africa*, and as the South African Nobel Prize-winning author Nadine Gordimer describes in her novel *Burger's Daughter*, the general parental preoccupation with politics generated feelings of abandonment and unimportance among many children of this era. Sometimes, parents were taken to prison in the early dawn and children were left in shock and alone. Politics may have led to a sense of parental remoteness from childish traumas and a general focus on "more important matters" pervaded such childhoods. After his wife Ruth's death, Joe Slovo, born in a Yiddish shtetl in Lithuania, a founder and leader of the South African Communist

Party for 50 years, as well as of the armed wing of the ANC, possibly began to understand his daughters' perspectives on their family life. He wrote in *Slovo – The Unfinished Autobiography*, "One thing is clear, however; the world would be a poorer place if it was peopled by children whose parents risked nothing in the cause of social justice, for fear of personal loss. If I regret anything, it is certainly not how my daughters turned out but rather that we might have found a way of easing the hidden traumas they were suffering. . . ." (Dolny 1995:111). Slovo lived to plan new housing for the poor as the first Minister of Housing in post-apartheid South Africa.

Most children of such activists suffered much greater disruption and dislocation than I ever did. I only lived this kind of life in South Africa for my first five years. Later, when I returned to South Africa in the 1990s, I came to know cousins and friends who had stayed through many traumatic years and, in fact, were the original models for the children in Gordimer's novel. One model for a fictional character in *Burger's Daughter*, who paid a high price for her family's political struggle, was my cousin, Sheila Weinberg, born in Johannesburg immediately after World War II. Her parents, after spending months in detention without trial and subjected to police interrogation, were banned for five years, which meant that they were confined to their own home and were constrained in whom they could meet or even with whom they could speak. Later, they left South Africa to live in exile in Tanzania. Sheila herself was detained without trial for 65 days at the age of 17 and had to take the full burden of responsibility when her brother died, suspected of suicide, while their parents were in prison. From 1994 to 2004, she served as a Member of Parliament for Gauteng in the new South Africa, concentrating especially on financial policies. In November 2004, at the age of 59, she died suddenly of a brain aneurysm.

My early memories of Johannesburg are few. I can visualize the nuns who ran Alexandra Clinic, where both my parents shared one doctor's position and another politically active couple, Michael Hathorn and Margaret Cormack, shared the other. I remember the long corridors where the patients waited. Even then I was aware of the daily racial inequities. The horror and urgency of apartheid in South Africa, vividly lived in Alexandra Township, was especially symbolized for me in images of the suffering of people coming to the clinic. Following so immediately after World War II and the Holocaust, as I was reminded as an impressionable young child by my parents, this seared images of fear and misery deep into my psyche. At that time, I had yet to develop the strong defenses or independent opinions in relation to my parents' overwhelming political and emotional engagement.

However, I also remember wonderful experiences from my childhood in South Africa – the freedom and the wild, wide-ranging sense of sun and fresh air on the large cooperative farm where we lived. I learned to swim in the small round pool with no shallow end. My four-year-old cousin swam across the pool under water like a mermaid, with her long scraggly blonde hair trailing after her, never coming up to breathe because she never learned how. Even at that age, I could proudly breathe and swim at the same time. We roamed freely across the farm as most of our parents were gone most of the time, and, anyway, they believed in greater freedom and exploration than I could ever allow my children growing up in the United States. I climbed right to the top of high trees with the six- and seven-year-old boys, after we helped each other up the first hard step of the bare but gnarled trunk. I remember clearly the exhilaration of reaching the top of a tree perhaps 20 feet high, with the wind blowing through the thin spiky branches. The children on the farm ran free with no shoes and we proudly compared the hard soles of our feet. (Even as somewhat disaffected exile-children in London, feeling out of place and unable to conform to English manners, my cousins and I would still compete over who could walk over the spikiest pebbles or glass.)

I remember the sense of warmth, well-being, and familiarity, playing in the sand on the long, wide crowded beaches at Muizenburg, a popular resort outside Cape Town. I would sit next to the parasol under which my grandmother set her chair, doubly protecting herself from the sun with a wide straw hat, a pretty blue ribbon tied around its brim. In spite of her apparent domesticity, my grandmother had been an early feminist and, also reflecting the adventurous outdoor esprit of white colonial South Africa, she was renowned in the family for staying in the ocean the longest of any swimmer. I heard many stories about my parents scrambling up Table Mountain with me in their backpack. We had family pictures of both of them climbing in the challenging and unpredictable Drakensberg mountains which stretched across the borders of South Africa and Basotoland (now Lesotho), encountering hair-raising adventures as streams suddenly turned into torrents or a sunny day was transformed into mist and cold.

In England, my brother slept under a Basotho blanket and our lampshades were contrived from hats made and worn by the Sotho peoples. My brother and I fought over the extraordinarily colored and smoothly warm and comforting blanket, and the name Basotho conjured up romance and mystery. However, although it was a household word to me, I could not have told you where on the map of southern Africa such a place existed. In London, my father read us the classic *Jock of the Bushfeld*, written in 1907 by Sir Percival Fitzpatrick. Fitzpatrick's recounting of his nineteenth-century colonial childhood, learning to track animals and survive in the bush with his dog, takes place in the Transvaal near where my father grew up. My father told us of his childhood on the remote tin mine where his father ran a small unprofitable hotel. He recounted his own exploits wandering through the bush, encountering snakes and hunting small deer. As an older child in England, these memories and stories painted a nostalgic image of the vast natural beauty of southern Africa.

In 1999, when I visited the old hotel, which was, in fact, still there, my father showed us his mother's grave. The tombstone was set apart, some meters distant from the other graves, because hers was the lone Jewish burial in this Christian cemetery.

In July 1955, my father had agreed to speak out publicly against an upcoming controversial case in the implementation of apartheid. Judge Oliver Schreiner, then one of the judges on the Supreme Court and one of the judges in the case, was also chair of the board of Alexandra Clinic. Schreiner objected to the fact that my father had agreed to appear on a critical panel organized by the African National Congress. Rather than agree to the political strictures of the Alexandra Clinic board, my parents left their shared job at the Township Clinic. With three small children in tow, they moved to my grandparents' apartment in Durban. My grandfather, Philip Stein, an early South African graduate of Caius College, Cambridge, was the first professor of mathematics at what was then a Technical College and is now the University of KwaZulu-Natal.

My most vivid memory of Durban at that time is of the enormous number of little monkeys that inhabited every tree in the vicinity. Our apartment complex stood near a little park where I used to swing and watch the Vervet monkeys, babies clamped on mothers' backs, careen through the trees. Sometimes, the sun came through after short-lived showers, creating a rainbow that my grandmother called a "monkey's wedding." My grandfather and I would walk past sugar cane fields, both chewing the cane he cut, as we climbed the terraced grounds up to his office at the university. When I returned for the first time in 1992, post-apartheid, urban development had left not a monkey to be seen.

My parents used the enforced free time of their unemployment in Durban to study with Sidney Kark, who was developing "community health clinics" – a concept and model later to be replicated around the world. Indeed, following Kark's model in South Africa, the first community health center in the United States was founded by Jack Geiger, now a family friend, in Bayou, Mississippi after he visited Kark in Durban on a student internship from Case Western Reserve Medical School. Similarly, Violet Padayachi Cherry, who ran the Englewood, New Jersey, Department of Social Services for 30 years, was inspired to pursue a career in community services by her early involvement with Kark's Community Health Center as a teenager in a poor Durban neighborhood. In an unexpected continuity, in 1997, when Richard Lee and I interviewed an extraordinarily active and effective community health director concerned with HIV/AIDS in Rundu in the Kavango region of Northern Namibia, it turned out that she, too, as a young African nurse in apartheid South Africa, had been trained under the auspices of Sidney Kark.

As a result of my parents' departure from Alexandra Clinic for political reasons, it was difficult for them to secure further paid employment in South Africa. At five-and-a-half years of age, I found myself aboard the steamer *Dunotter Castle* bound for Europe. I can still visualize the great ship majestically pulling out from Durban's Victoria Embankment. As we proceeded beyond the rows of sand reefs that rose up from the tide, bathers shouted and played far out in the ocean on their way to stand on these temporary islands. I, of course, had no idea of our future, but the scene remains in my memory as a momentous end to an era.

As my mother tried valiantly to keep three small children occupied after my baby sister woke up our cabin at dawn, we gazed for hours at the ocean and tracked the gulls and the flying fish. One afternoon the whole ship was alerted as we sailed past a large slate-like rock with water spraying out. Word was that it was an enormous whale but I was never quite convinced.

As we passed the equator, the ship's company and passengers indulged in a variety of folk rituals. They sprayed people with shaving cream and threw them and others fully clothed in suits and dresses into the swimming pool. They pretended to cut a lady in half, and to cut off people's legs, all in the name of crossing zero latitude. This was rather horrifying to me. I had not yet seen any television cartoons or the weekly newsreels with the pat comedy routines. For years afterwards, I looked warily for ladies with amputated legs. For this event, we were finally allowed into the area of the deck that was designated first class. True to the long tradition of British class division, dramatized in the sinking of the Titanic when the first-class passengers had priority access to the lifeboats, the *Dunotter Castle* was rigidly divided into first and second class. I already knew that first class had a large white tile-lined swimming pool in contrast to the dark green canvas-lined cavity held together by thick ropes in which we generally splashed, but this was the only time I stood near its edge. Apparently, crossing the equator had emerged over the centuries of exploration and colonial rule as a liminal experience in which British sea travelers temporarily violated rules of class and status.

It was on the ship, too, that I learned to read. British children started school earlier than South African children. In fact, my unshackled childhood owed much to this difference. Now that we were about to arrive in England, where children had already been in school for at least a year, my parents enlisted a nun on board ship as a teacher. While my brother and sister were assigned to day care, my tutor and I sat in deck chairs overlooking the ocean and reading sentences: "See Dick and Jane!" "See the ball." "See the dog!"

After three memorable weeks at sea, we landed at the British port of Southampton in the depths of winter. Snow was exciting but the cold was unfamiliar and brutal. My parents dragged us three children from one London boarding house to another over the grey damp winter months. In each new place, they were very careful with the shillings that we put in to extract a little heat from the electric burners. They paid little attention to what they viewed as "bourgeois" concepts of warm boots or other winter paraphernalia and they firmly believed in long, healthy walks. As a consequence we were frequently prone to frostbite as we marched off, colonials steeped in English folklore, to see such famous sites as the Peter Pan statue in Kensington Gardens. We wore waterproof boots and thin cotton socks. As we were told, in colonial admiration for all things English, these were the same garments sported by Christopher Robin in A. A. Milne's poem: "I've got great big waterproof boots on. . . ." Such comparatively cheap footwear, designed for summer rain, was not much use in snow and ice and most outings were accompanied by extensive crying and complaints.

As the oldest child, and expected by my parents to be responsible in difficult times, I was always most aware of the conflict we had left behind. I was both frightened and inspired by the implications of South Africa, as well as the slightly more distant stories of my father's military experience in World War II and my grandmother's accounts of relatives disappeared in the Holocaust. Her stories were eerily accompanied by letters from faraway places stamped "no known address" and returned unopened. My father's youngest uncle, Boris, and his three aunts, whose names were seemingly less significant but remembered by my father as Sophie, Bayla, and Masha, had stayed behind in the family home at Lutzen, 200 miles from Riga, now in Latvia, when the three older brothers migrated to South Africa. In 1933, posed laughing and looking surprisingly contemporary, sitting on the step in front of the Zusser butcher's shop, they were photographed by one of the brothers, George Susser, visiting from South Africa to check on their situation. In one photograph, which has come down through the family, the woman, who seems to be in her thirties, is dressed in a short sack dress, reminiscent of a flapper, with a cheerful sardonic look. In 1946, when my father's aunt returned to Lutzen to search for their relatives, no trace remained. She spent five years working with the Red Cross and other agencies devoted to tracing missing persons from the Holocaust but no one could suggest any leads to follow. Eli Weinberg, married to my father's cousin, Violet, and Sheila Weinberg's father, was long active in the anti-apartheid movement. He was quite explicit about the converging histories of fascism in Europe and apartheid in South Africa. He escaped anti-Semitism in a tortuous passage from Latvia and, in 1929, arrived as a young man in South Africa. When the Nationalist Party came to power in South Africa, he said that there was no point in running further. He had come all this way and found that this time he had to fight fascism where he found it. It was Eli who made a book of photos of me at two years old in the sand pit and on the swing. It would be hard to overstate the long-term effects of these collected histories on my thinking.

Wherever we lived after we left South Africa – London, Manchester, Kanpur in India or New York City – my parents were constantly involved and in touch with the anti-apartheid movement and were in fact founders of the anti-apartheid in London and Manchester. For the first year, we lived among exiles in London and my parents moved in a circle of South Africans. But even later, after we moved to Manchester and elsewhere, the London circle remained their touchstone, where we went for most holidays. We attended anti-apartheid rallies in London; we listened to South African Kwela music and to the historic South African musical *King Kong*, which we were immediately taken to see when it came to the UK. Although I followed events in South Africa, as I grew to be a teenager, I rebelled against what I viewed as excessive preoccupations with a South African heritage.

After we moved to Manchester, my parents formed a local anti-apartheid group and I remember the day, in 1963, when anti-apartheid activists Harold Wolpe and Arthur Goldreich, who had just escaped from a South African prison, came to speak in Manchester. Several times we marched along Wilmslow Road, in those days the street connecting the village of Didsbury to the central shopping area of Manchester. We were a bedraggled group, maybe 20 people strong, of whom half were young children, walking through the northern English drizzle, carrying anti-apartheid placards. I recollect that our little contingent was led by Mary Gluckman, the stalwart, progressive English wife of the well-known South African born anthropologist Max Gluckman.

I always felt different in England, perhaps privileged to be connected to a lively, cosmopolitan, artistic, and intellectual exile community and partly deprived and embarrassed because I was not a "normal" English schoolgirl. I was somewhat uncomfortable that my mother worked and did not stay home to cook and clean house, although, of course, I grew up to do the same. I was more embarrassed that we had no religion, despite out Jewish heritage. In my primary school in the 1950s, when morning prayers occurred I was sent off to a special room for Jewish children. At the age of six, my parents sent me to school on a Jewish holiday and I found myself all alone in the special Jewish room, a strong message about the differentness of our family. I discovered recently that my sister, four years younger and much more comfortably "English," simply went to the daily assembly and Church of England prayers. Ironically, my sons have told me that, like my parents before me, I did not give them an adequate historical knowledge of their own Jewish background. But, they are similarly steeped in the history of South Africa.

As a ten-year-old, I was still absorbing my parents' politics and as such I devised my own political activism. In May 1960, when the Sharpeville massacre took place in South Africa, I went to the principal of my primary school and requested permission to collect money to help the protesters who had been shot down by South African government helicopters. I proudly gathered a fund of about two pounds and eight shillings from my school friends and sent it to an organization in London. Although I had not realized, it was even difficult to send money directly to South Africa to help the protesters under the apartheid regime. In those days, South Africa represented the heart of my active political existence.

Even after we left South Africa, my childhood and early adolescence were darkened by the specter of apartheid, and intertwined with the excitements as well as desperation generated by the history of the anti-apartheid movement. We heard about the Rivonia trials and the arrest of the parents of many of our childhood friends and then more emigrants started to arrive in London. My cousins showed up several years after us, when my uncle was fired from his job. As the editor of *Drum*, he had printed a picture on the front cover of a white woman tennis player kissing a black woman tennis player who had just won an international match. Later, Monty and Myrtle Berman, an international with whom my mother had shared maternity clothes, and their four daughters arrived. South African exiles also came to Manchester, assisted by my parents and others at the University. My friends were the daughters and sons of South Africans in exile, underfoot at London parties, surrounded by African music, Kwela dancing, and fierce political discussion.

In my early teens, I became involved with the British Campaign for Nuclear Disarmament. However, even then I marched the four days from Aldermaston to London protesting nuclear proliferation alongside the children of South African exiles. We had digested our parents' general principles of the struggle for social justice, but we wanted to fight our political battles in the new countries where we had all tried so valiantly to fit in. Those very sons and daughters of Africa were to become leaders in the 1968 student protests at the London School of Economics.

In 1965, after my family emigrated to the United States, we were abruptly cut off from this vibrant political community, although we returned in the summers to stay with relatives in London. In 1966, a freshman at Barnard College, I joined other American university students protesting the Vietnam War. I made a conscious decision to live as an American and not to stay an exile forever. To me, trying to readjust as my family traveled from country to country, focusing on South Africa began to appear like avoiding a connection with my own daily reality. I distanced myself from my parents' ongoing commitment to the African National Congress. Nevertheless, in New York City, too, I found myself in the swirl of South African émigrés passing through, who often stayed with my parents or in my student apartment as they tried to establish new homes for themselves in the United States.

Trying to understand my own place in the world, I inhaled all the works of Doris Lessing, a southern African novelist and member of the London exile community. I read the *Golden Notebook* and the preceding volumes of the *Children of Violence Series*, took courses on politics in Africa, specifically at that time the independence movements and the war in Biafra, and majored in anthropology. As a result, I found myself reading the monographs on the Zambian copperbelt written by the Manchester professors among whose children I was reared.

In 1968, as a sophomore, I took a doctoral course with Immanuel Wallerstein who was greatly respected among politically active students at the time. Wallerstein was outlining his fledgling theory of the emergence of capitalism as an interconnected system, later published in his path-breaking volume *The Modern World-System* (Wallerstein 1974). I had a hard time following the lectures. I mainly remember little chalk circles on the board that apparently represented his view of multiple classes of professionals and businessmen in different societies. I also remember undergraduate men from Students for a Democratic Society, the largest student movement of the 1960s predominantly focused on ending the Vietnam War and very active on the Columbia campus, articulately and fearlessly standing up in class and arguing each point with the professor. That was the atmosphere of the times – for young men of political bent and white male privilege, inspired by anger at the Vietnam War and the omnipresent threat of being drafted. However, as an anxious young woman, I participated in all the demonstrations and activities but had neither the courage nor the encouragement and support to speak up whether in class or at meetings.

Eventually, I read Wallerstein's work on nationalism and ethnicity in Africa and chose to write a paper on a related topic. I took an incomplete and spent weeks of the following summer at the library of the London School of Economics in Gower Street reading rather aimlessly and trying to figure out what to do. Finally, I approached Ruth First, a leading South African anti-apartheid activist and a constant visitor at my cousin's house, and asked her for help. I believe she was writing her book *From the Barrel of a Gun* and she generously gave me a number of reprints on various aspects of political economy and ethnicity in Africa. That fall, after months of angst – and, most unforgivably, because of guilt about this project, skipping a trip to a certain music festival at Woodstock – I handed a paper to Wallerstein based on First's articles. I barely managed to achieve a C in his course.

Living in New York City, I continued to read most of what First wrote – from *117 Days* (1965), her description of life in solitary confinement under "preventive detention" (in other words, without trial), to her biography of Olive Schreiner (1980). Olive Schreiner had always been an important historical feminist figure in South Africa and one of my favorite writers. My cousin, who through her teenage years still swam only underwater like a bedraggled mermaid, was named after Schreiner's independent and rebellious heroine, Lyndall, in *The Story of an African Farm* (Schreiner 1924). First wrote about Schreiner, who like Doris Lessing and First herself was born in southern Africa but spent much of her life in revolutionary or at least progressive circles in Britain. Reading Schreiner, Lessing, and First informed my own struggles as a woman, adding depth to my understanding of what it meant to be a feminist, a white South African woman in exile, and a political activist.

Based in many places and rethinking, as each generation of women is forced to do – a woman's place in a man's intellectual world – Lessing and Schreiner were as much concerned with women's sexuality as their employment or country of origin. First chose to write about Schreiner, who perhaps was more like the early twentieth-century Russian analysts of free love Emma Goldman and Alexandra Kolontai than the austere figure I envisioned First to be. In fact, however, I was probably misunderstanding her. As a naïve and intimidated young girl, I imagined that First, a grown woman and sharp-witted, politically active scholar, must be without emotional conflicts and personal tensions. In reading some of the biographical material about her, I have come to think that First, renowned among her political comrades as a most beautiful woman, may also have been considering some of the dilemmas of sexuality and woman's place when she chose to research the life of Olive Schreiner. Sadly, in 1982 in Mozambique, Ruth First was killed by a letter bomb planted by the South African secret police – an act of state terrorism that also injured anthropologist Bridget O'Laughlin.

Clearly it was over-determined that I go into anthropology, or at least work in an international setting. My image of research was based on a romantic ideal of understanding the lives of people oppressed and undermined from apartheid rule, whom, in spite of my own extensive academic reading in the area (in completing a master's degree at the University of Chicago under the supervision of the Africanist anthropologist Lloyd Fallers), I envisioned in terms of the acclaimed memoir *Down Second Avenue* by my parents' friend Ezekiel (Es'kia) Mphahlele and the novel *Second Class Taxi* by my uncle Sylvester Stein. Both books were banned in South Africa. My uncle's book, a hilarious satire of apartheid in the 1950s, hardly sold but was finally hailed as a literary classic in Nadine Gordimer's recent review of South African literature.

In 1973, on entering the doctoral program in anthropology at Columbia University, an ongoing preoccupation with Africa was reflected in my application essay, stating that I wanted to research race and ethnicity and that for my dissertation I planned to go to southern Africa to do fieldwork in an urban township. In the end, however, I conducted my doctoral research in Brooklyn, New York, concerned with working-class social movements and the transformation of women's lives by the New York City fiscal crisis. An early harbinger of the dismantlement of the welfare provisions in the United States, and structural adjustment policies applied at home, the work was published as *Norman Street: Poverty and Politics in an Urban Neighborhood* (Susser 1982). Later, as the AIDS epidemic emerged, I focused on the possibilities for HIV prevention among homeless men and women in New York City and conducted fieldwork on the potential for community mobilization around HIV in a rural barrio of Puerto Rico where I had been working with my anthropologist husband and young children. We organized a conference at Columbia University in the early 1990s and co-edited with George Bond and Joan Vincent the book, *AIDS in Africa and the Caribbean* (Bond et al. 1997).

As South Africans began to fight free from apartheid, I redirected my research on the negotiations of men and women in community mobilization around AIDS in the effort to contribute to AIDS prevention in southern Africa and with Quarraisha Abdool Karim, Zena Stein, and several other people, submitted a proposal to the International Center for Research on Women (ICRW). It was in relation to this research that I made my first trip back to South Africa since boarding ship from Durban in December 1955. I traveled with my two sons, age three and ten and Zena Stein, who also worked on the grant, while she assisted me with the children, allowing me, a single mother recently split up from my first husband, to pursue my research.

During that first visit, I was walking past the luxury Carlton Hotel in central Johannesburg with the three-year-old in a stroller when shots rang out near the taxi stand. We had to take cover and then, in fact, look for a taxi to get back to where we were staying. That experience, among others, opened my eyes to the challenges of the transition from apartheid and to the violence that marked the struggle for change.

In the course of this first trip back, I met Dr. Nkosazana Dlamini-Zuma, who was one of the principal investigators on the original proposal. When she became the Minister for Health in South Africa she appointed Quarraisha Abdool Karim as the Chief Director for AIDS in South Africa. I returned in 1995 to follow up on the experiences of women in the informal settlements around Durban.

In 1989, the guerilla war led by the South West African People's Organization (SWAPO) against the apartheid South African army had resulted in Namibian independence. In 1996, with Canadian anthropologist Richard Lee, who had worked for three decades among the Ju/'hoansi of the Kalahari, I initiated a training program in social science research concerned with AIDS at the University of Namibia. For several weeks each year from 1996 to 2003, funded through the HIV Center at Columbia University, we worked with Scholastika Iipinge to train students, NGO workers, civil servants, and faculty in ethnographic research on the social context of AIDS. In 2000, we went to the historic Durban International AIDS Society Conference together with researchers initially trained in this program who presented abstracts at the conference. This project was later adopted by the University of Toronto and the University of Namibia and is still in operation. Over the past decade in conjunction with our training program, Richard Lee and I conducted research in Namibia and Botswana among the Ju/'hoansi and also among men and women in other areas.

I have been back to southern Africa more than 15 times since 1995, often for several months at a time, and become involved in anthropological research and training with respect to the social issues surrounding women and HIV/AIDS. In 2001, I was awarded a MacArthur Research and Writing Fellowship to conduct ethnographic research, titled *Spaces of Autonomy: Defining Sustainable Strategies to Combat HIV/AIDS in Sub-Saharan Africa* and also worked to develop a National Institute of Mental Health Ethnographic Training Project. The Training Project was funded from 2003–7, based at the University of Kwazulu-Natal and also at Columbia University School of Public Health. The concept and curriculum for this program, which involved training local researchers, including Sibongile Mkhize who has written a chapter for this book, had been initially formulated by Richard Lee and I in the program at the University of Namibia.

As a result of my research in AIDS and gender, I have learned from local and global activists as well as scientists and become engaged in working for gender and human rights in the AIDS world. With a number of committed activists, I helped to form ATHENA (Advancing Gender Equity in the Global Response to AIDS) and I recently, served as co-chair of the Social Science Track at the 2008 International AIDS Society Conference. Through these activities I have come to work with and learn from outstanding women, members of the International Community of Women Living with AIDS (ICW), such as Alice Welbourn, MariJo Vazquez, Dawn Averitt Bridge and Jennifer Mallet, from London, Barcelona, the United States, Namibia and elsewhere. ATHENA, in coalition with ICW and other groups, published a newsletter at the Mexico International AIDS Society Conference for which Zena Stein and I wrote pieces with feminist activists, sex workers, positive women, and researchers such as Marion Stevens, Tyler Crone, Johanna Kehler, Sue O'Sullivan, while my younger son, niece, and nephew worked as media volunteers to distribute it.

Although this book is based on extensive research, it represents a synthesis of the diverse experiences chronicled here in the attempt to understand the prolonged struggles for the recognition, treatment, and prevention of the AIDS epidemic among women and men in southern Africa and elsewhere.

# Acknowledgments

Like any author laboring for years over a book, I have incurred many debts. There is first the tremendous gratitude I owe to the people of southern Africa, who had the patience to put up with my questions and often welcomed me into their homes, workplaces, support groups, and communities as they creatively adapted to the HIV/AIDS epidemic.

Graduate students and researchers from universities in southern Africa also provided much important assistance and insight. At the University of Namibia, Scholastika Iipinge, a wonderful friend and colleague, worked with Richard Lee and I to establish an ethnographic training program in anthropology and AIDS. Among the many participants since 1996, our first research assistants, Pombili Ipinge and Karen Nasheya, merit particular gratitude for their friendship and guidance (plus patience with the hardships of camping). Particularly rewarding, also, was my time in the Center for HIV/AIDS Networking (HIVAN), directed by Eleanor Preston-Whyte, with members of the Partnership Training Program Sibongile Mkhize, Xoliswa Keke, Syenele Ndlovu, and a cadre of extraordinary, socially committed students and researchers.

At the University of KwaZulu-Natal in Durban, Jerry and Zubi Coovadia, Salim and Quarraisha Abdool Karim, Jane Kvalsig, Patrick Bond, Dennis Brutus, and many others provided an intellectually and personally welcoming environment. In 2007, I benefited greatly from the opportunity to present my ideas at the Center for Civil Society. In Cape Town, Zackie Achmat, Jack Lewis, Nicoli Nattrass, Mary Beth Mills, Marion Stevens, Steve Robins, Mugsy Speigel, and Susan Levine generously introduced me to people and places and assisted me with research. I discussed an early version of some of the ideas in this book at a seminar in 2005 in the Anthropology Department at Cape Town. The informative discussion there led me to refine key concepts.

Essential financial support came from the International Center for Research on Women, a National Endowment for the Humanities Fellowship, a National

Institute of Health Fellowship, a PSC-CUNY Award, National Institute of Health, Partnership in AIDS: Training Grant in Ethnography (Columbia University and the University of KwaZulu-Natal), a Fogarty Training Grant through the Columbia University HIV Center for Clinical and Behavioral Sciences, the National Science Foundation, and a MacArthur Research and Writing Fellowship.

Hunter College and its anthropology department kept me in touch with the vibrant, engaged, and diverse undergraduate and graduate students who emerge from the public schools and workplaces of New York City. Doctoral students at the Graduate Center of the City University of New York tested my ideas from a bracing range of intellectual standpoints. Funded through my Award from the National Science Foundation, Ted Powers, Kate Griffiths, Risa Cromer, Daisy Demampo, Kaja Tretjak, and Elan Abrell all conducted research in South Africa that contributed to the work presented here. I look forward to seeing their own work appear in print. Sam Byrd, Risa Cromer, Kaja Tretjak, Elan Abrell, and Lynne Desilva-Johnson energetically helped complete the citations and bibliography.

Overall, I have been sustained by the CUNY Graduate Center, home to the kind of incisive, informed, and collegial intellectual environment essential for research and writing. In particular, Jane Schneider and Shirley Lindenbaum created an anthropology department supportive of both students and faculty. They remain my role models. My colleagues Louise Lennihan, Don Robotham, Leith Mullings, Talal Asad, David Harvey, Neil Smith, Peter Kwong, Jeff Maskovsky, Setha Low, among many others, kept the dialogue going. The Center for Place, Culture and Politics at the Graduate Center directed by Neil Smith provided a one-year Faculty Fellowship and one year as associate director, which gave me essential time to write and offered a critically engaged and stimulating group of colleagues in an atmosphere of humane intellectual exchange. A year at the Humanities Center Seminar allowed me to present a chapter and plan of organization to an interdisciplinary group of scholars whose astute comments led me to reorganize the book. Whether the setting was the wonderfully contentious faculty seminar on Women and Globalization, organized by Linda Basch and Patricia Clough, or the current seminar, Rights to the City, led by Peter Marcuse, my thinking on the issues presented here was enriched by students, faculty, advocates, and activists from all over New York City.

At New York University, I learned much from the participants from many universities who gathered at a faculty seminar organized by Faye Ginsburg and Rayna Rapp. Emily Martin has been a particularly supportive and helpful colleague. Since its founding, I have benefited from the scientific exchange and immersion in central international debates among valued colleagues at the Columbia University HIV Center and from detailed reviews of research over the past five years as a member of the International Core, led by Richard Parker. It will be clear from the book itself how much I owe to global activists concerned with AIDS, to colleagues working with the International AIDS Society, to the members of the International Community of Women Living with AIDS and particularly to the ATHENA (Advancing Gender Equity in the Global Response to AIDS) Network.

To Richard Lee of the University of Toronto I owe a special debt. His years of knowledge and experience, not to mention his fluency in Ju/'hoansi, made our research in the Kalahari possible and added intellectual depth as well as historical context to the analysis.

Quarraisha Abdool Karim, Anke Ehrhardt, Elizabeth Tyler Crone, Marion Stevens, Sibongile Mkhize, Richard Lee, and Kate Crehan read carefully through chapters and drafts and provided a steady flow of valuable critique. Shula Marks generously sent me her insightful and comprehensive review of recent works on the AIDS epidemic in Africa in manuscript form just as I was finishing the final edits on these chapters. Christine Gailey and Frances Rothstein read drafts of the work. Their critical attention to the manuscript inspired me to keep going through diffi-cult periods. Over the past several years, Hester Eisenstein and I, each at work on a book, discussed every aspect of research and writing. She provided the best kind of constructive suggestions and encouragement.

Anything that might be worth while in this volume owes much to the intellectual contributions of my friends and colleagues; any errors or debatable interpretations are of course my own.

The editorial staff at Wiley-Blackwell have been patient, professional, and effi-cient. Jane Huber, my original editor, worked tirelessly with me to develop a more active and accessible style. Rosalie Robertson, Julia Kirk, and Deirdre Ilkson carried the project forward with insight and acuity while Paul Stringer, the project manager, handled last-minute emendations with a flexibility and generosity far beyond the call of duty.

Through the absences and stresses of writing a book, my family has consistently provided essential emotional grounding. The unstinting support and contemporary insight provided by my parents, Zena Stein and Mervyn Susser, is truly impossible to credit adequately. My aunt Paddy Bader generously offered a home away from home in Cape Town. My sister Ruth King helped to keep my family going dur-ing my absences in the field, while my brother Ezra Susser let me share his air-conditioned study in summers when he was toiling over his own book (and taught my boys soccer into the bargain). My sons, Philip and Jonah Kreniske, accompanied me into the field, their ever-present soccer ball a magnet to young people wherever we went. Later, they would find their own way, Philip to take part in the ethno-graphic training sessions at the University of Namibia and Jonah to work on the ATHENA Newsletter at the 2008 Mexico IAS Conference meetings.

Peter Parisi patiently and perceptively supported me through every stage and every page of this book.

*Ida Susser*
*New York City 2008*

Southern Africa

# Introduction

## *Global, Inequality, Women, and HIV/AIDS*

We may initially conceive of the HIV virus as a biological phenomenon, but it does not follow that it is free of social determinants. Much as we now refer to the environment as a product of long-term human interaction with the earth rather than as a sphere of separate and untrammeled nature, so the current manifestations of HIV/AIDS are shaped by 30 years of human interaction in a period of rapid global change. And just as the environment is losing protection under new forms of globalization, so too is the epidemic of HIV/AIDS exacerbated by global processes.

"Globalization has flattened the earth," says *New York Times* columnist Thomas Friedman (Friedman 2005). If we think of the instantaneous movement around the world of money, investments, media, and commodities, he is certainly right. When I began research in the Kalahari Desert in 1996, the only communication at the end of barely passable roads came through the unreliable, staticky radio phone (Lee and Susser 2006; Susser 2006). By 2003, I could rent a cellphone that would call New York City from the desert, and a landline was available in the newly opened Tsumkwe Lodge. In 1996, one local store displayed soap powder and a few dried goods on mostly empty shelves. By 2003 also, a brightly colored set of advertisements for Coca-Cola and pictures of skimpily clad women illustrating packages of Easy Rider condoms hung from the walls of two busy local stores. Not only were the pictures displayed, it was actually possible, for the first time, to buy refrigerated cold drinks (although not always condoms).

In contrast to the spread of communication and promotion, we find crevices gouged into the surface of Friedman's presumably level globe. Flexible capital flashes around the globe, leaving in its wake abandoned factories, barren land and chronically unemployed people, trapped in place in polluted environments and without rights to land (Brecher 2000; Castells 1996). For example, in 1969, Union Carbide, attracted by tax breaks, free land, and plentiful underground water, built a plant in Yabucoa, Puerto Rico, which employed nearly 1,000 workers. Over the next decade, the workers and local residents fought against the carcinogens and

**Figure 0.1**   Savanna II Supermarket, now closed, with Cool Ryder posters (Namibian Association for Social Marketing) still on display, Tsumkwe, Namibia, 2008 (photograph Adrianne Daggett)

other toxic effects the industry brought. Then, toward the end of the 1980s, when its tax breaks expired, Union Carbide abandoned the plant, leaving behind its toxic frame, a polluted water table, hundreds of unemployed workers and sick community residents (Susser 1985; Susser 1991).

Union Carbide's despoliation of Yabucoa and its free access to natural resources forecasted the local costs of globalization. Exploitation can take various forms. In the past decade, newly implemented neoliberal policies have expanded to privatized water and turned herbs into bio-commodities sold back to, and often unaffordable by, local populations (Escobar 1998; Gupta 1998). As I write, the San peoples ( a group once known as "Bushmen") are fighting to maintain and develop legal trusts to hold on to areas in Namibia and Botswana. In 2003, we saw water meters being installed in the Kalahari villages of Namibia to ration use and charge those who exceeded local allotments. In addition, reflecting a further assault on the resources of the San, the Hoodia cactus was developed by Pfizer as a herbal remedy without their knowledge. It is now advertised on the World Wide Web as anything from an appetite suppressant to a cure for nausea. But, again, in reaction to these depredations, representatives of the San have initiated legal negotiations with various companies to establish their rights to proceeds from these sales (WIMSA 2004; Hitchcock et al. 2006; Lee 2003; Solway 2006).

Information may flow faster as computer technology, the World Wide Web, and Internet become ever more fantastically capable but the poor lack the technology and training to use it (Castells 1996). Although they would surely benefit from access to the Internet, many do not have the general education that would allow them to make full use of it. For example, the children who wait in the parking lots outside Angkor Wat, Cambodia, to sell tourist guides, jewelry, and statuettes have memorized the capital of every US state and even write letters in English to sharpen their sales appeal, but cannot go to school because their families need their earnings. Similarly, poor people worldwide may be intimately familiar with Nike sneakers and other American consumer goods but are deprived of useful knowledge about medications for opportunistic diseases or the symptoms of sexually transmitted diseases. In 2003, people I interviewed in rural southern Africa were savvy about American hip-hop music, but did not know that effective treatment existed for HIV/AIDS. Nevertheless, globally, as among the San, local grassroots leaders and activists are working to change this situation.

First-world travelers can fly around the world to trek the ecotourist rainforest but for many of the poor, crossing a national boundary is fraught with danger and, if successful, brings life as an undocumented person, risking exploitation, arrest, and deportation. Fear of terrorism has led to even more restrictive, if still selective, barriers to migration (Kwong 2008).

Ironically, the AIDS virus, like dollars and data, finds no borders to block its spread (Parker 2001; Schoepf 2001). It travels to and from ever-more remote regions, like Phuket Beach, Thailand, borne by tourists for whom sexual exploration or drug use constitute the vacation experience. People in sub-Saharan Africa, the Caribbean, and South-East Asia sell sex to support themselves and their families (Altman 2001; Herdt 1997; Kreniske 1997; Manjate et al. 2000; Padilla 2007; Preston-Whyte et al. 2000; Schoepf 1988; Wilson 2004). The AIDS virus accompanies the vast movements of labor precipitated by ever-shifting global investment (Farmer 1992). In China, peasants struggling to support themselves in the face of declining communal agriculture (Walker 2006) were infected with HIV when they sold blood to government-sponsored agencies (Tyler 1996). In other regions, mercenaries, soldiers, guerillas, and roving bands, combatants in the ongoing, low-intensity warfare that has accompanied the destabilizing impact of globalization (Mamdani 2004), spread AIDS through rape and the general disruption of communities.[1] However, although the virus travels rapidly, poor people living with HIV/AIDS have been denied visas by countries such as Spain and the United States, and cannot themselves seek work or treatment elsewhere.[2] Once again, as with the San, we can see the effects of grassroots campaigns, as the United States finally reversed the 20 years of restriction on travel for people living with HIV/AIDS in 2008.

As scientific research has become more successful and sophisticated, science has identified the HIV/AIDS virus, its paths of transmission, and effective treatment. People with resources, knowledge, and options to change their lives can protect themselves or seek treatment. Over the past decade, concerted international organizing by groups such as HealthGap in the United States, ACT UP in many regions of the world and Treatment Action Campaigns in South Africa, Brazil, and elsewhere, have made treatment available to almost one-third of those in need over the globe.

Building on these outstanding successes, the next major effort has to address the social conditions that contribute to the epidemic. The poor in many places of the world are still deprived of the most basic barrier methods for protection from

HIV/AIDS, as well as many appropriate medications and treatment. Path-breaking scientific advances and behavioral interventions have not yet bridged widening gaps in knowledge and opportunity. The scientific advances and simple interventions, such as the female condom, have still not reached all the women and men who are becoming infected worldwide (Mantell et al. 2008). Thus, from 2004 to 2006, the number of people living with HIV increased in every region of the world (UNAIDS 2006a).[3]

Poor women are particularly disadvantaged by globalization (UNIFEM et al. 2004). Frequently, they must pay high prices to feed their families, must fetch and pay for privatized water, gather herbs for the sick, and cultivate grains on land they cannot own or inherit. Today, 40 percent of the world's workforce is women. However, because they consistently earn less than men, women make up 60 percent of the world's 550 million working poor (*see* aflcio.org/issues/factsstats).

At the outbreak of the AIDS epidemic, women in Africa were just as likely as men to be living with AIDS (Sabatier 1989). However, the chasm that separates poor women from the privileges of the globalized world is deepening. Now, in sub-Saharan Africa more women than men live with AIDS. Women, the large majority of whom are poor, make up 60 percent of the infected population (UNAIDS 2006a; UNIFEM et al. 2004). In addition, poor women shoulder the burden of caring for orphaned infants, those at risk of infection, and the sick in general.

Confronting the threat of HIV/AIDS in their most intimate relations, women, like men, confront tragic dilemmas, but the dilemmas are not the same for women as for men. In southern Africa, women contract HIV/AIDS in their early teens, on average ten years earlier than men (Abdool Karim and Abdool Karim 2005:75; Barnett and Whiteside 2002). At very young ages, women and girls must make life-defining decisions about possible sexual partnerships – if they escape sexual assault and are allowed to make decisions at all (Jewkes 2002; Jewkes et al. 2004; Schoepf 2001). Even if force were not a constant threat, precarious economic and social status or expected youthful sexual exploration can quickly lead women to infection and pregnancy. Unlike men, very young women face pregnancy and childbirth under the shadow of fatal infection. They must usually support their infants as well as themselves, whether or not they fall sick.

## Avenues of Hope

In concerning itself with the lives of poor women in southern Africa as they have been ravaged by the dual effects of globalization and HIV/AIDS, this book embodies no intention to reproduce the images of suffering, passivity, ignorance, and stigma which have dominated the representations of women – especially African women – living with HIV/AIDS. Rather, the research presented here envisions the possibility that, powerful as it is, globalization has not displaced the ingenuity and agency of people and groups at the local level. In pursuing this work, I have tried to describe avenues of hope, partly by searching for areas in which local women might be making decisions to protect themselves from AIDS and in which activists work across identity groups and national borders to shape policies that ultimately get decided at the global level. I am concerned with the small changes that poor women have implemented in their households or in community politics as well as the links between their actions and the more dramatic transformations precipitated by activists in global politics. As is well known, since the mid-1990s, social movements have emerged all over the world to combat neoliberal policies of globalization. I wanted to analyze the ways in which women and men in southern Africa have worked to change their own situations. I also strove to understand where they have joined, or acted in parallel with, people in Latin America, the United States, Canada, and Europe as well as Thailand and elsewhere, to confront the AIDS epidemic.

While women have been counted and targeted for intervention, the recognition of women as significant actors and agents of transformation has yet to be fully documented (Susser 2002). Although in southern Africa women are now the leading group living with AIDS (as well as the main care-givers and community activists), research on the strategies and agency available to women has lagged behind many other considerations.

Patterns of inequality by gender and income are neither natural nor unchanging; they are the product of historical processes, and are now operating on a global scale. To begin to explain the possibilities for agency among poor women in fighting the epidemic, we must also understand the political, social, and cultural variations that underlie the impact of globalization.

Several crucial concerns have guided my research on HIV/AIDS in southern Africa. The questions were always framed in terms of an activist approach to ethnography and in the search for pathways to change in a challenging era. Firstly, I hoped to explore the extent of women's autonomy or the spaces available to women for action and instances of adaptability and flexibility among families and households (Leacock 1981; Susser 2002). Secondly, I searched for examples of local mobilization and examined how the politics of HIV/AIDS on the local level might affect policies at other levels. Thirdly, I aimed to analyze government action and then evaluate its impact on women and men's collective action on the local and national level. This aim was based on the hypothesis that government cooperation and support is an almost essential component of the prevention and treatment of HIV/AIDS. Without government support for national campaigns and the widespread distribution of crucial resources, it seemed possible that a population could be literally sentenced to die (Campbell 2003). Fourthly, I aimed to explore the significance of international links among protest groups, from the local to the transnational, and how they might bring international pressure to bear on the state.

Throughout the research for this book, based, perforce, on multisited investigations over time, I was concerned with the ways in which ideas of gender and AIDS are intimately tied to the political economy of the state and ideologies of national transformation within the global sphere. From this perspective, the generation of internationally linked social movements becomes ever more central.

In the first chapter I outline the ways in which scientific questions about AIDS are themselves framed within a cultural context and the second chapter examines the impact of US politics on the trajectory of AIDS research and funding. The next two chapters discuss AIDS in South Africa, examining the legacies of colonialism and the injuries of class and racism as well as the cultural, social, and gendered situations which have shaped people's collective and individual endeavors to protect themselves. I show how new economic policies may institutionalize gendered difference and in some ways may perpetuate the very inequalities they are designed to counteract. I examine the ways in which gender is embedded in political ideologies and the ways in which images of nationalism may rely on moralizing discourses which serve as vehicles for racism, sexism, and other stigmatizing processes, thereby undermining women's autonomy. However, even within these opening chapters, I document people's ongoing struggles to redefine the situation of women in dynamic interaction with gendered ideologies, whether in science, in international funding, or in national discourses. In the subsequent six chapters, I document the local efforts and social movements among women, in South Africa, Namibia, and among the Ju/'hoansi of the Kalahari Desert, in the battle for treatment and prevention of AIDS in southern Africa. Chapter 11 analyzes the role of organic intellectuals in the struggles for social justice and women's autonomy and the ways in which such struggles can lay the basis for protection from AIDS. The concluding chapter addresses contemporary debates about AIDS prevention in the global arena and links the analyses of the book to policy recommendations.

The contrasts and variations between the experiences of different populations can help us sort out ways in which subsistence organization, gendered patterns of labor and kinship, sexuality and autonomy shape possible avenues of agency for women in a globalized world. As we shall see in the latter chapters of the book, the Ju/'hoansi women in both Namibian and Botswana villages still maintain an unusual degree of autonomy. They differed from other poor women of southern Africa in their sense of personal boundaries, in their experience of an egalitarian foraging society, and the particular forms of ecotourism developing around them.

The Ju also differed dramatically in their ideas of kinship and caring. Many women in the townships surrounding Durban, South Africa, with little help from their husbands, were involved in caring for their children and their neighbors, forming support groups, and seeking institutional resources from clinics and hospitals. In contrast, among the Ju, caring for the sick was the responsibility of a wide kinship network, both men and women. The activities of caring were carried out by different members of the kin networks and accessed in different ways. Among the Ju, for instance, both men and women shared caring tasks and, since people created their own shelters, many kin members could move to camp near resources. For example, we interviewed a sick man who had hitch-hiked with about seven close relatives, including his three adult sons, 30 miles from his shelter in the bush to settle in the yard of a folk healer. His new encampment was alongside the main road in the central administrative village. As a result, he was also accessible to the visits of the local nurse, who had approved the arrangement. Thus, while this book connects global processes to local conditions, I have attended in detail to differences on the ground, including the history of a gendered division of labor in the household and paid employment, marriage arrangements, and inheritance, as these frame collective efforts with respect to AIDS.

Since presenting the voices of women without education may foster a stereotypical image and simply retelling a narrative in my own words can entail an unintended hierarchy, Chapter 5 brings the narrative of Sibongile Mkhize, holder of an MA and an AIDS researcher in Durban. She was a participant in an ethnographic training program there and went on to write her own story of the damage to her own family wrought by the virus. Her courage along with her intellectual insight in themselves dispel many of the stereotypes about stigma, culture, and women as victims that have characterized discussions of Africa and AIDS both in the research literature and the mass media. An educated South African woman and mother of two, Sibongile describes how she was affected by AIDS, as one of two surviving children in a family of nine siblings. A brother and a sister as well as her uncle and other members of her family died of AIDS. Her story illustrates the dilemmas and resilience of many of the women I met.

## Ethnographic Methods: The Grass Roots, the National, and the Global

Against this background, the present study moves, as noted earlier, from the local to the global and from the personal to the national. The aim is to elucidate the way people themselves move within the structures of capital, state, and class and how they work to transform them. Early approaches to the ethnographic method were contrived in the twilight of colonialism and reinvigorated in the era of nationalist movements. As many have suggested, we are confronting a transformed global arena and need to rethink our methods (Burawoy 1998; Marcus 1995). In the effort to open up new questions, the extended case method, also known as situational or event analysis, offers a useful approach. Initiated by Max Gluckman in his classic analysis "'The Bridge': Analysis of a Social Situation in Zululand" (Gluckman 2002), systematically described by Jaap Van Velsen (1967), and much revisited (Burawoy 1998; Vincent 1978; Vincent 1986; Werbner 1984), such a processual analysis can lay a solid foundation for analyzing social change in the global era.

The work of the Manchester School emerged in critique of the operational assumption of a single unchanging culture in the early work of E. E. Evans-Pritchard and A. R. Radcliffe-Brown. In the 1940s and 1950s in what is now known as the Zambian Copperbelt, confronted with the labor migration of men from African pastoral populations to the new urban centers, Gluckman, Van Velsen, Victor Turner, Elizabeth Colson, William Watson, and others recognized that they could no longer rely on a single interpretive or symbolic understanding of a culture. Conducting research in both urban and rural areas transformed by colonial interests in the mines, the anthropologists were faced with diverse and contradictory values and people who adapted their responses to different situations. Under these circumstances, these researchers became aware of the way in which the analysis of conflict or the dramas of crisis and reconciliation could expose political fault lines and forms of social organization that might not be fully evident in the repetitions of everyday life. In addition, an analysis of unusual rather than customary events might illuminate the directions of future change.

Godfrey Wilson, the first director of ethnographic research on the Copperbelt, emphasized the creation of the migrant labor system in the interest of the colonial powers. After Wilson was fired for political reasons, his replacement, Max Gluckman, emphasized the need to posit a theoretical system in equilibrium: in other words, to assume that within a crisis or conflict there would be social mechanisms that would perpetuate or maintain the social system. As Benjamin Magubane pointed out, after Wilson lost his job, the creation of an urban proletariat by the British empire was never fully acknowledged by the Manchester anthropologists (Magubane 1971; Magubane 1979). However, many of Gluckman's students and colleagues rejected concepts of equilibrium and emphasized the significance of conflict in transformation. One such student, and later colleague, A. L. Epstein (1958) described the battles for labor representation among African mineworkers. Although the workers were rooted in many different language groups and tribal villages they recognized common interests in forming a labor union. Epstein demonstrated that extended case analysis – in this case, tracing the mineworkers' struggles as well as the responses of the mine owners over time – could be a powerful lens for making visible the constraints of industrial capitalism in a colonial context.

Nowadays, extended case analysis, which traces policies and people from the local to the global, might also be labeled a multisited analysis or "the peripatetic translative mapping of brave new worlds" (Marcus 1995:114). The project of this book is multisited in the attempt to map the cultural politics of AIDS from the meetings and literature of Western scientists and global activism to the national representations of the disease to the men and women most affected on the ground. However, extended case analysis is more than multisited. It is premised on the expectation that historical processes as well as government policies and corporate funding are crucially connected to everyday events and that these links can be traced and even explained through ethnographic and archival methods. The Manchester School emphasized history and process, so that the links between the sites, people, place, and time were a central aspect of the method (Vincent 1978; Vincent 1986).

Since the 1980s, much ethnographic research has shown that we can illuminate, through processual event analyses and on-the-ground participant observation, the connections between local experience and global decisions (Edelman 1999; Gill 2004; Nash 2001; Nash 2005; Susser 1982; Susser 1985). As extended case analysis was specifically invented to capture the possibilities for change, it seems particularly appropriate for the study of spaces of action in a rapidly transforming global era.

However, while global ethnography (Burawoy et al. 2000) provides a method for directing and analyzing participant observation, it lacks a sophisticated theoretical framework for understanding changing structures. We need to search elsewhere to conceptualize the major institutional transformations of our times. In a process which David Harvey described as "flexible accumulation" (Harvey 1990), since the economic crisis of the 1970s, transnational corporations have spawned new kinds of workplaces paying much lower wages in regions previously regarded as rural and where women were often the first hired (Nash 1983). As Manuel Castells (Castells 1996) first pointed out in his path-breaking analysis of the global era, this exportation of industry was facilitated and maintained, if not precipitated, by massive innovations in information technology.

Flexible accumulation was part of the answer to the fiscal crises of the state and the international shift in the power of oil (Klare 2004; O'Connor 1973); neoliberal policies were the other. Based on cooperation between corporate interests and the state ("public/private partnerships"), neoliberal policies emphasize market competition over collective and public endeavors, making commodities of resources previously held in common, and reducing public services (Robotham 2008). The ideas of neoliberalism, devised by Karl Hayek and developed by Milton Friedman at the University of Chicago, constituted a concerted assault on the welfare state (Harvey 2005; Robotham 2008).

As Naomi Klein has recently argued (2007) and as Jane Schneider and I demonstrated in *Wounded Cities* (2003), neoliberal policies are most easily implemented after a crisis, since most democratic societies resist the assaults on the public weal. Such policies were first implemented by General Pinochet in Chile after the 1971 coup. They were imposed by Margaret Thatcher in the United Kingdom in the early 1970s after the dramatic devaluation of the pound sterling and in New York City through the fiscal crisis of 1975 (Susser 1982). From the election of Ronald Reagan as President of the US in 1980, global institutions such as the World Bank and the International Monetary Fund exported the new neoliberal requirements to debt-ridden nations around the world (Stiglitz 2002).

Much of the scholarly work in anthropology of this decade is devoted to analyzing the local community in the context of these global transformations (Appadurai 1998; Friedman 2005; Schneider and Susser 2003). Authors in *Wounded Cities* (Schneider and Susser 2003) documented the ongoing processes of destruction and reconstruction that have characterized cities around the world in the era of globalization. In each case, from Beirut, Lebanon (Sawalha 2003) to Ho Chi Minh City, Vietnam (Chae 2003) to Palermo and New York City (Harvey 2005; Mulling 2003; Susser and Schneider 2003), contributors demonstrated the ways in which the reconstruction processes, based on neoliberal priorities, led to the exclusion of the city's poor and the exacerbation of the problems of housing, health, and education facing the urban working class.

Neoliberal policies, which involve the dismantling of the welfare state along with the constantly relocating investments of flexible accumulation, have led to lay-offs and insecurity in professional and white-collar jobs as well as those in manufacturing. They have also undermined the security of the middle classes, as such consequences as losing a job, losing health care, losing homes to a natural disaster or war are no longer cushioned by the benefits of the safety net provided by public investment. Ulrich Beck's concept of the risk society (Beck 1992) adds to this vision of insecurity the exacerbation and blurring of the natural disaster with the manufactured disasters in the environment created by "modernization". He highlights the increasing recognition of risks for people of the middle class, as well as the poor (albeit unevenly distributed by class and wealth), of global warming, with its accompanying floods, hurricanes, droughts and other disruptions, possible nuclear disasters and multiple forms of pollution.

Emily Martin gives a sense of the challenges facing individual subjects in the neoliberal era (Martin 1996), which she argues generates "flexible bodies," made malleable in the constant demand for workers to re-create themselves for new forms of work and we might add, following Beck, new environmental conditions (Martin 1996; Susser 1996a).

The wide dispersal of manufacturing and the speeded up global communications also precipitated what have been seen as hybrid subjects (Appadurai 1998). People all over the world were learning, adapting, and working in new kinds of jobs with a common set of global information and representations generated by the new information networks. At the same time, populations emerged from particular places with varying historical traditions and languages. Hybridity was one way of describing the multiple cultural understandings that made up the subjective experience of each individual.

One might argue that, as new forms of hybridity distance people from their communal histories, the shift toward the private may also engender a "neoliberal subject." As people lose their communal bearings, experience little security in the public weal, and lose faith in any common national purpose, the neoliberal subject focuses only on competing better for the needs of the self.

However, the all-pervasive neoliberal culture implied in discussion of the neoliberal subject is countered in the recent growth of anti-global social movements. The myriad varieties of globally connected social protests that have emerged since the late 1990s suggest that many people can still envision "the commons" as a public right even as, in much of the world, this public right is under assault.

It was some time before any internationally recognized opposition to neoliberal policies emerged on the global stage. In his analysis of eighteenth-century Britain, E. P. Thompson (Thompson 1963) argued that working-class consciousness emerged only in response to a new manifestation of ruling-class cooperation. One might argue that, along with the 1980s' Washington consensus at the beginning of the Reagan era, a new global elite came together to coordinate neoliberal policies and that the populations affected only became globally organized in reaction.

Since the 1990s, collective protests against globalization have been documented through detailed ethnographic case studies, grounded in a historical analysis of global investment and state institutions (Edelman 1999; Escobar 1998; Nash 2001; Nash 2005; Schneider and Susser 2003). Some of these might usefully be examined to help us contextualize the development of international protest around HIV/AIDS. With no claim to any exhaustive account, I have made an attempt to describe approximate periods of the development of global protest, starting with the Zapatistas in 1994 and followed by the 1998 Seattle protests. Disaffection and attempts at international coordination were present throughout the 1980s. However, the "global" focus and the increasing recognition of the widening gap between rich and poor worldwide (see Jones and Susser 1993) seemed to emerge over the 1990s and indeed ever-more clearly with the gray dawn of the third millennium.

Not surprisingly, some of the earliest anti-global opposition emerged in Mexico where neoliberal policies had been implemented since the fiscal crisis of the 1980s (Rothstein 2007). Latin America, always the experimental backyard of the United States, was the place where neoliberal economists had had their first opportunity to put their policies into practice. But, in 1994, the Zapatista demonstrations flashed across the international stage and become almost instantaneously emblematic of global protest in the information age. The local drama of Mayan protestors marching out of the forests masked and armed combined with their sophisticated communication techniques as they faxed their contemporary message through the international news networks to catch the attention of world media.

June Nash (2001) argues that both our critique of globalization and our very vision of alternative possibilities have been influenced by indigenous groups such as the Mayans. Nash argues that the Mayan villagers who participated in the Zapatista protests were steeped in a collective past that sharpened their sensitivity to contemporary deprivations instigated by new policies of neoliberalism. Their previous experiences of communal society provided them with the shared values and social organization from which to generate contemporary collective protest. Nash shows the ways in which, in their fight against the impact of neoliberal policies on their livelihood, the residents of Chiapas negotiated national and international politics with well-informed political strategies.

To Manuel Castells (1996), the Zapatistas were prototypical of the new anti-global movements in their self-conscious management of an exotic identity as well as brilliant efforts to represent their demands globally. Thus, their masks and arms were less a realistic effort to take over the government than a dramatic upstaging of the Mexican army.

While Castells perceived the significance of the new forms of protest in the global era, Nash and her students, who were conducting fieldwork in Chiapas at the time, describe in detail the ravages of neoliberal policies from which the protests were generated. Although most of the protesters were of Mayan heritage, some had been relocated, often multiple times, from their areas of origin and resettled with people from many different villages in a barren neglected area designated as an environmental preserve (Doane 2007). Deprived of education, health services, or adequate roads, they rose up in protest, inspired by activists from a number of different leftist and liberationist perspectives.

While recognizing the centrality of identity politics in this prototypical protest, we can also stress the complex nature of identity (Appadurai 1998; Castells 1996).

Although based on shared languages and communal histories, the disinherited, and disenfranchised people of Chiapas re-crafted and redefined their cultural identity and worked with many well-connected urban activists to fight for the resources and public services of the modern state.

In Seattle, major, self-consciously "anti-global" demonstrations shut down the Third Ministerial Conference of the World Trade Organization, which was attended by 135 nations in 1998 (Borosage 1999). Similar demonstrations had already taken place the previous May in Geneva. Nevertheless, the newscasts from Seattle showing heads of state and corporate executives trapped in their hotels while protesters flooded the streets clearly recorded an emblematic moment. Many people world-wide first heard of the WTO in that encounter.

In Seattle 1998, as among the Zapatistas in 1994, although many different groups converged, a clear message of what exactly was "anti-global" was still in process. In the US, anti-sweatshop campaigns aimed initially at Nike were one central concern. In Europe, protests targeted Monsanto's genetically engineered food. The French sheep farmer and leader of a farmers' union, Jose Bove, led objections to turning Roquefort into a "brand" through the use of the label Roquefort for cheese any-where but in the eponymous region. In 1999, Bove drove his tractor into a proposed McDonald's franchise to protest free trade policies (Lloyd 2000). One of the major issues that has emerged on the "anti-global" stage has been the question of fair trade and agricultural subsidies. A central controversy concerns how much farmers in poor countries are paid for their produce. Agricultural tariffs set by wealthy Western governments combined with the subsidizing of Western agriculture, in general, force down the prices for farmers in poorer countries (Kaufman 2005; White House 2005). However, with respect to AIDS, the anti-global protests have focused on the Trade-Related Aspects of Intellectual Property Rights (TRIPS).

In 1994, at the creation of the World Trade Organization, TRIPS were intro-duced as part of the shift to global governance and the extension of the reach of global corporate influence. Although many countries of the global South have his-torically been relaxed in the enforcement of copyright and other such laws, nations that refused to go along with the new stipulation were now threatened with sanc-tions through loss of investment and the inability to export goods. In the finding and patenting of new drugs, the new intellectual property laws allow corporations to turn common goods into private commodities. TRIPS then protect corpor-ate profits in the subsequent sale of the medications by preventing local manufacture.

Patents, newly enforced on an international level, allowed corporations to prevent the manufacture of generic drugs and deprive needy people of life-saving medica-tions. With respect to HIV/AIDS, as well as many other diseases, global protesters began to question the right of pharmaceutical corporations to use the new interna-tional patent laws to remove their research findings from the public realm. As a measure of the success of these struggles, many corporations negotiated lower prices for specific medications for poor countries. Meanwhile, they continued to expand the global reach of patent regulation to ensure their profits for the long term.

While global regulation of intellectual property has increasingly limited the possibility for industries of the South to produce generic medications at affordable prices, the same laws have allowed pharmaceutical companies to patent herbal folk remedies. A recent global ethnography (Gupta 1998) documented the corporate patenting of indigenous herbal substances in India by corporations protected by the new trade-related intellectual property regulations. Similarly, social movements emerged in the struggle of Peruvian peasants to protect the wild herbs of the Amazonian rain forest from patenting by large transnational pharmaceutical companies (Escobar 1998). In India and the Amazon, the legal issues concern the control of local herbs and their scientific properties. Who owns the herbs – the local people who first identified their healing properties and on whose lands the plant has grown or the pharmaceutical companies who have extracted the essence of the herbs, documented their properties, and retailed them for profit?

Indigenous battles against pharmaceutical companies which claim intellectual property rights to turn herbal folk remedies into patented drugs parallel the battles over AIDS drug treatments. In South Africa and Brazil, activists have fought against the patents of the same pharmaceuticals, seeking to allow the manufacture of affordable generic drugs for the treatment of HIV/AIDS.

Under the unequal global conditions created by TRIPS, we can begin to see how internal debates in South Africa that pit herbal remedies against Western medications can easily be portrayed by some antagonists as a battle with Western corporations for indigenous rights. Ironically, in South Africa, echoes of these political battles in support of indigenous healing have been used by corporate manufacturers of herbal medicines against health activists demanding public access to life-saving anti-retroviral therapy.

Trade-Related Intellectual Property Rights, which, as we have seen, limit poor people's access to both indigenous herbal remedies and HIV/AIDS drugs, have featured as a central bargaining chip in global policy decisions. With respect to agriculture, as it has been with many other issues, negotiations about TRIPS and life-saving pharmaceuticals have been juggled with the need to reform agrarian tariffs. In some instances, poor countries have had to choose one or the other. At Doha, after the 9/11/2001 attack on the World Trade Center in New York heightened fears of terrorism, an emergency demand for vaccinations and medications on the part of Western nations led the WTO to negotiate with respect to pharmaceutical patents while refusing to discuss agricultural subsidies (Bello 2001, 2002). In contrast, in October 2004, India was forced to abide by WTO patent regulations in exchange for agricultural trade agreements. This affected the herbal remedies of Indian Ayurvedic medicine as well as the manufacture of generic drugs. Since India is a major world supplier of generic HIV/AIDS drugs, this decision could have contributed to higher prices for HIV/AIDS treatment in southern Africa.

Ironically, in January 2008, in Mexico City, as the Joint Planning Committee for the Mexico 2008 International AIDS Society Conference was planning a session on TRIPS and global regulation to be organized by Anand Grover, the Project Director of the Lawyers Collective HIV/AIDS Unit in India and a leading lawyer in the court cases with respect to TRIPS regulations in India, we had to cut the meeting short because a million people were expected to march past the hotel in a protest against the latest provisions of another aspect of global regulation, the North American Free Trade Agreement (NAFTA).

On January 31, *campesinos*, led my men and women on tractors and men riding horses, some dressed as Zapatistas, protested the end of protected prices for their produce of maize and beans. In the march, a contingent of people from the rural areas – small, wizened old ladies with walking sticks alongside young women – carried signs calling for the right to family planning, contraceptives, and abortion. Meanwhile, youths with green and pink hair marched by as a rainbow coalition for sexual rights. The huge demonstration, which shut down Mexico City for the day, with the cooperation of a supportive, progressive city police, portrayed in full living color the linked dilemmas of globalization which were being discussed at the conference.

HIV/AIDS activists from southern Africa have commanded the global stage and entered the arena of anti-global protest in a long, arduous and dramatic struggle to provide affordable drugs for HIV/AIDS. Again, the question of international pharmaceutical patents has been central to this battle. In 2000, at the International AIDS Society Conference in Durban, South Africa, Edwin Cameron, a Supreme Court of Appeals judge in South Africa, who had access to life-saving treatment through his professional benefits in a country where most people could not afford it, discussed the contrast between himself and the poor (Cameron 2005). In public disclosure of his own HIV-positive status and a powerful speech advocating universal access to treatment, he urged that the rest of South Africa be given the right to live.

In 2002, in Barcelona, Spain, during the next International AIDS Society Conference, Zackie Achmat, a brilliant South African activist, demonstrated before the world the dilemma of living in a country where others are dying of a preventable and treatable disease. On a video shown during the plenaries, he announced his refusal to take AIDS treatment, which he could in fact afford. He risked his own death in order to pressure the South African government to make AIDS treatment available to people throughout the South African public health system.

In the context of such local and global activism as well as the desperate need on the local level, ethnography itself calls for an activist approach. Engagement and partnership has been a crucial grounding for most anthropologists working with HIV, such as Paul Farmer, Merrill Singer, Brooke Schoepf, and Richard Parker. This stance implies not only being explicit about one's critical perspective, while talking to all actors or representatives of institutions involved, but also "participating" with people most affected by the issues to understand and work actively to transform conditions.

The interpretive/reflexive approach to ethnography calls upon us to question our own hierarchical position in relation to our research subjects and topics, and some have called for decentering anthropology, away from its identification with the subaltern (Marcus 1995). In contrast, it seems crucial under the current critical circumstances, to follow an older tradition of engaged anthropology. Along with other AIDS researchers, I have taken the pursuit of social justice as a primary tenet. This activist perspective, with an emphasis on community partnerships, emerged from early work in the 1930s (Lewis 1998) and was reinvented in the 1970s (Brodkin 1988; Sanjek 1987; Susser 1982). Such personal and political engagement was also a tenet of feminist ethnography (Brodkin 1988; Gailey 1998; Mascia-Lees et al. 1989; Morgen 2002), as well demonstrated in Sandra Morgen's participation in the struggle to save a women's health clinic, documented in *Women and the Politics of Empowerment* (Morgen 1988).

In my research on HIV/AIDS, I have seen myself as an advocate and activist trying to work with people to better conditions. Ethnography and participant observation require personal relations and the establishment of trust and attendant, ongoing human responsibilities. Under these conditions, it is practically impossible to study a place where people are becoming infected from a preventable disease without advocating for preventive resources. It is equally untenable to conduct ethnography among people who are dying for lack of an available treatment without joining the struggle for treatment.

It seemed essential that ethnography in such situations include intervention. From the first research project described here, my work in HIV/AIDS has involved community activism in the effort to foster collective responses, as well as advocacy for attention to women and the South on the global level. Hopefully such efforts are enlightening in their failures as well as the successes. As this book illustrates, activism itself became one subject of research. When did it work? How did it work? What did people do to struggle for better health and what barriers and obstacles stood in the way of their efforts?

This book relies on ethnographic work that I have conducted with many other people in southern Africa since 1992 as well as ethnographic analysis of international institutions such as the International AIDS Society Conferences in Durban, Barcelona, Bangkok, and Toronto and as the co-chair of the Social Science Track in preparation for the 2008 Mexico City IAS Conference. As noted in the preface, over time I became involved in helping to form a global network focused on women's needs in the AIDS world, ATHENA: Advancing Gender Equity and Human Rights in the Global Response to HIV/AIDS. Thus, I have engaged with and observed people at all levels of the international world of AIDS policy.

Obviously, there is the risk here that one can make major mistakes and advocate for policies that backfire on the downtrodden; however, that is a risk we all take as citizens of the world. Since we indeed make our own history in conditions not of our own making, anthropologists too have an obligation to act on their findings. Nevertheless, as engaged anthropologists, we need not limit our attention to one side of an argument. Even effective activism requires that we document conflicting perspectives.

To be sure, understanding the problems for women with respect to protection and treatment for HIV/AIDS is a long way from transforming their conditions. Many of the problems discussed in the following pages are so well known that they can engender hopelessness and consequent neglect because solutions are not clearly on the horizon. The main aim of this research is to highlight not only the difficulties inherent in women's lives but also ways in which possibilities for people to transform their situations might emerge.

However challenging, working through these issues is crucial not only to addressing AIDS but also to understanding the significance of global protest in the struggle toward democratic processes, protecting rights with respect to gender and sexuality as well as class and race, both in the global North and in the South.

The more I have come to understand HIV/AIDS in southern Africa, the more it appears to be not simply related to globalization, but a stark and deadly paradigm of globalization's effects. In turn, the protests around the globe and coordinated efforts among affected populations and activists with respect to HIV/AIDS have appeared as rays of hope in the battle for the construction of any form of vital democracy as well as effective prevention and treatment of HIV/AIDS in the global state.

# 1

# The Culture of Science and the Feminization of HIV/AIDS

Since the mid-1980s, researchers and grassroots organizers have been calling attention to the social and political context of AIDS and to the specific situation of women struggling to protect themselves, but with scant effect (Bond et al. 1997; Farmer et al. 1993; Long and Ankrah 1996; Stein and Flam 1986; Susser and Gonzalez 1992; Dlamini-Zuma 1988a, b). The sharp critiques of the early period could be repeated and expanded today with no loss of cogency or point (Epstein 2007; Hunter 2003). Even as this book was delivered to the publisher in February 2008, a *New York Times* editorial lamented a new surge in AIDS infections among young men in New York City (New York Times 2008), leading the Executive Director of the New York City Civil Liberties Union to write a letter asking pointedly why only teenage boys were discussed: 48 percent of the increase was in teenage girls (Lieberman 2008). Why are women so invisible?

In discussing plans for sessions on gender at the 2008 Mexico City International AIDS Society Conference, some planners contended that men who have sex with men (MSMs) were the most important risk group for Latin America and themselves highly stigmatized. Women's issues, it was said, would get the attention they needed. However, at the same time, HIV-positive women in Mexico City were struggling for representation on the planning panels. One of the problems raised by organizers was that most of the women did not speak English. Among the positive men in Latin America, English-speaking professionals could represent the concerns of MSMs. But, it was suggested, most positive women were poorer and less educated than the men. In the end, Violetta Ross, who has a graduate degree in anthropology and is a member of the International Community of Women Living with HIV/AIDS (ICW) from Bolivia as well as Patricia Perez, a founding member of ICW, spoke eloquently at the 2008 IAS Conference. In addition, one plenary paper was allotted to review the issues of gender and the vulnerability of women and girls. A special request was added to the call for abstracts asking researchers to specify whether their data was broken down by gender. Still, the controversies concerning the representation of gender and the voices of positive women highlighted the ongoing struggles, even in the most enlightened precincts, for women and girls to combat erasure of their needs for prevention, treatment, fertility, and sexuality with respect to HIV/AIDS.

In the following chapters, we examine the ways in which ideologies of gender and everyday practices of subordination interact with political and economic forces to reproduce inequality. Working to address ideologies embedded in everyday practice has required continuous, and frequently controversial, efforts by public health practitioners, activists and grass-roots movements. This chapter briefly outlines the inclusions and exclusions of women in the history of research and scientific perspectives on AIDS.

As noted above, from the 1980s some researchers have grasped the necessity for a social, political, and economic perspective on AIDS transmission and prevention. As might be expected from a discipline that emphasizes holistic, qualitative approaches, anthropologists were a significant presence among this group (Baer et al. 2003; Bond et al. 1997; Farmer 1992; Schoepf 2001). Public health researchers, too, recognized that "because the social context determines to an enormous extent the lived realities of women, men, and children, social barriers to prevention must be recognized, understood, and directly addressed" (Mann and Tarantola 1996:xxxiii). And the Director of the HIV Center for Clinical and Behavioral Sciences at Columbia University writing in 1987 could outline a women's agenda for AIDS as follows:

> The epidemic will shake the very foundations of our society . . . any prevention and intervention program aimed at changing behavior must be designed with careful attention to the realities of women's lives. These include ethnic, cultural, and religious standard, gender roles and the legal and economic conditions of women (Ehrhardt and Exner 1987:38).

However, 2003 brings a similar call for such considerations not yet fully taken into account:

> A common thread in most of the reviews of the HIV prevention literature previously cited [those on women] is a call for more prevention initiatives that attempt to tackle the larger systemic barriers . . . that undermine attempts to decrease sexual risk behavior (Exner et al. 2003:129).

In the late 1980s, Elizabeth Reid, who led the effort to bring AIDS policy to the United Nations Development Program, called not only for attention to the context of women's lives but also for a recognition of the power of women's collective action with respect to AIDS. "While women individually may feel and be powerless to change men's behavior, women collectively can effect extraordinary changes. There is a need to look for models of women's collective action which have changed men's HIV-related behavior" (Reid 1997:163).

In fact, in 1992, women sex workers in Calcutta were already organizing the Sonagachi Project to protect themselves from HIV infection. This project emerging as it did from the demands of a heavily marginalized community in conjunction with health activists and international donors, has become a model for women's collective action (Cornish and Ghosh 2007; Jana et al. 2004).[1] But we find again that researchers are just beginning to recognize the importance of collective approaches in 2007![2]

Not only was women's collective action not widely acknowledged or supported, but women's particular vulnerability to AIDS worldwide frequently went unrecognized. One major reason often given for overlooking the situation of women was that men were at the center of the Western epidemic. In the United States, initial estimates suggested that positive men outnumbered women by about 10:1 (Sabatier 1989:40). However, while all members of minority groups in the United States were three times more likely to have AIDS than whites, minority women were proportionately more at risk than men from minority groups. A black woman was 13 times more likely to have AIDS than a white woman and a Latino woman was 9 times more likely (Sabatier 1989:40). Twenty years later, in August 2008, in a report entitled *Left Behind: Black America: A Neglected Priority in the Global AIDS Epidemic*, the Black AIDS Institute noted that in the United States, "AIDS remains the leading cause of death among Black women between 25 and 35 years and the second leading cause of death in Black men between 35 and 44 years of age" (2008:16). The neglect of women in the United States, from the early 1980s on, points to a potent combination of racism and sexism.

Initially and understandably, among African Americans, fear of being stigmatized made many people reluctant to discuss AIDS (Black AIDS Institute 2008:4). The Minority Task Force on AIDS and several other activist groups concerned with women and minorities were founded in the 1980s. However, in the course of field-work, I learned that as late as 2001, an editor of a major US women's magazine, who had been working with the United Nations representatives to highlight gender subordination as a central facilitator of AIDS transmission, decided not to run an article on women and AIDS. Her stated reason was that any such discussion would simply further stigmatize people of color. The 2008 Black AIDS Institute report confronts these issues directly and points out the combination of structured inequality and failures in government that has contributed to the neglect of the black epidemic in the United States (Black AIDS Institute 2008).

Initial research in Africa in the 1980s showed women infected equally with men. However, some researchers argued that the epidemic in the United States and Europe was different and that women were not at risk. In fact, in 1988, the US Secretary of Health and Human Services announced, "We do not expect any explosion into the heterosexual population" (Sabatier 1989:38). We have to assume here that the Secretary of Health was referring to white women.

Public perceptions were dramatically evidenced by Michael Fumento's much-publicized book entitled *The Myth of Heterosexual AIDS* (1990, reissued to great acclaim in 1993). Major foundations such as the American Foundation for AIDS Research (AmFar) and Gay Men's Health Crisis turned down proposals for research among women. This was most likely because gay activists had raised donations for these foundations and fought hard for federal funds. In the United States, the plight of men who have sex with men loomed so urgent, so controversial, and so neglected by the federal government that only this research seemed to merit support. Nonetheless, this approach resulted in the neglect of research about women worldwide. What is now recognized as a classic article outlining the need for research on preventive methods for women and introducing the concept of microbicides (Stein 1990) was turned down by three journals before it was finally accepted by the editor of the *American Journal of Public Health* after a second submission and still over the objections of reviewers.

It was not until the 1990s that many researchers and funders began to accept that women were at risk from heterosexual sex (Corea 1992).[3] As Long and Ankrah argued, "by taking women's and girls' experiences seriously, both men and women will be able to do a better job of preventing HIVAIDS" (1996:2). By that time, according to estimates, over 11 million women had become infected worldwide, as well as over 3 million children and more than 15 million men (Mann and Tarantola 1996:11).

Even when the idea of heterosexual transmission was accepted in the US, women were chiefly conceived as vectors of the disease for men and infants more than victims themselves and sometimes this emphasis remains the focus of research (Exner et al. 2003). Back in 1993, as we might have expected, researchers calculated that two-thirds of US federal research funding for women was spent on children (Long and Ankrah 1996:2). However, even at the 2007 Sydney International AIDS Society meetings on HIV pathogenesis, treatment, and prevention, a survey of abstracts submitted or accepted found that less than 20 percent addressed women's issues and many of these were focused on mother–child transmission of AIDS rather than women themselves (Collins 2008).[4]

The fact that AIDS would continue to press inexorably forward along fault lines of inequality had been clearly spelled out in the initial years of the epidemic (Bond et al. 1997; Mann and Tarantola 1996). Panos characterized AIDS as "a misery-seeking missile" (Sabatier 1989:ii). Accordingly, through the 1990s, the drama of rising rates of HIV/AIDS moved from men and women in Africa to families selling blood in destitute Chinese provinces to young unemployed drug users in the depressed cities of eastern Europe (Baer et al. 2003).

However, in spite of the general recognition that subordination and vulnerability had emerged as the driving forces of the epidemic and in spite of the inequality of women's situation in most countries of the world, the idea that, over time, more women than men would become infected (UNIFEM et al. 2004) was far from generally anticipated. There was still "a *zeitgeist* that, at best, minimized women's needs and perspectives" (Exner et al. 2003:119).

One major change occurred at the first United Nations General Assembly Special Session (UNGASS) on HIV/AIDS meetings in New York City, June 2001. Noeleen Heyzer from UNIFEM and her deputy Stephanie Urdang, led the discussion of gender and AIDS. Heyzer's closing speech documented the new recognition of the centrality of gender to the epidemic:

**Figure 1.1**    "Survival," 2003, an installation by Fiona Kirkwood (South Africa): 24′ × 4′11″, male and female condoms, resin, Perspex. The first artwork created from the female condom

> If the strong gender perspective that has been incorporated into this joint commitment is reflected in all policies, resource allocation and actions from this point forward, we can truly turn the tide of the HIV/AIDS pandemic.[5]

Other international spokespeople such as Peter Piot (2001), Executive Director of UNAIDS, and Kofi Annan (Annan 2002), Secretary General of the UN, also began to recognize that the worldwide epidemic was driven by gender subordination. However, even at the 2006 Toronto International AIDS Society Conference, HIV-positive women and women health activists felt compelled to organize a "Women and Girls' Rally." Speakers from "fourth world" women in Canada, women in poor countries, women prisoners, and women drug users highlighted the gender challenges they faced. Well-known international representatives such as Stephen Lewis, former UN Special Envoy for HIV/AIDS in Africa, and Mary Robinson, UN High Commissioner for Human Rights 1997–2002, also decried the continuing lack of attention to the problems of women and AIDS (Susser 2007).

## History of Diagnosis: AIDS Symptoms Among Women and Populations of the Global South

From the first signs of the disease, race, class, and gender shaped the scientific and cultural understandings of AIDS. Ironically, gender may even have played a role in the patterns of scientific recognition for basic research on the HI virus. In 1983, Francoise Barre-Sinoussi at the Pasteur Institute in Paris isolated the HIV-1 strain of the virus. Barre-Sinoussi, a woman researcher in Luc Montagnier's laboratory, was listed as first author on publication in *Science*.[6] However, two men, Luc Montaignier, the director of the research team at the Pasteur Institute, and Robert C. Gallo, then the director of a research team at the National Cancer Institute, have competed for public credit for this discovery (Crewdson 2002).

The common misconception that HIV/AIDS was exclusively a gay men's disease began with the identification of the disease in 1981. The Centers for Disease Control (CDC) published an early warning about a new phenomenon found among patients at several hospitals, including Mount Sinai in New York City (Centers for Disease Control 1981). The cases identified by the CDC were all men, mostly with access to good medical care. The CDC were alerted by doctors concerned about the strange disease that was killing young middle-class men who could, in most circumstances, expect to be extremely healthy (Shilts 1987). Hemophilia, a major cause of blood transfusion, is inherited only by men. For this reason, in the early 1980s, even those who contracted AIDS through infected blood were predominantly men, although a few early documented cases included women.[7]

Once alerted by the cases among middle-class men, researchers soon discovered similar symptoms among migrant sugar cane cutters in Belle Glade Florida. There, men and women workers from the Caribbean, employed at minimal wages by US agricultural business, displayed the characteristic rashes and other symptoms which had already been identified with the mysterious new disease. Within a year, poor and minority men and women in New York City were also found to be infected (Baer et al. 2003).

Later researchers demonstrated that since the 1970s there had been an increase in deaths among poor drug users in the United States which could be attributable to HIV/AIDS misdiagnosed as tuberculosis and pneumonia (Freidman et al. 1990).

Although migrant farm workers and poor black and Latino/Latina New Yorkers had been dying of the new disease, their cases had not precipitated a medical alert. Either their deaths did not appear out of the ordinary or they did not seek care as often or, when they did seek medical help, their cases were not as carefully documented as the men in private care. The fact that both men and women in these poor and vulnerable populations were infected did little to change the public and scientific discourse, which, as noted above, continued to concentrate on men (Ehrhardt and Exner 1987).

By 1985, with a viral test available, men and women living with HIV/AIDS had been tested in Zambia, Kenya, and what was then Zaire, and in each case the ratio of men to women infected was approximately equal. Evidence of AIDS infection in Central Africa was later traced back to 1975, which was approximately as long as in the United States and western Europe (Iliffe 2006; Sabatier 1989). However, in Africa, as among poor people in the US and the Caribbean, the disease caused by the virus was not identified among African populations until the symptoms had been described in the United States and researchers were attempting to map its spread. Thus, the epidemic had been missed until Western, middle-income, predominantly white men began to die.

From early on, researchers understood that since the main characteristic of HIV/AIDS was that it destroyed the immune system, the actual manifestation and symptoms of the disease might vary in relation to the surrounding environment. Clearly the opportunistic diseases to which a person with HIV/AIDS might be exposed in any particular setting would differ dramatically in sub-Saharan Africa, Europe or the United States. As a result the symptoms or manifestations of HIV/AIDS would vary with culture and geography. Nevertheless, since Western research framed the cultural constructs, scientific understandings, and economic investments in treatment, the models developed with respect to gay middle-class men became the basis for diagnosis of HIV among both men and women internationally. As Panos noted, "Typical symptoms" are "based largely on North American and European experience; the syndrome varies considerably from one part of the world to another and less clinical research is available on AIDS patients in developing countries" (Sabatier 1989:6). Diagnosis did not originally include the opportunistic diseases that were most common in sub-Saharan Africa.

Thus, the original Western criteria limited the possibility that either men or women in many parts of Africa could recognize that they had the virus. Kaposi's Sarcoma (KS), a skin lesion almost never seen before in the United States, was used as a diagnostic criterion of AIDS by the Centers for Disease Control. However, Kaposi's Sarcoma, which seldom occurred in women, was endemic in many African countries and therefore not immediately or usefully a symptom of AIDS in that region.

Among middle-class gay men in the West, unusual forms of tuberculosis were an immediate flag that AIDS might be present. However, among poor women and men in the US, as well as in most regions of Africa, Latin America, and even Russia and eastern Europe, there is much untreated tuberculosis. Drug-resistant forms can be found apart from AIDS and are thus not a good indicator of AIDS infection.[8]

Just as diagnoses based on the symptoms of gay Western men with AIDS made AIDS diagnosis difficult in other parts of the world, early diagnostic criteria also made it difficult to diagnose AIDS in women, even in the US (Marte 1996:230). In fact, the Panos report, generally one of the most enlightened of its time, does not even mention women's symptoms, although, as noted above, it was careful to point out the lack of research on the symptoms of Third World AIDS. Oral thrush (oral candidiasis), a yeast infection in the throat, was identified early among Western men with HIV. However, for many years, vaginal yeast infection (vaginal candidiasis), associated with HIV in women, was not officially identified with AIDS. The difficulty in assigning a diagnosis of AIDS to women in the United States limited their access to medical benefits, treatment, and disability assistance. Because of the definition of symptoms for AIDS, many poor women died before they were allowed the official AIDS label, which would have made them eligible for financial assistance (Marte 1996). As a result of women's protests, in 1994 the Centers for Disease Control broadened the diagnostic criteria for AIDS to include vaginal candidiasis and other symptoms more common in women.

After the isolation of the virus in 1983, research on treatment became possible. For the first decade, many Western middle-class men, in desperate straits and also becoming extremely well organized, had early access to treatment through experimental drug trials. Women were not included in these trials, partly because AIDS was seen as a predominantly men's disease, partly too because most of the women were poorer, less educated, and less well organized, and partly because women were routinely excluded from drug trials in the United States (Farmer et al. 1996; Heise and Elias 1995; Susser 2002). To join possibly dangerous experimental drug trials, men and women sign away their rights to legal recourse in the event of toxicity. However, this agreement does not cancel the legal rights of the fetus. Legally, the problems of an infant can be traced much more easily to a mother's exposure than to the father and for this reason, among others, the pharmaceutical industry has historically been wary of including women in trials. Even today, this remains a major obstacle in trials of microbicides, which would involve an invisible vaginal gel to protect women from the virus. Women who are or become pregnant have to be excluded from the trials to protect the fetus. Some current trials re-admit women after the birth of their babies.

Exclusion from early access to experimental drugs, much contested by the women's health movement, had even more profound ramifications. The US Food and Drug Administration (FDA) regularly insisted that new medications be licensed only to the age and sex groups included in the trials, which meant that women had less access to treatments once drugs were tested. The exclusion of women from trials and therefore neglect of treatment possibilities for women and infants was particularly damaging for poorer countries where many more women were infected and where the majority of cases of transmission of the virus from mother to child became concentrated.

Since 2000 and the advent of microbicide trials, vaccines, and research on mother-to-child transmission, contrasting problems of the ethics of experimental research among poor populations of the global South have become a central concern (Craddock 2005). With the highest prevalence of AIDS now occurring in poorer countries, trials must be conducted there. The trials need a large at-risk population in order to measure whether the intervention has shown any preventive effect. Such trials have raised difficult ethical questions. A major issue concerns the equivalence and continuity of care ethically required for people engaged in such trials. A subsidiary but quite thorny issue involves the lack of high-quality or continuing care for mothers who participate in trials of drugs that will reduce AIDS transmission to their infants but not necessarily help the women themselves. A second ongoing challenge, to be discussed later, involves the dubious advocacy of replacement feeding in situations where breastfeeding has for many decades proved the most healthy approach (Coovadia et al. 2007).

The Women's Interagency HIV Study, initiated in response to women's demands and established in 1993, was set up specifically to fill the gender gap left by the original research on men. Federal funding did not permit comparison between men and women through the selection of a similar men's group. However, since its inception the Women in Health publications have printed over 340 articles on the experiences of women in treatment for AIDS (Gollub 2008) and with respect to such issues as cancer of the cervix (Harris et al. 2005).

In spite of these developments, "In reviewing how vertical transmission programs aimed to treat mothers and their unborn" Marion Stevens pointed out in her paper at the 2008 Mexico International AIDS Society Conference, programs have prioritized "preventing transmission to children over treatment for mothers" (Stevens 2008, reviewed in Susser, Stein, and Stevens 2008:2). Clearly, she argues, we need to start working toward guidelines for women of reproductive age and map out the options that serve both women and children well.

The history of women's exclusion from drug trials and medications has had a cumulative effect. The data gathered for men in the global North over many years of taking the medications was not available for women, mostly from the global South. Positive women say that, even now, although some data exists, they have less access to networks with information about how women respond to AIDS medications (personal communication, members of the ICW).[9] On a panel at the 2008 Mexico City International AIDS Society Conference, Gracia Violetta Ross powerfully described her own experiences, which dramatically highlighted the need for more engagement with the issues of treatment, reproduction, and fertility with respect to AIDS. As an HIV-positive woman from Bolivia, 31 years of age, Ross wants very much to have her own children. As a member of ICW, she is a highly informed and educated global activist and spokesperson for people living with HIV and, as she noted, she is expected to be a model of behavior. Fearing widespread condemnation, she courageously announced that she wanted a baby just like any other woman and was having unprotected sex in the effort to conceive. In a discussion afterwards, Ross noted that she had explored every avenue and that since her viral load was undetectable, she felt that she was doing the right thing. Ross called for more research and public discussion of the real and complex decisions with respect to childbirth for HIV-positive women (Ross 2008, reviewed in Susser, Stein, and Stevens 2008:2).

In 1996 when effective anti-retroviral medications were discovered, they became life-saving for middle-class people all over the world. However, most men and women in poor countries were completely excluded from access to the new and expensive treatments. Over time, this economic discrimination, with its deadly consequences, became the focus of a continuing worldwide campaign. Conditions have shifted dramatically. In Brazil, Argentina, and other countries of Latin America, highly active anti-retroviral treatment (HAART) is now distributed through national health services. Assisted by funding from the Bill and Melinda Gates Foundation and elsewhere, Botswana is committed to providing universal access to HAART. By the time this book is published, some affordable treatment is likely to have become available in South Africa, Uganda, and other regions of Africa as a result of powerful social demands.

As I write, in 2008, women are receiving an estimated 59 percent of the HIV care.[10] Although more treatment for AIDS is available today than anyone imagined possible ten years ago,[11] the ways in which the availability and types of treatment will be distributed by income and gender is open to debate.

A recent United Nations Development Program study from India found that, as we might expect, "a significant proportion of new infections are found in women in monogamous relationships but have been infected by husbands or partners who have taken multiple sex partners." However, they also found that, since women are overrepresented among care providers, they find it difficult to seek treatment. "There are significant gender differences in the percentages of untreated opportunistic infections . . . Not only is the percentage of women's illnesses which go untreated higher than that of men, but in the case of women, financial constraints turn out to be an important reason for not seeking treatment."[12] In India, once widowed by AIDS, women often find it easier to go for treatment than when their husbands were alive. Freed from the burden of care and the domination of their partners, widows in India have begun to form strong activist networks (Anandi Yuvaraj, personal communication; Periasamy 2008, reviewed in Susser, Stein, and Stevens 2008).

Many people access health insurance through their work. A few capital-intensive, strongly unionized industries, such as the Anglo-American Mining Company and Coca-Cola Company in South Africa, offer HAART. Since women tend to predominate in low-capitalized, non-union waged work or in the informal sector without any benefits, it remains to be seen whether the trend toward treating more women than men will continue.

In addition, with women continuing to suffer from subordination and oppression internationally, the dearth of women-controlled preventive measures has not yet been fully addressed. Worldwide, women and men are becoming infected faster than treatment is being implemented. In 2007, for every one person who received anti-retroviral treatment, six more were infected (AIDS Vaccine Advocacy Coalition 2007). In fact, estimates suggest that the rate of infection actually escalated worldwide between 2005 and 2007. Thus, clearly, in concert with treatment, technological preventions, and the socially effective distribution of condoms, we need to consider broader social transformations with respect to gender inequality.

## Gender Inequality Increases Childhood Mortality

As noted above, doctors, women, and pharmaceutical companies were initially concerned that anti-retroviral treatments would harm the fetus. It was not until about 15 years into the epidemic that physicians in the US were permitted to try treatments for pregnant women. Only then was it discovered that, in fact, drug treatments during pregnancy and labor reduced the number of children who would test HIV positive after the first year.

Drug treatment during labor and early infancy has become one of the leading tools of prevention for children in the battle against the virus. As a consequence, in the United States and western Europe, the problem of infants who develop HIV/ AIDS almost disappeared in the late 1990s. However, in sub-Saharan Africa, anti-retroviral programs for mothers and infants have only been extensively implemented since the turn of the millennium. By the time such preventive treatments became available, 500,000 infants in sub-Saharan Africa had already been infected at birth (UNAIDS 2000).

Typically, in poor clinics in which there is a program to protect the newborn child, the mother herself still has not been treated. As a result, the infants may be saved to become orphans. In a welcome contrast, newer programs are offering anti-retroviral treatment to infants, mothers, and other positive members of the household (Bassett 2001; ICAP 2007; Rosenfield 2002).[13] So far, this policy initiative is in operation in certain areas but has been delayed by the shortage of clinics, trained personnel, and government commitment in many parts of the world (UNAIDS 2006a). Children have suffered inordinately as the result of the neglect of women's health concerns. Although clearly noted among women researchers in the 1980s (Reid 1997), the significance of the mother–child dyad and the importance of the mother's survival in saving the child was little examined and even now is little emphasized.

In the global South, concerns for children were the leading edge of prenatal prevention. Breastfeeding is one such area. Paying attention to both the mother and the child did not emerge for another ten years. Recently, it has become clear that in many African countries, exclusive breastfeeding, avoiding the pollution of water and bottles, and allowing the mother's immune responses and hormones to be transmitted to the baby has saved more babies over time than the provision of formula (Coovadia et al. 2007; Kuhn 2007). In addition, when the mother is receiving effective anti-retroviral treatment, her breast milk hardly transmits the virus.

It has taken 25 years for research on breastfeeding to develop and the subject is still highly marginal among medical researchers in AIDS. Breastfeeding was not mentioned at the plenaries of the 2006 Toronto International AIDS Society Conference. A panel on breastfeeding was organized as an independent satellite, and no other breastfeeding research was presented at the meetings, despite a plenary presentation on nutrition.

In May 2006, the World Association for Breastfeeding Action (WABA) organized a pre-conference meeting ahead of the 2006 Toronto IAS Conference to address the issues of breastfeeding and AIDS. The event itself, like many other AIDS events, had taken several years to organize from both sides. Women and AIDS activists were concerned about WABA's focus on the infant rather than the woman. WABA activists did not all see AIDS prevention as an appropriate issue for their organization. However, members of several feminist NGOs, including ATHENA, Blueprint for Action on Women and HIV, and the Canadian Positive Women's Network, were invited to the WABA pre-conference in Toronto in 2006. As a result of this pre-conference and other women's organizing efforts, including such advocacy groups as International Committee of Women Living with HIV/AIDS (ICW), Center for Health and Gender Equity (Change), The World Wide Young Women's

Christian Association, and others, a member of WABA was included in the 2008 Mexico City IAS Conference and the category "Nutrition, infant feeding, and food security" was added for abstract submission. As another consequence of these cumulative efforts, Anna Coutsoudis was invited to deliver a pathbreaking presentation in a high-profile session packed with over 500 people at the Mexico 2008 Conference (Coutsoudis 2008). The fact that Coutsoudis's presentation instigated by far the most questions testified to the overwhelming interest in breastfeeding options at this time.

In a picture shown by Anna Coutsoudis, we saw a mother with twins where the hospital had recommended she breastfeed the boy and formula feed the girl. The boy thrived while the baby girl, clearly malnourished in the photo, died the following day. Coutsoudis's main point, sharply illustrated by the photograph, was that breastfeeding promotes child survival. In countries with an infant mortality rate higher than 25 per 1000, exclusive breastfeeding saves babies' lives in the long term. Replacement feeding may eliminate the transmission of HIV only to increase the rates of death from diarrhea and other diseases. Coutsoudis called for a return to the normalization of exclusive breastfeeding, widely practiced in most of the world before the commercialization of formula and baby cereals. She recommended that women in poor countries could exclusively breastfeed, with support for expressing milk and saving it when they worked, even quickly heating it to kill the virus. She suggested that, in light of all the advantages of breastfeeding (which we now know even contributes to brain development), women in middle-income countries should be allowed the option to nurse their babies using similar methods (Coutsoudis 2008).

Although, the significance of the mother–child dyad to child survival was established by Dr. Cicely Williams in the 1950s,[14] in the AIDS literature this is often recognized only implicitly in the gender-specific definition of orphans as those whose mothers have died or who have lost both parents (Barnett and Whiteside 2002:9). However, the failure to address women's concerns with respect to HIV has also dramatically increased the tragedy for children. Even foster-care providers for orphaned children are usually female relatives, who are forced to take on extra responsibility in the face of the epidemic and, as women, are themselves at greater risk of infection (Botswana 2000; Kalipeni et al. 2004). Anthropological studies have described a broad network of kin who have taken care of children in the past (Etienne 1997; Gluckman 1965). In many cases, the concept of kinship obligations extends far beyond any biological relationships (Lee 2003). However, in the face of the ravages of the AIDS epidemic, children without mothers and orphans in general have lost social supports (Hunter and Williamson 1997).

An approach to treatment and prevention which always counseled and treated the woman, pregnant or not, would save the mother as well as the child. The mother could breastfeed, adding to the child's chances of survival. Care providers would survive. Such an approach still has the potential to transform the face of the epidemic in southern Africa.

## Unequal Prevention

In spite of the millions of dollars spent over the past decade on the search for a preventative microbicide or a vaccine, only two proven methods prevent the spread of the virus through sex: the man's condom and the woman's condom. In conventional terms, "condom" usually refers only to the man's condom, but, in fact, a female condom has been available for over 15 years. Both the male and the female condom, if used correctly, have been shown to prevent the spread of the HIV virus at least 90 percent of the time. In addition, the woman's condom is made of an extremely strong form of polyurethane and is less likely to break than the male condom.

A man's condom, whether provided by the man or the woman, is clearly under the control of the man. It has to be put on at the moment of intercourse and requires that the man have an erection. A woman's condom, designed to fit into the vagina, can be inserted by the woman, even several hours before sex. Although, once inserted, the edges of the female condom can be seen by the man, it is under the control of the woman and can be perceived, like the diaphragm, as part of the woman's effort for reproductive health (Mantell et al. 2006; Mantell et al. 2008; Susser 2001; Susser 2002; Susser 2007; Susser and Stein 2000).

In southern Africa today, many of the women becoming infected with HIV/AIDS are married and have already become accustomed to taking responsibility for family planning (Piot 2001; Sinding 2005). Family planning measures, such as Depo-Provera, provide no protection against HIV/AIDS. It is in this context that the woman's condom may prove most useful to HIV prevention.

However, there has been a worldwide disparity in the provision of the woman's condom as opposed to the man's. The man's condom was made available practically as soon as the sexual transmission of AIDS was understood. In the 1980s and 1990s, it was provided in great quantities, free of charge, by the US government and international agencies both in the United States and in many other countries around the world. No requirement was instituted for testing the man's condom to see if it prevented HIV infection before it was distributed universally in the campaign to halt the AIDS epidemic. When men did not like the male condom and did not use it, it was not withdrawn from the market. Until recent policy reversals by the Bush administration discussed in Chapter 2, extensive education and social marketing campaigns were introduced, using film and rock stars on education videos. New colors, aromas, and flavors were used with some success to sell the male condom and make it more appealing. Men who had sex with men had never before used condoms and became a target population of the new "sexy" condom marketing.

The fate of strategies for women to protect themselves from the virus has been different. At least three styles of women's condom were developed in the 1980s in response to the AIDS epidemic. Seeking greater erotic appeal, a European company

**Figure 1.2**   Women and Girls' Rally, International AIDS Society Conference, Toronto 2006. "Survival," 2005, by Fiona Kirkwood (South Africa): 24′ × 4′11″ digital print onto polyester fabric

developed what was known as the "bikini style." It tied around the hips and evoked the sexiness of thong underwear before thongs were as fashionable as they are now. All three female condom styles were subjected to extensive testing and bureaucratic regulation. Only one company survived the ordeal financially. In 1992, after seven years of trials and legislative hurdles, the Reality Female Condom was approved by the US Food and Drug Administration. In 1993, the Reality brand was also approved by the US Medicaid system to be available at reduced costs to women eligible for Medicaid.

However, 15 years later, in 2007, while 11 billion male condoms were distributed worldwide, only 26 million female condoms were circulated (Female Health Company 2007; UNFPA 2007). Little effort or funding from either US or African governments or international agencies have been used to promote this strategy – it is said that women will not use it, or that they already have the man's condom (see Mantell et al. 2006 for review of current literature). Why spend money on promoting a condom for women? A voluminous literature documents the usefulness, feasibility, and cost-effectiveness of the woman's condom (Aggleton et al. 1999; Gollub 2000; Mantell et al. 2006; Wellbourn 2006).

Here I cite some of the most convincing and thorough studies, many of which have been available for over a decade. In Brazil, it was found that when the woman's condom was introduced by knowledgeable and supportive providers, many couples used it and unprotected sex decreased considerably more than when only the man's condom was made available to women (Barbosa et al. 2007). In Senegal and Mexico, UNAIDS experimental programs demonstrated that some women preferred the woman's condom and were more likely to use it than to be able to persuade their husbands to use a man's condom (Mane and Aggleton 2000). In South Africa, when UNAIDS made women's condoms available free to women sex workers in Mpumu-langa Province, the workers reported that men offered to pay more for the woman's condom because they preferred it to the man's condom. In 1998, in Zimbabwe, 30,000 women signed a petition requesting that the woman's condom be made available. (For a review of the studies of the female condom in the United States and elsewhere see Aggleton et al. 1999; Gollub 2000; Mantell et al. 2006; Mantell et al. 2008).

In 2006, at the Toronto International AIDS Society Conference, CHANGE (Center for Health and Gender Equity), led by Jodi Jacobson, launched a campaign to promote the female condom. Much unofficial effort was devoted by feminist health activists to the promotion of the female condom, including an art creation by Fiona Kirkwood, "Survival," which was a textile poster composed of male and female condoms and placed in front of the podium at the Women and Girls' Rally.

The following year, 20 years after the female condom was first manufactured, a major international initiative was funded through the United Nations Fund for Population Activities (UNFPA), also known as the Population Fund, to distribute the female condom. The Society for Women Against AIDS in Africa (Society for Women Against AIDS in Africa 2006) and the Program for Appropriate Technology in Health (PATH and UNFPA 2006),[15] also contributed to the female condom initiative.

Sadly, some of this new recognition of the female condom might be attributed to recent setbacks for the microbicide trial, the diaphragm and the vaccine trials, all in 2007 (AIDS Vaccine Advocacy Coalition 2007).

On November 13, 2007, the *New York Times* "Science" section finally published a spread that highlighted the usefulness of the female condom. However, even in this report the science writer highlighted, as had many other earlier reports, the "yuk" factor as the reason female condoms had not been distributed up till now.[16] Notwithstanding any unaesthetic factor for middle-class Americans, female condoms are now in use in 75 countries and since funding has become available for their distribution, many more women in sub-Saharan Africa and elsewhere are using them (PATH and UNFPA 2006; Society for Women Against AIDS in Africa 2006).

There has been extensive testing of vaginal microbicides, gels that would not be seen or felt in sexual interactions but would kill the virus, which would clearly be preferred by men and women around the world. However, it was announced in July 2000 in Durban that none of these had yet been successful. Seven years later, in January 2007, people were waiting with bated breath for results of further micro-bicide tests and again the results showed that using a microbicide might in fact raise the risk of HIV infection for women (AIDS Vaccine Advocacy Coalition 2007).

An invisible vaginal microbicide that would kill the virus but allow pregnancy is a powerful and important goal but one that is not yet under test, although at least one of the candidate microbicides could do this. Some microbicides now in testing stages would kill the sperm as well as the virus and even then are expected to be less than 50 percent effective. The research on the diaphragm, which would also be invisible in intercourse, has not yet proven conclusively that the method is effective in the prevention of HIV infection although there are possible indications that it may be as good as the male condom (Padian et al. 2007).

The idea that women worldwide should wait for the microbicide option, without having access to the female condom in the interim, suggests an inflexible representation of sexuality for both men and women, at least among a professional elite. It would appear that many national governments, funding agencies, and global non-governmental organizations prefer to wait for an invisible method, possibly more conducive to "beauty" and sexual fantasy, than to promote access to any other method that will save women's lives *now*, even if more clumsy and awkward (Susser 2001). Women are dying for lack of the immediate and secure option of the female condom.

It is sometimes the elision of biological difference, and at other times its emphasis, that contributes to the unequal access for women to strategies for HIV diagnosis, treatment, and prevention. For example, women were denied access to experimental drug trials because the medical community feared the impact of the drugs on pregnancy, a denial based on the biological differences between men and women. In contrast, in the distribution of the male condom, it was assumed that women were somehow equivalent to men. If women had access to male condoms, it was as if women themselves had them – inequality justified by ignoring biological difference.

Whether women are viewed as the same as or different from men, female needs have rarely been met and, as a result, the lives of children and men have been ravaged by the various forms of cultural blindness that continue to plague efforts to prevent disease.


## Gender Inequality and the Relentless Inevitability of Infection


The ongoing costs of gender and sexual inequality outlined here can be tracked again in the shifting demographics of HIV/AIDS worldwide. In the early 1980s in sub-Saharan Africa, HIV was found in a ratio of one man to one woman. In the same region by 2000 more women than men were infected, and while men were dying between the ages of 25 and 45, women were dying of HIV/AIDS between the ages of 15 and 25 (Botswana 2000; Piot 2001). By 2000, twice as many young girls as young boys, age 15–24, in Namibia, Botswana, and throughout southern Africa were living with AIDS. In Namibia, 20 percent of young girls aged 15–24 were living with AIDS and 9 percent of young boys. In Botswana, 34 percent of young girls between 15 and 24 were living with AIDS, as compared with 16 percent of young boys (UNICEF 2000). At that time, one community sero-prevalence study in Ndola,

Zambia found four sero-positive girls age 14 for every one sero-positive boy of the same age (UNAIDS 2000). In 2007, if the growing gender disparity among youth is any indication, as girls are living with AIDS at a rate three times that of boys in sub-Saharan Africa, the epidemic of the future bodes even worse for women (Physicians for Human Rights 2007).

As noted earlier, similar trends toward the greater infection of young women can be traced in the United States. Although proportionately few women were infected in the early 1980s, by 2006, 25 years into the epidemic, many more women had become infected. black women were still particularly at risk:

> During 2001–2004, in 35 areas with HIV reporting, 51 percent of all new HIV/AIDS diagnoses were among blacks, who account for approximately 13 percent of the US population. Of these, 11 percent (12,650) of HIV/AIDS diagnoses in men were in black men who were infected through heterosexual contact, and 54 percent (23,820) of HIV/AIDS diagnoses in women were in black women infected through heterosexual contact. In the US today, women account for approximately one quarter of all new HIV/AIDS diagnoses and, in 2002, HIV infection was the leading cause of death for black women aged 25–34 years (Centers for Disease Control: Fenton and Valdiserri 2006).

In the United States, HIV has even shifted regionally from its main concentration in the urban north. Poor young Black women in the rural south infected through heterosexual sex are a new and fast-growing population (Centers for Disease Control: Fenton and Valdiserri 2006). Clearly we are watching the interplay of inequality in race, class, and gender reflected in the medical and health experience.

HIV/AIDS affects women differently than men and worldwide affects as many, if not more, women than men. With respect to every aspect of HIV, transmission, diagnosis, treatment, access to care, care-giving, reproduction, and stigma, women have particular experiences and needs different than men. Historically, women were diagnosed later than men, and treated, if at all, later than men. Apart from (or, more accurately, in association with) the biological, women have different kin and household responsibilities and expectations, different demands at different points of the life cycle, and, of course, very different access to employment and resources.

I am not arguing here for an essentialist perspective on "woman" but rather for a holistic and practical vision which takes women's lives in terms of class, inheritance patterns, gendered violence, and employment opportunities into account, along with obvious biological differences. This is the kind of vision that is being generated by Physicians for Human Rights in their studies of Botswana and Swaziland when they begin their Executive Summary with the statement:

> HIV/AIDS interventions focused solely on individual behavior will not address the factors creating vulnerability to HIV for women and men in Botswana and Swaziland, nor protect the rights and assure the wellbeing of those living with HIV/AIDS. National leaders, with the assistance of foreign donors and others, are obligated under international law to change the unequal social, legal and economic conditions of women's lives which facilitate HIV transmission and impede testing, care and treatment. Without these

immediate and comprehensive reforms, they cannot hope to halt the deadly toll of HIV/AIDS on their populations (Physicians for Human Rights 2007:1).

## Reconsidering Biology: Some Notes on the History of Public Health Terms

The representation of women's issues within public health and AIDS research was overdetermined in a number of ways. Clearly, Western funds and Western research emphasis was initially on the first identified Western problem of the gay epidemic, as it was called early on. As the disease was recognized, the tragedies of early death among middle-class Western men led through denial to outrage (Shilts 1987). Both men and women, as represented most dramatically in the gay and lesbian cooperation in such important and effective protest groups as ACT UP, called for action (Brier forthcoming). They protested the lack of funds and research and demanded the speed-up of drug trials. In fighting the stigma of homosexuality and defining the human right to confidentiality, activists framed the AIDS debate in terms of what was most progressive and enlightened for the Western epidemic among gay men (Oppenheimer 1988; Oppenheimer and Bayer 2007).

However, as has been argued with respect to the general discourse on human rights and enlightenment values, rights must be framed within a situated understanding of poor people and women of color in the West and women in different contexts worldwide (Asad 2000; Nussbaum 1999). We need to also consider the situated rights and challenges of women with biological and socially different positions from the gay men who framed the important demands of the Western epidemic.

In the early 1990s some activists recognized the different problems of poor and minority people living with AIDS. For example, New York ACT UP worked to prevent evictions of poor people with AIDS who could no longer pay their rent. They blocked traffic with furniture and through a variety of strategies fought successfully for the rights of people with AIDS to government-subsidized housing (Eric Sawyer, personal communication, 2003). However, as mentioned earlier, in this period, most poor women did not survive to present the symptoms which would allow them to access that right.

The much-criticized public health focus on "risk groups" also led to a lack of understanding of women's issues (Baer et al. 2003; Patton 1990). As discussed earlier, risk groups such as IV drug users, partners of IV drug users, and sex workers were singled out in the literature without attention to their lives as men or women in the social context of families or neighborhoods (Baer et al. 2003; Patton 1990). From early on, in the US, Uganda, and elsewhere, it was evident that married women, women civil service workers or even professionals were also contracting AIDS (Mann and Tarantola 1996). However, partially reflecting the power of the "risk group" characterization of women sex workers, even today, one speaker in

2006 at Toronto said, "We sex workers are never included in panels that are about 'women.'"

A third issue that led to the misunderstanding of the epidemic among women stemmed from the epidemiological perspective that focuses on the modes of transmission. Here we return to terminology. The very terms that have been used to describe the women's AIDS epidemic have sometimes obscured our understanding of the processes of transmission. "Heterosexual transmission" is the term most frequently used in the public health literature to index the problem of women contracting HIV through sex with men. Talking about and measuring "heterosexual transmission," while appearing to construct a scientifically specific image, makes invisible the actual differences in behavior as well as minimizing the differences in risk of infection between men and women involved in a sexual encounter. Such an apparently objective rendition of behavior as "heterosexual sex" erases gender differences and confuses scientific questions with respect to the transmission of HIV/AIDS: the biological, the cultural, and the social.

If we look at the research literature since 2000, we can see some of the confusing aspects. One review illustrates the problem:

> Heterosexual intercourse is the most common mode of transmission of HIV in poor countries. In Africa slightly more than 80 percent of infections are acquired heterosexually, while mother-to-child transmission (5–15 percent) and transfusion of contaminated blood account for the remaining infections[3]. In Latin America most infections are acquired through men having sex with men and through misuse of injected drugs, but heterosexual transmission is rising. Heterosexual contact and injection of drugs are the main modes of HIV transmission in South and South-East Asia (Lamptey 2002:207).

When this writer says "heterosexual transmission is rising," he means that more women are becoming infected. However, nowhere is the problem stated this way. In this paragraph the words "men", "mother" and "child" are used, never "women." We are never told whether the drug users are men or women, but implicitly "drug user" is coded as "men" and, as we shall see later, the consequent heterosexual transmission referred to in the article is to partners of drug users almost universally read as "women." In the rest of the article, the differences between men and women's experiences are reduced to a general concern with "women's vulnerability." In the literature, transmission of the virus to men through female sex workers is stressed, but sexual differences in the behavior of women, in general, are seldom raised. Often, women, 50 percent of the human population, are classified as "vulnerable groups" and problems related to the infection and treatment of women are incorporated into general themes such as "culture."

A detailed review of the 2006 Toronto IAS Conference Track categories and the proposed categories for 2008 reveals what tended to make invisible the differences between men and women. In Toronto, categories such as "culture" and "vulnerable groups" became the general terminologies under which issues of women's subordination or women's different opportunities might be classed. The problems of women as a whole – biological challenges and opportunities, social and economic inequalities, and cultural subordination – were rarely highlighted.

Firstly, of course, only women contract HIV/AIDS through the vagina, though, of course, heterosexual relations for women can be vaginal or anal. Anal sex may be even more risky for women than vaginal sex (Exner et al. 2008). Since women are much more subject to gender-based violence (Jewkes et al. 2004), it can be assumed that women are more likely to have participated or been forced to participate in anal sex than men. In regions such as Puerto Rico, with its long history of Catholicism and emphasis on virginity, extremely high rates of anal sex between male and female young college students have been documented. These particularly high rates of anal sex might suggest that the women are trying to avoid pregnancy and the "violation" of their virginity while acquiescing to their male partner's demands (Cunningham 1994).

Overall, since the measures of "heterosexual transmission" do not in themselves imply the differences in cultural, economic, age, or physical power between the two groups, the "men" and "women" incorporated indiscriminately in the term "heterosexual" are in fact apples and oranges. Such confounding of categories makes it difficult to sort out the social and cultural pathways of risk and vulnerability. Although there is much speculation and some evidence that women are more likely to be infected through sex with men than men are infected through sex with women, 30 years into the epidemic, definitive data on this question is still not available. Just as there has been extensive discussion in the social science literature of the ways in which blindness to racial difference does not address racial discrimination (Baker 2001; Harrison 1995), so an insistence on terms such as "heterosexual" and even "gender" serve in many ways to erase important differences in the experiences of women and men, including the subordination of women.

As mentioned earlier, the other category that usually designates women and somewhat vaguely overlaps with "heterosexual transmission" is the term "partners of IV drug users." This term almost universally implies women who do not use IV drugs and became infected through sex with men: in other words, a specific form of "heterosexual transmission." As we can see, women disappear from the scene as researchers write:

> Three cases of pediatric AIDS in children born in 1977 provided the first evidence for HIV infection among drug users in New York ... Their only known risk factor was that they were born to IV drug using mothers ... The first 5 known cases among heterosexual IV drug users occurred in 1980 when there were an additional 3 cases with IV drug use and male homosexual activity as risk behaviors (Des Jarlais et al. 1992:280).

Here, although obviously we know, we are not told that the drug-using mothers also took part in heterosexual sex. One might ask, was the cause drug use or sexual transmission? We are to assume it was drug use, as this is the categorical hierarchy of the CDC. We do not know if the "5 heterosexual IV drug users" are women or men, only that the other three were men who had sex with men. If a woman uses drugs, she is assumed to have contracted HIV through drugs not sex. A man's drug use and sex with men is classified as possible sexual transmission (Exner et al. 2003). The particular article cited above, on the history of IV drug use and AIDS, concludes with a call for more attention to drug users themselves, rather than to their transmission of the virus to women, heterosexual men, and children. However, it fails to discuss the differences between men and women drug users or men and women's sexual experiences (reviewed recently in Gollub 2008).

The superficially objective "behavioral" distinction "partners of IV drug users" blurs much of the most useful information for understanding the increasing transmission of HIV/AIDS to women and young girls. We read sentences like this confusing quote taken from the recent AMSA report, *AIDS has a Woman's Face* (American Medical Student Association 2005). Speaking of eastern Europe and central Asia, the investigators write:

> . . . Most of the IV drug users are young and sexually active, characteristics leading to an increasing prevalence of sexual transmission as a mode of transmission.

In each continent this publication shows that women and young girls are becoming the largest group infected with AIDS. Each time IV drug use is mentioned, the sexual consequences are noted in the same vague way, without any examination of which group is using the drugs and which group is subsequently receiving the infection through sexual intercourse.

Clearly, sexual behavior is changeable and culturally determined. However, the biological, social, and cultural differences between the experiences and behavior of men and women which are hidden in the terms "heterosexual transmission" and "partners of IV drug users" simply illustrate the challenges faced by women as well as possible programs for intervention and prevention. Such differences are far from captured in the passing addition of women to a list of "vulnerable" groups, often including "orphans" (as noted above, another term that elides its gendered implications often meaning boys and girls without *mothers*) and poor people in general.

Recent controversy surrounding the important preventive success of medically supervised adult male circumcision has also been sparked by a seeming inattention to women. Demographic evidence has long suggested that male circumcision may reduce transmission among both men and their partners in the overall circumcised population. We also know from extensive data in three randomized control trials that medically supervised adult male circumcision performed in such trials reduced infections among men by 50–60% (AIDS Vaccine Advocacy Coalition 2007). In other words, male circumcision is much less effective than a condom or a female condom, when actually used, but possibly of great benefit in the light of the fact that many couples use neither of these. This promising finding is the basis on which current policy recommendations are being considered.

In the crucial need to scale up prevention and the disappointing results for microbicide, vaccine, and even to a certain extent the diaphragm trials, this recent data on male circumcision, which shows that although it does not consistently protect men from infection, it reduces the probability that a man will become infected through sex, has been hailed by the scientific community with relief.

However, the differing prevention effects of male circumcision for men and women have not been much considered in the currently published research (Berer 2007).

We do not know from any randomized control trials whether male circumcision reduces or possibly increases the risk for transmission of the virus to women or, in fact, to male partners of men. Following the pattern of leaving out women in previous research, of the three recent studies of male circumcision as a protection from HIV infection, only the one directed by Dr. Maria Wawer included any follow-up of women partners (AIDS Vaccine Advocacy Coalition 2007). All three studies showed that an HIV-negative man was less likely to turn positive if he was circumcised. However, there was obviously no protection from the circumcision for an HIV-positive man and possibly some increased vulnerability for his partner. The demographic effects predicted by modeling sexual interactions suggest that if enough men are circumcised (estimated around 70%) over a number of years, male circumcision should contribute to a reduction of HIV infection in the general population.

The one study that included the women partners of circumcised men did not include enough women to show whether women were protected or possibly put at risk by male circumcision. As noted above, there is some indication that if the man is HIV positive, his participation in a male circumcision program may increase the risks for his partner (AIDS Vaccine Advocacy Coalition 2007).[17] As Marge Berer pointed out astutely at the Mexico 2008 IAS Conference, male circumcision is the first preventive measure yet invented that protects only one of the partners in a sexual encounter (Berer 2008).

Ironically, if we were considering women's protection, perhaps there should have been a move to advocate male circumcision over 20 years ago when researchers established that it protects women from cervical cancer. Instead, the American Association of Pediatricians dropped its recommendations for infant male circumcision some time after that finding was established.

As noted above, a demographic argument has been made that if male circumcision reduces men's likelihood of being infected by women, it will reduce the overall rate of infection. However, this will be less effective if men, feeling safer, simply increase their sexual activity without using condoms or if, as many men have done, they have sex before the wounds of the operation have healed (Berer 2007; AIDS Vaccine Advocacy Coalition 2007). Although more systematic research data is not yet available, women have also reported that men have used the fact that they had had the cut to argue or even force women into unprotected sex. Under these conditions, the rates of infection for some women may rise.

If male circumcision is introduced as – or simply believed to be, in spite of careful health education messaging – a sure-fire protection from AIDS, its ultimate failures to live up to such certainty may backfire and, in fact, contribute further to the general suspicion of Western technologies already prevalent in many regions. In addition, if circumcision works as a partial preventive measure, it was suggested jokingly at a meeting I attended that perhaps we should also be advocating simple hygiene measures. Nevertheless, considering the current dearth of effective prevention measures, it is clear that male circumcision should be added to the armamentarium of harm-reduction technologies for sexual encounters. The way in which it is introduced will go a long way toward determining how effective it will be as a form of harm reduction.

In the face of the continuing scarcity of women-controlled HIV prevention methods, Zena Stein has suggested that we should revisit the findings on the diaphragm as a reasonable form of harm reduction. In article entitled *The Diaphragm Lives!* she argued that "careful study of the findings of Nancy Padian's pathbreaking randomized control trial (RCT) of the diaphragm suggest that the diaphragm probably did act as 'harm reductive'. Thus the efficacy of the diaphragm was suggested by the findings that although many of those in the experimental group abandoned the condom and used the diaphragm alone, the two groups achieved equally good results" (Stein et al. 2008).

As Stein points out, almost since the epidemic began, she and others have wondered if the vaginal diaphragm might not have a "harm reduction" role in protecting women. Used by generations of women as an alternative to the male condom in preventing pregnancy, it did reduce, although not absolutely prevent, conceptions. It also gave some protection against other sexually transmitted infections. As understanding of HIV emerged it could be argued that the diaphragm gave protection to the cervix, the site of many of the cells that are infected by the semen.

Stein notes that the degree of protection the diaphragm achieves is uncertain but its known merits have been neglected for too long. The evidence for protection given by the male condom never included Randomized Control Trials (RCTs) that examined the protection they give to women. In fact, as Stein emphasizes, the trials only traced the protection from sexually transmitted infection that they gave to sailors, spending their time ashore. In recent years, however, reports of male condom use – still not RCTs – among discordant couples have been persuasive that consistent use gives protection for both partners.

Women's experience differs dramatically from men's in many ways beyond the biology of sexual transmission. It becomes necessary to state the obvious: only women can become pregnant and in this way transmit the HIV virus to their children (Reid 1997). This crucial biological difference means that an HIV-positive baby can be directly traced to her positive mother. Thus, women generally find out in a much more public way than their sexual partners that they are HIV positive (Reid 1997). A man can continue to deny an AIDS infection, but a woman with a sick baby cannot. As mothers all over the world have discovered, an infant with

AIDS deprives its mother of the right to choose whether to be tested and in fact makes such a choice irrelevant. Many of the discussions of voluntary testing and counseling turn a blind eye to this issue which, again, has dramatically different implications for men and women.[18]

Equally, only women can transmit the virus to children through breastfeeding. Correspondingly, only pregnant or breastfeeding women can transmit protective or harmful medications through their bloodstream to infants. All of these differences have had profound consequences for the experience of HIV/AIDS for women. As will be seen in the discussion of poor women in southern Africa, when HIV/AIDS affects the very basis of social and biological reproduction, a woman's ability to bear a child and create a family, this carries very different implications for lifetime decisions than the possible transmission of HIV/AIDS from man to man, or even through female and male sex workers.

The human and emotional dilemmas for women in their role as partners and mothers are dramatized in the fact that many women sex workers require their clients to use condoms. Nevertheless, the same women cannot easily make the same demand of their boyfriends or lovers (Cleland et al. 2006). The conflicts facing women in the constitution of family life are particularly challenging in the era of HIV/AIDS.

Clearly, condom use is universally situational and men too will behave differently with sex workers or casual partners than with their wives. A man may wish for children in his relations with a woman and therefore refrain from condom use. However, as we have seen, it is the woman who is at most risk of infection from such a decision and, in many sexual situations, the woman is subordinate to the man and he defines the nature of the relationship. Of course, it is also the woman who will have to bear the infant and often take the responsibility for raising the child whether or not her partner, herself, the baby or other children in the family are subsequently living with HIV/AIDS.

Thus, before we even begin to outline the historical, social, and economic discrimination women have suffered, combined with the lack of access to equal inheritance, and education and employment today, we have to recognize that biology has framed the experience of women in this epidemic differently than for men.

In conclusion, in poorer countries, where sexual transmission between men and women is dominant, women are in a central and, from this perspective, powerful position with respect to the HIV epidemic. As the first diagnosed by dint of bearing an HIV-positive infant, they are regularly exposed to blame and victimization for their positive status. As mothers who can protect their infants from transmission of the virus breastfeed to promote child survival and, in maintaining their own health, prevent a child from becoming an orphan, they hold a potential key to limiting the devastation. Approaches to treatment and prevention may either counteract or exacerbate existing patterns of inequality and discrimination by gender. As was first said in 1997, only by putting women in the center of thinking about the epidemiology of HIV/AIDS can we fully address the increasing rates of transmission throughout the world (Reid 1997).

## Social Context of AIDS Research

Paula Treichler, Shirley Lindenbaum, and others early on, drew our attention to the problem of the Western gaze on AIDS (Lindenbaum 1997; Patton 1990; Treichler 1992). Scientific theories were developed based on a medical paradigm which did not take the local realities or perceptions into account but drew rather on Western representations of, for example, "darkest Africa." In particular, Treichler commented on the heavy reliance on statistics to deal with the unknown. When nothing is known, the way statistics are used can also lead to paradigms that fit stereotypic conceptions. She called for a diversity of voices in the attempt to introduce diversity into science (Treichler 1992). Although many of these problems persist, there is no doubt that, after a prolonged struggle, qualitative work and anthropological analyses have gained more credibility and funding in contemporary AIDS research (e.g. Farmer et al. 1996; Hirsch et al. 2007; Lee and Susser 2006; Parker et al. 2000).

Although incorporating history and political economy into our understandings of the HIV/AIDS epidemic has long been recognized as essential to an ethnographic analysis of AIDS (Barnett and Whiteside 2002; Bond et al. 1997; Parker 2001; Schoepf 2001), it is also crucial to examine the historically changing relations of men and women within this context and to sort out which generalizations apply to men and which to women (Morrell 2001; Schoepf 2004; Susser 2002).

Nevertheless, even in much of the sociologically informed literature on AIDS with respect to gender, the unmarked category tends to assume privilege and refer to men. For example, Barnett and Whiteside's volume *AIDS in the Twenty-First Century* (2002) is written in terms of "sociological" categories such as "individuals," "people," "wage earners," and "parents" without in-depth consideration of how men and women differ in ways they take on or experience such roles.

In discussions of the economic impact of AIDS, Barnett and Whiteside stress "households." However, like the word "heterosexual," the word "household" obscures more than it reveals. In addressing AIDS effectively, it seems important to consider further the implications of the exploitation of women's labor in the household, documented in the development literature in many parts of the world (Kabeer 1997). As we have often been reminded, the global economy frames the possibilities for governments, women, and men in dealing with AIDS (Altman 2002; Parker 2001; Susser 2004). Thus, we need to understand the interplay of the ideologies of gender and race with local, national, and international politics.

## Global Strategies: Women's Rights To Health

The international recognition of the feminization of HIV/AIDS has been both temporary and erratic. Indeed, the current political climate leaves little assurance that women's demands for protection, care, and treatment will progress in any concerted fashion in the coming years. While much attention has been paid to maternal transmission of the virus, the protection of women from infection has been less considered.

In 1990 at the San Francisco International AIDS Society Conference, plenary speakers Mindy Fullilove and Helen Rodriguez-Trias both articulately raised the issues of women's subordination. The Women's Caucus of the HIV Association was formed at this meeting. The 1992 International AIDS Society Conference was held in Amsterdam after people refused to accept a conference proposed for Boston due to US restrictions on allowing people living with HIV/AIDS to enter the US.[19] The decision was made rather late, which left little preparation time. Jonathan Mann, co-chair of the conference, was adamant that human rights and community participation – especially including people living with HIV/AIDS – would be a key theme of the conference.

At that time, a group of women living with HIV/AIDS in the Netherlands wanted to establish connections with other HIV-positive women around the world. The women's group of the HIV Association and members of ACT UP The Netherlands proposed holding a pre-conference meeting that would unite positive women and help prepare them for navigating the conference. Fifty-six women from 27 countries attended this initial event and over the years ICW came to represent an extremely central group of women activists.[20] As a result of this history of women's activism, a plenary at the 1994 Yokohama IAS Conference focused on "Methods Women con Use' (Stein 1994).

In Durban during 2000, at the International AIDS Society Conference, Geeta Rao Gupta (2000) gave a plenary speech concerned with women and AIDS. This was the first conference to be held in the global South. To enter the scientific conference required a hefty registration payment. Community-based women leaders and global advocates collaborated to create a forum parallel to the Durban conference that would be open to the public. "Women at Durban," as this initiative would come to be called, highlighted the need for open forums where community members could engage the International AIDS Society Conferences and led to the initiation of "Women at Barcelona" and "Mujeres Adelante" at the subsequent IAS Conference in Barcelona, Spain. "Women at Barcelona" was organized to bring together advocates and researchers on women and HIV at the conference. Organized by ICW in Barcelona, "Mujeres Adelante" was a parallel forum, open to the public, which focused on the engagement of local community women living with HIV. However, Mujeres Adelante staged a march at the closing ceremony to highlight their frustration with the neglect of issues important to HIV-positive women. The difficulties for women to be heard in the conference persisted.

Together, these initiatives set the stage for the International AIDS Society to incorporate a forum at the IAS Conferences that would be open and available to local community members and conference delegates alike. The Global Village became institutionalized at the IAS Conference in Bangkok, Thailand where the Thai Women and AIDS Task Force set forth a feminist platform.

At the 2002 Barcelona conference, the Women's Caucus of the International AIDS Society convened to draw up a set of principles for the health rights of women and girls, which became the Barcelona Bill of Rights. The Barcelona Bill of Rights, which included the controversial right to abortion among such issues as rights to land and inheritance, was reiterated and carried forward at the 2004 Bangkok International AIDS Society Conference. *ATHENA: Advancing Gender Equity and Human Rights in the Global Response to HIV/AIDS*[21] was formed after Bangkok to connect feminist, human rights, and AIDS networks in global activism. Building from this history, ATHENA, ICW, Blueprint, and Voices of Positive Women joined to convene the inaugural Women's Networking Zone in the Global Village of the IAS Conference in Toronto. Since that time, a Women's Networking Zone has been designated at international AIDS meetings, and panels related to women's claims and women's marches have been organized (Susser 2007).

One of the many interventions that takes women's lives into account is a "one-stop shopping" clinic for women and girls that includes family planning, HIV/AIDS prevention and treatment, and prenatal care. Since the 1980s, some public health activists, recognizing the centrality of women's experience of reproduction to the spread of the HIV/AIDS epidemic, have recommended that family planning clinics integrate HIV/AIDS services into their routine interactions with women. As long as they included all services, from sex education for young girls, fertility planning for positive women, harm reduction programs to well-baby clinics, this would certainly be a significant intervention. Indeed, in 2000, this was adopted as one of the Millennial Goals of the United Nations. Mary Robinson, who was then the UN Commissioner for Human Rights, and many others have advocated for these goals on the international stage ever since.[22] However, such an obvious and seemingly logical, practical, and economical approach to HIV/AIDS prevention has seldom been put into practice. Since 2000, as we shall see in the next chapter, family planning itself has come under attack. For this reason, the comprehensive approach to family planning and AIDS visualized in one-stop shopping care and prevention programs seems like an even more remote possibility, though still eminently worth striving for.

In related developments crucial to protection from HIV/AIDS, the 1995 Beijing Conference on Women represented a pinnacle for the international recognition of women's sexual and reproductive rights. But significantly, while Beijing and the 1985 Conference on Women in Nairobi were high points in women's rights and reproductive and sexual health, there was little link to HIV despite this parallel course. It has only been in the past few years that a tighter link between the reproductive and sexual health community or the women's rights community and HIV has been crafted.

Women's ability to negotiate care and prevention of HIV/AIDS has recently been constrained by newly initiated international contestation of sexual and reproductive rights (Baer et al. 2003; Petchesky 2003). In line with US support for global restrictions on women's reproductive health and sexual rights, the US funding constraints with respect to international policies including sex education and abortion and the encouragement of faith-based initiatives and abstinence are also limiting and shaping the global possibilities for AIDS prevention and care.

## A Theoretical Reevaluation: The View Over Time

Having thus reviewed both the exhilarations and frustrations of struggling with the issues of gender and AIDS in terms of public health interventions and social movements, in the following chapters I step back from the fray in order to develop a more comprehensive theoretical framework for understanding the culture and politics of gender with respect to AIDS. I have tried to explore the reasons why, in spite of high visibility in global and even national discourse, women's needs with respect to AIDS are still far from addressed. In this effort, I outline the particular historical processes that have shaped women's experiences on the ground as well as contemporary ideologies of gender. I describe public health professionals, political actors and activists, and grass-roots leaders as they frame public discourse at particular historical moments. Through multiple voices, attention to changing global and class relations, gender, and social movements, I examine how the tragedy of AIDS plays its part in the public sphere and frames the domestic lives of women. I explore how the ongoing politics of sexuality, gender, race, and class in South Africa, Namibia, and among the San of the Kalahari have shaped women and men's options as they continue to fight for a future of their own making.

# 2

# Imperial Moralities and Grassroots Realities

*Our knowledge of HIV remains inadequate. And yet we are drowning in evidence which is not applied, driven by theological and moral beliefs over fact-based, accurate information. (Elisabet Fadul, first youth plenary speaker at XVII International AIDS Society Conference, Mexico City, 2008)*

As we have seen, biology, culture and social organization, low incomes and the lack of services conspire to render women extraordinarily susceptible to HIV infection. Under these conditions, it is crucial to examine whether women's abilities to negotiate gender roles have been further limited or enhanced through the regulation of funding by the United States and other international players. And, in fact, the US government's funding policies do directly affect the particular constraints women face in southern Africa and throughout the world. Here, I outline the contested policies with respect to HIV/AIDS in the United States. We shall explore how, as with the framing of scientific perspectives, such policies are intimately related to US political battles fueled by ideologies of gender and race. We then trace the ways in which these different approaches are transmitted through US funding to poor countries.

As I write, in 2008, the President's Emergency Plan for AIDS Relief (PEPFAR) contributes the largest proportion of money available for treatment and prevention for the global epidemic.[1] Doubtless, funding for treatment provided by PEPFAR and other major funders is saving countless lives. The fact that the money for treatment exists is a major tribute to 25 years of health activism around the world. In 2006, however, only one in five of those in need were receiving HAART (highly active anti-retroviral therapy) (UNAIDS 2007). By 2008, this had increased to one in three, which is an extremely hopeful sign. However, we are still not near to meeting global needs. In addition, simply sustaining treatment over the lifetimes of those already receiving HAART constitutes a major global challenge (UNAIDS 2006 Report on the Global AIDS Epidemic).

It is generally recognized that the next great step must be, as one plenary speaker at the XVII International AIDS Society Conference at Mexico City put it, "Highly Active HIV Prevention" (Cohen 2008) combined with a much more stalwart and broader commitment to address the social context of AIDS (Richter 2008). The PEPFAR funds are central to the scaling up of treatment; however, even as treatment becomes available, it becomes ever more critical to examine PEPFAR restrictions on social programs for prevention in order to slow the rate of new infections.

Health professionals, activists, and governments understand the importance of continued US funding for saving lives worldwide. Many have argued that it is counterproductive to criticize PEPFAR regulations but better to adjust to them within each program. Health professionals in several African countries told me that although regulations are restrictive, they are able to carry out prevention without interference from local PEPFAR representatives. To such health providers, questions about the impact of US regulations on stigma, gender hierarchies, and prevention in general have seemed relatively unimportant. In fact, an editorial from *The Lancet* in 2004 asked whether it was not "churlish" to criticize President Bush over his spending policies (Lancet 2004).

However, an evaluation of global AIDS funding which compared Mozambique, Uganda, and Zambia noted: "Overall resources from all three donors appear to be disproportionately focused on treatment and care at the expense of prevention" (Oomman et al. 2007:xii). They point out that "PEPFAR funding is least conducive [among the three major global funders] to allowing recipients to implement comprehensive approaches that combine elements of treatment, prevention, and/or care."

The evaluation of global funding in the three African countries proceeds to stress that, for the United States, "achieving its globally set programmatic targets and its accountability to Congress take precedence over any other feature." In line with these targets, the distribution of PEPFAR funds is remarkably uniform across countries with different epidemiological features. As the evaluators note:

> PEPFAR funding is largely allocated based on requirements set by the US Congress for the treatment, prevention, and care of patients as well as orphans and vulnerable children. The distribution of funds is strikingly similar across the three countries, with the largest share going to treatment (Oomman et al. 2007:ix).

Thus, the politics of the United States are central to the framing of PEPFAR and to the inadequate funding of prevention worldwide. This gap in funding for prevention, combined with constraints on comprehensive sex education and reproductive health, limits the possibilities for women and men to protect themselves from HIV infection.

As the epidemic increases even faster than treatment is being provided (Beyrer 2006), as noted above, prevention becomes ever more central even to the long-term sustainability of treatment programs. Women's sexual subordination and centrality in reproduction and childrearing are crucial to prevention. For this reason, the moralities explicit in US funding and the ways in which these constrain women's ability to protect themselves worldwide are of prime importance.

## What is PEPFAR?

In January 2003, George W. Bush announced the creation of the President's Emergency Plan for AIDS Relief, PEPFAR, a program to funnel US funding for prevention and treatment primarily to 15 countries selected by the administration.

From its inception, PEPFAR put treatment first. Fifty-five percent of its funding was mandated for the purchase of patented US pharmaceuticals rather than the cheaper generic drugs. This requirement raised the costs for treatment and substantially reduced the number of drugs that could be bought worldwide (Center for Health and Gender Equity 2004). Twenty percent of the funds were assigned for prevention; 15 percent for care; and 10 percent for orphans and vulnerable children. Over the past few years, PEPFAR has strayed little from these proportional guidelines (Oomman et al. 2007).

Under PEPFAR, support for what is known as "harm reduction" is minimal. Harm reduction is based on the concept that if drug users do not stop using drugs they can still learn to protect themselves from AIDS (Friedman and Lipton 1991; Friedman et al. 2007). Harm reduction programs, among other projects, involve helping drug users to exchange dirty needles for clean or providing them with condoms to prevent the sexual transmission of HIV. Such programs have been shown to be extremely effective in reducing the spread of AIDS worldwide (Wodak et al. 2004). However, in 2006, those funds for "injection safety activities" – as included in the prevention budget – represented only 2 percent of the PEPFAR allocations (PEPFAR 2006: Planned Funding for Prevention, Treatment and Care in 15 Focus Countries).

PEPFAR, instead, promotes what has been designated by the Bush administration as the "ABC" approach to prevention – so called in reference to its major tenets:

*A*bstinence-only, *B*e faithful, use a *C*ondom

This approach is outlined as follows: firstly, a declaration to abstain until marriage. Unfortunately, this program (which is required for teenagers) also "abstains" from sex education, discussion of sexual orientation, contraceptives, and family planning. The directive "be faithful" encourages monogamy in committed couples. The condom and its proper use are not taught in abstinence-only education and any mention is directed largely at sex workers. Central to understanding this approach is its financial incentive, a ruling that 66 percent of all money for prevention *must* be spent on abstinence-only and fidelity.

ABC, as promoted by the Bush administration, focuses only on heterosexual relations. It also ignores the long-accumulated data demonstrating that marriage is a major risk factor for women in terms of their likeliness to become infected with HIV (Hirsch et al. 2007). Single people are often taught abstinence only and encouraged to adopt "secondary virginity" after they have already been sexually active. Institutions which receive PEPFAR funding internationally must sign a pledge condemning sex work and trafficking and risk the loss of funds if they are associated with any programs related to reproductive choice or abortion.[2] Condoms and other prevention, including blood safety, injection safety, comprehensive sex education or work with men who have sex with men are not mandated for any percentage of prevention funds. Counseling and testing for HIV infection are also not mandated expenses. Any of these issues could be neglected altogether without violating PEPFAR requirements.

The failure to provide comprehensive sex education or counseling with respect to issues of sexual orientation or reproductive choice, in fact, violates human rights requirements (Freedman 1999; Human Rights Watch 2005). Women, men, and children have the human right to know about their own bodies and risks to their own health (Freedman 1999; Santelli et al. 2006).[3] In 2006, the BBC gave back over four million pounds sterling which they had been granted for televised AIDS education in Africa when USAID required them to sign a pledge condemning sex work and trafficking (Reproductive Health Matters 2006:6–16).

Recently a study of the $50 million a year federal funds mandated for abstinence-only programs in the United States has demonstrated that they had no significant effect in persuading teens to abstain from sex. Similarly, teens who had been trained in the programs had no less unprotected sex than those who had not (Trenholm et al. 2007). A general review of abstinence-only programs throughout the US found that they "are undermining comprehensive sexuality education and other government-sponsored programs . . . by withholding information and promoting questionable and inaccurate opinions" (Santelli et al. 2006).

In the United States, lack of comprehensive sexual education and reproductive health programs have had a particularly deleterious impact on poor women and women of color. Regarding the challenges facing women and girls in South Carolina and Florida, McGovern notes what she identifies as a "unique" contradiction that "policymakers are working to control women's reproductive choices and sexuality, and restricting sex education, but doing little to address the overall lack of access to quality reproductive health care" (McGovern 2007:119; McGovern et al. 1999). In fact, she has pointed to a profound and widespread contradiction in US policy both domestically and abroad.

Thus, the regime of President George W. Bush has reoriented both national and international funding in the direction of ever-more constricting moral imperatives. Through US contributions to the World Health Organization and the United Nations – which constrains UNAIDS, UN Population and Family Health and UNIFEM (the

**Figure 2.1** US President George W. Bush holds an African child as he announces his request to Congress for $30 billion for the second round of PEPFAR funds, May 30, 2007

United Nations Development Fund for Women) – the United States has influenced policy worldwide with respect to comprehensive sex education, sexuality, abortion, gender-based violence, substance use, and women's reproductive health.

The next sections of this chapter demonstrate first the major impact such policies have had on poor countries and then return to the US to explore the background of the policies. The chapter considers three main precipitants of what might be termed the new imperial morality in the US: firstly, increasing domestic inequalities associated with globalization and cutbacks in government services; secondly, the alliance of the US Republican Party with the religious right; and thirdly, the neo-conservative policies associated with the war in Iraq. I argue that each of these processes contributed to a heightened emphasis on sin and morality as well as gender subordination. Such imperial moralities were reflected in constraints on sexuality, sexual orientation, women's reproductive choice, and health and harm reduction. They contributed to stigmatizing vulnerable groups and damaged AIDS prevention possibilities worldwide.

## "All the World's a Stage . . ."

At the 2004 Bangkok International AIDS Society Conference, Yoweri Museveni, President of Uganda, internationally renowned for 20 years for his unusually pro-gressive and non-judgmental policies on AIDS, gave a plenary speech that sent shockwaves around the world. Standing at the podium, Museveni expressed his gratitude to President George W. Bush for the $94 million from PEPFAR that Uganda had received in 2004–2005 (Museveni 2004). He then revised Uganda's well-established support for a comprehensive approach to AIDS prevention and claimed that, in his personal opinion, condoms were not really "masculine." He said that condoms were not "optimum" and added that men who were drunk would not use them.

In fact, although they were in his plenary speech, the words about the problem with condoms were nowhere in Museveni's written presentation, which was most likely developed by public health officers in his administration.[4] The notes for Museveni's presentation list the increased use of condoms as one important aspect of a multipronged prevention program. His published notes also cite a study from the international journal *AIDS*, which claimed that between 1989 and 1995 condom use in Uganda had risen from 15.4 to 55.2 percent among men and from 5.8 to 38.8 percent among women (Museveni 2004).

Since the late 1980s, when President Museveni took up the cause of AIDS prevention, policies of "zero grazing" or "be faithful" have been accompanied by the government advocacy for the use of male and frequently even female condoms (Bond and Vincent 1997; Lyons 1997). In fact, Uganda was one of the first countries in Africa to widely distribute the female condom (Rosenfield et al. 2001).

Immediately after the plenaries, journalists from the US and elsewhere packed the press-room to meet with Museveni and question him on his presentation. One woman journalist said to me, "Can you believe it? Did I hear right? Has he reversed his position on condoms?" I was no better informed than she, and just sat down next to her at the press conference.

She asked: "Have you reversed your long-standing policies?"

To which Museveni replied, "Nothing has changed."

This answer is representative of the ambiguity of Museveni's position from then on. He ricocheted in his answers, at one point supporting condom use, at another denigrating condoms.

In 2004, Museveni's speech, wavering from his previous two decades of strong support for condoms, and the ambiguity of his new AIDS prevention messages corresponded with start of the flow of millions of dollars of President's Emergency AIDS funds from the United States to Uganda. President Bush, in his public speeches, identified Uganda as his model for the successful implementation of a newly minted US policy of ABC. In fact, evaluations of US AIDS funding noted that Uganda had received an unusually high share of the resources.[5] Thus, one might understand that President Museveni felt particularly obligated to the US government and President Bush (Human Rights Watch 2005).

Funds from the US to Uganda increased by 50 percent between 2004 and 2005 and Uganda was scheduled to receive $258 million from PEPFAR in 2007 (Oomman et al. 2007:13). Indeed, it seems Uganda was expecting only about $235 million and when an extra $22.2 million was forthcoming they were not quite sure what to do. "We had to go through the process of planning again . . . It is becoming difficult to absorb more funds . . . All partners are at the limit," says a dismayed member of Uganda's PEPFAR field staff (Oomman et al. 2007:21).

However, at the same time, evaluators quote one puzzled official:

> You find in this country we spend about US$200–300 million on HIV/AIDS through different ministries and agencies but still we don't cover a big ground. So there is a problem on how to manage that money. Aid comes but somehow it goes to the wrong targets (Human Rights Watch 2005:13).

Meanwhile the contributions of the Ugandan government to AIDS treatment and prevention have remained stable – only around 5 percent of the total (Oomman et al. 2007).

Clearly, the sharp difference between what the Ugandan government has contributed to AIDS funds and the millions contributed by PEPFAR suggests the importance of this funding to President Museveni and possibly even to the stability of his regime. Under these circumstances and considering that Randall Tobias, the PEPFAR director in 2004, had himself disparaged condoms (ACT UP 2004), Museveni's statements seem hardly surprising. As we shall see, under President Bush the Centers for Disease Control supported the US Abstinence-Only Programs' claims that condoms did not prevent AIDS (Cohen 2004; National Council of Research on Women 2004). It therefore seems somewhat over-determined that President Museveni should himself waiver in his promotion of such a method.

After the press conference with Museveni, a second press meeting was arranged with three representatives of the health administration in Uganda, including one woman, Dr. Lydia Mungherera. Dr. Mungherera reiterated that the health services in Uganda were continuing to advocate the use of condoms and outlined the importance of a multipronged policy. No mention was made of ABC by these three Ugandan representatives and, in fact, in the written report of Museveni's speech there is also no mention of ABC. As noted above, the published report talks of comprehensive sex education in the schools and the multipronged approach that the health administration representatives emphasized. This approach, including the social marketing of male and female condoms and peer education programs among sex workers, had been central to prevention in Uganda and espoused by a multitude of government and international agencies (Nalugwa 2003). When I met Dr. Mungherera at a meeting at Yale University six months later she told me that she and the other two Ugandan panelists had felt compelled to organize the second press conference in order to straighten out the record with respect to HIV/AIDS policy in Uganda.

One revealing description of the way abstinence was previously used by women in Uganda evokes the Greek drama of Lysistrata, where women refused to have sex with their husbands until they ended the Peloponnesian war. To quote Kavita Ramdas, at that time, 2004, president and CEO of the not-for-profit Global Fund for Women[6]:

in Uganda . . . they didn't use abstinence in this sort of puritanical or even moralistic sense . . . rather, entire groups of women in villages would get together and talk to their husbands and say, "All of us, collectively, none of us are going to have sex with you . . ." And this was then combined with a sex education program that was remarkable . . . It involved adolescent girls, young men, husbands, grandfathers, and uncles . . . Brought them in to talk about sex, power, and changes in sexual behavior.

However, Museveni's plenary speech signaled a major policy shift in Uganda as, in line with the massive contribution of Bush's AIDS funds, the administration became less than friendly to the condom and moved in the direction of the moralistic advocacy of abstinence-only. As a senior official in the Ugandan Health Ministry, Sam Okware, explained:

PEPFAR really shifted the emphasis to A and B [Abstinence-only and Be faithful] just because of the amounts of money being put into these programmes (Murphy et al. 2006).

In fact, as policy analysts have noted, "ABC" as described by the Bush administration and applied under PEPFAR "is a uniquely American intervention." The research shows "nothing in the demographic or historical record suggests that 'abstinence education' as conceived by the United States is what contributed to Uganda's HIV prevention success" (Brocado 2005).

At the Bangkok meetings, at the plenary level where Museveni spoke, criticisms of ABC were never discussed, although many other important issues were debated. However, the implications of this shift were discussed in one packed and contentious session, CNN vs. ABC (CNN = condoms, needles, and negotiating skills; ABC = abstinence-only, be faithful, condoms), which was actually translated into Mandarin Chinese, Spanish, French and Thai.[7] ABC in Uganda was defended by Edward Green an anthropologist who says on his curriculum vitae that he introduced ABC to the Bush administration.[8] Green directly opposed prevention interventions that stressed risk reduction (which he identified as relating to "condom and drug" interventions) and describes ABC as the policy of the Ugandan government.

This panel starkly portrayed the gendered impact of the new ABC regulations. Green was accompanied on the CNN vs. ABC panel by a Ugandan man, seemingly in his late twenties or early thirties, who claimed to be "practicing" virginity. This was apparently "secondary virginity" as he talked about a religious rebirth in which he changed his previous behavior.

The leading scientist who spoke in opposition to ABC was Stephen Sinding, the previous Executive Director of International Planned Parenthood Federation, an organization that had refused to follow the PEPFAR regulations and was not receiving funds. Sinding was accompanied by a young Indian woman who spoke about women and girls who could not "practice virginity" as many of them had already been married at a young age or were subject to sexual force and violence. The problem of women's protection is particularly significant in Uganda, where, in 2002, "six girls were reported to be infected with HIV for every boy" (Human Rights Watch 2005:15) and in Botswana and South Africa where, as noted in Chapter 1, the ratio of infection for girls is similarly many times that of boys.

In 2004, we saw the initial stages of conservative reaction as the billions of dollars of US government funds began to trickle across the world. In that same year, sudden religious revivalism emerged in Uganda (Epstein 2007). In 2006, the US provided US$39 million to Museveni's wife, Janet Museveni, for a family planning program based on Moon Beads. The program promoted the old but notoriously unreliable rhythm method in a new religious form. In order to prevent pregnancy, a woman could count the days of her ovarian cycle based on the rosary. Janet Museveni announced that she thought such an approach was very useful for a "backward" population. Some might wonder whether the promotion of such an ancient and unreliable method indicated some "backwardness" rather on the part of the US government and not in Uganda.

### Moon Beads as FP Device in Uganda
Uganda's First Lady Janet Museveni has launched a new family planning device called **Moon Beads.** The device is composed of a string of 32 colored beads and requires an individual to move a ring around different beads with different colors everyday starting from a red bead. Once the ring touches white beads, it means it is not safe for unprotected sex. When the ring moves to brown beads, it would be safe. "I know that teaching or practicing family planning for a backward population is very hard. But I urge you to work selflessly," Museveni was quoted as saying. The device is to be distributed throughout Uganda in a five-year project funded by the USAID (Xinhua News Service 2006).

Although the epidemiology of AIDS in Uganda varies widely by region, in 2004 a definite decline in prevalence seemed to be evident (UNAIDS Global Report 2006). However, by 2007, after three years of PEPFAR funding, the numbers seemed to be on the rise again (AIDS Vaccine Advocacy Coalition 2007).

## The History of Moralities in the US

Since millions of US dollars are being channeled into poor countries with obvious impact, at this point I return to the history of the conservative policies in the US reflected in the PEPFAR restrictions.

Since at least the 1980s, the United States, the World Bank, and the International Monetary Fund have promoted neoliberal policies. Besides the "restructuring" of government services for health and education, such policies promote the privatization of public assets, such as water and communications, and the expansion of global investment in poor countries (Harvey 2005; Stiglitz 2002).

Many analysts have suggested that the global imposition of such neoliberal policies has been associated with authoritarian values (Brenner and Theodore 2002; Mitchell 2003; Peck and Tickell 2002; Smith 2003). This argument hinges on the idea that since neoliberal policies have increased the gap between rich and poor, and simultaneously undercut the middle class and civil society, they necessarily require an increased authoritarian approach to governance.

If this is so, we need to ask what exactly does such authoritarianism entail. Is an argument concerned with the widening gap between rich and poor connected also to racism, women's subordination, and restrictions on sexual orientation and reproductive rights?[9] Are neoliberal policies on an international level also accompanied by a trend toward authoritarian policing of sexuality and gender?

To explore these issues, let us briefly outline the changing patterns of gendered labor and the history of racism in the US, which form the basis for the particular dispossessions related to race, class, and gender of our neoliberal era (Collins 2009; Mullings 2005). The formation of the US welfare state in the first decades of the twentieth century, partly in response to working people's struggles and also in the interests of maintaining a stable labor force for industrial capitalism, has been termed Fordism, following initial distinctions developed by Antonio Gramsci (Harvey 1990:126). Incorporated in the Fordist idea of a "fair day's wage" was the image of the woman as a dependent, not entitled to adequate wages herself and newly devoted to household, children, and community (Fraser and Gordon 1994; Gordon 2000). As a result, through the 1930s, women were excluded from many of the benefits of the New Deal, which laid the groundwork for the modern welfare state.[10] As one of the ongoing consequences of the brutal politics of race in the US, and in spite of the protests of many, African Americans, both men and women, mostly outside the formal industrial labor force and working as domestics, agricultural workers, and hired hands, were largely excluded from New Deal benefits (Wiesen Cook 1999).

After World War II, the later stages of industrial capitalism were associated with the strengthening of unions and the increasing demands for welfare state provisions for the elderly and the disabled. However, such entitlements were still fundamentally predicated on the image of the woman as loving, unpaid domestic worker dependent on a man's support (Abramovitz 1996). Meanwhile, African American men and women were discriminated against in the workplace and forced into the informal economy. They were then viewed as "undeserving" poor because the men did not have formal employment and the women could not stay home to rear their children (Gordon 1998; Susser 1993; Susser 1996b; Susser 1997). In the 1970s, just as, in response to the civil rights and feminist movements, legislation was introduced to outlaw discrimination by color and gender, industries began to leave the United States to look for cheaper workers elsewhere.

We can perceive the globalization of manufacturing and the expansion of global trade and investment as associated with post-Fordism and the dismantlement of the US welfare state (Harvey 1990). As manufacturers left the United States, domestic wages also began to decline (Bluestone and Harrison 1982). Over time, with lower wages for men and the reduction of state services, women were redefined as workers and the "fair day's wage" no longer included support for a family (Abramovitz 1996; Roberts 1995; Susser 1997). Women were still expected to provide the same unpaid domestic labor as before. However, now, as African American and other minority women had long been forced to, all working-class women were supposed to take care of domestic responsibilities while they were working. They still earned much lower pay than men but could no longer depend on the assistance and security provided by the entitlements of the welfare state (Lawinski 2007; Piven et al. 2002; Susser 1997).

Indeed what some have labeled "globalization" was fundamentally an attack on labor through the exportation of industry and the hiring of women worldwide at lower wages than men could command (Harvey 1990; Nash 1983; Susser 1996b).

Although the rhetoric describing neoliberal policies and globalization includes such terms as "free market" and "deregulation," in fact, such policies involve a deregulation of corporate interests and re-regulation of the private lives of individuals in terms of the new moralisms (Ain-Davis 2006; Peck 2001; Roberts 1995). As the entitlement of women and children to support with the labor, costs of childrearing, and health care has been erased, the "risk" or, more accurately, the social problems created, have been enshrined in religious morality as "blame" for individual men, women, and even children (McGovern 2007:119). Since the poor are disproportionately members of minorities, such "blame" has also been associated with racism (Ain-Davis 2006; McGovern 2007:120; Roberts 1995).

Thus, as we shall see, the dismantling of the welfare state opened up a new or possibly renewed avenue of moralistic politics in the United States. The Republican Party had relied on an underlying racist ideology to mobilize voters ever since the Democratic Party under President John F. Kennedy mobilized the African American vote in 1960.[11] It was along this moralistic avenue that the Republican Party now strove to motivate its conservative constituencies and to link marital discord, divorce, and poverty with race (Krugman 2007; Piven 2004).

The shift towards conservative moralism about women, reproduction, and sexuality, blended with racism, can be traced in Republican Party policies from the early 1970s. In 1973, in the US, as a response to strong feminist demands among women who were just entering the formal workforce in massive numbers, the Supreme Court decision of *Roe vs. Wade* established a woman's right to have an abortion. However, the exportation of industry of the 1970s precipitated a decline in wages and employment for American working-class men and a conservative backlash against women's autonomy. Almost immediately, women's reproductive rights came under assault as a Republican majority passed the Hyde Amendment, which prohibited US international funds from funding abortions. Thus, although there was strong domestic support for women's reproductive choice, conservatives were able to deny that right to women internationally who received US funds.[12]

In 1981, as soon as Republican President Ronald Reagan was elected, the Republican Party Congress passed the first "abstinence-only policies," which were included in the "Adolescence Family Life Act." Under Reagan and then under Herbert

Walker Bush in 1988, such policies were interlocked with racially tinged assaults on public assistance programs (Krugman 2007).

Although, in 1992, the Democratic President Bill Clinton was elected on a progressive platform to increase social services, and particularly to improve health care for all, Clinton also enthusiastically promoted free trade policies and globalization. During Clinton's first term, in 1994, massive Republican wins in the US Congress led to a new assault on the poor and particularly women of color. Newt Gingrich as Republican Speaker of the House led a *Contract for America* to implement major cutbacks in all social services and destroyed any hope of a unified health system or indeed any support for government services for the next decade (Krugman 2007).

In 1996, a beleaguered Clinton took the lead in implementing the *Personal Responsibility and Work Opportunity Reconciliation Act* (PRWORA: US Congress, 104th Session, 1996), which was promoted as "welfare reform." This was a major dismantlement of the public assistance programs of the US, which had been in place for half a century. This Personal Responsibility Act was an assault on poor women, undermining both health care and family stability, and, because women of color are disproportionately poor, particularly women of color.

The Personal Responsibility Act was also important for the metaphoric and representational values it codified. In its very title, this new Act signaled a shift from a recognized public responsibility for the support of women and children to the institutionalization of private risk and individual responsibility in the face of economic change (Roberts 1995; Susser 1997).

At the same time, as the new welfare provisions institutionalized patterns of unemployment and low-paying jobs available to women and minorities, it codified gender and racial stereotypes to justify the reductions in family supports. Newly mandated limitations on the time that people could access assistance precipitated the abandonment of poor women and their children to the erratic shifts in the new economy (Lawinski 2007). The new Personal Responsibility Act also left many poor women and children without access to health and reproductive care to which they had previously been entitled.[13] This decline in support was combined with stringent regulations limiting political advocacy among neighborhood community organizations that received government funding.[14]

Significantly for discussions of sexuality and morality, Clinton's welfare revisions assigned 20 percent of the federal public assistance money for "marriage funds." The new policy added limits and sanctions for the number of children a woman might have and instituted marriage requirements. In addition, states were financially rewarded for instituting ways to reduce out-of-wedlock childbirth and for implementing abstinence-only education (McGovern et al. 1999).

In this way a whole new territory for blame was created: the behavior of the mother, pregnancy, childbirth, and marital discord. This new policy attributed poverty to divorce, with heavy racist and sexist connotations, denying the decades of research demonstrating the social and economic roots in the problems of poor households. A new derogatory label, "deadbeat dads," came into currency to refer to men who, due to unemployment, illness or whatever other reason, were not keeping up on their mandated child support payments and could be put behind bars (Roberts 1995).

Thus, as noted above, US neoliberalism's deregulation was applied to the corporations not the population. The government and corporations were able to reduce their responsibility for the support of households in the face of economic shifts. For individuals, the Personal Responsibility Act was re-regulation, as the new funding for poor people included a little-noticed moral agenda of sexual policing.

While the undermining of social supports evident in the Personal Responsibility Act was a clear instance of neoliberal policies, the neoconservative provisions concerning abstinence, marriage, and, as we shall see, religion were promoted by the majority Republican Congress. Such neoconservatism, as associated with restrictions on gender and sexuality, and closely linked with racism, is not only associated with neoliberal economic policies but also reflects a political shift.

The Republican Party built its resurgence on an alliance with the religious right (Kaplan 2004). Since at least the early 1990s, right-wing religious groups had allied themselves with the Republican Party in return for a platform that was clearly opposed to abortion, contraception, and sex education in schools. In fact, from 1988, it became clear that these "value" issues could mobilize a sector of the population to vote Republican. In the 2004 election, opposition to gay marriage was used in the same way to mobilize a religious right constituency. In turn, the religious right was rewarded by Republicans in Congress with a fundamental blurring of the constitutional separation of church and state which had been sturdily maintained for more than half a century (Klein 2006; Kranish 2006; Milligan 2006; Stockman et al. 2006).

In 1996, at the very same time as women were turned into poorly paid laborers and support for rearing children, health care, and other costs of social reproduction were cut back, the Personal Responsibility Act began to demolish the wall separating church and state in government funding. Ironically, working-class families, left without state services, were in desperate need of the new faith-based services, accompanied by evangelical proselytizing, now funded by US tax dollars (Ehrenreich 2004).

Religious organizations had always been eligible for government funds. Many religious organizations, such as Catholic Charities and the United Jewish Appeal, had been active in social services for a century. What are known as "voluntary" hospitals, not-for-profit medical care, has been dominated by federally funded religious institutions equally as long. However, in these settings, employment in the administration or access to the services of federally funded programs did not require membership in any particular religion. Federally funded programs could not require participation in religious rituals and other religious obligations.

However, the passage of PRWORA in 1996 began the erosion of the legal separation of government-funded social services from faith-based practices and requirements. After 1996, faith-based organizations receiving federal funds were less constrained. In other words, from 1996, faith-based organizations were allowed to hire and, indeed, proselytize among their clients while funded by US taxpayers' money.

The sexual policing and funding of religious teaching has become much more manifest under the Bush administration. After George W. Bush became president in 2001, he immediately increased religious funding and relaxed even further the restrictions on the faith-based funding. This shift in the availability of funds for religious institutions led to an accelerated emphasis on marriage, motherhood, virginity, and abstinence.

Again in 2001, within weeks of becoming president, Bush reinstated the global gag rule, which denies US funding to any international agency that practices, advocates, or educates about reproductive choice. This rule was originally implemented under the Reagan regime of the 1980s and withdrawn during the Clinton presidency. Since the US Supreme Court ruled abortion legal in 1973, the gag rule does not apply domestically but, as noted earlier, the US does not always allow rights worldwide which are required domestically (Center for Reproductive Rights 2003).

After 2001, much information about birth control, condoms, and abortion disappeared from federal websites. Department of Health websites actually changed to say that condoms can cause infection and do not prevent AIDS. Notices appeared claiming that abortion causes breast cancer. Some of the worst cases of misinformation, such as the two noted here, were toned down after an outcry from public health professionals (National Council of Research on Women 2004).

The policies of the Bush administration have contested and undermined the freedom of women in their access to reproductive choice and even "morning after" pills (National Council of Research on Women 2004). In the rhetoric concerning gay marriage in the 2004 US elections, sexual orientation also became a related arena of battle (Girard 2004).

The specific moralisms of US AIDS policies reflect the political decisions of the neoconservative regime (Robotham 2009). The neoconservatism of the George Bush presidency has been spearheaded by such figures as Richard Cheney, Donald Rumsfeld, and Paul Wolfowitz, who have been working together since the 1970s, dependent on the mobilization of voters from the Christian right (Kaplan 2004). Such moralistic and constricting ideologies, based on racism and patriarchy, appeal to and reinforce US nationalism. As we shall see, these particular nationalist ideologies are also directly associated with neoconservative military ambitions.

## War and AIDS Funding: The Basis of
## Compassionate Conservatism

Since 2001, as the United States has turned in the direction of war, women are sent to fight in Afghanistan and Iraq. At the same time, their reproductive rights are restricted rather than expanded. Thus, the emphasis on war and nationalism in the United States today has been accompanied by the effort to regulate marriage and abstinence before marriage. Women are "freed to join the military," to risk sexual violence from male fellow soldiers, and even forced to leave their children when called up. How can this be squared with the increasing government emphasis on moral rules about women's sexuality and reproductive roles?

Much work by anthropologists has linked women's subordination to processes of state formation as well as colonial projects (Gailey and Patterson 1987; Leacock 1981; Leacock and Etienne 1980; Nash 1980; Silverblatt 1980; Stoler 2002). Current feminist literature, drawing on these themes, views reverence for motherhood and constructions of femininity as intimately related to images of nationalism (Abu-Lughod 2004; Aretxaga 1997; Das 1995; Kligman 1995; Petchesky 2003). In her detailed study of the history of a military base at Fort Bragg, North Carolina, Catherine Lutz demonstrates the ways in which the military history in the US has been directly interlocked with racism, the subordination of women, and discrimination with respect to sexual orientation. She describes how the training at Fort Bragg contributes to increased authoritarian perspectives and violence at home as well as the glorification of masculine violence in war (Lutz 2001).

As we shall see, the new funding for AIDS has been a central plank of the Bush platform and has been directly associated with war. Rhetorically, HIV/AIDS funding has been cited at crucial moments to demonstrate the Bush administration's efforts to "do good" while also going to war. We can begin to discern the association of AIDS funding with war rhetoric in President Bush's State of the Union Speech, January 28, 2003, the speech in which the President's Emergency AIDS funding was first announced, six weeks before the United States went to war with Iraq.

Twice Bush yokes mention of war on "evil doers" to mention of the war on AIDS, justifying his bloody intentions in Iraq with his compassionate AIDS funding. Bush proclaims: "we have the opportunity to save millions of lives abroad from a terrible disease . . . we will answer every danger and every enemy that threatens the American people."

A few pages later, President Bush announces the new funding for AIDS again, following it immediately with a sentence on the "war on terror":

> I ask the Congress to commit US$15 billion over the next five years . . . to turn the tide against AIDS in the most afflicted nations of Africa and the Caribbean. The nation can lead the world in sparing innocent people from a plague of nature. And this nation is leading the world in confronting and defeating the man-made evil of international terrorism.

This statement appears in the center of the speech. For the entire second half of his speech, using coded religious rhetoric, Bush warns the world of the "evil" states and, particularly, Saddam Hussein. He does not directly announce his imminent intention of going to war in Iraq but repeatedly implies unspecified recourse and "removal" as in the following sentences:

> And tonight I have a message for the brave and oppressed people of Iraq: Your enemy is not surrounding your country – your enemy is ruling your country. And the day

he and his regime are removed from power will be the day of your liberation . . . If
Saddam Hussein does not fully disarm . . . we will lead a coalition to disarm him.

Thus, as we have seen, Bush consistently twinned two international objectives –
one explicitly to kill people; the second apparently to save lives with AIDS funding.
The money for AIDS was one way to make palatable a pre-emptive war, with no
clearly stated cause.

On July 7, 2005, as a series of bombs exploded in London, Bush again linked his
commitment to AIDS funding with his commitment to war. At that moment,
George W. Bush and the British Prime Minister Tony Blair were at the Edinburgh
meetings of the G8.[15] Outside the meetings, masses of people demonstrated under
the rubric "Make Poverty History." During this summit, nations of the global
South, led by countries such as South Africa, were demanding the removal of agricultural subsidies for farmers in Europe and the US, which undermined efforts by
farmers in poorer countries to sell their produce on the global market.

Within hours of the bombings, at 1:30 p.m. on Thursday July 7, 2005, from the
Gleneagles Hotel in Auchterarder, Scotland, President Bush offered condolences to
the people of London in a two-minute televised speech. At this critical moment, in
such a short window of time, Bush again juxtaposed assistance for AIDS with the
"war on terror":

> The contrast between what we've seen on the TV screens here, what's taken place in
> London, and what's taking place here is incredibly vivid to me. On the one hand, we
> have people here who are working to alleviate poverty, to help rid the world of the
> pandemic of AIDS, working on ways to have a cleaner environment. And on the other
> hand, you've got people killing innocent people. And the contrast couldn't be clearer
> between the intentions and the hearts of those of us who care deeply about human
> rights and human liberty, and those who kill – those who have got such evil in their
> heart that they will take the lives of innocent folks. The war on terror goes on . . . We
> will find them . . . we will spread an ideology of hope and compassion that will over-
> whelm their ideology of hate.

Considering the surprising centrality of AIDS funding to the Bush administration's election claims of "compassionate conservatism," we might understand the
president's AIDS funding as an effort to provide a moral shield for imperial policies
of war.

The $15 billion earmarked for AIDS has also gone a long way to promote a
conservative agenda of stigma and moral condemnation domestically and internationally (Brocado 2005). In very concrete and explicit ways, the current neoconservative government has changed laws with respect to gender and sexuality on a global
level – cutting funding for science and technology, women's reproductive health,
and studies that mention sexuality – but at the same time funding faith-based
groups worldwide (Girard 2004). We can see this most clearly through the US global
policies on HIV/AIDS.

The promotion of a conservative moral agenda internationally has emerged partly from the actual regulations of PEPFAR outlined earlier. But, for poor countries receiving PEPFAR, there are many more implications than the immediate moral imperatives about abstinence. With the destruction of the wall between church and state, relaxing the rules against funding religious practice, and not requiring a multipronged approach to prevention, Bush's new AIDS funding has precipitated a dramatic increase in faith-based funding abroad. According to Marge Berer, the editor of *Reproductive Health Matters*:

> In the past, faith-based groups took upon themselves the unambiguous role for good of providing care and support for people living with HIV and AIDS . . . Now, however, tempted . . . by Bush's prevention dollars, many (though thankfully not all) have also taken on abstinence-only education and are disguising it as HIV prevention. Bush's money made it easy for them – it exempted them from promoting comprehensive life skills, sexuality and relationships education by requiring them to promote abstinence before marriage and faithfulness after it (Berer 2006).

US-based churches with fundamentalist moral agendas, which had no experience in AIDS prevention and treatment, even in the United States, and had never operated internationally have been funded under this initiative. Indeed, the US government has created a special set of funds designated for faith-based organizations and other non-governmental organizations with no previous AIDS experience (Stockman et al. 2006).

In addition, agencies have been denied funding because of association with reproductive education. USAID denied funds to highly regarded AIDS prevention programs in Africa while granting funds to a consortium of evangelical groups with no expertise in HIV/AIDS or international work (Stockman et al. 2006; Klein 2006; Kranish 2006; Milligan 2006).

In 2004, the US government withdrew $34 million from the United Nations Family and Population Administration (UNFPA) because they were accused of funding programs in China that were associated with Marie Stopes. Although Marie Stopes does support programs where abortion information is available, the particular programs funded by UNFPA were for unrelated services elsewhere (Marie Stopes International 2002). The decision by the US government to slash the money allotted to UNFPA had an immediate and intimidating effect on all UN agencies.

One indicative reverberation of this loss of funds was that United Nations agencies specifically concerned with women, such as UNIFEM and the Family Population Administration, had to disassociate themselves from the Barcelona Bill of Rights. As noted in Chapter 1, the Barcelona Bill of Rights was a list drawn up by the Women's Caucus at the Barcelona 2002 International AIDS Society Conference to represent the rights of women with respect to AIDS and it included the right to abortion. In 2002, the Barcelona Bill of Rights had been ratified by an international network of feminist and human rights organizations, such as Human Rights Watch and the Center for Reproductive Rights. In 2004, after the UNFPA were sanctioned by the loss of $34 million, the Barcelona Bill of Rights was perceived as much more contentious and threatening than it had seemed in 2002.

## Conclusions

Thus, authoritarian rule and reproductive constraints do not simply diffuse across the world. We must confront their funding and promotion by the current US government in much more systematic ways. From the point of view of cultural construction, the links with the shifts in US global reach need to be made transparent. Very soon, if not already, the changes we are seeing will be read by most, and especially the US media and policy makers, as the "exotic other" mired in their conservative sexual traditions (Di Leonardo 2000). With mission hospitals come the expectations of mission morality (Bosmans et al. 2006). At the most basic levels, sex education is not discussed, condoms are not distributed, and options for sexual negotiations, especially for women and youth, are prematurely shut.

Under current policies of globalization, populations are becoming poorer and the elite–mass gap greater than it has ever been (Stiglitz 2002). As social service provisions have been cut back and more and more women in the poorest countries of the world have been forced to work in non-unionized sweatshops at minimal pay (Nash 1983; Schneider and Susser 2003; Stiglitz 2002), contemporary US national projects attempt to curtail women's reproductive choice and emphasize images of women as mothers. Women are portrayed as powerful symbols of national or religious continuity confined to their role in procreation. This has nothing to do with "traditional" societies versus "modern" ones, as we can see from the US funding and promotion of "traditional" and unscientific methods of family planning.

The apparent contradiction of a "modern" society promoting "traditional" values can be explained. In fact, religious and "traditional" values provide the powerful moral foundation from which to generate individual blame for the social disorders that have accompanied cut-backs in social services, health infrastructure, and other government investments that were aimed at the support of women in the social reproduction of households.

However, sexual conservatism and gendered subordination is not a necessary consequence of neoliberal economic policies. In many western European countries, gender has not become the ideological football it has in the US. In the United Kingdom, Sweden, and other countries, women's reproductive choices are not being progressively constrained. In neither of these countries has the welfare state been undermined to the extent it has in the US. Nevertheless, in these specific historical contexts, increased racism and nationalism have certainly accompanied the growing inequalities exacerbated by neoliberal economic policies (Clarke 2004; Pred 2000). In the past decade, neoliberalism in the US has been directly intertwined with the construction of gender and coded messages of morality, racism, and blame (Collins 2009; Mullings 2005). Indeed, in the US, the emphasis on marriage for people who receive public assistance is also a coded and racist message that poor people, who are assumed to be black, are morally failing (Roberts 1995).

Neoconservative policies promoted by the US are being spread dramatically to poor countries by US funding for AIDS. The faith-based, fundamentalist platform of the United States Republican regime – with its particular restrictions on women and reproduction as well as neglect of comprehensive sex education and stigmatizing of sexual orientation, sex workers, and drug users – may be leading to the deaths of many people. Such policies are likely to lead to higher rates of infection even as the availability of treatment is on the horizon.

These shifts have been highly contested on the ground in South Africa and Uganda, and elsewhere. Many international women's groups are fighting the conservative moral agenda: International Women Living with AIDS, SIECUS, CHANGE, and others. Nevertheless, the new moral regime was strongly reflected at the International AIDS Society Conference in Bangkok in 2004, where the ABC policies went unquestioned in the plenaries. It was even further reflected in the AIDS plenaries at the 2006 Toronto IAS Conference where the topics of sexuality, violence against women, breastfeeding, condoms or comprehensive reproductive health programs were not mentioned except by Louise Binder, a health activist and a leader of positive women. Major speeches by Bill and Melinda Gates and others called for high-technology/scientific solutions and treatment. Melinda Gates actually mentioned sex workers and condoms and decried the discrimination against marginalized groups and the neglect of condoms by many governments. However, Bill Gates praised the PEPFAR policies without critique. None of the constraints surrounding this funding were discussed in such central forums.

At the Mexico 2008 IAS Conference, partly as a consequence of extensive organizing by a gender alliance described in Chapter 1, many of these issues were re-inserted into the global agenda. The restrictions represented even by the nearly $50 billion renewal of PEPFAR in 2008 were articulately challenged by the first young woman plenary speaker, Elisabet Fadul, Country Coordinator of Global Youth Partners. "What does HIV look like today? It looks increasingly young, significantly female, and unjustly marginalized," she said, as she pointed out that even though 18-year-olds can be recruited to the army they still cannot access comprehensive sex education. She continued, "This is a violation of our human rights driven by theological beliefs rather than evidence-based research" (Fadul 2008).

A few days later, Elena Reynaga, the Founder and Executive Director of the Argentine Association of Female Sex Workers, delivered the first sex worker plenary speech (Reynaga and Crago 2008). "We want sex work to be recognized as work." said Reynaga. "Sex workers are not the problem; we are part of the solution."

Starting with the historic Sonagachi project begun by women sex workers in Kolkata in the 1980s (and discussed in Chapter 1), Reynaga demonstrated that sex workers have organized through their work to protect themselves from AIDS. Sex workers in Kolkata have a 5.17% prevalence of HIV infection while other cities in

India such as Mumbai have rates as high as 54% (Reynaga and Crago 2008). Sex workers have mobilized all over the world to overturn criminalization, to meet with the Global Fund and UNAIDS.

However, in spite of these major successes in international recognition, Reynaga pointed out that sex workers are subjected to violence through government anti-prostitution policies. They are often imprisoned with their condoms confiscated and their treatment stopped. In Cambodia, and elsewhere, "anti-prostitution policies have been approved under great pressure from the US – and now, as a result, sex workers are being arrested under the pretense that they are victims of slavery and trafficking" (Reynaga and Crago 2008).

In the face of concerted political efforts, both national and international, based on the growing recognition and evidence summarized in this chapter and elsewhere, on July 18, 2008, the Senate authorized the renewal of $48 billion for global AIDS relief with restrictions still intact. The new bill required 50 percent of prevention funds in countries with generalized epidemics to be devoted only to "abstinence-only until marriage" and "be faithful programs" (without comprehensive sex education) while retaining the requirement for fund recipients to pledge opposition to prostitution and trafficking.[16]

As we shall see in Chapter 4, over the decade from 1998 to 2008, a similar conservative shift as that described here for the United States, also linked to neoliberalism, gender, and ideologies of nationalism, can be discerned in the policies of the Mbeki administration in South Africa.

# 3

# The Transition to
# a New South Africa:
# Hope, Science, and Democracy

## AIDS and the Transition in South Africa

The tragic confluence of the remarkable victory of the African National Congress over apartheid rule in South Africa with the rising mortality of the AIDS epidemic has only slowly emerged. In 1990, HIV prevalence in antenatal clinic attendees was estimated to be 0.7 percent. By 2003, it had risen to 27.9 percent (Gouws and Abdool Karim 2005). The latest figures for Hlabisa, a region in KwaZulu-Natal a few hours' drive from where the women described in this chapter lived, show a prevalence of 57.5 percent for women of 26 years of age (Welz et al. 2007).

In the face of transformations and crises of such epic proportion, ideas about science, medicine, Western influences, and capitalism have been re-examined. In some situations, sorcery, witchcraft, sin, and punishment have also been brought into play to explain the shocking conditions (Ashforth 2000; Ashforth 2005; Comaroff and Comaroff 2001a, b; Leclerc-Madlala 2001; McGregor 2007; Scorgie 2002). Since, in southern Africa, AIDS is integrally linked to heterosexual transmission, childbirth, and infant feeding, such perspectives have an uneven impact on women.

In any setting, the interrelatedness of death and sexuality is explosive. However, the South African debate is also set within a historical context of racism, colonialism, modernity, and what some have labeled millennial capitalism (Comaroff and Comaroff 2001a, b). Widespread illness and multiple deaths have framed political power and resistance over the past decades in southern Africa and have had profound effects on the particular ways in which women, sexuality, and AIDS have been perceived.

Thus, this chapter necessarily starts with the history of the apartheid regime, which structured the gendered and racial divisions of South Africa over the past 50 years. Under apartheid, in line with an authoritarian fascist government, we see ethnic/racial discrimination mixed in a potent brew with a nationalist patriarchal fundamentalist religious rhetoric. In this era, AIDS among the African population received little attention.

Later during the transition, we see the strands of resistance and the fight for new visions of rights and a progressive AIDS agenda. The chapter documents the hope and visions for democracy and sexual equality that were generated in the opening years of the new South Africa. I outline perspectives on the epidemic from the point of view of women in the informal settlements in the early 1990s, while pointing to the underlying tendencies that provided the fuel for the turn-about in terms of denialism and the failure to address the epidemic adequately, which will be discussed in Chapter 4.

## AIDS and the Politics of Apartheid

There is no question the raced and gendered migrant labor system which the British set up in the late nineteenth century to excavate the mines – gold, diamonds, and, to a lesser extent, tin and platinum – has been a defining characteristic in the political, social, and economic conditions of the population for the past hundred years (Bonner et al. 1993; Wolpe 1980). In the service of colonial priorities, African men were forced to leave their tribal lands to work on the roads, in the mines, and in the towns, while women were originally confined to the rural areas.

The mass of the population, descendants of the African pastoral Bantu-speaking peoples, were only defeated in the early twentieth century in a series of famous and bloody battles. Thus, images of masculinity among the African population, as they worked in the mines and elsewhere, were strongly associated with war and resistance to colonialism (Hunter 2005; Morrell 2001).

South African history, while overwhelmingly defined by the black and white division of colonized and colonizer, also reflects two centuries of competitive interaction among colonizers as well as a long history of the importation of labor from other colonized territories. As part of the global processes of capitalism, imperial powers imported indentured workers from Malaysia and India to work the lush tropical farms of the Cape as well as areas in KwaZulu-Natal. A hierarchy of discrimination against Indians and other populations who were the descendants of indentured labor was later enshrined in the apartheid constitution. Such divisions, along with specific gender hierarchies, were lived spatially and socially in everyday lives.

The British won the Boer War in 1901 and by 1910 the Union of South Africa was created as a white settler state within the British Commonwealth (Marks and Trapido 1979). The British takeover of the land from the Boers or Afrikaners, descendants of early Dutch settlers, contributed in the first half of the twentieth century to the emergence of a poor white population, both farmers and mineworkers, with strong nationalist and religious aspirations. This poor white population frequently competed with African cattle herders for land and needed African labor on their farms (van Onselen 1996). In addition, they were easily convinced that maintaining their wages as workers depended on the maintenance of a color bar and a major differential in black and white earnings. It was this population that became the base of support for the apartheid regime (Vestergaard 2001).

When soldiers returned from fighting for the British at the end of World War II, South Africa was a burgeoning industrial nation, still racially and ethnically divided, but with lively populous cities where men and women listened to jazz, drank Coca-Cola, danced Kwela, and drove immense American cars. However, South Africa did not follow the erratic route of other former colonies toward the independence of the African population. Instead the Nationalist Party, representing a large White settler population, constructed a modern neofascist regime within the framework of racial division forged under colonial rule.

In 1948, the Nationalist Party, promulgating an apartheid ideology, won an election where almost no people of color could vote. Over the next 20 years, the Nationalist Party generated a heavily armed police state in which habeas corpus and freedom of speech disappeared. In ways similar to Hitler's legislative assault against the Jews in 1930s Germany, although without the murderous "final solution," first the legislation was changed and then, over time and unpredictably, people of color were subject to increasingly restrictive and punitive regulation. In 1949, significantly for research on gender, the prohibition of intermarriage between whites and blacks and the 1950 Immorality Amendment Act, which made adultery between blacks and whites illegal, were among the first pieces of racial legislation.[1] Over the 1950s, having made both legal and more informal interracial partnerships criminal, the Nationalist Party then passed legislation requiring people to register their "race" and thus reify a racial status that could be traced among their descendants for future policing.

Perpetuating and spatializing the skeletal framework of a post-colonial settler society (Marks and Trapido 1979), the 1950 Group Areas Act (Act no. 41) assigned Africans to live in barren infertile reservations in tribally designated areas. The government proceeded from 1951 with a series of laws forcing blacks into such "Bantustans," later described as ethnic homelands. In 1970, even urban Africans were assigned to "ethnic homelands" and deprived of South African citizenship and passports. As these policies were unsystematically but unrelentingly implemented over more than 25 years, segregation was enforced through the brutal dispossession of large urban and rural populations. Each of these changes had implications for gender, as women, children, and the elderly were pushed back into "ethnic homelands," increasingly dependent on the remnants of largely, but not exclusively, patrilineal inheritance patterns.[2]

While the levels of repression and the interaction of gendered and racial hierarchies were particular to the politics of the apartheid state, the political economy of South Africa after World War II also had to address some of the dilemmas of industrialization common to capitalist nations of the period. In a distorted and divisive way, the implementation of modernizing policies in housing, education, and health care by the apartheid state was responding to the needs of a growing urban population whose labor was the basis of the economy (Bonner et al. 1993; Marks 1993:354).

The apartheid government developed policies of community destruction and extensive resettlement in the same era as many Western capitalist countries were also building working-class housing subsidized by the welfare state. However, in South Africa, communities were destroyed with little warning or compensation and the rebuilt housing was segregated in regimented cement blocks far from the central cities and frequently without electricity or clean water. Processes of destruction and resettlement varied according to specific politics of the national government, the changing economy, and the provincial negotiations (Bonner et al. 1993; Sapire 1989). Although from the early 1950s regulations were in place which would allow such dislocations, the actual processes of dispossession were much more contingent on history.

In the 1950s, Sophiatown, a famous and historic African township in Johannesburg, was destroyed and its residents dispossessed (Lodge 1981). For decades, Sophiatown had been home to the destitute, the working class, and middle-class Africans as well as some whites and people of other backgrounds. In the early 1950s, similar to Harlem in the period of the Renaissance, Sophiatown was a hotbed of art, music, and political ferment. It was the crucible for the politically dynamic and internationally respected African magazine *Drum*, with now-famous writers such as Ezekiel Mpahlele and Todd Matshikiza. (Chapman 2001; Stein 1999)[2] Matshikiza was the composer of the first South African musical, *King Kong*, which played on the London stage to much acclaim. It was as a singer for *King Kong* that another Sophiatown resident, Miriam Makeba, captured international attention.[3] Amid outrage and protest, the brick houses and shacks of Sophiatown were bulldozed to the ground. Black residents from such old and vital urban communities were forced to leave their homes and this has often been cited as one of the sources for the newer but now even more famous settlement of Soweto (Southwest Town) further from the center of Johannesburg.

Many of the songs and political memories of South African urban life are captured in the District Six museum in Cape Town, which commemorates the destruction of a vibrant heterogeneous, class differentiated neighborhood. District Six, named in 1867 as the sixth Municipal District of Cape Town, had been settled for over 100 years by urban Africans, Indians, and people known under apartheid categories as "Cape Malays," reflecting the local black population as well as the numerous indentured workers brought over to work on the vineyards at the end of the nineteenth century. By the 1960s, over 60,000 people lived there. Many were poor and working class but others were "artists, politicians, businessmen, musicians, writers, teachers, sheikhs, priests, gangsters, sportsmen, housewives and always lots of children" (Ebrahim 2001:8). On February 2, 1966, the Nationalist Government officially declared District Six a white district and, over the next ten years, the homes of this mixed population were bulldozed and the people were evicted.

Under the apartheid regime, Africans were relocated to townships far from the cities and were then limited in their movement into urban white settlements by pass laws. An African man who was stopped by the police on city streets and found not to have a stamped pass that certified he was currently employed in that area was subject to arrest. In the 1950s, the regime attempted to implement this regulation with respect to women. Interestingly they started with the requirement that nurses show passes to their matrons in hospitals (Marks 1993). However, widespread demonstrations erupted (Bonner et al. 1993; Walker 1991). As a result, women avoided the pass laws and made their way through the interstices of the system, helping in the process to undermine the segregation and control of the apartheid government (Bonner et al. 1993). Women primarily worked in the urban areas as domestic servants, living in rooms behind their employers' houses.

In 1953, the Nationalists passed the Bantu Education Act, no. 47. Following the Bantu Education Act, the apartheid state required that African children must be taught only the curriculum that "suited the requirements of the black people."[4] Formulated by Hendrik Verwoerd, the Netherlands-born future Nationalist Prime Minister of South Africa, the Act was meant to ensure that people who would never be eligible for jobs needing any Western academic training should not have access to skills above their station. Previously, mission schools, the only source of education for the African population, had taught academic subjects in English and Afrikaans. Now, in the primary schools developed by the apartheid state, teachers were required to teach only in African native languages and to focus on such topics as crafts and folk culture.[5]

The colonial processes of missionary education, while contributing to a silencing of the colonized, had also educated men and women who would initiate the resistance movements of the early twentieth century (Comaroff 1997; Hyslop 2001). In 1959, consolidating their racial policies in the Extension of University Education Act, no. 45, the Nationalist Party, against much multiracial student opposition, began to seal off the possibilities for African higher education. They planned to set up separate institutions for whites, Asians, and Africans. The very opportunities through which, among others, the ANC leadership and Nelson Mandela himself had managed to obtain law degrees at major South African universities were reduced in the next generation.

In the dispossession of black and heterogeneous urban communities as well as in the displacement of sometimes even prosperous black farmers from the land (van Onselen 1996), the "dis"education apparent in the insistence on "Bantu Education," and the provision of overcowded, under-resourced, and segregated health care for the Black population (Stein and Susser 2008), we see the "racial cleansing" which was necessary to transform the racist colonial regime into a fascist apartheid system. Through it all and even after the transition, the labor migrant system for the fueling of the mines remained central although not unchanging.

By the 1980s, South Africa was ruled by a white supremacist regime in which Africans were not allowed to vote, to attend schools in English, to go to white hospitals or to live in cities unless they could prove they worked there. The ruling Nationalist Party had systematically constructed a repressive, apartheid, modern capitalist regime, based on the regimentation of the migrant labor system. It also incorporated the exploitative vision of poor African women, at the bottom of the hierarchy represented in the gaze of the white colonial man (McClintock 1990).

The migrant labor system, raced and gendered, involved women not only being left behind in the rural areas but also being drawn into paid work on agricultural plantations, as domestics and later in the factories on the borders of rural regions (Bozzoli and Nkotsoe 1991; Hart 2002; Walker 1990a). In addition, different jobs for Africans, Indians or Whites also involved different employer definitions of the work by gender (Beall 1990). However, African women and men were constantly interacting with and negotiating with the impositions of this regime, fighting, striking, and repositioning themselves to counteract the racist and sexist regulations of the migrant labor system as well as the constraints of domestic employers, the church, the segregated health system, and the authoritarian state (Adler and Webster 2000; Bonner 1990; Bozzoli and Nkotsoe 1991; Flint 2001; Walker 1991). In fact, women were central in resistance movements against the state, whether in fighting the pass laws or in leading the bus boycott (Bonner et al. 1993; Walker 1991).

African women worked as nurses, in spite of apartheid regulations. Up until 1957, Black women had also had access to nursing training and employment with white nurses. However, with legislation that enforced institutionally hegemonic "notions of black inferiority and white superiority [which] were both common place and common sense" (Marks 1993:352), black nurses were pushed to segregated settings. Very soon, there was a general shortage of nurses, as white women, finding more professional occupations opening to them, were no longer willing to train for so long to take such hard work for such low pay and low status. In spite of all the ambiguities of race, gender, and sexuality in interaction with medical hierarchies, black nurses were eventually hired in most medical settings (Marks 1993).

Nevertheless, the apartheid state was superimposed on the rural/urban gendered and raced divisions of migrant labor. The Africans, mostly women, children, and elderly, who were left in the rural areas were constantly subject to dispossession (Delius 1996; Hart 2002). As apartheid policies forced people back onto the barren areas of land designated for the different tribes, the Bantustans became ever more overpopulated and the people poorer. Gender relations became tense. In 1959, one rural woman outlined the issues:

> We do not get enough food. Our husbands pay more than two pounds in taxes. The employers do not pay them anything. Our husbands are stuck at home. If husbands come home from Durban because of sickness they cannot go back to Durban. Because of these things we are dying (Walker 1991:233).

Women were central to the rural economy, but they had less and less land to cultivate and were more and more dependent on remittances from men. Another rural woman tells us:

> We pay money for cattle ... cattle have died ... We cannot start ploughing. There is a tractor we can hire but it costs us lots of money. Our husbands get little money ... We have not enough fields to plough (Walker 1991:233).

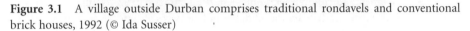

**Figure 3.1** A village outside Durban comprises traditional rondavels and conventional brick houses, 1992 (© Ida Susser)

Under worsening conditions precipitated by the long-term impact of the apartheid policies, violence – and specifically violence against women – proliferated. This is perhaps indexed by shifts in the identification and punishment of witches documented in the Northern Transvaal (Delius 1996). Whereas, even in the 1950s both men and women could be accused as witches, by the 1980s in some areas, the majority of people accused of witchcraft were women. Under terrifying conditions rather than, as before, subject to gossip or other less brutal sanctions, women were burned as witches (Delius 1996).

The apartheid government was accompanied by a fundamentalist, nationalist religion promoted by the Dutch Reformed Church. Under the aegis of this religious nationalism, patriarchal domination was the rule of the day in the segregated white congregations and promoted by paternalistic white Dutch Reformed pastors in the black churches (Crapanzano 1986; Du Pisani 2001). The moral precepts of this nationalist religion also maintained a legal ban on abortion in the apartheid regime and a searing discrimination against South Africa's gay population (Oppenheimer and Bayer 2007). Here, we see the confluence of a repressive state with the effort to control women's reproduction and a violation of the rights to sexual orientation that resembles the congruence of the Christian right with the George W. Bush presidency in the United States. These moral constraints clearly reflected government interests under apartheid. In the post-apartheid years, their power and influence was much contested but still not inconsiderable (Du Pisani 2001).

The health system under apartheid was segregated and inadequate (Bassett 2000; Benatar 2001; Susser 1983) and the early stages of the AIDS epidemic were characterized by neglect and overcrowding in the public hospitals and clinics (Oppenheimer and Bayer 2007). However, as part of this racial domination, few statistics about the African population, such as a nationwide census and health statistics, were collected (Stein and Susser 2008). The settler regime differed

**Figure 3.2**  Women and children wait outside a rural clinic in 1992. Waiting for a bus or walking long distances, a trip to the clinic could be virtually an all-day affair (© Ida Susser)

from an earlier colonial government in that British and other colonial administrations throughout the world collected demographic data with respect to the colonized populations. In fact, such data, including some health statistics, were erratically available in South Africa until the 1950s. Under the apartheid regime, while there were extensive statistics recording the health of the white population, health statistics for the African population generally applied only to specific urban areas. It was difficult to generate figures for African infant mortality or any other indicators that might provide surrogate measures of social inequality.

Social indicators can be used by international agencies as well as political activists to evaluate health systems worldwide and to hold governments accountable. The French theorist Michel Foucault emphasized the controlling and invasive aspects of the collection of such data, which he understood to contribute to a certain form of restrictive governmentality common to the modern state (Foucault 2003). However, at least in terms of health, it appears that the political clarity and insights provided by statistics and the scientific implications of disease trends and other figures can be a major threat to a repressive capitalist state. The apartheid regime in South Africa, predictably, neglected the spread of AIDS among the black population and, if anything, was suspected of welcoming the decimation of the African population that such a disease might bring (Dlamini-Zuma 1988a). One of the major battles of AIDS treatment organizations today has been to document AIDS mortality and to evaluate and monitor the availability of treatment (Nattrass 2007).

## The Transition

In spite of the repressive policies and seemingly unbeatable armamentarium of the apartheid regime, there were growing cracks in its ability to separate African workers from the cities. In the late 1980s, by the time the pass system was dismantled, there were already many hundreds of thousands of squatters living on the outskirts of South African cities, undermining the strict migrant labor system. Informal breaches in the apartheid code took place to provide a civilian labor force for hospitals and other advanced capitalist needs within the gendered and raced inflexibilities of apartheid (Marks 1993). In addition, as capitalism involved greater and greater global interrelationships, corporate capital could no longer function in the international isolation apartheid had precipitated (Muller et al. 2001).

The 1960s had seen the formation of the armed wing of the ANC while in the 1970s the Soweto school children took to the streets in protest. In the 1980s, the broad oppositional alliance of labor, churches, and other civil society groups known as the United Democratic Front (UDF) and the massive strikes among the African unions took place. By the 1990s, after two turbulent decades, the leaders of the Nationalist Party were forced, through international sanctions and internal unrest, to cede power. This was symbolized by the freeing of Nelson Mandela, the revolutionary leader of the ANC. On February 11, 1990, to massive national and international acclaim, Mandela was released from 27 years of imprisonment. It was then that epidemiological figures on AIDS among the African population began to be collected. In 1990, the first set of figures showed an infection rate of 0.8 percent (Marais 2000:5). It was in the early 1990s, also, that the South African government began to institute AIDS education and to develop a preliminary AIDS prevention approach, involving antenatal clinics, nurses, and an effort to reach children in the schools.

Under apartheid, there were several strands of organizing with respect to AIDS in South Africa. On the one hand were the mostly white, middle-income men who were part of the cosmopolitan Western epidemic among men who have sex with men and the responses to that epidemic.[6] Many of these men, and the women from the lesbian/gay networks who supported them, also worked with the worldwide movement with respect to AIDS and some were strong supporters of the ANC, which was at that time an armed underground liberation movement (Mbali 2003; Mbali 2008; Oppenheimer and Bayer 2007). Such groups were also active in the transition in making sure that the new constitution reflected the rights of sexual orientation.

Building on the historical strength of women's organizing in South Africa, both as feminists and against the apartheid regime (Bonnin 2000; Hassim 2006; Walker 1991) leading up to the transition, women's health advocates were already considering the interface of contraception and AIDS as it might affect poor women (Klugman 2000). The Women's Health Project was active in reframing demands for sexual rights for women at the international women's conferences and also in making sure that the new South African constitution reflected women's reproductive choice (Klugman 2000).

In these early days, members of the African population had not yet experienced the full devastation of AIDS and knowledge of the disease was not widespread. There was, however, a social movement mobilized around health. Following a historic tradition that went back to the cooperation between the communist doctors of the 1950s and the ANC, this movement was led by African and Indian public health professionals. Many of the activists were cosmopolitan in their experience and outlook and members of the National African Medical Doctors Association (NAMDA), a doctors' organization formed because neither African nor Indian doctors were allowed to join the white doctors' association. Both Indian and African medical students were primarily trained at the Medical School of the University of Natal, which continued to practice non-racialist policies through the apartheid era. It was here where such African medical students as Steve Biko, a founder and leader of the South African black consciousness movement, and Mamphela Ramphele, Biko's partner and co-organizer,[7] became outspoken activists. In 1977, when Steve Biko died after his arrest by apartheid regime police, the African doctors' association took up his cause (Guttmacher and Susser 1985). Some of these doctors also took part in the ANC's struggle against the apartheid government and were supportive of the armed wing of the ANC.

Because of the hierarchies of racism and gender in the histories of South African settlement, intellectuals emerged in a number of different ways and contemporary intellectuals generated different relationships within the new South Africa. As was noted from the 1950s in studies of the Zambian Copperbelt, class was as salient among black workers as white (Burawoy 1972; Epstein 1958; Mitchell 1956). However, the complex history of colonialism, labor migration, and apartheid policies led to a range of educated middle-class people, divided by historical boundaries of color and gender, just as it divided workers along the same lines. As we have seen, for over 100 years, mission-educated black men have joined both the teaching and clerical professions while African women became nurses and teachers. African ministers, lawyers, doctors, and anthropologists obtained degrees at South African universities. Indians whose ancestors had been brought as indentured workers became doctors and lawyers.

Like Nelson Mandela, Oliver Tambo, Walter Sisulu, and many members of student movements, the health activists formed part of what might be understood as organic intellectuals in Gramsci's sense (Gramsci 1971). Like the international progenitor of non-violent resistance Mahatma Gandhi, who began his lifetime of organizing as a lawyer in Durban, such intellectuals were not necessarily all from among the poorest. However, in their endeavors they worked for social justice in opposition to the hegemonic apartheid state. Mandela was adopted by and in line to succeed a hereditary chief among the Xhosa. In this sense, as well as through his law degree, he represented the small but substantial educated middle-class African population that had emerged in South Africa over the previous 100 years (Sampson 1999). Many of the health advocates and feminist and lesbian/gay activists could also be characterized as organic intellectuals from different sections of society working to articulate and address class inequalities. Along with the ANC in exile, they were among the earliest groups in South Africa to recognize the threat of AIDS.

Another group of South Africans who were becoming experienced with AIDS were the ANC guerilla forces based in Angola and Mozambique, areas with high rates of HIV infection. In 1961, after peaceful protests had been banned, the ANC was forced underground, as had their colleagues in the South African Communist Party ten years before them. The ANC leadership decided to continue through armed struggle – Umkhonto we Sizwe (MK) or Spear of the Nation. It was these plans that were exposed at the Rivonia Trial, after which many underground activists, such as Mandela and Govan Mbeki,[8] ended up with life-term prison sentences.

Over the next decades, a few South African freedom fighters, like the youthful Thabo Mbeki and the future ministers of health, Manto Tshabalala-Msimang and Nkosazana Dlamini-Zuma, with the assistance of ANC contacts and international support, escaped abroad to continue their education and provide hope for future leadership. Interestingly, Thabo Mbeki and Manto Tshabalala were among a small group of ANC youth who escaped together and both at some point ended up in the then Soviet Union where Tshabalala was trained in health. Mbeki primarily studied economics at Sussex University and later returned to various sites in east and southern Africa to work with the ANC in exile. Other exiles such as Jacob Zuma had little access to international education and made their way directly to nearby African countries to set up guerilla bases and to provide training for youthful revolutionaries who, especially after the school boycotts of 1976, began fleeing South Africa in large numbers.[9] By the late 1980s, many of the ANC guerilla recruits were high-school age. Members of the ANC in exile went so far as to make a film to inform the young guerillas about the dangers of AIDS. This film was later shown at the 1990 ANC Health Conference at Maputo, Mozambique.

The gay activists, the women's health advocates, and NAMDA were in touch with South Africans in exile. Many worked with each other or were members of both, and were well-informed with respect to the worldwide epidemic of HIV/AIDS. Although approaching AIDS from different perspectives, all heavily criticized the scandalous passivity of the apartheid state in the face of the epidemic. However, as we shall see, the differences etched into the life experiences of these disparate groups by the discriminations and brutalities of apartheid policies were also to lead to divisions and differences in the implementation of AIDS policy in the new South Africa.

## Maputo 1990: ANC Policy on HIV/AIDS

In April 1990, in the expectation of the ANC's imminent accession to the government of South Africa and joining the cause of AIDS prevention with the cause of liberation, the ANC co-sponsored a conference in Maputo, Mozambique, confronting the question of health in southern Africa.

There were preliminary conferences that led to the organizing of the historic Maputo event.[10] In 1988, at one such conference in New York City, Dr. Nkosazana Dlamini-Zuma,[11] who was to become the first Minister of Health in the new South

Africa, talked eloquently about issues of health for women among those living in the informal settlements, the importance of clean water, and the general struggles of poor women. She made the point that women must be viewed as members of the black working class first and women second.

In the 1970s, while in medical school, Dr. Dlamini-Zuma had been active in the ANC underground and served as Deputy President of the South African Students Organization, which had just been formed by Steve Biko. Forced into exile in the United Kingdom, she completed her medical training at the University of Bristol and was married for some years to Jacob Zuma. Both Dlamini-Zuma and Jacob Zuma were to have central public roles in the HIV/AIDS narrative and in 2007 Jacob Zuma was elected President of the African National Congress.

At the 1988 conference on *Women's Health and Apartheid* in New York City, we hear from Dr. Nkosazana Dlamini-Zuma, representing the ANC, calling for more action on HIV/AIDS:

> We have all heard how the migrant labor system disrupts families. Besides disrupting families, it does two other things. One it accentuates poverty, because instead of the man's salary being used in one household, he must divide it between where he lives in the city and his family in the rural area . . . Two . . . it is going to be a problem also with the new disease, AIDS, because these men are not allowed to take their families into the cities . . . And people will say, well, part of the prevention of AIDS is to have one partner, or few partners, but how do you expect someone who is away from home eleven months out of the year to have one partner? . . . I think it is going to be a recipe for the spread of AIDS . . . (Dlamini-Zuma 1988b:15).

In examining the typescript volumes prepared from these preliminary conferences, only Dlamini-Zuma mentions AIDS.[12] In fact, as in this instance, work on AIDS in southern Africa was frequently spearheaded by women. Dlamini-Zuma suggested that the next conference be in Maputo, co-sponsored by the ANC, and that it should address the new threat of AIDS, a suggestion strongly supported by Zena Stein, who was then co-director for the HIV Center for Clinical and Behavioral Studies at Columbia University.

It took two years to raise the money and organize the conference that was eventually held in Maputo in 1990. The final Maputo conference represented a cross-section of groups, public health workers, unions, and ANC representatives. Manto Tshabalala-Msimang, appointed Minister of Health in 1999 after Mbeki promoted Nkosazana Dlamini-Zuma to Secretary of Foreign Affairs, came from exile in London. Many others traveled from Europe and the United States as well as other countries in Africa.

In 1990 in Maputo, Chris Hani (born Martin Thembisele Hani, 1942–93), leader of the revolutionary wing of the ANC, clearly stated, "We cannot afford to allow the AIDS epidemic to ruin the realization of our dreams. Existing statistics indicate that we are still at the beginning of the epidemic in our country. Unattended, however, this will result in untold damage and suffering by the end of the century" (Frohlich 2005:369; Marais 2000:4).

Echoing Hani's concerns at the Maputo Conference, representatives of the South African mineworkers' union called strongly for action on AIDS, showing that people in South Africa were fully aware of the situation, even in the late 1980s. Once again citing the migrant labor system, Bafana Seripe, a representative of the National Union of Mineworkers (NUM) Workplace Information Group, stated:

> Denied access to land and jobs, many people are forced to leave their homes and families to seek work . . . Men and women who are away from home for long periods may seek companionship and comfort in new relationships. In the rural areas, women left behind may also take lovers for comfort, companionship and financial help. Women also migrate to seek waged employment. Many women, denied access to a meaningful place in the economy, may need to sell sex to survive. The more sexual partners a person has, the greater the risk of contracting a sexually transmitted disease like AIDS. It is clear, however, that merely addressing people's sexuality will not solve the problem. We also have to challenge the socioeconomic and political conditions of people's lives . . . (Seripe 1990:99).

The NUM was struggling specifically against a government policy of "repatriation" to the Bantustans of mineworkers who tested positive for AIDS. The mineworkers' union adopted a number of resolutions although they did not manage to absolutely defeat the policy. The South African Chamber of Mines agreed not to "deport" those "foreigners" (the apartheid language used for Africans who were regarded as belonging to Bantustans defined out of South Africa by apartheid policy) who were not sick, although they retained the right not to renew their contracts (Seripe 1990:101–104).

As the speaker for the NUM made clear, unions were beginning to take leadership on AIDS: "In 1989 many unions made important progress around AIDS and AIDS education, with unions assuming an increasingly leading role. A number of resolutions around AIDS were taken by COSATU [Coalition of South African Trade Unions] and its affiliates" (Seripe 1990:104).

This presentation was in fact criticized in another paper, by Dr. Liz Floyd,[13] at the same meetings. She pointed out many of the major difficulties in reaching trade union members and township residents with respect to warning about the coming epidemic: "The traditional medical sector says that the only way to stop HIV is education and condoms. The progressive sector says you have to eradicate the conditions that promote the spread of HIV. In addition people need to know how to protect themselves" (Floyd 1990:86). Floyd proceeds to argue that, in fact, unions were not involving their membership and that youth and others were more concerned with the ongoing political struggle for liberation from apartheid than they were with AIDS.[14]

If we take these statements without some examination, prescient as they are in predicting the problems of the transition with respect to AIDS, we could believe that the progressive health sector never took a broader approach and that was why AIDS spread so dramatically in the 1990s. However, in the same proceedings we find an extract from a letter to the South African Chamber of Mines, dated January 28, 1990 (three months before the Maputo discussions), from Cyril Ramaphosa, General Secretary of the National Union of Mineworkers. Ironically for the future of the AIDS epidemic, Ramaphosa was later edged out of the ANC political leadership in favor of Mbeki:

> The National Union of Mineworkers approaches the negotiations in an AIDS policy for the mining industry with the realization that the implications are momentous. The results are likely to affect the quality of life of millions of people, not only mineworkers and their families. Employers in other industries are likely to take their cue from these deliberations, and some of the principles regarding major public health issues will have been established through them (NUM 1990:107).

The principles listed in the statement are informed by the recommendations of the World Health Organization and the International Labor Organization as well as Panos (Sabatier 1989). Clearly the NUM was both integrating its AIDS concerns with other negotiations and connecting with the most informed global health research on AIDS.[15]

Cyril Ramaphosa, like the other famous spokesperson on AIDS, Chris Hani, was a leading member of the ANC at this time and clearly could have led the ANC toward a strong program with respect to AIDS. He became the ANC's chief constitutional negotiator, and was considered a strong candidate for Mandela's successor as the head of the ANC (Sparks 2003). When Ramaphosa was passed over by ANC leadership in favor of Mbeki, he stepped aside into the business world.

Rounding out one of the most progressive and farsighted social perspectives on AIDS in Africa, other presentations at Maputo discussed the impact of US instigated "low-intensity warfare" in Africa on the spread of AIDS (Baldo and Cabral 1990:34–46), something that has perhaps as much resonance now as it did in the Cold War era (Mamdani 2004). While reminding us that the legacy of Victorian misogyny, where "female sexuality was seen as dark, dangerous, disease-ridden and in need of direct control," had led feminist movements to deny women any sexuality at all, Megan Vaughan called for "a new discourse on sexuality or sexualities [that] might be developed by communities in Africa that are struggling to resist dominant and oppressive representations of themselves" (Vaughan 1990:124).

Such views expressed at this conference in Maputo were not sole voices crying in the wind. As Chapter 1 notes, already at that time, a systematic view of the issues of war, racism, misogyny, labor migration, and the significance of community involvement was being generated globally (Bond et al. 1997; Fee and Fox 1988).[16]

Not everyone at the conference saw AIDS as a high priority for health care. Some ANC representatives from South Africa, less familiar with the disease than those in the training camps in Angola, emphasized primary health care in general, as, in fact, most of the participants had outlined in the 1988 New York City conference. Objections were voiced to the lectures by leading medical personnel from Uganda, Mozambique, and Zimbabwe, who were describing the ways that their governments, coping with dramatically higher rates of AIDS than South Africa at the time, had confronted the epidemic (De Sousa et al. 1990; Latif 1990; Serwadda 1990). Conference participants preferred to have general discussions about the needs of South Africa and were not willing to listen to lectures about a topic they did not necessarily view as crucial (Zena Stein, personal communication, 2006). Some of these divisions, evident in discussions quoted from the Maputo Proceedings, were to widen precipitously over the next 15 years as the African National Congress became the ruling party of South Africa. Nevertheless, the concluding statement of the Maputo Conference reflected the high priority set on AIDS emphasized by Chris Hani and based on his experiences in east Africa where the disease had taken hold a decade earlier. Participants "acknowledged research that shows that human immunodeficiency virus (HIV) infection and acquired immune deficiency syndrome (AIDS) is an established epidemic in South Africa and throughout southern Africa . . ." (MCHTSA 1990:136). They recognized that "The magnitude of the epidemic is increasing rapidly" and "agreed that if no significant intervention is made within the next few months, there would be little chance of avoiding its disastrous consequences" (MCHTSA 1990:136). Recognizing that the South African government response "had been totally inadequate," the statement noted that "The African National Congress has a major role to play in this regard" (MCHTSA 1990:136).

Finally, the delegates developed a broad preventive plan for AIDS with attention to all social sectors, such as employment, youth, and education as well as public health. A National AIDS Task Force was proposed, and, in fact, a conference was later convened in South Africa which led to the formation of the National AIDS Coalition of South Africa (NACOSA), chaired by Nkosazana Dlamini-Zuma. Explicitly echoing Maputo, The National AIDS Coalition developed a comprehensive strategy for addressing the AIDS epidemic in South Africa. However, the plan was never implemented.

Immediately after the Maputo Conference, Mervyn Susser and Zena Stein met with Mandela, who had just been set free, to welcome him back and explicitly to discuss the issue of AIDS. In 1990, Mervyn Susser had been invited by the South African medical student association to tour South Africa and speak about AIDS. He had in fact written an open letter to Oliver Tambo, copied to Nelson Mandela, outlining the threat of AIDS to the liberation regime. According to Zena Stein, at their brief meeting, Mandela asked about their children and grandchildren and they discussed the years since they had known each other in the liberation struggles of the 1950s as well as AIDS. However, in the middle of the conversation, Mandela received an urgent phone call from Mangosuthu Buthelezi, the leader of the Inkatha Freedom Party. Since this was at the height of the violence involving Inkatha prior to the transition, Zena Stein told me that she felt that Mandela was extremely concerned to address this bloody conflict and could not take any further time to focus on the AIDS discussion. Stein and Susser walked across the hall to talk with their old friends Walter Sisulu, renowned ANC leader, and Ahmed Kathrada, who was of a slightly younger generation of freedom fighters and a prison inmate with

Mandela. They never really had the planned conversation about Maputo and AIDS with Nelson Mandela. Perhaps this brief experience highlights an argument that the immense strains and conflicting demands of the transition diverted the new government from a focus on the looming tragedy of AIDS (Marais 2000).

It is possible, with hindsight, to understand the lack of attention to AIDS in the immediate process of transition. In light of the lack of health care, adequate sanitation or education for the African population, opposition to the apartheid state had historically been framed from a modernist, liberationist perspective. Demands for state investments in public health, including biomedicine and a concern for women's reproductive health and maternal mortality, were central. An emphasis on AIDS was viewed by some as reflecting a Western bias and shifting attention from what were perceived as the much broader and more pressing needs of an emerging African state. Contraception was suspect as the apartheid government had in fact advocated condoms in its efforts to prevent an increase in the black population (Dlamini-Zuma 1988b). As a result, among the black population who had not yet experienced AIDS mortality, the idea of AIDS – and that men should use condoms – was often seen as a new Western plot to limit population. During the transition, the shadow ANC Health Ministry pronounced free primary care for all as the main health policy for the future democratic regime. Primary health care, which, in fact, has an inherent emphasis on women and children, was seen as a crucial and democratic first step. In this context, AIDS was not singled out as a central problem in need of attention beyond the primary health care plan.

## The Politics of AIDS in the Transition

In 1992, the ANC entered a power-sharing arrangement with the apartheid government in preparation for the 1994 elections. These were to be the first national elections in which the majority African population would vote. The ANC was expected to win overwhelmingly. In 1993, Chris Hani, who had been the leader of the militia in exile and had emerged as a major figure in the new South Africa, was murdered, most likely at the instigation of a White conservative backlash. Hani's assassination may be seen as the first step in the gradual defeat of the AIDS agenda. Hani's much-quoted support of the AIDS initiative, combined with his major influence and credibility among the youth of South Africa, might have led to a different outcome. The failure of political will with respect to HIV/AIDS in the 1990s was to cost South Africa dearly as the rate of AIDS rose from under 1 percent in 1990 to 22.8 percent in 1998 (Marais 2000:7).

The question of what happened to prevent the implementation of the NACOSA plan in South Africa and the ensuing tragedies of the following years has been much discussed and a number of issues have been highlighted. Helen Schneider emphasizes the structural decisions to confine AIDS to the Ministry of Health (Schneider

2002; Schneider and Stein 2002). NACOSA envisioned a multisectoral approach and direct access to the president. In the administration of the new South Africa, the problem of AIDS was instead relegated to the Department of Health, headed by Dr. Dlamini-Zuma. As Schneider argues, rather than harnessing the energies of the HIV/AIDS movement, the new government structures deprived them of their previous direct access to ANC health policy.

Hein Marais stresses the enormous energies required for the transition. Throughout the 1990s, as central ANC leaders focused on issues of housing, racial equality, and income, concern with AIDS became marginalized. In addition, the new administration had to learn the rules of the inherited bureaucracy and to negotiate with provincial hierarchies. Even within the Department of Health, which did focus on AIDS, high-profile scandals involving financial mismanagement of *Sarafina II!* (a health education AIDS drama)[17] and the invention and promotion of a new drug, Virodene, which turned out to contain industrial solvent, also destroyed the credibility of new government policies with respect to AIDS (Marais 2000; Nattrass 2007; Schneider 2002; Schneider and Stein 2002).

Ironically, in terms of the AIDS epidemic, the 1994 victory over apartheid allowed the opening of borders to migrant labor from the rest of southern Africa, which may actually have accelerated the spread of the virus (Marks 2002). In addition, the gendered inequality of the liberation movements was to come back to haunt the new republic as liberation heroes such as Jacob Zuma adopted militaristic and patriarchal approaches to women. This was clearly one of the issues that arose both in court and in the streets when Zuma was tried for rape a decade later (Motsei 2007).

## South Africa in the Early 1990s

Dr. Nkosazana Dlamini-Zuma's own research provides a sense of the future ANC government's perspective on AIDS. In 1992, Dlamini-Zuma was a leading member of the Gender Advisory Committtee, discussing the new South African constitution. As the wife, in those years, of Jacob Zuma and herself a prominent leader in the ANC, she had unusually direct access to future government leaders. She was conducting a survey of the perspectives of the political leadership on AIDS as a component of a research project focused on AIDS in the community (Abdool Karim and Morar 1994).[18] At a small informal seminar where we discussed our plans, she reported her experience with amusement.

Of Nelson Mandela and a number of other leading men from the ANC, Dlamini-Zuma joked: "When I call them for an interview, I say it is about AIDS policy and they do not seem to have much to say. They put off the interview for several weeks ahead and then they get the information together, so that by the time I see them, they are more knowledgeable." At the time, she noted with approval that this was an important educational process and hoped it would contribute to effective AIDS prevention in the future. She could not have foreseen the future complexities involved in government recognition of the problems of HIV/AIDS.

At this time, it was evident that Dr. Dlamini-Zuma, born in KwaZulu-Natal and, again, a long-time member of the ANC, had a strong local following among the poor African population on the outskirts of Durban, the major city in the province. In 1992, as discussed further below, Dr. Dlamini-Zuma was greeted with enthusiasm at a community meeting about AIDS and was clearly viewed as a "daughter" of Durban. As we shall see, people in this setting welcomed her speaking candidly about AIDS, sexuality, and women's possible options.

## Colonial/Apartheid Heritage in the New South Africa

To comprehend the significance of Dr. Dlamini-Zuma and the later dilemmas and conflicts facing the new South Africa, we must take a detour here, to outline still salient features of the colonial heritage. KwaZulu had been the center of the old Zulu kingdom and also the crucible of explosive cultural and political contestations from the apartheid era through the transition. It was the "traditional" base of the Inkatha Freedom Party (IFP), which had first emerged in the opening years of the twentieth century and had originally represented the Zulu landowners and farmers as opposed to the landless peasants (Marks and Trapido 1987) but was revitalized in 1975 under the apartheid regime.

The Land Rights Act of 1913 had provided the legal groundwork for the eventual relegation of Africans to less than 13 percent of South African land. Nevertheless, in some regions Africans managed to maintain land and to continue reasonably successful farms (Hart 2002; van Onselen 1996). However, in the 1960s, in line with similar acts of dispossession in central cities and elsewhere, the apartheid government precipitously escalated major displacements of black farmers and landowners from the land around Durban (Hart 2002).

In 1970, in line with the homeland policy, Chief Mangosuthu Buthelezi, who had participated in the ANC youth league as a student and was a graduate of the University of Natal, was appointed Chief Minister of the KwaZulu Authority by the apartheid government. Buthelezi's acceptance of this position was viewed by many ANC members as the self-conscious exploitation of tribal differentiation and interpreted as allegiance to or at least cooperation with the apartheid regime. In 1975, it was Buthelezi who reinvigorated the nationalist Zulu organization, the Inkatha Freedom Party. Over the 1980s a split developed between Inkatha and the ANC and Inkatha became the leading African opposition to the ANC. In the 1990s, Buthelezi enlisted the support of the Zulu king against the African National Congress and enshrined Inkatha in the symbolic raiments of traditional Zulu allegiance. However, even the province of what came to be known as KwaZulu-Natal, a name negotiated in 1994 by the ANC and Inkatha, was split between the ANC and Inkatha.

Throughout the transition years between 1990 and 1994, murderous conflicts erupted in the rural areas of KwaZulu-Natal between Inkatha and the ANC. During this period, in the contestation over political control of the nation, migrant workers living in hostels, dressed in Zulu traditional garb and carrying spears, precipitated armed confrontations with ANC members. The violent conflict between the ANC and Inkatha was inflamed in part by the Third Force, a little-known group which the Truth and Reconciliation Commission of South Africa later exposed as a loose network of operatives linked to the apartheid regime (TRC 2003:584).

In the new South Africa, Inkatha won the provincial elections in KwaZulu-Natal for ten years. In 2004, the ANC finally defeated Inkatha in KwaZulu-Natal, perhaps in part by adopting the "traditionalist" approaches, including the control of customary land rights for chiefs which had provided the bedrock of support for Inkatha.

Ironically, KwaZulu-Natal, the center of traditionalist opposition to the ANC, was also a major center in AIDS research and one of the first places where treatment was offered to mothers and children. In fact, in 2002 Buthelezi himself gave speeches in support of treatment and criticized Mbeki for his refusal to distribute the medicines that would prevent mother-to-child transmission of the HIV virus.

Jacob Zuma, who on December 18, 2007 defeated Thabo Mbeki in the elections for President of the African National Congress, is of Zulu heritage while Mandela and Mbeki are of Xhosa background, representing two closely related pastoral societies. However, rather than taking a "traditionalist" stance and advocating herbal treatments, Zuma's acceptance speech called for government treatment for AIDS as his third priority, after addressing income inequality and crime. In spite of his infamous remark that he would "take a shower" to protect himself from AIDS, Jacob Zuma provided an openness for AIDS treatment in South Africa rare in the Mbeki administration. Such contradictory perspectives on AIDS, culture, and gender may help to illuminate the complex and historically framed politics of today.

## Town and Country

There were other historical divisions besides those of tribal affiliation among the African population that laid a foundation for the fateful evolution of the AIDS epidemic. Beyond those of class and ethnicity were the urban and rural identities originally created and reinforced by the long-term and still continuing migrant labor system. Such identities were also connected with the Inkatha–ANC contestations as the performance of the rural was associated with "traditionalists," long linked to Inkatha, but later with the herbal remedies promulgated by the ANC Minister of Health, Manto Tshabalala-Msimang.

Contestations over cultural representation associated with town and country identity and the inheritance of land and resources were described by Philip Mayer in the 1950s (Mayer 1971). Mayer outlined the local distinction of School versus

Red among the Xhosa population of East London, in the Eastern Cape, several hundred miles south of Durban. School Xhosa wore Western clothes and attempted to establish their financial security in a Western-defined arena. Reds, dressed in traditional blankets, were careful to maintain their kinship status and access to resources in the tribal hierarchies of their rural villages. These urban/rural distinctions, however interpreted, are still in use today. In fact, they are discussed in Steinberg 2008, with reference to the Xhosa and the Mpondo-speaking peoples, in terms of the "ochre" (who wore "traditional" blankets) and the "dressed"(who wore Western clothes). He documents the life of Sizwe Magadla, an HIV-positive man from an "ochre" background where participating in youth ritual and associations rather than school are seen as the appropriate role for young boys. As soon as Sizwe's father leaves town, his mother insists that her sons go to school, rejecting the "ochre" or traditionally oriented upbringing his father envisioned for him (Steinberg 2008:39).

The very categories Mayer discussed were seen by the Copperbelt anthropologists as the product of the situational fluidity of identity required by the migrant labor system (Vincent 1986). Bernard Magubane later noted that these analysts had taken colonial occupation for granted and that the system, as Godfrey Wilson once wrote, was created to serve an imperial economy (Magubane 1979; Wilson 1941). Nevertheless, situational analysis suggested that people strategized with respect to the adoption of identities according to particular historical and political situations. As Ferguson points out for Zambia in the 1990s, when unemployment hits, situational exigencies lead many people to re-create or remember their rural kin ties in the search for an economic safety net (Ferguson 1999).

Relevant to the current era is the idea that the return to a dependence on kin ties in rural areas places people under the control of the "traditional" chiefs and opens the way to the complex gendered differentiation of customary law. Customary law itself was not static and had been in the process of transformation through the colonial era and apartheid and in the new South Africa. However, in spite of historical transformations, customary law presented a different paradigm with respect to gender than Western constitutional law (Mikell 1997; Ngubane 1977). Western constitutional law is fundamentally based on the image of the individual (even in its regulation of corporate behavior) while customary law takes a broader social perspective. However, in southern Africa and elsewhere, the combination of the two over time has clearly favored a patriarchal praxis which marries the male bias of Western colonialism to the patrilineal customs of the cattle complex societies, to be described in more detail in Chapter 4 (Bozzoli and Nkotsoe 1991; Mikell 1997; Morrell 2001; Walker 1991).

If we avoid the possible reification of situational identities, Mayer's symbolic and economic differentiation among rural-based and urban-identified populations can be conceptually useful also for understanding the differentiation among "women from the country" and urban women still made among the predominantly Zulu women I worked with in the informal settlements in Durban. It can also be understood in the echoes of Zulu tradition embraced by Inkatha in competition with the ANC.

In the 1980s, in an era of massive protests and strikes organized by COSATU (Congress of South African Trade Unions), the pass laws were relaxed and many men and women flocked to the urban areas. By the early 1990s, due both to the dispossession of Africans in the rural areas and the demise of the pass laws, a million people were living in informal settlements on the outskirts of Durban, the main city of what came to be known as KwaZulu-Natal. Many of the households were made up of single women with children who had left the rural areas to come to the city looking for work and some way to support their children. Some viewed themselves and were seen as "rural-based" and others as urban (Preston-Whyte and Rogerson 1991).

As we have seen, there were many forms of differentiation among the women in the informal settlements around Durban, including class and education, urban–rural and Inkatha–ANC. Each of these historical processes of differentiation was woven into emerging responses to the AIDS epidemic.

## Durban Settlements

As noted earlier, in 1992, Dr. Dlamini-Zuma was wildly acclaimed when she addressed a group of community women activists in Zulu, in the community hall of a densely populated informal settlement. At that time, houses were made of corrugated iron and old cardboard with occasional outhouses of the same materials. There was no running water, but women activists had managed to force the government to provide community water faucets. Roads were not paved and were often precipitous and winding so that driving through the area was nerve-racking. Since the settlement was outside any official municipal district, there were no local clinics or schools and children had to walk to a formal municipal district to attend school. However, there was an active ANC presence and, as outside researchers, we did have to stop to inform the urban civic council leaders when we entered the area.[19]

At this informal settlement, there were no telephones and a community health organizer announced a women's community meeting about HIV through a bull-horn. People gathered in a small hall behind a grocery store, and Dlamini-Zuma spoke in Zulu about HIV and the empowering possibilities of the female condom. I had brought some female condoms with me and these were passed around for illustration. The first printing of the new ANC constitution in Zulu was distributed and a tremendous sense of excitement was palpable in the room. Some of the approximately 50 participants at the meeting were women who had been part of a crafts cooperative in the settlement. They asked questions about AIDS and talked publicly about sex and forcefully about the desperation among poor women which sometimes led them to sell sex to feed their children.

In Dlamini-Zuma's presentation and her presence in this early period of the transition to the new South Africa, the fight against HIV/AIDS, the fight for women's empowerment and employment, and the birth of the ANC constitution were all integrally connected as the stage was set for freedom from apartheid. She managed to inspire poor women facing widespread dangers of political turmoil and living in shantytown conditions to read the ANC constitution and to demand the female condom.

These events were even more remarkable for the fact that they took place at such a moment of political turmoil in KwaZulu. One evening when we met for dinner, Dlamini-Zuma was looking after seven children, some her own, some orphaned by violence, and was herself moving from place to place to avoid assassination. She told us she visited many funerals each week and that there might be as many as 14 funerals to attend in a weekend.

As noted earlier, although the majority of ANC supporters were of Zulu background, the mobilization of "traditional" allegiances by Inkatha, in cooperation to some extent with the apartheid government, provided the template for the power as well as the gendered nature of tribal connections for use in future political contests. The political conflicts of the transition exploited the images of armed masculinity in African history and violent conflict came to characterize migrant workers. Even among men in the increasingly powerful unions, which supported the ANC, violent conflict and the subordination of women who had no access to such unionized work characterized images of masculinity (Morrell 2001).

Many men lived in hostels where an urban woman's entitlement to a bed depended on her serving the man food, doing his laundry, and providing sex (Ramphele 1993). Some women lived on the margins of mines, working as sex workers under the domination of men who maintained their positions through violence (Campbell 2003; Jochelson et al. 1991). When such men returned to wives in the rural areas, they looked to the chiefs to maintain patrilineal control of resources (Bozzoli and Nkotsoe 1991). As we shall see, to the detriment of the situation for women, the symbolic manipulation of difference in the support of customary rights and traditional healers became a major strategy in the process through which the ANC sought to capture the majority of votes in KwaZulu a decade later.

## Hopefulness Among Women of the Grass Roots

In 1994, the ANC was finally elected to power, having ruled jointly with the defeated Nationalist Party, inventors of apartheid, for two years. Nelson Mandela became president and implemented many changes immediately. Housing was built. Water pipes were laid. Informal settlements became municipal districts, entitled to schools, clinics, and libraries. Nkosazana Dlamini-Zuma was appointed the Minister of Health and Quarraisha Abdool Karim, the principal investigator of the earlier research, was appointed by Dlamini-Zuma as the national director of South Africa's AIDS program.

By 1995, in the informal settlement where the 1992 meeting had taken place, a new brick assembly hall was built in recognition of the community's historic support for the ANC in a heavily Inkatha region. The women in the Durban settlements became even more politically active, articulate in public, and aware of the threat of HIV/AIDS. At a meeting about AIDS called by the same community health educator, local women again called for the female condom. Now, with a sense of empowerment generated by the new South Africa, they went even further in their willingness to confront HIV. They said that in their houses there was no room for privacy and this made it difficult to negotiate sexual relations with their partners. They also talked more explicitly about employment possibilities and pointed out that if they had work, they could tell their husbands that they wanted to avoid pregnancy to keep the job. In this way, they could legitimately ask to use the female condom. The women demanded training as community health workers.

At the meeting, a woman who had been trained as a community health worker provided a dildo which the women used nonchalantly as they talked about how to put a condom on a man and how the female condom worked. Although there was a lot of laughing and general cheer and camaraderie, women were very open in their discussions of sexual anatomy and contraception. They were generally outspoken, hopeful, and demanding. At one point, a male ANC official came into the meeting. He laughed and joked with the women. When he was asked whether he would use a condom, he pulled out his wallet and showed that he was carrying one with him. When the women showed him the demonstration female condoms and asked him how he would respond if a woman wanted to use a female condom, he answered that it was all right for her to use such a thing if it was in her room. There was little sign of embarrassment. A general willingness to tackle the issues of sexuality in public obtained. It is important to recognize the openness of the women to such discussion as far back as 1995 when it comes to evaluating the "traditional" values that have become so prevalent in discussion of AIDS prevention in the past few years.

The women at this meeting regarded Nkosazana Dlamini-Zuma as their representative and knew that she had now become the Minister of Health. Newly empowered in a democratic state, and clearly expecting results, the women wrote a letter and signed petitions to Dr. Dlamini-Zuma, demanding the woman's condom.

Dr. Dlamini-Zuma's national AIDS program director Quarraisha Abdool Karim, committed to women's issues and energized by the ANC victory, had already ordered 90,000 female condoms to be distributed by provincial health departments to two pilot clinics in each province. Some commentators actually criticized the Department of Health for spending the money on such an "expensive" prophylactic, but this evaluation should be put in the context of the cost of 97 million male condoms that were also distributed but were not viewed as too costly. Clearly, the cost of AIDS, even days of absence from work, far outweighed any condom costs. As noted earlier, pursuant to an agreement between the outgoing Nationalist Party and the ANC, provincial departments of public health were still controlled by remnants of the old regime. Perhaps for this reason, or simple lack of efficiency, the female condoms were not distributed for more than a year. By the time the female condoms appeared in local clinics, the expiration date had passed. The Ministry of Health had in fact spent the preceding year educating the population about the expiration dates of medications (Quarraisha Abdool Karim, personal correspondence, 2007). Ironically, health activists, perhaps already beginning to feel politically excluded themselves, accused the clinics of "dumping" US expired goods on South African women. As a result, the female condoms were actually recalled.

As the government began to edge aside the progressive groups that had brought the ANC to power, women paid the price by losing access to the female condom. An active feminist health movement, which included at least two highly visible publications, *Agenda: Empowering Women for Gender Equality* and the *Women's Health Project*, mobilized for ten years for the woman's condom but it only became available in some public clinics in 2003.

This is an early and unrecognized instance of access to resources for HIV prevention being stopped by the accusation that US capitalist corruption was the problem. The "dumping" of expired medications from the United States to poor countries has been clearly documented in the past and, in other situations, might have been a well-founded suspicion. However, it is hardly appropriate in the case of the female condom, which is known to be made of polyurethane and could probably last several thousand years. It is certainly stronger than male condoms. The unsubstantiated conspiracy theory operating here is an early indication of the contradictory ways in which attacks on women's access to resources and perhaps a fundamentalist backlash was already undermining democratic processes and taking a toll on AIDS policy.[20]

During this period, feminists, like the AIDS activists represented in the National AIDS Coalition, were also working for a voice in government and, in fact, were incorporated into the institutional framework of government through the Women's Government Initiative. Feminists won representation in government and, in the early years of euphoric victory, were able to de-criminalize abortion and fight for maintenance grants for poor women. However, as discussed briefly in the next chapter, in a process that parallels the history of AIDS activism, feminists found themselves isolated in government and largely unable to advocate effectively for the needs of poor women (Hassim 2006; Govender 2007).

The ANC and the South African government have traversed a very erratic route with respect to HIV/AIDS, much of it played out as a drama on the world stage. As we shall see, over the next few years, Dr. Nkosazana Dlamini-Zuma continued to be involved in a number of international problems relating to HIV/AIDS. Her policies were in some cases ill-considered and costly, and this eventually resulted in the resignation of Quarraisha Abdool Karim, director of the national AIDS program, and of Olive Shisana, the director general of the Department of Health, diminishing hope for a vital HIV/AIDS program (Schneider 2002; Schneider and Stein 2002). It also signaled the end of the simple, modernist approach to HIV/AIDS and the end of direct feminist impact on the epidemic.

## Suspicion and Superstition

The main point I wish to demonstrate by this short period piece about South Africa from 1991 to 1996 is to dispel the impression that "traditional" beliefs framed early public responses to AIDS. In the early 1990s, people were hopeful about the incredible victory over apartheid, the prevalence of HIV/AIDS was less than one percent, and the new constitution was still being hammered out, claiming revolutionary rights for women and sexual orientation as well as the right to health. In this early dawn of a new democratic state, activist groups were calling for a holistic public health approach to HIV/AIDS prevention and, within this, access to women's barrier methods.

Beneath this hopeful veneer, contradictory forces slowly began to surface. Some problems were already evident. In 1992, a community health study in a rural village documented the fact that women knew much less than men concerning sexually transmitted diseases (Abdool Karim and Morar 1994). In that same village in 1992, some of the men at a public meeting outside the clinic told us that the disease we called HIV/AIDS was actually a disease identified by local folk healers as a punishment for infidelity.

As the anthropologist Harriet Ngubane, herself educated in Catholic missions of KwaZulu but of Zulu origins and language, has noted, traditional healing practices among the Zulu peoples have always centered strongly on women and reproduction. To quote Meyer Fortes' introduction: "most critical family tensions arise in relation to rights over the reproductive powers of women . . ." (Fortes, in Ngubane 1977:x).

In the rural village mentioned above, women would not speak to us in front of their men and only men ran for election for the village council or for ANC positions. However, in the hopeful 1990s these issues seemed open to change as the chief himself was an active ANC member and, for example, a few years later, a nearby Zulu village chose a woman as chief. Local folk healers were talking with public health practitioners about cooperative work around HIV/AIDS (Abdool Karim et al. 1994). There were hopes that cultural and "traditionalist" expectations could merge with constitutional law to implement a "pragmatics of difference" (Comaroff and Comaroff 2004).

In a different but equally prophetic vein, in the urban areas in 1992 we met with numerous local religious groups, many dressed in the long white robes of the synthetic Zionist churches.[21] At the same time, we heard that the corrugated iron houses of people known to be diagnosed with HIV/AIDS had been burned to the ground and the people chased out of the informal settlement on the margins of Durban where they had been forced to live.

Such underlying forces of women's subordination in the tribal areas, fundamentalist religious beliefs, and sorcery accusations certainly supplied the available grist for a public culture built on suspicion and repression, rather than the human rights and social justice celebrated in the new constitution. However, in the early 1990s health activism characterized the public voice of the ANC, as represented by the Maputo Conference and the formation of NACOSA (Mbali 2003; Mbali 2008).

Nevertheless, from around 1991 to 1996, conflict and turmoil raged in the rural areas of KwaZulu-Natal, represented by political competition between the African National Congress and the Inkatha Freedom Party. Although, as noted earlier, the violence was associated with the "Third Force," which was later connected to the White nationalist supporters of apartheid, Inkatha was also representative of the Zulu Kingdom of KwaZulu-Natal Province. In 1994, immediately before the first national elections, Buthelezi announced his support for the ANC. Inkatha won the province of KwaZulu in the national elections of 1994. The ANC won the national elections and Buthelezi was appointed Minister for Home Affairs.

For eight years, Inkatha governed KwaZulu-Natal and, as noted earlier, contrary to "traditionalist" expectations, supported HIV/AIDS education, prevention, and treatment. In contrast, over time the ANC, possibly in the effort to compete with Inkatha in KwaZulu, adopted a more "traditionalist" stance to sexuality and HIV/AIDS. This could be interpreted as a conciliatory offer to attract the entrenched tribal hierarchies. We have already seen the ways in which the distribution of the female condom might have been undermined by opposition to women's sexual autonomy. As we shall see in more detail later, in opposition to the new constitution, "traditionalist" groups were permitted to strategically mobilize customary law in order to subordinate women and their rights to land and inheritance. In 2004, the ANC won the provincial elections in KwaZulu-Natal.

As the events of the early 1990s illustrate, public culture at that time was contested but vibrant and democratic. Biomedical understandings of health and HIV/AIDS dominated the discourse as did activism with respect to social justice for women and sexual orientation. In the broader public sphere, between 1994 and 1996 the government, represented by the priorities of the ANC, invested in subsidized housing for the poor, roads through informal settlements, access to clean water, primary health care, male condoms, and schools.

Tragically, by 1996, South Africa, Botswana, and Namibia began to manifest the highest rates of HIV/AIDS infection in the world. At the same time, the South African government instituted massive structural adjustment and privatization policies through the Growth, Employment and Redistribution policy that came to be known as GEAR. As has been true all over the world, structural adjustment hits women particularly hard because it universally involves cutbacks in social services, health, education, and welfare upon which women and children depend heavily. However, as we shall see, these policies had an even more serious and detrimental effect on women in the context of AIDS.

# 4

# Of Nevirapine and African Potatoes: Shifts in Public Discourse

This chapter explores the impact of the shift to neoliberal policies from 1998–2004 in South Africa. It examines the association of economic cutbacks with the beginning of HIV denialism, the government mistrust of biomedicine, and the stress on herbal healing and African masculine traditions.

The years between 1998 and 2004 were crucial for the implementation of AIDS treatment and the clarification or obfuscation of government discourse. As we have seen from Maputo, NACOSA, and other sources, public health policy provided clear models for effective interventions at that time (Abdool Karim and Abdool Karim 2002:39). However, "[n]one of these steps were approached with the foresight, vigour and urgency that were called for"(Abdool Karim and Abdool Karim 2002:40). It will be a critical challenge for South Africa today to counteract the impact of the deaths, community destruction, and gendered framing of the AIDS epidemic precipitated by the policies of this era.

In 1996, the government of South Africa explicitly shifted its economic priorities to implement Growth, Employment, and Redistribution (GEAR). This economic program delayed funding for public welfare in a concerted effort to pay off the international debt and ostensibly to attract international business investment.[1] As a result of this program, from 1998, the gap between middle income and poor increased, the implementation of social programs slowed, and the promises of the early liberation era began to seem more distant.[2]

The much-contested change in economic priorities away from domestic welfare had a predictable impact on poor women, on health, and on the possibilities for AIDS treatment and prevention. At the same time, there was a dramatic shift in the public discourse on AIDS as, led by President Thabo Mbeki, the biomedical understanding of the AIDS virus as well as the efficacy of anti-retroviral treatment were questioned (Nattrass 2007:40).[3] Under these stringent economic conditions, we also find a renewed, although not consistent, public discourse on a nationalism, which stresses women's subordination and African men's "traditional" patriarchal rights (Posel 2005; Fassin and Schneider 2003; Marais 2001).

As mentioned in the previous chapter, women won some concessions in the early years of the transition but, by 1999, policies that addressed the unequal poverty of women or their reproductive rights were no longer successful. Pregs Govender's description of her experience in parliament and as the chair of a parliamentary committee on the status of women shows that, while "[i]t was not easy trying to get agreement that women's issues should be prioritized by the ANC and parliament," some success, such as in the invention of the Women's Budget, was possible in the early years (up to 1998–9) (Govender 2007:158).

Govender outlines the ways in which she led efforts to implement laws addressing violence against women and talks of the short period from 1994 to 1999 when women's issues could be raised. In 1999, as the Mbeki government was convened, Govender was re-elected as chair of the committee on women and initiated hearings with respect to the violence "of rape, witch-burning, battery, femicide, adult incest with children as well as the everyday humiliation of sexual harassment" (Govender 2007:187). As she said: "Our job . . . [is] only done when we see the laws function and when they're effective" (Govender 2007:189). Govender and her committee were challenged at every step and received very little support from parliament. In 2001, in her role as chair of the committee on women, she did break the silence on AIDS in the ANC and led the first public parliamentary hearings on HIV (Feinstein 2007, Govender 2007).

There is no question that the equal representation of women on government committees and the appointment of women in the cabinet was a main theme of the African Renaissance called for by Mbeki. Nevertheless, in parallel with the historical shifts toward GEAR and global economic investment discussed in this chapter, after 1999, women in leadership found it extremely difficult to address the needs of poor women. Govender writes: "Another factor in the lack of impact is that, globally, decision making has shifted to unelected, unrepresentative institutions which protect the interests of capital above human rights. At the same time, more women have been elected onto representative institutions such as parliament than ever before. There they are confronted by conservative macroeconomic policy, trade agreements, and patents that undermine women's rights. In South Africa the national budget has ended its 1998/99 commitment to the Women's Budget" (Govender 2007:169). As many might expect, women in parliamentary positions do not or cannot always represent the needs of poor women or even women in general.

In the general process of neoliberal restructuring, which included cutting back on social services, education, and other expenditures, funding for health was also cut back (Benatar 2001). Under the apartheid state, well-equipped hospitals largely served the white population but primary health care for the poor black population was minimal. As progressive medical professionals redesigned the health care system in the post-apartheid state, decisions were made to invest in free primary care, such as new health facilities, prenatal clinics, vaccines, and other minimal low-technology services. Pregnant women and young children receive free health services. In line with the emphasis on primary care, there was some reduction in investments in the tertiary sector. From 1996, as radical structural adjustment programs were implemented, the health funding structure became much less progressive; proposed investments in primary care slowed, so that many clinics essential to the primary care program lacked health personnel, equipment or medications while the decline in tertiary or hospital investment continued (Benatar 2001). Data indicate that inequities in access and utilization between socioeconomic groups have not improved as a result, among other factors, of staffing loss as well as the costs of transport for the poor to access care and their worsening household economic conditions (Gilson and McIntyre 2007). Again referring to the impact of neoliberal policy shifts, the authors note that in 1995, the key problem of staffing was addressed by large salary increases while "the stagnating public health budget in the second half of the 1990s led, in practice, to reductions in staffing levels" (Gilson and McIntyre 2007:685).

As has been the common result of structural adjustment internationally, in South Africa the gaps in access to health care between rich and poor have actually widened dramatically. This is despite the fact that it has been estimated that during this period about 800 people were dying each day from AIDS (Abdool Karim and Adool Karim 2005). To quote an overall perspective of health care following structural adjustment: "While public sector health care expenditure has been relatively stagnant in real per capita terms over the last decade, expenditure in the private sector has continued increasing at rates far exceeding the rate of inflations despite medical schemes covering a declining share of the population" (McIntyre and Thiede 2007:35).

In 1996, the same year as structural adjustments were introduced in South Africa, newly effective, life-prolonging AIDS drugs became available in the United States and western Europe. The possibilities for AIDS treatment massively expanded and with this success the gap between the options for people in rich and poor countries starkly widened. To add to the situation of global inequality, just as AIDS treatment became available, the World Trade Organization initiated a multistage process of international patent laws, known as Trade Related Aspects of Intellectual Property Rights (TRIPS) that limited, among many other things, the manufacturing and distribution of new AIDS medicines. In Latin America, activists fought the measures in court and through popular movements using new constitutions that recognized people's right to health. In Brazil the combination of popular protest and legal suits resulted in widespread access to treatment for people with AIDS (Parker 2003).[4]

In 1997, as part of the search for affordable treatment for AIDS, the South African Minister of Health Dr. Nkosazana Dlamini-Zuma challenged the TRIPS agreement by amending the Medicines and Related Substances Control Act to allow South Africa to buy the cheaper generic drugs manufactured by pharmaceutical companies in India and elsewhere (Health Systems Trust 2006; Nattrass 2007:50). In February 1998, retaliating against Dlamini-Zuma's initiative, 39 US pharmaceutical companies brought a suit against South Africa for violation of the TRIPS agreement. Thus, the battle over affordable treatment was launched on a global scale. Ironically, by the time South Africa won this battle, the government was not willing to translate their international victories into action. The Minister of Health refused to allow the distribution of free medications, such as nevirapine, although, by this point, some provincial leaders in KwaZulu-Natal, the Western Cape, and Gauteng had broken ranks with the administration and supported treatment initiatives (Nattrass 2007:98).

As the South African government entered the global scene with GEAR and then in its challenges to the World Trade Organization over the costs of AIDS drugs, activists too shifted to global battles. The South African Treatment Action Campaign (TAC), founded in 1998, supported and energized Nkosazana Dlamini-Zuma's battle with the pharmaceutical companies over the TRIPS agreement and eventually filed an amicus curiae brief in support of the ANC government challenge. In this way, the group that became the largest movement for the treatment of people with AIDS in South Africa seemed to be working with the government in very progressive ways (Friedman and Mottier 2004). Just as South Africa was becoming a player in the global South, its government was also addressing one of the most pressing issues – the right to medicines at affordable prices.

In 1998, Geneva, the International AIDS Society Conference was entitled "Bridging the Gap." However, as one US health activist noted, while there was international discussion about equal access to treatment, for Africa, with the poorest populations and the highest rates of AIDS in the world, concrete proposals were missing (Berkman 2003). As a result, following Geneva, anti-globalization activists focused on the United States' responsibility for global inequality, adopted the demand that people in poor countries could and should have equal access to treatment immediately, no matter what the cost. It was at this point that the newly formed South African TAC joined with Health GAP[5] (Global Access Project), ACT UP, and other organizations to fight against TRIPS and for affordable treatment.

The South African TAC had a broad social agenda with respect to AIDS. It was initiated by a small group of South Africans who came out of the old liberation networks and NACOSA (National AIDS Coalition of South Africa) and were well connected to the international gay movement as well as the African National Congress.[6] They were fully aware of the treatment available in wealthy Western countries (Nattrass 2007). They had been among the groups influential in writing the new South African constitution, making sure it was one of the most progressive in the world and assured the rights of women, sexual orientation, and also the rights to health (Constitutional Court of South Africa 1996). They self-consciously crossed lines of gender and ethnic identity, class, and race to demand access to treatment. Over time, the South African TAC linked with public health activists, churches, trade unions, the women's health movement, and the demands of poor South African men and women, organized in coalitions like those of the Durban informal settlements, an historic stronghold of the ANC.

From early on, the South African TAC has attracted many if not more women than men into its ranks, although not as effectively into the leadership (Friedman and Mottier 2004). From the point of view of gender, the TAC was fighting an important battle for women to have access to treatment just as they fought for men. However, at this early stage, 1998–2001, the battle for universal treatment was still thought to be a long way off. The TAC was among those leading the fight in South Africa for women's access to the medications that would prevent mother-to-child transmission of the virus. In July 2000, Boehringer Ingelheim Pharmaceuticals agreed to provide nevirapine free to developing countries. Nevirapine administered to the mother ante-natally reduced the cases of mother-to-child transmission. TAC efforts focused heavily on the distribution of nevirapine to women in childbirth to prevent the transmission of AIDS from mother to child (Nattrass 2007; Petchesky 2003).

The battle for nevirapine evoked the question of saving the child and not treating the mother. Babies whose mothers received nevirapine might survive as orphans. There was always the contradiction, raised by women's health advocates at the time, in funding the free and one-time medication for the child but not the expensive life-long medications for the mother. This also led to the question of how such an orphan would survive without a mother to take care of him or her (Bassett 2001; Rosenfield 2002; Susser 2002). More recently, questions of the mothers' resistance to treatment following the administering of nevirapine in childbirth have also been raised but these were not particularly known or relevant at the time since few mothers had any access to treatment for themselves. Since universal treatment access was the keystone of the South African TAC, the fight for nevirapine might not be understood simply as the neglect of the mother for the child, but rather the implementation of an initial milestone in a long struggle for treatment for women and men.

We might also consider here the centrality of fertility and children to both women and men among many groups in South Africa. As previously noted, Fortes points out in his introduction to Ngubane's ethnography that, "most critical family tensions arise in relation to rights over the reproductive powers of women" (Fortes, in Ngubane 1977: x). In traditional settings, men wish for children to assure the survival of their lineage. In addition, in patrilineal societies while women may be subordinate in marriage, they wield much influence as mothers. Rearing children can be essential to a woman's social position. Under these conditions, the fight for nevirapine to be available at childbirth was answering the wishes of both women and men for the survival of the family. Feminists are rightfully wary of the neglect of women's needs incorporated in saving only the child. However, at least in South Africa at the time, one might perceive the effort to save the child through an easily administered and cost-free medication as in fact representing the fulfillment of wishes by both women and men for the continuity and status that children represent.

## South African Politics

In 1990, AIDS rhetoric was involved in the critique of the apartheid government and in 1992, as we have seen, Dr. Nkosazana Dlamini-Zuma had linked the rhetoric of fighting AIDS with the ANC constitution and the empowerment of women. However, Mandela almost never mentioned AIDS in his speeches (Nattrass 2007).

Meanwhile, the Ministry of Health, faced with a major disaster and low government priorities, was beset by a number of problems. First was the outcry over *Sarafina II!*. After receiving over 14 million rand in AIDS funding from the European Union, the Minister of Health committed money to support the development of this new play – apparently without the necessary EU authorization (Office of the Public Protector 1996). The play, which was to open on December 1, 1995 in recognition of International AIDS Day, was conceived by Dlamini-Zuma as a community education program that would travel around the country performing in rural and urban areas to alert people to the AIDS epidemic.

Although the play was attacked for financial irregularities (Schneider 2002; Feinstein 2007), according to Dlamini-Zuma the assault was also fueled by some groups who objected to the play's message to teenagers that, "if you cannot abstain, use a condom" (Dlamini-Zuma 1996). As mentioned earlier, the Ministry was also under attack for the purchase and distribution of female condoms. Such controversies might be interpreted as an assault on rights to sexual knowledge or women's autonomy. As we trace the loss of government support for AIDS prevention and treatment over the next decade, it would be well to remember that the early controversies with respect to AIDS policies revolved around the acceptance of condoms and sex education for teenagers and women's access to the female condom.

Another problem for the Ministry of Health concerned the promotion by Thabo Mbeki and the ANC government of the untested drug virodene, which was later found to contain industrial solvent (Epstein 2007; Nattrass 2007). This was sought and funded as a possible African solution to the AIDS epidemic. Thus, in these early crises we see the nascent issues of gender, sexuality, and nationalism emerging in contestations over the response to the epidemic.

To summarize briefly, in 1996, the ANC government adopted the stringent structural adjustment policies represented in GEAR. The administration appeared to be fully embracing the priorities of global capital to service international debt and theoretically kickstart economic growth before addressing the health and social needs of the society (Marais 2001). However, when in 1997, the South African government challenged the international pharmaceutical companies with respect to patented drugs this appeared as a heroic stand against Western capital. Thus, the administration developed an anti-West, anti-capitalist, and anti-colonial rhetoric around AIDS in the same few years in which decisions about the economy were molded to fit the global capitalist scene.[7] Dlamini-Zuma, although stymied and in some cases misguided in her attempts to effectively confront HIV/AIDS at the level of the state, took on the AIDS crisis as a battle with pharmaceutical companies and the new licensing restrictions of the World Trade Organization. The amendment to the Medicines Act, if actually implemented, was clearly pathbreaking and heroic on a global scale.

In 1999, President Mbeki took office. He appointed Manto Tshabalala-Msimang as Minister of Health and promoted Nkosazana Dlamini-Zuma to Secretary of Foreign Affairs where she was no longer involved with AIDS and its controversies. As noted earlier, in 1962, like Thabo Mbeki himself, Tshabalala-Msimang had escaped from South Africa to become one of the young ANC in exile, hopefully to be trained and available when the ANC came to power. She later joined the ANC in Tanzania. She is the wife of the former ANC Treasurer Mendi Msimang who helped revitalize the ANC with Mandela in the early 1950s (Sampson 1999). Before her appointment as Minister of Health, she was Minister of Justice.

In early 2000, Mbeki adopted the views of scientifically marginal scientists, often called AIDS denialists, and led by Berkeley researcher Peter Duesberg. Duesberg had for years claimed that the HIV virus was not the cause of AIDS. In an appropriation of revolutionary rhetoric, Mbeki portrayed these researchers as dissidents similar to the ANC revolutionaries who had fought apartheid in South Africa (Gevisser 2007; Nattrass 2007).[8]

In early 2000, Mbeki formed a President's Advisory Committee, which gave international status to the AIDS denialists (labeled dissidents by the Mbeki government). Representatives of the denialist point of view from all over the world were flown in first class and placed on a committee with several AIDS researchers. Zena Stein, as a long time advocate for health in South Africa, after much soul-searching felt obliged to accept the invitation from President Mbeki although she knew that many local scientists were refusing to participate. As Nattrass records, Stein was shocked and felt demeaned by the experience, which did not approximate any scientific examination of the evidence (Nattrass 2007). However, this Presidential Committee accorded the AIDS denialists an international platform such as they had never achieved before. Science and evidence were not the issue. Through the President's invitation, in South Africa, the denial of the AIDS virus was set on an equal footing with decades of the most sophisticated research findings about HIV (Nattrass 2007).

Mbeki asserted that there were African solutions to the disease (Epstein 2007; Fassin 2007; Specter 2007). One particularly destructive aspect of this new theory was the claim that available medications were toxic, possibly an intentional poisoning of the African population on the part of the Western medical establishment, and, therefore, should not be distributed in South Africa (Nattrass 2007:75). In spite of much well-informed counsel, both national and international, as South Africa has for decades been home to some of the best medical research in the world, Mbeki refused to reconsider his policies.

From 2000, Mbeki began to attribute AIDS to poverty (Mbeki 2000). Although the denial of the AIDS virus did not fit with medical knowledge or with an appropriate prevention and treatment of the disease, this argument fit the general rhetoric and approaches to governance Mbeki was developing. Clearly, poverty was a product of colonial history and the incursions of global capital and therefore AIDS could also be attributed to capitalism. Such rhetoric allowed the South African government to adopt drastic fiscal policies, reduce support for the health system, increase the gap between rich and poor, delay medical treatment for the hundreds of thousands of people with AIDS, and find Western capital the source of the problem (Butler 2005; Epstein 2007; Nattrass 2007; Oppenheimer and Bayer 2007). Here we can see how Dlamini-Zuma's court case against the drug companies could be integrated into anti-capitalist rhetoric without the ANC mentioning the viral transmission of AIDS or sexuality. Such denialism, which came to synthesize nationalism, pan-Africanism and patriarchy in its discourse, had divisive implications for gender as well as ethnicity.

In late 2001, President Mbeki gave an address at the University of Fort Hare, saying that people "who consider themselves to be our leaders take to the streets carrying their placards, to demand that because we are germ carriers, and human beings of a lower order that cannot subject its passions to reason, we must perforce adopt strange opinions, to save a depraved and diseased people from perishing from self-inflicted disease" (Mbeki 2001). With some historical justification (Mbeki 2001),[9] Mbeki claimed that AIDS had been blamed on African men and contributed to the representation of Africa as the source of disease and unrestrained promiscuity. However, rather than combat this stereotype with effective HIV policies, he chose to undercut the policies and simply use the negative representations as a reason to avoid addressing the problem of AIDS at all.

Deborah Posel suggested that the crisis of AIDS forced the government to confront the changing sexual mores of the new South Africa and precipitated a patriarchal backlash among leading members of parliament (Posel 2005). In some of the controversy around the condom message of *Sarafina II!* and in the condemnation of the supply of female condoms, we see the shadows of a "traditionalist" backlash. In the same few years, a national religious movement grew, advocating virginity (Leclerc-Madlala 2001). However, such fundamental moralism also matched well with the nationalist fundamentalism of the previous apartheid state (Marais 2001).[10] Adapting to such pressures might have enouraged President Mbeki and other members of the administration to claim a "nationalist" or "traditionalist" and patriarchal perspective in relation to the AIDS epidemic (Fassin and Schneider 2003). In addition, such an approach also served as a way to stave off demands for preventive measures and treatment (Butler 2005).

## AIDS Policies Contested

From 2000, government denialism over the connection between HIV and AIDS dominated public discourse. Health activists had suddenly become oppositional intellectuals and public health messages no longer carried consensus value. Building on the mobilization from the 1998 Geneva International AIDS Society Conference, and carried forward in the face of Mbeki's AIDS denial, the Durban International AIDS Society Conference in 2000, "Breaking the Silence," became the next scene for oppositional discourse. In a high-profile street demonstration before the opening ceremony, culminating in a speech by Winnie Mandela, herself an extremely controversial figure (though here standing for the survival of African women), the South African Treatment Action Campaign, involving hundreds of young men and

**Figure 4.1** Global and South African AIDS activists parade towards the opening of the International AIDS Society Conference, Durban 2000 (Gideon Mendel, Positive Lives, www. artthrob.co.za/02mar/images/mendel01a.jpg)

women, connected with New York ACT UP, Philadelphia ACT UP, and Health GAP to demand access to treatment.

In contrast, in his speech at the opening ceremony in Durban, maintaining his position of AIDS denial in this international drama, Mbeki continued to stress the primacy of poverty and its relationship with AIDS (Mbeki 2000; Sidley et al. 2000). He never specifically mentioned a virus, sexual transmission, or the prevention or treatment of HIV/AIDS. Instead he called for an end to poverty as the solution to the epidemic, borrowing a form of political economic determinism usually deployed by progressive groups.

In direct contradiction of Mbeki's statements, the Medical Research Council had prepared a report that showed incontrovertibly the tragic patterns of AIDS mortality in South Africa. The statistics demonstrated the rising mortality rates, particularly among young women and men, that could only be attributed to the disease (Bradshaw et al. 2003; Bradshaw and Dorrington 2005). As Mbeki gave his speech at the opening ceremony, statistics highlighting the AIDS epidemic were published across the front pages of Durban newspapers.

The plenary sessions of the Durban Conference opened with an impassioned speech by the white South African judge, Edwin Cameron, who announced that he himself was HIV positive and that he was taking medications that cost $400 per month. He called for access to treatments for poor populations.[11] Equating the fight for AIDS with the fight for liberation, Cameron contrasted the treatments he could afford with the lack of treatment available to the majority of South Africans (Cameron 2000). Many TAC members, like many members of Mbeki's cabinet, were, in fact, entitled to expensive treatments through well-funded insurance policies. This theme was reiterated at the 2002 Barcelona International AIDS Society Conference when Zackie Achmat (a founder of the South African TAC) refused to accept this class privilege and take medications for AIDS. He demonstrated that he would rather die from AIDS than live while the South African government denied the rest of the population their right to health.⌉


## International Activism and South African Activists Converge


The 2000 International AIDS Society Conference in Durban, the first in a country of the global South, was also the first to merge scientific research and activism concerned with women's issues. As stated in Chapter 1, outside the conference, for the first time, women's international and local organizations (reflecting both US, European, and South African feminists) organized continuous community speak-outs about women and HIV and the plenary speeches were broadcast to community settings.[12] This collaboration was able to bring together grassroots women, research-ers, policy makers, scientists, sociologists, and activists for the first time at a free and independent parallel conference on, by, and for women. This group of women worked across national borders so that local women could benefit from, and have an impact on, the Conference. They made sure that women's voices, especially community women's voices, were heard within the Conference. Grassroots organi-zations among the poor gained access to the public debate and the issue of access to treatment became a vision, or an imaginary, of the poor populations of southern Africa, and even other poor regions of the world. This community impetus was a powerful reflection of the still-vital hopes for a vibrant although much-contested new democratic state in South Africa.

Publicly contradicting Mbeki's position for the first time, Nelson Mandela closed the Conference with a speech broadcast across the world. He called for action to address the crisis of HIV/AIDS in southern Africa. What was not broadcast was the remarkable drama in front of an audience of fifteen thousand people, when a doctor jumped up in front of Mandela and spontaneously burst into a praise song in Xhosa celebrating his courageous speech.

Within months after the Durban 2000 meetings, with the support of the United Nations and other international organizations, pharmaceutical companies began to make deals for cheaper treatments in poorer countries. It should be noted here, from the point of view of women, that both at the Durban Conference and in the later international agreements, the issues of prevention with respect to the subordination of women and such simple technology as the woman's condom dis-appeared from the public agenda. The money was being collected to pay for phar-maceuticals and to treat people once they were infected, as if little was possible beforehand.

Just one year later, on April 19, 2001, after extensive campaigning worldwide and a campaign by the TAC to support the South African government's position, the 39 pharmaceutical companies who had sought to sue the South African govern-ment over TRIPS were defeated (Craddock 2005). However, by this time, the TAC support for the treatment battle was much stronger than the South African government. In the very courtroom within minutes after the successful decision, Manto Tshabalala-Msimang announced that winning the case did not mean the South African government would now make any drugs available to the population. In recognition of the global significance of the case, both the TRIPS decision and Tshabalala-Msimang's statement were broadcast live, locally and internationally.

The TAC, which, in line with its excellent professional connections, had extensive access to the South African media as well as legal recourse, proceeded to bring a case against the Mbeki government to make nevirapine available to pregnant mothers to prevent the transmission of HIV to their newborn infants. But, even after TAC won the case in December 2001, the government still refused to supply nevirapine. Indeed a full year after the TRIPS case had been won, nevirapine was still not available to pregnant women in South Africa. After a series of further appeals, on April 4, 2002, the Constitutional Court of South Africa ruled that "the government make nevirapine available in public health facilities," pending a further appeal by the government to be heard on May 2 (Barnard 2002; Nattrass 2007).

In May 2002, after 60,000 leaflets were distributed arguing the case of the dissidents, a major party meeting was held. The ANC finally reversed itself. In a resounding victory for the TAC, the unions, and the social movements for AIDS treatment in general, the government published advertisements in six major South African newspapers saying that AIDS was spread by a virus and that nevirapine was not toxic and would be made available to pregnant women. However, government decisions have wavered back and forth on every one of these issues since then (Nattrass 2007).

[Meanwhile, Health Minister Manto Tshabalala-Msimang began to advocate garlic, beetroot, and African potatoes as a nutritional approach to treating HIV/AIDS (Nattrass 2007). Thus, the arguments about poverty causing AIDS were joined with discussions of nutrition. Diet was claimed to be both the cause and the cure of the epidemic. Anti-retroviral drugs were portrayed as toxic and seen as the reason people were dying.]

[Highlighting the deep-rooted power and gender implications of this controversy, a widely renowned woman journalist, Charlene Smith, once a member of the ANC underground, was publicly derided by Mbeki as a White racist with no respect for Black men when she talked about her own experience of rape and the issues of violence against women in South Africa (Smith 2001). When she contradicted the prescription of garlic as a treatment for HIV/AIDS, she was again attacked by Mbeki, an incident that was widely quoted in the international press (LaFraniere 2004). Since her rape in 2000, Charlene Smith has fought unstintingly to make PEP (Post-Exposure Prophylaxis) available to women immediately after rape. PEP is a form of AZT that is thought to prevent infection by the HI virus if taken within 12 hours and is part of a package that people working with sexual violence all over the world have been trying to implement (TAC 2006a). Smith has frequently been accused by Mbeki of racism in relation to her efforts to protect women from the effects of sexual violence through advocacy of "Western" medications.]

In the course of the legal battles, the struggle over the universal accessibility to nevirapine and treatment involved the unions and provincial governments as well as the Pan African Congress (a small opposition party founded in 1959) in the fight for AIDS resources. After 2001, the Congress of South African Trade Unions (COSATU) supported access to nevirapine and when the government claimed nevirapine was possibly toxic and needed further testing, COSATU directly contradicted this position (Mothapo 2003). In KwaZulu, which has some of the highest rates of AIDS in South Africa (Welz et al. 2007), the provincial government supported the provision of antenatal nevirapine. The Pan African Congress also set up clinics, which provided nevirapine and anti-retrovirals treatment for mothers. The two South African heroes, Nobel Prize winners, and world icons Nelson Mandela and Bishop Desmond Tutu both publicly called for access to treatment.

As a result of a protracted three-year struggle, conducted by lawyers, doctors, unions, non-governmental organizations, grassroots women's movements, and opposition parties, nevirapine became available in pilot sites of the public health service where the medical providers had approved its use. As part of the struggle for treatment, in 2001, Médecins Sans Frontières was invited by the TAC to demonstrate that AIDS treatment could work in low-resource settings. In partnership with the Western Cape Provincial Department of Health, they set up a clinic in Khayelitsha, a poor district on the outskirts of Cape Town. Also, through the efforts of activist health professionals, a few mission hospitals and designated clinics were providing treatment funded by the Bill and Melinda Gates Foundation, the Global Fund to fight AIDS, Tuberculosis, and Malaria, and other major foundations. Funded by such outside organizations, where possible, South African health providers and researchers, together with health professionals from Columbia University, Harvard University, and other international institutions, worked in many settings to provide treatment and care for AIDS. As a consequence of the unrelenting mobilization for treatment, both in South Africa and internationally, in late 2003, the South African government agreed to start providing AIDS treatment through public clinics.

But, counteracting such efforts to promote treatment, in a similar attempt to frame discourse and give status to denialist ideas as we saw with the President's Advisory Committee, President Mbeki created a Presidential Council on Traditional Medicine. Herbert Vilakazi, a US-trained sociologist who has claimed that anti-retroviral treatment is a poison sent by the West to kill Africans (Specter 2007) was appointed as Chairman (Nattrass 2007). Here again, we see the emphasis on the "traditional" in the bolstering of Mbeki's political base.

At the 2006 Toronto International AIDS Society Conference, the South African Minister of Health highlighted garlic, lemons, and olive oil at the Conference booth. Mark Heywood and Stephen Lewis both decried the misleading emphasis on nutrition and the inadequate roll-out of treatment in South Africa (Heywood 2006; Lewis 2006).

In 2001, the female condom was still not available in public health sites in South Africa in spite of the struggle that began ten years before. By 2003 the female condom was being distributed from a few designated government clinics in South Africa but it was not until 2007 that major funders began to support its distribution (McNeil 2007).

## South Africa in Global Context

In the global economic and political arena, South Africa was striving to become a global state and, as such, directed state power toward capturing global investment and addressing the wishes of global financial institutions and corporate investors. Political officials oriented their policies to the demands of global interests in the privatization of public resources and utilities, and in the encouragement of international corporate investment. A global state is not one "run" by global interests; it is a state whose power structure envisions its economic future in connection to the global (Castells 1996). The priorities of its own middle-class and poor population are not set first on the agenda.

New York City, hailed as one of the first global cities, was also an early site for the implementation of drastic structural adjustment policies. Following the fiscal crisis of 1975, business representatives transformed the social and economic climate of the city. They created what was initially called a "Dual City" because of the clearly documented increasing gap between rich and poor. Later this was recognized as a prototype global city. New York City's recovery represented the glamour of global investment, combined with the stripping of historic social services to the extent that the showcase of the global world became also the center for a new poverty and homelessness not experienced in the First World since the Great Depression (Castells 1996; Martin 1996; Mollenkompf and Castells 1991; Sassen 1990; Schneider and Susser 2003).

Clearly there can be degrees of globalism and the struggles in contemporary democracies may foster or attempt to block global allegiances. The policies of the new South Africa demonstrably reflect these struggles (Desai 2002; Muller et al. 2001; Saul 2005).

South Africa is a middle-income, industrialized state at the tip of a poor, under-industrialized continent. As such it is the magnet for migrant labor from all over southern Africa and the source of investment funds for many sub-Saharan countries. With apartheid legislation abolished and an exemplary constitution instituted, the new South African ANC government has established a small African elite alongside the more established white wealth. The government has had much less success in reducing the enormous gaps between rich and poor that they inherited from the apartheid regime. In fact, many argue that the majority of poor Africans, urban and rural, may be comparatively poorer than they were a decade ago (South African Institute of Race Relations and Cronje 2007). For this reason, in 2006, COSATU, the powerful African trade unions organization that had formed the backbone of the United Democratic Front and, with the South African Communist Porty, were part of the tripartite coalition of the ANC, threatened to withdraw support from the government (Mbeki 2008). Since 2004, a number of riots have been occurring in the poor urban areas protesting the decline of services. Eventually, in 2007, delegates to the African National Congress Party Conference elected Jacob Zuma, seen by his supporters on the left as more open to the needs of the working class and the poor, as leader of the party.

The current global state in South Africa has to contend with increasing inequalities while the government negotiates for investments within the global arena. In South Africa's bid for global status, Mbeki became an active member and indeed leader of the poorer nations in bargaining with the World Trade Organization over agricultural subsidies and even intellectual property regulation. Mandela, Mbeki, and other South African representatives have been constant participants at Davos, the World Economic Forum where global corporate leaders meet on panels with the world's most powerful politicians.

As South Africa strode confidently into the world arena, the ANC government implemented structural adjustment programs, lowering investment in the public sector in order to service the national debt. This increasing global orientation and local inequality has been accompanied by a continuing ideological misrepresentation of the AIDS pandemic on the part of the South African government. These are not unrelated phenomena. Mbeki's AIDS denialism draws distortedly on a long history of leftist critique of the US and Western medicine. The government initially rejected millions of dollars for treatment,[13] while simultaneously accepting millions in business investment. Resting precariously on an explosive situation of income inequality and overwhelming death, the South African government deployed the critique of imperialism and Western capitalism to justify its creation of a global state. As the AIDS crisis inevitably worsened and thousands of people were dying daily, Mbeki drew on "traditional" images of patriarchy and masculinity. In its effort to garner support from older tribal elites as well as the historically patriarchal far right, such an ideology divided the South African population by gender rather than confronting the realities of inequality and death.

Divisions by ethnicity and race have also been exacerbated in the government denial of the AIDS epidemic. The transmission of AIDS in South Africa, as in the United States, breaks down quite obviously, by race, class, and gender, as white gay men constitute one group and African men and women, the large majority of whom are poor, represent a different and far larger constituency. While the virus has certainly spread to a lesser extent among the Indian and other populations, the invisibility of this problem has contributed to a lack of recognition and preventive strategies among these groups. In a further complication of ethnicity and class, the public health and medical professionals who have fought for AIDS treatment come from the predominantly white and Indian middle class. This has, sadly, contributed to the ability of the current South African government to dismiss the concern with AIDS as a Western issue by dividing and stereotyping the professional population, many of whom were life-long fighters for the ANC.[14]

## Conclusions

Under these conditions of chronic hostility, Mbeki's reliance on African Renaissance rhetoric and the African remedies along with, as we shall see later, Jacob Zuma's defense of the African man can be understood as a gendered nationalist response to a devastating crisis.

The very fact that the South African government aims to be, if it is not already, a major player on the global scene may have helped to slow down the grassroots and international efforts to address the treatment and prevention of HIV/AIDS. John Saul has argued:

> A tragedy is being enacted in South Africa. [Here], in the teeth of high expectations arising from the successful struggle against a malignant apartheid state, a very large percentage of the population – amongst them many of the most desperately poor in the world – are being sacrificed on the altar of the neoliberal logic of global capitalism" (Saul 2001).

Saul was not speaking specifically of HIV, but this is one way to interpret the AIDS policy from 1999 to 2007. In South Africa, people were literally dying in the face of the restructuring of the neoliberal economy. AIDS activism in the light of crisis was one vital movement that helped to shift the balance towards an imperfect democracy. In fact, since much of South Africa's international debt has been reduced, the government has increased redistribution and funding for infrastructure and services. For example, assistance grants have been extended to children under 12. Since 2007, the National Strategic Plan, a new effort to roll out highly active anti-retroviral treatment (HAART), has also been underway.

However, from the initial decision for the adoption of GEAR, a major bid for acceptance by global capital was coupled with a critique of Western capitalism. From 2000, building on this initial approach, three interrelated governing strategies have emerged: first, denial of the viral cause of the disease accompanied by a lack of figures or diagnosis; second, an emphasis on "traditionalism" or "nationalism" – garlic, *African* potatoes – and an effort to bring together traditional healers; and, third, a support of traditional patriarchal practices, including the upholding of patriarchal and chiefly rights to land and inheritance.

On the face of it, these particular strategies are different than the descriptions of US neoconservatism and the governmental strategies associated with it, as described in the previous chapter. Nevertheless, the South African regime under Mbeki mirrored the neoconservative shift towards anti-scientism and patriarchal regulation generated in the United States over the past decade. Perhaps because of the divergent colonial histories and the government's lesser investment in technology, neoliberalism in South Africa does not seem to involve the same level of invasion of personal privacy or imposed domestic constraints that have been documented in the United States (Mitchell 2003; Peck and Tickell 2002; Roberts 2002).

However, in terms of poverty and AIDS, it seems to involve some of the suppression of scientific and empirical evidence associated with more authoritarian regimes.

The intimate relationship of South Africa to the globalizing world is indicated by the efforts on the part of former President Clinton and others to remind Mbeki of the scientific basis of HIV (*News Hour with Jim Lehrer* 2000). This represented an attempt to mediate between the great pressure on the global elite of South Africa to cut back expenditures on health care and the effort to maintain what some have designated "low-intensity democracies" as the safest, most stable form of state for international capital investments (Mamdani 2004).

Under the Bush administration, no presidential advice to accept scientific evidence has been forthcoming. Instead, Mbeki's denialism has been complemented by the neoconservative religious strictures that have now limited education with respect to sexual and reproductive health worldwide. In fact, as we have seen, the Bush administration has funded abstinence-only programs which also deny well-known scientific findings, teaching that the AIDS virus can be spread by kissing and that condoms are not effective barriers to disease.

In tracing the public discourse and contestation around the nature of AIDS from 1992 to 2006 in South Africa, I have attempted to set the stage for understanding the conversations about AIDS, sexuality, treatment, and prevention among poor African women from the informal settlements around Durban and its rural hinterland. The next two chapters describe African women's participation in bead working and support groups centered around AIDS clinics, mostly between 2001 and 2003. They illuminate some of the ways in which Tshabalala-Msimang's emphasis on nutrition and Mbeki's denialism on the one hand and the TAC's vision for treatment on the other bear upon women struggling with the disease and its consequences in their everyday lives. I have reprinted here, in the following chapter, Sibongile Mkhize's story of her efforts to find treatment for her sister and the way in which AIDS penetrated and wounded all members of her family, both affected and infected. It expresses these tensions on the scale of individual lives.

# 5

# The Difference in Pain: Infected and Affected

*I am affected by HIV/AIDS. I know that I feel more pain compared to the one who is infected or suffering from the epidemic. Am I wrong for being sensitive?*

## Sibongile Mkhize

It is very important to explore exactly the level or the degree of pain for those infected versus those affected by the epidemic. Being infected by HIV is when you find out that the virus is in your blood system. The pain you experience is when you think of your future knowing that in the meantime there is no cure for AIDS. Death will be the end result if the virus is not controlled in your system.

People who are infected can live healthy lives for many years as long as they eat healthy food, take their treatment, and practice safe sex. Under such control the virus does not develop into full-blown AIDS. There are many people who die from other illnesses not associated with AIDS, leaving the infected people behind living a healthy life. I know people who have been living with the virus for more than ten years who are healthy and who are still continuing to live healthy lives.

There are many projects taking place in the fight against HIV/AIDS. There are research undertakings done by social scientists to come up with recommendations about how people can live their lives and also about how the state can intervene. Medical institutes are conducting research to find the cure.

There are counseling sessions, which are made available to those people who discover that they are HIV positive and they are being educated about how they can live positively but healthy. The media is broadcasting information on the epidemic as well. This could be through drama, educative pamphlets, and fliers.

Presently one can proudly say that through medical research, the lives of the unborn children can be saved. A child has a chance of being HIV negative at birth even though her mother is HIV positive. That is because expectant HIV-positive mothers can take anti-retrovirals (ARVs) during their pregnancy, which is known to be the best cure in preventing mother-to-child transmission.

People who are HIV positive can undergo treatment that will help them not to progress to an AIDS stage. Recently, health centers are rolling out powerful anti-retroviral drugs to treat the fully blown AIDS patients. So, this means that there are several alternatives for keeping people healthy and preventing further deaths from the epidemic.

Infected people have a lot at their disposal to fight the virus and the epidemic at large. For them knowing that they are infected is good because they can take measures in ensuring that their condition does not reach an AIDS stage. I cannot dispute the fact that with some people, when they get their positive results they get devastated and do awful things like committing suicide. However, with awareness campaigns put in place, there are few HIV suicide cases.

Given the above discussion, I believe that the person who is infected is better off because they have the knowledge that they are infected and things have been made easier for them to do something about it. There are many people who live with the virus but who are not sick and, as mentioned earlier, have lived with it for a long time. They know that they have the virus and they know that they will die at some stage. They know that they can prevent that from happening soon by seeking advice and treatment and doing as they are told.

I believe that the pain felt by the infected is possibly easier to bear than the pain felt by people who are affected by HIV/AIDS. It is very painful to hear that your loved one is infected by the virus, which will later progress to a deadly disease that is incurable. You struggle inside and feel more pain when trying to understand what they feel or think about their future.

To understand the case of being affected, may I draw your attention to the times when people suffer from AIDS whilst relatives do not know what to do to help them; when relatives try anything at their disposal but find out that the immune system of the person is too weak to respond to treatment. Given the background of HIV/AIDS, others may suffer from it but not tell the cause of their illness and maybe refuse to go for testing and blame their illness on other things. It is in this context that I would like to show you the severity of the pain of the affected person.

It is painful to see your loved one suffering, in case the virus complicates to AIDS. It is painful to see them fighting helplessly for their lives. I use "helplessly" in the context where a person is sick and they have no access to medical treatment and people who are taking care of him are not well informed of the resources that they can draw on for help to save his life. This is the experience of people living in rural areas where they have to travel long distances to the health centers. And, when they reach those medical centers, they find that there are inadequate resources: for example, being short staffed; no medication or specific drugs; ill-treatment because of stigma; and many more.

Personally, I am really feeling the pain because I am affected. I have more than ten relatives who died of the epidemic. At that time it was difficult for me to help save their lives because I was not well informed about the epidemic. I tried all I could but nothing seemed to work for my relatives. They eventually died, one by one. Seeing them suffering from one opportunistic illness to the next and sometimes suffering from a number of them at the same time broke my heart. The opportunistic infections could be cured but at that time there was this problem of stigma, so they preferred to be secretive about their illnesses with a hope that they will get better while unfortunately they got worse. They were hiding their illness just because they were told that they have the virus so they were afraid to seek medical attention. The reason for their lack of interest is that at that time the stigma was a stumbling block and also there were reports about medical staff being harsh to people.

Again, the way HIV/AIDS was introduced to people was really disheartening because it was mostly portrayed as a disease caused by sexual intercourse. So, amongst Africans, sex is respected and if it is done outside wedlock it is not acceptable. Not to mention when it gives you diseases, then it is a humiliation. So if a woman finds out that she has a disease that is known to be sexually transmitted, she will opt to keep it a secret because if it can be known then fingers will be pointed and she will be made to feel bad about her actions.

On her last days, my sister did not feel the pain. When I asked her where exactly the pain is she said there is no pain. She ended up failing to talk. I could see in her eyes that she wants to say something but words could not come out. Her eyes changed colour and the iris became blurred. I noticed that she could not see me anymore. She was gasping day and night. I would feed her by pouring the porridge down her open mouth but she would not respond by licking her lips or swallowing. The food just went down her throat. I felt the pain of not knowing exactly where I can touch to make her feel better and bring her back to her real self again. It was painful for me to see my sister fading or deteriorating in front of my eyes. She felt no pain, but on the other hand I felt more pain when seeing her going through that phase. I tried everything and all the medication but she slipped through my fingers.

I loved her so much, especially for the courage she had. She disclosed her status to me and we kept it as a secret from our parents for four months. I would buy this and that from Durban that people said would help an infected person. I would go home every weekend to administer the medication. At that time, she was still strong. She told me: "You know *Sisi*, I will not die. I want to work for my children and see them growing." I had to help her to see her dream coming true. I remember there was a time when she got very ill, skinny, and extremely weak. That is when the truth came out to our parents that their daughter was HIV positive and she reached a full-blown AIDS stage. Fortunately, with the support of the family, we all joined forces to help her fight the disease. We tried this and that until she regained her strength. I believe that her will to survive, the love and support we gave her together with the medication helped her to be back on her feet again. She went back to work and generated income for her children and parents. It was known in our township that she had HIV and she was open to people about it because she said she wanted to help others deal with it.

I remember one day we were in a taxi, she said, "*Sisi* I am paying this taxi fare but someone I am with in this taxi is getting a free ride. That is HIV in my system as it is going everywhere with me but it does not pay. I am the only one paying." That was a joke and people were amazed to hear her talking like that about the disease that is "dirty" and feared by all. She said to one old lady who was shocked to see her on her feet after the long illness she had been through, "*Mama*, the reason

I survived my long illness is because I looked down the grave and saw how deep and dark it was. I got such a fright and told myself that I am not going there. I will use the last strength I had to pull away from the grave." I was so impressed, but the way she was saying it was in a joke form, as she was a sweet lady, always smiling.

In 2001, there was a problem of stigma. At the same time, the anti-retrovirals were not available by my home and I knew nothing about them. She had reached a full-blown AIDS stage when one nurse prescribed Bactrim for her. I gave those to her, including the vitamin tablets, but I think it was too late. I tried everything at my disposal but she eventually died. I felt guilty for failing her.

The burning pain I felt was like a burning arrow shot through my heart. With all my relatives, my heart went into pieces when they reached the stage of dying in front of me and me not knowing what to do. What am I going to tell their children? I had to be strong. I remember having to sit and untangle the braids that my sister had plaited on her hair. I had to do that to her while there was no life in her body. I was all alone, but strong and not scared of her. The undertakers came to fetch her lifeless body away.

My sister's son was watching because he was ten years old at that time. He saw exactly what happened. He was in his grandfather's car watching the whole process. When the undertakers left, he cried alone in the car. I saw that and went straight to him. I did not know the words I was going to use to make him feel better because I was in pain myself. However, God is wonderful. I could not believe myself when I said to him, "My son, you have me now to be your mother because your mother is gone. I am happy to have you as my son. It is painful to me to see you crying like this. Your mother was very ill for a long time. You saw that we tried everything at our disposal to help her. If doctors and other forms of medication do not help a person, it is important that a sick person die. This is the last alternative to free her from pain. As much as it is the hard one but it is for the best if anything else does not work. Did you want your mother to live the painful life as she did?" He said "No." "That is the way she had to rest from all the pains, okay. Please understand this and know that God has done this on purpose. He will be with you all the way. He knows exactly how you are going to grow up without her. I will be there for you; grandpa and your uncles as well." He looked at me and wiped his tears. I then begged him to eat his food because he had not eaten for two days. To my surprise, after that long talk and hugs, I saw him eating the food he prepared himself. Later he went to play with his friends.

Well, problem one solved. Another problem was how to tell the three-year-old of her mother's death. How am I going to tell my own two-year-old son as well? He wanted my attention and he needed to suckle my breast but I could not let him. I am the one who was preparing the corpse, so it is believed that the spirit of the dead may harm the suckling baby in a certain way, so I wanted to save him. I called my husband and told him the news and asked him to come and fetch my baby so that I can prepare for the funeral at ease.

The final blow was not knowing where we were supposed to get the money to prepare for the funeral because my father had only 50 rand in his savings account.

My sister was 30 years old when she passed away. She was already not covered by my father's funeral policy. This meant that we had to pay all the costs. I was not working since we had been spewed out of our teaching jobs due to the program they had of reconstruction and redeployment. Funerals are so expensive. No one will be prepared to help you with money unless you borrow it and will return it with interest. My brother had a low-paying job at the restaurant and he was always penniless. My youngest brother was still studying at the university. Knowing that we had no money I felt more pain. My father and I tried all we could to prepare for the funeral. Finally she was buried peacefully a week later.

The reality that I had to face after the funeral was that I had to take care of the children that she had left behind. It was painful for me to know that I have to leave the children and go to Durban to look for a job. I could not find a job and I had difficulties dealing with the loss. I decided to register at the university and do a master's degree. I knew that it was going to be demanding and require me to be fully committed to my studies. However, I did not mind the challenge, because that was exactly what I wanted to help me take my attention from thinking about the pain of losing my sister. She was feeling no pain, resting peacefully in the land of the dead. I was left behind feeling the pain that no painkiller could cure. It was worth it to do my master's because it took my pain away. I was so proud on graduation day to hear my name announced on the list of those who made it. I owe this success to my late sister.

My sister's children lived with my parents. Later on her son remained with the grandparents and we sent the little girl to live with her father. I believed it would be good for her to bond with him. They were happy to have her back. However, my mother was not happy with the idea and she tried everything she could to deprive the father of his paternal rights. We tried showing her the importance of this decision because her father wanted her badly and he is working at the hospital and he promised to take good care of her. The trauma I went through seeing that the little girl wanted to live with her father but my mother preventing her made me feel a lot of pain. Finally, her father with the help of her grandmother, succeeded in keeping the little girl.

My mother is abusive by nature and self-centered. She and my father live with my late sister's son who is schooling at a multiracial school. The pain I feel is about not being there for him all the time. My mother would not punish him as kids used to be punished. She would bang his head on the wall. Sometimes she hit him using anything that she could find, including wires, hosepipe, big sticks, and many more. It was painful to me. I would make sure that he came to Durban to visit me, spending holidays away from my mother.

One day, the little boy overslept and was late to go to school. Seeing this, my mother took a rope, which was used to tie the goats, and she used it to strangle him while banging his forehead on the floor. The boy was helpless and could not cry for people to come to his rescue. Fortunately someone heard the noise of the banging and tried pushing the door. She called people who helped in setting the boy free. He called me, crying, and related the whole story. My abusive mother! It was so painful to me to realize that the boy trusted me with his life but I was too far away to come to his rescue. I advised him to go and open a court case. He did. He was later removed from home by the magistrate and placed at another house far away from my mother. This was very traumatic for my father and deepened the pain to me.

The legal case concerning my nephew was not a child abuse case but an attempted murder case, which was putting my mother in a very difficult position. She went on trial on several occasions, for about two-and-a-half months to be specific. To my horror, the case was dismissed because the investigating officer did not bring the witnesses to the trial in time. That was even more painful for me. If my mother was set free, then the little boy would be removed permanently from home because of fear that he would be a victim of abuse again. My father did not know what to do. We were all crying. I felt more and more pain. My sister is resting in peace and feels no more pain but I continued feeling more pain on top of the other pain.

My brother's case was different from the one discussed above. The whole family had a gathering and he was also there. We were all happy and he came to our bedroom, saying that he will not sleep. He will watch us so as to protect us from anything that might come our way in our sleep. We cracked jokes and then he left. After the gathering, we all left our parents' home and went to Durban where we worked. Two weeks after that gathering, he called to say that he had to see the doctor because his body was so stiff and he could not move. He said it was aching too. He promised that he would take the medication and that he would be fine.

I called my younger brother and asked him to check his brother often. He promised to do so. He would report to me that he is okay. One day my late brother called me saying that he was hungry he needed food. I hired a car and went straight to check him because this request to me sounded so strange. When he came out of the room he was renting I was very shocked with the sight. He was so skinny and his lips were red. He was gasping. His nose was dripping and he could hardly walk. I nearly fainted. I tried to be strong and asked him to sit next to me and tell me what he wants. We then drove to buy food. I then took him to the doctor who told me that his chest is not good; he may have bronchitis. We took the medication and I helped him with it and the food. I asked him if he had HIV. He said no; that is the last thing he might get in his life because he uses a condom.

We went back to his room. After I had tucked him warmly in his blankets, I left. I remember it was Wednesday. On Thursday I went to see him early in the morning. He was alive but he was really sick. He was shivering and he said his feet were sore. As time went on, he was saying things which were not making sense. He ended up confusing the people he was seeing in the house. I asked my younger brother to drive us home. It was after six in the evening. He was sitting quietly on the back seat. When we were about an hour away from home, he had fits (epilepsy), which he never had before. We were so shocked. When stopping the car, we realized that it was too much. This is because he could not see us. We called the ambulance and he was hurried to hospital. He was admitted on the same Thursday night.

I came to spend the weekend with him and he was just fine, talking and laughing, saying how grateful he was that he was alive. We left on Sunday. On Monday we were called with the news that he was getting confused. I had to come back on Monday. He was really confused but surprisingly when I entered the ward he recognized me and greeted me. I fed him banana and juice. He ate very well but the element of confusion was still there. Next day he was fine and was transferred to the ward of stabilized patients. I left for Durban. On Thursday we spoke on the phone and he told me how much he loved me and that he wanted to go home because he was feeling much better. I asked him to be patient, hoping that before the end of the week he would be out. On Friday, after 2 p.m., I called my father who broke the news that my brother died at about 11 a.m. I was so confused and angry. I felt the deepest pain, as if some part of me inside has been ripped out. I went to his ward and they told me that he went to have a bath nicely and came back. They said he was so jolly that morning. They said he got off the bed and took few steps and fell on the back of his head. He did not get up. When nurses came to him, he was cold; dead. I felt the pain so much that as from the day of his death it is still difficult for me to accept. I remember that I could not turn off the light in my room for more than three months because I was hoping that he would come back and tell me what happened and what really the cause of his death was. This is because the doctors wrote in his death notice that he died of natural causes, which was strange.

My father tore my heart when he said, "my son is dead and that is painful to me but more pain is exerted by the thought of having no money to bury my son." Fortunately, I was working and his death happened a few days after my pay day. I assured him that everything would be fine, so, with the help of my husband and my little brother, everything was well prepared. The saddest part was when my father sobbed, saying: "I had nine children but now I only have two left. I buried all those children. Who will bury me when I die?" Seeing the pain he was going through I had to stay strong for him. I wanted to close the gap left by my six siblings in his heart. It was painful to me to know that I do not have the power to do that.

My brother left behind his five-year-old daughter. On the funeral day, she was confused and crying. She did not even want to come inside our home. She did not want us to touch her or to go and pay "ashes to ashes" respect to her late father. It was so painful to think of her future without him. She was his adorable angel.

## HIV/AIDS Treatment Availability and Accessibility

This then draws this discussion to an issue about HIV/AIDS treatment in South Africa. The first time I heard about this epidemic was 1983 when my cousin's girlfriend passed away of the virus. My cousin himself eventually died in the late 1990s. At that time there was a problem of ignorance, stigma, and the fact that drugs were not available. People would blame their illnesses on being bewitched because of ignorance or denial.

Others would go to the clinics and hospitals but find no help because the drugs were not available at that time. There were treatments available for the opportunistic infections. However, people were not accessing them because they preferred staying at home and hoping that the infection would eventually go away. Others would go to the clinics but would be treated badly by the nursing staff and then decided not to set their feet there anymore.

I remember that eventually, people had access to the drug called Bactrim, which was known to be helpful. With the growing demand, nursing staff were so selective when giving them out. So people ended up depending on different kinds of medications, including traditional medicines.

Currently, drugs are available in South Africa for HIV/AIDS. There are health centers where they are paid for. Only some people can afford to go to those centers for treatment and care. This leaves out those people who are poor. This is very bad because they are the people who have to be targeted given that it is known that AIDS is prevalent amongst the poor people.

Fortunately, there are also health centers that are funded to provide the drugs free of charge to their patients. However, since the waiting list is very long, there are many patients who die before their turn comes to access free drugs. Others die while they are still undergoing adherence training because they cannot be put on drugs before the end of the training.

The health centers that have free drugs are mostly in towns and far away from the poor needy people. This discourages them and they end up not reaching them because of financial constraints. More often these centers set the rules, including that they will only offer service to people who are on certain location boundaries, thus leaving lots of people out. People who become excluded are mostly those in rural areas and the illiterate. One can argue that, yes, treatment is available, but it is not yet accessible to all and this problem needs to be addressed urgently.

## My Siblings' Experience with the Epidemic

We were nine children at home, five boys and four girls. Two brothers and a sister were stillborn because my mother was diabetic. Another baby boy died in the mid-1970s when he was a few months old. Our eldest brother was shot dead. So, two sisters and two brothers grew up together knowing that we were only four children in the household. We girls were older than our brothers. We girls were so close to each other. I loved my sister so much – in such a way that I never had a friend in my life just because there was no space for one since my sister and I were always together. We even ended up in the same class at school.

She went to Johannesburg to work at a restaurant. She came back home eight months pregnant with a second baby. She gave birth in Johannesburg. When we met again to see her little one, I noticed that she was so slim, which is so unusual with a recently delivered mother. I asked her about her condition and she said that things are tough at work. After a few months she came back and I noticed that she had grown even thinner. She told me again that life in Johannesburg is tough. I advised her to get a transfer so that she would work closer to me in Durban. So, she did, but again she never gained weight.

After four months of patiently trying to get through to her, she finally disclosed that she was HIV positive. She told me that she found out about her status when she was pregnant. Strangely enough although in those times all those who were positive were taken for a caesarean section delivery, she had a natural birth. We had to keep this a secret because my parents were very strict. My mother was thinking that HIV was other households' problem and would never be a problem for our household. We loved and respected our father and we thought that if he heard about this, it was going to break his heart and we did not want that to happen. We kept quiet.

I visited home often because I was bringing the medications to my sister. Anything that I would be told of in the community or be advised by pharmacists to buy I would surely buy and secretly give it to her. She was still strong and working in a manufacturing factory. Her financial contribution was significant. Unfortunately one day, I got a call from my father stating that my sister was terribly ill with excessive diarrhoea. He said that she disclosed that she has HIV. He was so heartbroken but he remained strong for her. He told her that he would support her all the way. On the other hand my mother was harsh and cursing everyday. This was really hurting my sister.

I hurried home and, to my shock, my sister was so skinny and was mentally disturbed. When I entered the room, she quickly recognized me. I fed her a food supplement as she was not eating because of thrush. I then gave her vitamin tablets and other medications I had brought along. I monitored her. In about an hour's time, she said she wanted me to take her to the dining room so that she could watch television. I did. She watched but one could see that she was still disturbed. I monitored her for three days and then when I saw that she was well I went back to work.

My sister was independent and had recovered amazingly. She would visit me in Durban, traveling alone. She would come to buy medication on her own. She returned to work. We were all happy and we were so supportive of her. I do not know what happened, but her condition changed and got worse in my absence. We tried everything we could but nothing seemed to help. She unfortunately passed away on January 7, 2001, leaving behind her ten-year-old son and a three-year-old daughter to grow up without their mother.

There have been developments in my sister's story. I was worried about the growth of the little girl because she was skinny and always ill-looking. Her grandmother worked in hospital, so she took good care of her and knew exactly what medication was needed by a child her age. I was suspicious of her status. I wanted to know if she was tested for HIV but it was very difficult for me to explore that area because I did not want them to think that I was implying something. I had to swallow it and allow the pain to grow in me.

Her daughter's father got married five years after my sister's death to a lady who was about ten years younger than him. In December 2006 I visited them and they told me that he was in and out of hospital and doctors' rooms because he was very sick. He did not look like a person who had episodes to me. I only noticed the black marks on his fair body. I then thought he had an outbreak of sores during his illnesses. When asking what the problem was, hoping they would tell me what was making him sick, there was no clear answer, which could be leading to what one could suspect. In February 2007, it was on a Tuesday, his mother informed me that he was very sick. She said she does not know the cause of his illness but she described his condition. She said, he was not eating, talking or even seeing his visitors in the ward, though his eyes were open and he was still alive. While I was still planning to visit him on the weekend, I was called on the Thursday to be informed of his death. I counted that it took him exactly seven years living with the virus. I thought of the daughter that he was leaving behind with his new bride, both depending on him. I was so sad and the pain is growing even more.

My pain grew as I thought of the new bride. I spoke to her and she told me that he died of the epidemic; he was diagnosed positive during the episodes he had. I was angry to hear that because they kept this a secret when I asked them about it. I then had to calm down a bit, realizing that it must have been difficult for them to accept and deal with it. I knew that it would be even worse to know that somebody else knows about it. She told me that she also tested positive but she is fine because her CD4 count is way too high. We then spoke about testing the little girl and she promised that she would take her to the nearest health facility and let me know of the results. I assured her that I would provide them financial assistance.

During his funeral, I was very shocked to learn that he had four children from four different mothers. My sister was dead and she had the eldest, others were born after my sister's death. When thinking of the reality of what that implies for the children and their mothers, my pain grew even more.

I am going through difficulties accepting the death of my siblings. That is a reason why I felt that I better put my feelings on paper; that I really feel the pain and I believe it is more than the pain of the one who suffered from HIV and died because that one knew the problem in his system. For me watching the person deteriorating is even more painful.

So in conclusion, there is more pain felt by people who watch their relatives struggling for their lives. It is more painful to see them dying. When they are dead, they do not feel pain anymore, but the people left behind have to bear the consequences. Those consequences include having to adapt to the new life without this dead person who was very much part of the household. There is the pain of seeing the sorrow in the eyes of children they leave behind. It is more painful to realize that, as much as one can play the parent role for them, it will not match the love their biological parents gave them. Sometimes others die before marriage; therefore, children are always left with the partner who will later find his or her own life. This life will have consequences for the lives of the children. Usually, the consequences are not good. In this case, this inflicts more pain on you as their relative to see the hardships they experience and be unable to do anything about it. You feel that you owe it to your dead brother or sister but the situation is too strict for one to act. It is so painful to realize the problem but see again that there is nothing you can do about it. So that is why I say that I feel more pain by being affected by HIV/AIDS rather than infected. When a person is suffering it is painful to see the struggle. You want to share the pain but circumstance cannot let you because you are not the one who is sick. You think that if you take the share you will be able to handle it. You sometimes feel that it is so unfair for your sick relative to go through this pain, wishing to shift it to someone who can manage the pain. It is painful to listen to his children, spouse, and parents lamenting the pain they feel as they see their loved one suffering. It is even worse when they talk about the loss when a person has passed away.

It is so sad to see the difficult lives that their children go through. The experience is so painful. I believe that there are many people who go through the same experience. The dead people are dead and they do not feel the pain caused by their death nor see the suffering of people left behind. I wish there could be programs put in place to help us to be prepared for these experiences. It could be the support groups or the counseling services. Those will be appreciated if they can be available in rural areas as well.

With the pain I am experiencing, I can say that I am feeling so empty and helpless. There is no painkiller that can ease this pain. This pain feels like it is from a bleeding wound that takes long to dry. As soon as one is hoping that the pain is going down, something else comes up. It can either be in the family or outside but what is common is that the suffering manifests itself in a similar way. That on its own makes these wounds bleed more. For an affected person like me, there is limited access to a cure and if that is not accessible, it makes it more painful. The infected people do have other medications that are available to help deal with the illness. There also is more research taking place to come up with the cure. However, the affected people have no medications and that is more painful, making them lose hope.

Nevertheless, there are glimmers of hope. In December 2007 I took my sister's little girl to a clinic for testing. She tested HIV negative. I related the good news to her grandmother and my father. They were so happy and relieved. It is interesting to note that even though my late sister had a natural delivery for this little girl, she was born negative and she will be 10 years old in August. This is a huge breakthrough when we recall that, in South Africa in 2001, there were few interventions for prevention of mother to child transmission (PMTCT).

## Note

Sibongile S. Mkhize is a Social Science Researcher in the Research Program of Health Systems Trust (HST). The paper was started while working for the School of Development Studies (SoDS) in the University of KwaZulu-Natal, continued at the Centre for HIV/AIDS Networking (HIVAN), and finalized at HST.

# 6

# Contested Sexualities

Under the difficult conditions described in the previous chapters, what can women do, what are they doing, and what is happening on the ground? In the next two chapters I describe the perspectives of women in support groups I observed in KwaZulu-Natal in 2003 and 2005. The present chapter outlines the discussions and expectations of sexuality and family relationships among the women and the following chapter explores volunteer activities, activism, and possibilities for transformative action among the same women.

Here, I examine the discussions among women in two support groups and distinguish between moral condemnation and pragmatic perspectives of the epidemic. Adopting the mode of situational analysis (Burawoy 1998; Gluckman 2002; Vincent 1978; Vincent 1986; Werbner 1984), I draw out the implications of these conversations in terms of the historical patterns of marriage, reproduction, and spaces of women's autonomy, with attention to contemporary echoes as well as changes. Finally, I consider how recent massive economic restructuring may have worsened the dependence of women on men. This in turn, may have contributed to the epidemic among young girls and women as well as to the increasing manifestation of gender-based violence (Jewkes 2002).

As we can see from Sibongile's story, many women did not shut their eyes to AIDS and used whatever strategies were available to them to fight for survival. Sibongile stresses the ways in which relatives and friends, who were themselves tragically affected by the epidemic, supported people who disclosed they were HIV positive and tried to help them in practical ways. Families did not necessarily reject their positive sons and daughters but tried to find some kind of treatment and to look after them when they fell sick. As we shall see, Sibongile's story, including her devotion to her sister and brother, reflects the experiences of many of the people she calls the "affected." Many women, having come into contact with the ravages of the disease, went searching for further knowledge and for training and education so that they could help others in similar situations.

Sibongile Mkhize, an educated woman, was seeking to do the best for her sister, who was open about her diagnosis and desperate to find a way to stay alive and rear her two children. However, neither Sibongile nor her sister found out about the treatments available in the South African private health sector. In the late 1990s, at the time Sibongile's sister was ill, such treatments were already part of the public health services in Brazil and countries of the global North. Sibongile learned about possible treatment after both her sister and brother had passed away.

Over and over, as the observations of the next two chapters will show, women and men, in whatever ways were available to them, sought information about the disease, about caring for the sick, and about prevention. Nevertheless, although people sought information, the kinds of information available, the context in which such information was forthcoming, and people's previous knowledge and education (what Pierre Bourdieu might call their *habitus*) also limited the usefulness of their searches. In these ways, the distinctions of urban and rural based (or "Red" and "School" as Mayer characterized the groups among the Xhosa) carried powerful implications for the meaning of AIDS. As we shall see in Chapter 7, practical difficulties also arose for people trying to cope with the epidemic, such as access to transportation and adequate sources of water.

In the early 1990s, when AIDS was just starting to affect members of the African population, we saw women in the informal settlements around Durban open to learning about sexual options such as the female condom. They exhibited the condom and laughed and talked with practical sense about the need for prevention.

In 1992, we saw women asking for income-generating activities, and reading the ANC constitution. Later, in 1995 women were writing letters to the ANC government and asking to be hired as community health educators. The women were self-confident and strategic. They looked for resources and at the same time offered to work in prevention in practical ways. They understood the opening up of the political sphere within the new South Africa and they expected their voices to be heard.

## Common Sense, Practical Sense

Gramsci has distinguished "practical sense" – which people learn from analyzing their own experiences – from "common sense" (Crehan 2002:110; Gramsci 1971:326–330). Common sense gains its credibility from its echo of hegemonic ideas. To capture the counter-hegemonic mobilization with respect to morals, so essential to AIDS discourse, I have adopted the Gramscian distinctions between "common" sense and "practical" or "good" sense. In colonial and post-colonial terms, common sense is linked with a set of moralisms, often but certainly not always related to Western religious teachings (Comaroff 1985). From this perspective, common sense is a partial reflection of easily assimilated hegemonic sayings or givens. Gramsci sees practical sense or good sense, in opposition to common sense, as derived from people's pragmatic evaluation of everyday experiences. Practical sense derives from people's conscious efforts to resolve the contradictions between received discourses and their material challenges understood as counter-hegemonic. Pragmatic sense, in this context, evokes the possibilities for transformative action among women coping with the epidemic.[1]

Although the distinctions are not always clear, the contrast of "common" versus "pragmatic" sense offers a useful guiding light in trying to sort out the changes that were taking place in people's perspectives on AIDS. Such distinctions are particularly useful in the effort to understand the impact of a confusing public discourse on the understandings of grassroots women.

At the same time as the health activism of the 1990s was taking place, in the rural areas, many women were afraid to speak up in public or to talk in front of their elders. Witchcraft was under discussion and land was controlled by patriarchal tribal elders (Delius 1996; Walker 2002). Here, I would suggest a difference between the urban- and rural-based women in the ability to maintain autonomy.

This difference has to be seen, not as a concrete characteristic of the particular women, but rather as changing over time and even changing as women move from one setting to another. Many of the women in the informal settlements had recently arrived as single mothers from the rural areas and found ways to support themselves on the fringes of the urban economy (Preston-Whyte and Rogerson 1991). In this way, they were somewhat freer to articulate and, where possible, act on their own practical sense. However, other more "traditional" women, marked by their beads and long straight skirts, were associated with the rural areas, although they might spend time in the urban settlements. Rural-based dress might also be associated with political representation (Marks and Trapido 1987) since, as noted earlier, allegiance to Inkatha involved a reemphasis on "traditional" garb.

Historically, women who stayed in the rural areas were much more dependent on their male partners for cash and on the tribal elders for the right to stay in their homes or to work the fields (Bozzoli and Nkotsoe 1991; Walker 2002). To quote from a woman in the 1950s: "I am a woman, a mother, but I am not married. . . . If I went home I would be under orders from my brother or his wife" (Mayer 1971:244). Also: "after my husband's death I first tried staying on at his place with his elder brother and family. The wife of this elder brother bullied me, and used to order me about as if she were a mother-in-law instead of only a sister-in-law" (Mayer 1971:242). As we can see from these quotes, if we view the categories of Red and School as dynamic, we can understand how a woman in need of help from her kin may return to her rural village and find herself as isolated and lacking in autonomy as the women who never left. We can also understand how, even in urban areas, the insecurity and poverty of the informal settlements and the exacerbation of unemployment under austere economic debt-repayment policies, may lead many people to rely on the connections of kin in the rural areas and, as a corollary, the reification of patriarchy in the contemporary era.

Peter Delius,[2] speaking of the devastation caused by the apartheid policies in the late 1980s in the rural Transvaal, notes that:

> It was regarded as essential to a properly ordered society that women should remain under male authority. . . . The ambiguity of women's positions within the villages had been intensified by the processes of change at work which had not altered their formal status and had increased their dependence on cash income, but had also extended their control over households and their centrality within village life (Delius 1996:202).

He then emphasizes the explosive clash of both generation and gender in the violent abuse of women:

> . . . young men, who had been raised to expect to exercise control over women, instead found themselves trapped in social limbo and unable to assert either male or adult authority . . . They . . . collided with the women who controlled pensions, remittances and households (Delius 1996:202–203).

It is in this context, in fact, that Delius finds women most vulnerable to accusations of witchcraft and murder. Such descriptions suggest that rural women's fears of speaking in public or taking leadership positions, which I noted in 1992, were based on recent experience of violent sanctions and conflict.

However, even after the transition to a new South Africa, Cherryl Walker notes that rural-based women are still among the poorest. In the late 1990s, "in the context of rising job losses, many migrants are returning to their rural homes with no prospect of finding formal jobs in the cities or mines again" (Walker 2002:26). Although the barrenness and overpopulation of the rural areas has undermined the importance of agriculture, Walker notes research that shows that agriculture is still the third most important "livelihood tactic" for households in the rural areas and that, in fact, it is the poorest households that still rely on supplementary agriculture (May et al. 2000; Walker 2002).

Under these stressful conditions, the historical patriarchal emphasis of the rural areas again puts women in a difficult position. As Walker points out:

> Women are restricted from inheriting land and, while they are often the workers on the land, their decision-making powers and control over the product is curtailed . . . (Walker 2002:28).

## Bead Workers and Hope Workers

In 2003, we find varying approaches to political action among the women who sought treatment in a mission hospital in Durban. Rural-based women seemed more isolated from or less willing to listen to news about science, treatments, and political dissension.

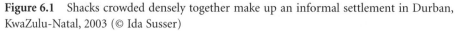

**Figure 6.1**    Shacks crowded densely together make up an informal settlement in Durban, KwaZulu-Natal, 2003 (© Ida Susser)

These distinctions were embodied in the women who participated in two support groups: a group composed mostly of rural-based women, whom I shall call the Bead Workers, and a group made up largely of women from the urban settlements, called here the Hope Workers and described in more detail in the next chapter. Although religious narratives were integral to both groups and religion was an extremely important support for many of the women (Hlongwana and Mkhize 2007), we see the emergence of a clear practical sense of AIDS among each group as well as the barriers for women in different contexts to act on such understanding or to access adequate information to inform their understandings.

By 2003, over ten years into the epidemic, treatment was still too expensive for all but the wealthiest members of the population. However, women had organized in many ways to address the epidemic. In 1992, in public discussions of AIDS prevention, women had explicitly asked for income-generating activities to reduce the necessity of what has been called "survival sex" or the transactions of sex for funds for immediate household needs (Preston-Whyte et al. 2000; Susser 2001). By 2003, many small income-generating activities were operating: bead making, sewing, selling CDs, selling AIDS buttons. Many women had been trained as care providers in the ways they had been demanding since 1995. However, the vast majority of carers were working for free. Support groups had been formed. They visited sick members, helped to pay for funerals, and generally allowed people to talk through the devastating situation on a personal level.

## Discussing Sex and AIDS

In 2003, more than 20 years after AIDS was identified among women, in terms of sexuality and women's options, much was contested, yet little was won. Condoms, female and male, were still the only source of prevention for married women. Female condoms were rarely available in South Africa. Even if universally available, condoms also prevented pregnancy but, for both men and women, having children was extremely important.

Let us listen to a discussion about sex and AIDS with the Bead Workers. Many weekday mornings, Bead Workers traveled for several hours each way from the outlying informal settlements or even rural areas outside Durban; others slept in makeshift shelters in the urban areas. They came together to make elaborately designed multicolored bead necklaces, belts, pins, and bracelets to help pay for medical needs at a mission hospital. When the program started, their beading supplemented the cost of doctors' visits and the treatment of opportunistic diseases.

In 2003, since the rollout of government treatment was still in dispute, this hospital was one of the few places in South Africa where HAART was available. However, few, if any, of the Bead Workers could afford such treatment, which cost, at that time, about 900 rand (roughly $200) per month.

Sitting on the wooden floor of a light, pleasant, but virtually unfurnished room adjacent to the hospital, the Bead Workers expressed a wide range of responses to the crisis. They spoke about AIDS in Zulu, translated simultaneously by two young women research associates (Syenele Ndlovu and Xoliswa Keke). By the time I joined them and these conversations took place, the Bead Workers were on familiar and friendly terms with my research associates, who had sat with the group on many occasions.

First, we heard a common refrain, often reported in the international news. A woman, possibly in her thirties, sitting on the floor threading beads and dressed in colorful Western clothes with a red bandanna over her hair, wearing many bead necklaces herself, said, "I would like to use a condom but my husband would never agree – I have tried, but he refuses."

But, in this context of about 20 women in a room, beading and talking, this statement was not left to stand. Another, older, woman answered: "The condom is not pleasurable but one uses it for the sake of one's life."

A little later during the same discussion, another young woman, dressed in a modishly tight long skirt and beautiful colored necklaces and bracelets, kneeling on the ground to do her work, spoke up: "Relationships between men and women would be dead without making love – I would not even look forward to making him tea."

Another woman responded, "People can live without sex. I have not done anything since 1999. My child is now three years old and I have not had sex because my boyfriend was sleeping with people I did not trust."

A third woman argued, "That's because you don't live with him. If you did, there would be no peace in the family if you refused to make love." A fourth woman replied, "I'm married to my husband but I refuse to sleep with him because I know the person he slept with and what is happening with her. My husband refuses to test for HIV, so I refuse to make love with him." Another responded vehemently, "If my husband forced me to remove a female condom and forced himself on me, I would report him to the police station."

Several important issues emerge from these remarks. First, words such as virginity and sin were not used in the meetings that I observed; nor were they in the field notes recorded by my associates. In the meetings I attended, as in the informal settlements in 1992 and 1995, women talked about sexuality openly.

The conversations recorded above clearly show that women talked about both husbands and boyfriends without raising judgmental or moralistic issues of marriage, sexuality, or the "legitimacy" of the child. This is particularly significant given the claims of religious groups or "traditional" leaders that "virginity," "abstinence," and other rules about sexuality emerge from belief systems ingrained in the local population.

Boyfriends and the children born from such relationships were discussed directly without qualification, embarrassment or apology. The term "boyfriend" (the term used in translation by Kake and Ndlovu) might suggest that a woman's partner or the father of her child lived elsewhere. "Husband" did not necessarily refer to a legal status or a customary marriage but indicated that the woman lived with her partner and that he expected all the many amenities suggested in the simple idea of "making his tea."

Many of the remarks among the Bead Workers suggested that the women were trying to exercise "practical sense" and did not echo a moralistic "common sense" about faithful sexual relations expected in marriage. They did not condemn the other sexual relations of their partners but were largely concerned when they "did not trust" the other women. As one woman says, she acknowledges her husband but she refuses to sleep with him because she knows her husband's mistress and "what is happening with her."

The Bead Workers had been formed to help poor women supplement their incomes or to subsidize their family's medical needs. Many were intimately tied to the rural areas. On questioning them, several commented that there was no local clinic near to their homes but a mobile clinic came twice a month.

The Bead Workers were all too familiar with AIDS. When the group started, it had been linked to costs in the hospital so that members who sold beads only paid half the cost of a regular visit to the clinic – 50 rand (about $10) instead of the 100 rand ($20) a visit cost at the time. There were no men or teenagers there on the days I visited, although, in fact, one man did join the group with his wife and they beaded together.

Among the Bead Workers, the main issues raised were those that I heard over and over again. Among the Hope Workers, the same sexual contestation could be heard. Even among graduate students and others in our ethnographic training sessions in Durban, similar conversations took place.

In all these situations, the discussion did not turn on a moralistic argument about sex and sin, or virginity, faithfulness, and marriage. Religious or "traditional" expectations were not invoked. In all these settings, the conversation turned to practical perspectives on contested sexual relationships similar to those outlined by the Bead Workers. Women could see few clear options in the face of a reasonably well-understood threat of disease.

## Bead Workers as Carers: Contested Knowledge

Among the Bead Workers, some of the women described themselves as volunteer health educators and "carers" trained by mission centers through a government AIDS education program.[3] Several of the women talked about the kind of effective contributions they believed their visits and education were making. We hear a "common sense" kind of comment by one Bead Worker:

> I would not know how to talk to my children about HIV prevention. Traditionally, I can't do that. I feel that if I were to show the children how to use a condom, it would be like encouraging or teaching them to have sex before they themselves had started on their own.

Pum,[4] another Bead Worker who had sought training as a volunteer carer, counteracted this "common sense" with "practical sense." She tries in her own way to generate solutions to the threat of the new disease:

> I go around in my community [as a community health worker] educating people about HIV – especially young people . . . to abstain; wait until at least there is a cure . . . Young people listen to us . . . we found some people who want to commit suicide or spread the virus to everyone but when we talk to them, they listen and appreciate it.

Although this woman educator did not discuss access to treatment or talk about sexual options, such as female and male condoms, in telling youth to abstain from sex she was not promoting a moral option. Interestingly, she said, "Abstain . . . until there is a cure." Nevertheless, she did not tell youth to use a condom or mention the availability of treatment, even in addressing those who talked about suicide. The government training, emphasizing nutrition, left Pum with a limited repertoire of initiatives.

## Religion and Faith-Based Initiatives: Perspectives on Sexuality

To fill the gaps in public responsibility for the sick, missions, churches, and multiple faith-based organizations have emerged as important resources for HIV care. Up until August 2003, mission hospitals were one of the few places where people could access anti-retroviral therapies for AIDS, although at a price prohibitive for most. Religious organizations also tended to be one of the main trainers of home-based care providers. In addition, religious organizations have been crucial in supporting care for orphans and children in need.

Churches have historically recruited women to donate their labor to look after the sick in the parish. The men may have been paid as pastors, but the women were supposed to visit for reasons of charity. Thus, even before AIDS was recognized, churches were recruiting and training women as volunteers to visit the disabled and the needy.

Most of the groups I observed started their meetings with a prayer. However, the influence of religious belief was far from predictable. Although connections between religion and AIDS caring, community health education, and even health activism were evident, I did not hear condemnations of the sick or discussions of sin and stigma among the carers.

In recent years, both men and women have been appointed as pastors. Significantly, in terms of breaking down gender stereotypes, men pastors were visiting the homes of people with AIDS and discussing sexuality and AIDS prevention with young people, often in informal and non-judgmental ways. In Namibia, two men pastors came to our AIDS research training course saying they wanted to find some way to help the youth in the many families they visited on the parish rounds. They did not raise any issues of sin but said to us that they felt helpless in the face of the epidemic and came to the course in search of direction (see Chapter 8). In 2003 in Durban, I watched a well-educated and articulate African woman pastor discussing the explicit aspects of AIDS prevention through barrier methods as well as AIDS treatment. Notwithstanding her religious affiliation, she was straightforward, detailed, and even humorous in her public presentation concerning condoms and female condoms and the importance of access to treatment, which had not yet been approved by the South African government.

Nevertheless, the centrality of religious involvement in AIDS prevention and treatment brings with it questions of the maintenance of gender hierarchies, images of good and bad women, and an emphasis on sin with respect to sex. Such a tendency can be detected even among the most lenient and welcoming health providers. As one well-meaning mission administrator said to me in an interview, "After all, AIDS has its source in sin." I had heard the same statement 15 years earlier from a woman who was a leading member of a Pentecostal church in Puerto Rico (Susser and Kreniske 1997).

A more judgmental faith-based initiative, which emerged in South Africa in the 1990s, involves public rituals in which mothers brought their daughters to be tested for virginity. Examiners walked past hundreds of girls lying on the ground as they raised their skirts for visual inspection. Failing a vaginal examination could lead to humiliation and punishment (Leclerc-Madlala 2001; Scorgie 2002).

In some cases, faith-based initiatives may be led by women looking for a way to bolster and protect their teenage daughters and their own rights to live safely without HIV infection. As has been documented all over the world, the hope expressed by women under siege is that strong religious adherence might stop men from "straying" to other women or drinking (Mintz 1960; Robbins 2004; Susser and Kreniske 1997).

However, faith-based movements may reinforce and legitimate women's inequality, such as in stressing the need for youth to remain ignorant of sex and by punishing girls who do not or cannot maintain their virginity. In early 2002, I first heard a middle-aged African pastor in Johannesburg give a rousing speech about a "virgin power" movement he was launching nationally, which gave some premonition of more constraining approaches that were to come.

In 2003, new PEPFAR funds from the United States were introduced with a number of restrictions around reproductive health and education. The constraints on the funding initially led many South African medical institutions to question whether they should accept the money. On the other hand, faith-based organizations accepted the funds with alacrity. This, as noted in Chapter 2, increased the likelihood that youth would learn about abstinence only. In fact, one administrator involved with such an international NGO said, "We have Bush funding so anything that mentions condoms gives us the jeepers." Since the events I am describing unfolded before the full impact of the PEPFAR funding – in fact, before such funding had been widely distributed in South Africa – the lack of arguments that rely on sin, virginity, and other religious discourse is significant. If the same research were to be conducted three years later, perhaps the influence of this increase in funding for abstinence and virginity would be more marked.

## Customary Law: Historical Reification of Patriarchy

Clearly, contestations about meaning, sexuality, and autonomy were sharply evident in the contemporary scene and echoed in the religious sphere. However, before immediately attributing such perspectives either to tradition or religion, or to the new politics and AIDS, it seems important to understand the history of contestation about women's autonomy and sexuality as well as the definitions of men's and women's roles that can be traced since the colonial era. To quote Mayer once again:

> For School widows there is an added complication as regards the taking of lovers. The Christian expectation that a widow should remain chaste [short of remarriage] runs directly counter to the Xhosa expectation that she should have regular and authorized lovers. This clash of two moralities has never been resolved. Young School widows in the country do, in many cases, take lovers, like their Red counterparts, but with an extra burden of shame and secrecy (Mayer 1971:242).

From the middle of the nineteenth century, customary law had been adapted by the colonial regime, with a bias toward the recognition of men's prerogatives and the undercutting of women's status.[5] Colonial regimes appointed men as chiefs, hired men as interpreters, and generally regarded men as the appropriate mediators and beneficiaries of administrative power. In promoting chiefs who supported colonial policies, the colonial administration undermined patterns of descent and the local legitimacy of leaders (Mamdani 1996; Marks 1990).[6] Nevertheless, men's leadership and advantage, naturalized in Western eyes through both politics and religion, became the general expectation (Comaroff 1997; Mikell 1997). However, women have struggled throughout to negotiate their own situation and to deal with the changing political regimes (Etienne 1997; Flint 2001; Potash 1989; Walker 1991).

Prior to colonialism, women maintained ongoing links and obligations with their natal lineages, which gave them some independence in relation to their family of marriage. Among the cattle-centered groups such as the Xhosa and the Zulu, the groom's lineage brought cattle to the prospective bride's lineage as an indication of possible engagement. One of the animals might be slaughtered for a major feast, bringing the surrounding villages together in recognition of the possible marriage alliance. Others would be distributed among the bride's male kin and negotiations would take place between the lineage heads of the groom and bride about future obligations. Later, when the wife went to live with her husband, similar feasts and cattle might be exchanged (Evans-Pritchard 1951; Gluckman 1965). Interestingly, according to Max Gluckman, among the Zulu at the time of his fieldwork, a groom would pay two cattle for the initial *lobola* if the woman was regarded as a virgin and one cow if she was not. No moral sanctions are discussed by Gluckman with respect to this distinction at that time (Gluckman 1965:44).

On the birth of a child, the husband's lineage would be obligated to pay the wife's natal lineage in cattle and if it was a boy more cattle were expected. If a woman was not happy with her husband, she could return to her natal lineage. The elders, with the strong incentive to maintain their own alliance and the future exchange of cattle, could try to negotiate with the couple to improve relations. Eventually, if the woman refused to return to her husband, the natal lineage was under a long-term obligation to return the cattle wealth they had received for her (Evans-Pritchard 1951; Gluckman 1965).

However, the return of cattle would be complicated by the presence of children. If the children were raised with their mother, but returned to their father at some later date, then the husband's lineage might regard this as a negotiated settlement. It was the future labor of the children for the father's lineage that was regarded as particularly valuable in this situation. Thus, in spite of many ritual expectations for the payment of bride wealth by men for women, there was enormous flexibility in the system. Anthropologists have documented the multiple ways in which men and women were able to live autonomous sexual lives under such apparently regulated kinship systems (Delius and Glaser 2003; Evans-Pritchard 1951; Gluckman 1965).

The distinctions between sexuality and marriage for both men and women were among the important insights of early anthropologists (Evans-Pritchard 1951; Gluckman 1965). While a woman might be married with *lobola* paid, she could often live where she chose and have sexual relations as she preferred, as long as the children were returned to their patrilineal lineage in the long term. Marriage had much to do with defining legal succession and place for children and less to do with biological or genetic definitions of kinship in the Western sense.[7] Adoption, such as the adoption of Mandela by a Xhosa chief, was also a common practice for establishing succession and inheritance (Etienne 1997; Nyamnjoh 2002). A woman's ability to bear children was highly valued and for this reason under scrutiny. The birth of a child before marriage under these conditions could enhance the worthiness of the bride by guaranteeing her fertility.

The links between cattle and marriage, as well as the inherent flexibility of many kinship systems in terms of women's autonomy, have been documented extensively throughout the pastoral populations of sub-Saharan Africa (Evans-Pritchard 1951; Hunter 1936; Hutchinson 1997; Hutchinson and Jok 2002). However, the connection of such well-documented and highly respected rituals to HIV bears further examination. For example, it was possible for a man with many cattle to marry the sister of his wife in order to help with the farm duties (van Onselen 1996). In the light of such historical arrangements, as we see among the Bead Workers, women may look without strong disapproval at the "outside" sexual partners of their men. But, as Helen Epstein notes in her discussion of the significance of concurrent partners in the spread of AIDS in Uganda (Epstein 2007), in the era of AIDS such patterns are no longer practical. This would help to explain the clear distinctions evident in the remarks of the Bead Workers. In the conversations I recorded, the women did not condemn their partners for their other sexual liaisons but explicitly noted that they refused sex because they "did not trust" his other women or "saw what happened to his other women."

Even in 2003, in South Africa, the system of *lobola*, or bride wealth, was still strongly in place, especially among women from families that could establish the value of their daughter and the expectation of a customary marriage. Women with education who worked in such positions as nurses, professors, and social workers often came from such families and had been married in the customary way, with the payment of *lobola*. However, as was the case for one of my research associates, the groom and his family took some time to collect the resources and make arrangements and the actual ceremonial event often took place several years after the birth of the first child. I was told that, currently, an initial payment of *lobola* legitimized sexual relations between a man and a woman although it might be many years, if ever, before they were fully married. Childbirth before marriage, or outside of marriage, as noted in the Bead Workers' conversation, was not viewed with the reprobation that might be forthcoming today among fundamentalist Christians in South Africa or the United States, or among the British colonials of an earlier era. However, in some cases, if *lobola* was paid after the birth of a child, that child might not belong to the father's patrilineage.

## The Rigidifying of Patriarchy: Custom, Colonialism, and Apartheid

As noted above, domestic flexibility was a feature of many pre-colonial societies, whether patrilineal or matrilineal. Domestic arrangements among different groups allowed women to travel frequently between their natal lineages and the lineages of their husbands. After the birth of an infant, and sometimes following postpartum rules, women often returned for several years to their original home with the new baby and possibly older siblings.

However, the migrant labor system enforced the separation of husbands and wives for long periods of time. In addition, in the appointment of men in leadership and mediating positions, colonial rule frequently undermined both the legitimacy of chiefs and the roots of women's autonomy. The new chiefs were dependent on the support of a colonial administrative hierarchy and less likely to respond to any local demands, particularly those of women (Platzky et al. 1985; Swartz et al. 1966; Trust for Community Outreach and Education 2004; Turner 1957).

In terms of a contrasting public discourse of sin and virginity, we have already discussed the nationalist ideology and moral code imposed by the Dutch Reformed Church in the apartheid era, the remnants of which still frame debates within the South African government (Crapanzano 1986; Du Pisani 2001; Vestergaard 2001). However, another source of moralistic constraints on women was to be found in the colonial interpretation of customary law with its patriarchal underpinnings. In nine-teenth-century Natal, colonial legislation requiring bride-wealth payments to be made in one lump sum rather than over time fixed women much more firmly in the purview of their husband's lineage. The long, slow negotiations with respect to marriage settle-ments, children, and lineage alliances were undermined. The one time bride-wealth payment reduced women's autonomy in the balancing of their natal lineage with their husband's lineage and limited their ability to return to their natal homes. In addition, in Natal province women were legally regarded as minors and, in general, colonial law seldom recognized women as owners of land or cattle (Walker 1990b).

As noted in Chapter 3, the history of migrant labor, as it was developed under colonial rule and later under apartheid, meant that women, youth, and the elderly were often forced to stay in the rural areas, dependent on the meager agricultural production possibilities. Thus the division between rural and urban was also clearly gendered. While men migrated to the towns in search of work, poor African women predominated in the rural areas, in a situation dominated by patrilineal inheritance (Walker 1990a).

Under apartheid, new chiefdoms and patronage were created in relation to the Bantustans. As we saw in Chapter 3, large segments of the population were dispos-sessed and forced into overpopulated, overgrazed homelands which, as Walker notes, could barely be classified as rural any longer (Platzky et al. 1985; Trust for Community Outreach and Education 2004; Walker 2002). Under these conditions, chiefs began to demand payments for land distribution, education, and other village needs. A wealthy group of chiefs with little local legitimacy was established and took charge of dispensing patronage (Delius 1996; Walker 2002). It was these chiefs, represented by Mangosuthu Buthelezi of the Inkatha Freedom Party, with whom Mandela had to bargain when the ANC came to power.

The abolition of the Pass Act in 1986, with the massive migration of the poor into informal settlements in the cities has not severed rural relations nor undone the gendered patterns. Throughout the post-colonial regions of southern Africa, access to land has for generations been sought as "security" for times of unemployment, disability, and old age (Ferguson 1999; Hart 2002). Land available to poor African women in South Africa remains governed by a system framed partly by patrilineal inheritance and reinforced by Western patriarchal patterns.[8] Thus, in spite of the enlightened new constitution and legislated rights, women still struggle in many situations with subordination to men (Hart 2002).

The transition to the new South Africa, was built on a broad-based coalition that included the "traditional" patriarchal elite, many of whom owed their position to reification of masculinity and corporate property perpetrated by the history of colonialism and apartheid (Bozzoli and Nkotsoe 1991; Walker 1990b). This negotiation of patriarchal rights in return for allegiance to the ANC was, as noted in Chapter 3, extremely important in KwaZulu-Natal, the political stronghold of Inkatha led by Chief Buthelezi. As Ramphele notes (2001), the coalition constructed to lead the new South Africa agreed to the codification of what Cherryl Walker (Walker 1991) calls the "shell of customary law" in the new regime. In terms of marriage, some women may still be somewhat protected by and wish to continue *lobola* as a confirmation of the obligations of both men and women in customary marriage. On the other hand, under this "shell" local chiefs determine access to land in the rural areas and elder men's councils decide whether women or youth should be allocated plots.

As has long been understood in South Africa (Bentley 2004; Bozzoli and Nkotsoe 1991; Small and Kompe 1992; Walker 1991), this rendition of customary law fosters the exclusion of women from deliberating councils as well as from inherited land. When a man dies of AIDS, whether in the rural areas or an urban settlement, such rules allow members of his lineage to evict the wife and children from his home and to take possession of his property. One tragic well-known example of such an event occurred when Khabzela, the nationally renowned DJ from Soweto, was dying of AIDS. As Khabzela became sicker, his mother and sister accused his wife of witchcraft and eventually evicted her from Khabzela's home (McGregor 2007).

Whereas, previously, the children of fathers were claimed by the patrilineage for their labor, nowadays, especially in the urban areas, children are often living with their mother and may be evicted with their mother. Children's labor is of less use than it might have been in a cattle-raising society, Thus, the concentration of power among the men who are elders also leads to the neglect of the needs of children and youth (Ramphele 2001:6). Since youth are at the greatest risk for AIDS and young girls are more than three times more likely to contract AIDS than young boys, this uneven situation in terms of customary law and land rights has multiple implications for the epidemic.

## Land Rights in the New South Africa

As noted earlier, the Land Rights Act of 1913 allocated only a small percentage of the land to the black population, which constituted 80 percent of the total population. By the late 1990s, the black population was still concentrated on only about 13 percent of the land (Walker 2002). Thus, the repeal of the Land Rights Act has been a major symbol for the new South Africa. Since the early 1990s, land rights have been a central demand of progressive civil organizations (Walker 2002).[9] Land had not been a central priority of the ANC except in terms of eliciting the support of rural chiefs. Besides the pioneering work of Govan Mbeki, Thabo's father, the ANC had had few connections in the rural areas since the early twentieth century (Delius 1996; Hart 2002). A number of reallocations of land were initiated over the first decade of the ANC government. However, the major response to land reform in the communal areas was legislation enacted in 2004. Amid much public attention, the Communal Land Rights Act transferred the title to some 17 million hectares of communal land back to "communities" in the former homelands. Considering the slow pace of the ANC's land reform process up to then (Hall 2004; Trust for Community Outreach and Education 2004), the lengthy bureaucratic processes required before communities had administrative rights over their land displeased communities. The process outlined was not as fast as many poor people might wish. However, the crucial decision of great import for women was that tribal authorities were permitted to be in charge of the land redistribution and administration processes in communal areas.[10]

The land that was not already under "communal" (or more accurately, chiefly) control was allocated in a neoliberal policy to support a small number of black commercial farmers (Centre for Development and Enterprise 2005; Walker 2002:54–59). The communal land was maintained firmly in the control of the tribal elders whose patriarchal power had been amplified both under colonial rule and later under apartheid. By reducing women's autonomy, such decisions were implicated in increasing even further the massive vulnerability of women and girls to AIDS.

## A History of Spaces for Autonomy

As noted above, under the migrant labor system, which was enforced during the apartheid years and still persists, men went to work in the mines and women were left in the rural areas. By the early 1900s, some women had followed the men to work on the margins of the settlements in the informal economy, brewing beer and selling crafts or sometimes exchanging sexual favors for support or cash. However, as noted earlier, even in the rural areas, women in divided households found some avenues of flexibility and autonomy.

Historians have begun to re-analyze early ethnographic studies to highlight the presence of women who were neither wives nor daughters, but mature independent widows, divorcees, and single women. Such women had control over their own sexual choices and might take lovers as they wished, among both the married and single men of their community (Bonner 1990; Delius and Glaser 2003). Much historical and ethnographic research confirms the long-term existence of women with a degree of sexual autonomy in both the rural and the urban areas, as well as the ongoing practice of extramarital affairs, among both men and women, along with polygamy. Although such patterns most likely existed before the implementation of migrant labor, the preponderance of extramarital relationships was much increased by the creation of the mining economy.

In the late twentieth century, as the rural communities lost resources and were unable to support such autonomous women, the women were forced to rely more on forms of transactional sex and migration to the cities. Nevertheless, even some of the poorest sex workers circulating around the gold mines today comment appreciatively about the autonomy from men that such an occupation allows (Campbell 2003).

Whether such women maintain their independence through sex work or beer brewing, or a mixture of both, they are also attaining a degree of autonomy with respect to the burden of care. The connection between care and sexual partnership was stated clearly in the Bead group when one woman said, "If there was no sex, I would not even want to make him tea." Many of the quotes from women without partnership obligations, both historically and nowadays, comment on the freedom from the daily "domestic routine of cooking, cleaning and child-care that would have been required . . . at home" (Campbell 2003:77).

As Mayer wrote[11] over 30 years ago:

> Some older women live it up when their husbands are away. One can see them moving around from one beer drink to another, exactly like men. "Now nobody asks me any questions about why I was not in the house all the time. I need not bother about cooking the food for him, and washing his clothes. I go where I like and come home any time that pleases me" (Delius and Glaser 2003).

Today, talking of the women sex workers on the mines, Campbell writes:

> On the one hand, their choice to become sex workers had resulted in the dangers and stresses of their present daily lives. On the other, abandoning their claims to conventional respectability (in coming to the mines, abandoning their children and setting up lives as single women with few responsibilities to anyone except themselves) represented a radical break from the drudgery and restrictions of conventional womanhood (Campbell 2003:77).

However, obviously, the burden of care for children, at least, is being taken up elsewhere by other women, usually the grandmothers, so that the narrow choices for autonomy are not in any way a solution to the burden of care for women in general.

But, in other ways, women still take care of one another. Single women are helped and taken care of, to a certain degree, by other women who act as landladies and beer brewers. Campbell (2003) cites cases of sex workers bathing their sick co-workers and some ways in which they act collectively to protect one another from the violence of clients. Still, here, as we shall see later for the volunteer carers in the bead and support groups, the difficult issue of transportation arises because women are unable to take sick people to hospital without paying exorbitant fees to the unemployed men who serve as taxi drivers in the settlement.

However, although this historical approach emphasizes the spaces for single women, the more significant point to be garnered from the ethnographic record may be the desperation and increasingly dependent circumstances to which such women have been reduced in the past few decades (Bentley 2004; Delius and Glaser 2003; Kehler 2001).

## Contemporary Contexts: Neoliberal Economic Policy and AIDS

Clearly, the history of colonialism, migrant labor in the mines, and the ruthless policies of apartheid forced men to leave their homes and women into desperate dependence on remittances and hard work on small inadequate landholdings.

As we have seen, by the time of the transition, the Bantustans were too densely populated for agriculture to yield enough to feed households and both men and women were migrating to the cities in search of employment.

Unfortunately, since the late 1990s in South Africa, in spite of early investments in public housing, water, and education, the fundamental contradictions institutionalized in the urban–rural system have been exacerbated rather than reduced. Neoliberal economic policy concentrates on investment in the formal economy with, in South Africa, a predominantly male labor force. The implementation of structural adjustment policies and stringent economic constraints has led to increasing male unemployment as well as the commercial sale of privatized land to the highest bidder. As Delius notes for the transition: "Efforts were made to allay the anxieties of local businessmen, and leading figures in the ANC appeared to embrace precisely the chiefs and homeland leaders whom youth and some migrant workers regarded as principal foes" (Delius 1996:206). Land redistribution in the rural areas has been relatively slow and dominated by patriarchal policies in the communal areas and support of commercial black farmers for the rest (Walker 2002).

Researchers have argued that these policies have undermined men's ability to support families (Hunter 2005; Morrell 2001). As Ferguson documented for Zambia under similar conditions (Ferguson 1999), increasing unemployment may have led to a hardening of brutal male behavior in the pursuit of sexual liaisons with numerous women rather than for the establishment of a domestic base (Morrell 2001). Where men previously might claim two wives (or a rural wife and an urban mistress), now they routinely claim to have eight or nine women as sexual partners (Hunter 2005), including a wife who is expected to accept such behavior. We see this perhaps sad practical acceptance among the Bead Workers but also in DJ

Khabzela's narrative, as his wife chooses to stay with him, knowing of the girlfriends always in the background (McGregor 2007).

However, rather than emphasize men's unemployment alone, we also have to consider women's unemployment more centrally. As in most societies, women's lack of steady paid work is made less visible by the preponderance of women involved in unpaid labor in both the rural and urban areas as well as others earning meager sustenance in the informal economy (Bentley 2004; Kehler 2001).

Even though more men may have become unemployed, overall many more women are excluded from the formal economy. If one examines the employment and income figures for South Africa, rural black women continue to be the poorest population (Bentley 2004; Seekings and Nattrass 2005). As we have seen for the rural areas, predominantly associated with women, women are at a disadvantage in accessing the land they have worked for over a century. Thus, the idea that a prosperous formal economy, which may yet be developing in South Africa, will support women, children, the elderly, and the disabled is premised on the expectation of men sending remittances to the rural areas. Such remittances combined with public assistance grants for children and the elderly are seen as an assumed hidden income which supposedly sustains the 40 percent of the population who are unemployed (Seekings 2007; Seekings and Nattrass 2005).

However, such a sanguine presentation of neoliberal economics bears further scrutiny. Firstly, we do not know who the remittances are sent to, what is expected in exchange, or even how much is sent (Walker 2002). Secondly, such an economy, in effect, exacerbates gendered subordination, as it employs some men at reasonably high incomes and a few at extremely high sums and then expects the women to depend on men to support their children. In the rural areas, processes of dispossession erratically progressing since the early twentieth century have been re-instituted with exacerbated gendered implications. Women may have lost more bargaining power with respect to communal land and neoliberal policies subsidize a small number of new black commercial farmers in the effort to address historically inherited racial inequality (Walker 2002). The issues of rural development have been heavily debated in South Africa in the past few years and obviously vary greatly by region. However, in a detailed analysis of how land reform is working in the Eastern Cape, published as a special issue of the journal *Social Dynamics*, the editors point out that, in fact, the shifts toward neoliberal policies which occurred in the rural areas after 1996 did not necessarily lead either to successful market reform or to better living conditions (Bank and Minkley 2005). In the urban areas, since 1994, much informally settled land has been allocated to the urban dwellers and new working-class housing built. However, in some areas, when it is sold on the currently rapidly gentrifying housing market, poor women and men may lose their homes and livelihood. When people lose their homes, as in 1980s Zambia under structural adjustment programs, (Ferguson 1999), "survival sex" is almost underwritten by economic policy: ". . . relations involved trade-offs of money and sex, with women using their emotional and sexual leverage to extract economic resources from men, and men using their wage-earning power to command the domestic and sexual services of women" (Ferguson 1999:186). As

Mamphela Ramphele documented in her pathbreaking ethnography of men's mining hostels under apartheid in South Africa, women were not allowed beds in the oppressive boarding houses assigned to the men (Ramphele 1993). As a result, women came with their children to illegally share a bed with the worker and in exchange for the "bed called home" carried out extensive domestic chores. Such mining hostels have changed since the end of apartheid. However, when most women are excluded from formal employment and often from the housing associated with it as well as from rights to land and decision making, many women must attract the attention of a few well-paid men to supplement their meager earnings or to encourage them to send remittances.

Child grants and disability grants, and even pensions, institutionalize women as responsible for the burden of care in society without, in fact, providing women with sufficient livelihood to support themselves or their households. Some have labeled the institutionalization of entitlements rather than employment as the production of a rural pensionariat rather than a rural proletariat (Beinart, quoted in Bank et al. 2005:15). When women do have access to more entitlements than men, this may also exacerbate gendered and generational conflict particularly focused on older women. In at least one region under apartheid, in association with witchcraft accusations, widows have been murdered or brutalized for their pensions (Delius 1996).[12] Young women in the rural areas may still have to accept men's behavior on the chance of receiving remittances, access to housing, and rights to land. In addition, the erosion of educational and health services, particularly in the rural areas, rebounds back in troubles for the women, young and old, who are trying to rear both boys and girls with little hope for their own futures. The combination of gendered policies implicit in the neoliberal paradigm for development with the general lack of investment in the capacities of the population is a recipe for disaster with respect to AIDS.

Unveiling the gendered nature of neoliberal development policies and the lack of support for capacity building suggests that young girls, who are regarded as recklessly chasing the 3Cs – cellphones, cars, and cash – in their relations with older men (Phleta 2007), are in fact pursuing the main route to income available to them. Following this economic logic of neoliberal investment, we can clearly see why young girls in South Africa are now five times as likely to become HIV positive than young boys the same age.

Campbell's work dramatically illustrates one extreme of the sharpening of inequalities between men and women as well as the degradation caused by the widening unemployment. She describes the unemployed men who control the lives of women sex workers on the edge of the mines, largely through a combination of threats and violence (Campbell 2003). A related phenomenon (Niehaus 2003) concerns a recent trend toward the naturalizing of the rape of women in the talk of men on the mines. Others document the epidemic violence against women in the contemporary era.

Feminist or women's groups in South Africa have mobilized against gendered violence since the 1970s (Bennett 2001; Hassim 2006; Park et al. 2000). Many argue that such violence has been exacerbated by the twin forces of HIV/AIDS and economic insecurity for men and women (Jewkes et al. 2002). I would suggest that it is in some ways fostered by formal economic policy.

Under apartheid, people who became ill were often pushed back to the rural areas and even today people may return there to survive with less money. With the onslaught of AIDS in the 1980s, it became the official policy of the mines to force people with AIDS, seen as "foreigners," to return to their "homelands." This was the inhuman and ideologically framed policy criticized in the 1990 letter from Cyril Ramaphosa, President of the National Union of Mineworkers, discussed in Chapter 3.

In the post-apartheid era, as Anglo-American and other major industrial investors in South Africa have confronted AIDS, they have begun to fund treatment through the benefits of the formal economy. However, since men still predominate in these jobs, women find themselves dependent on men being willing to name them as partners in order to access AIDS treatment (Lurie et al. 2003). In addition, since employers are in a position to limit treatment for women as partners of such employed men, women must compete with one another to have their liaisons officially recognized by men in the hopes of accessing HAART.

Women have also been the recent target of marginal transnational corporations established in the rural areas (Hart 2002; Mikell 1997). Such plants, which sprung up throughout the rural areas in the late 1960s and increasingly under the global economy of the 1990s, hire predominantly women. However, in contrast to the highly capitalized and unionized mining industry, very little or no consideration has been given to AIDS treatment or prevention by the low-paying, low-capital, non-unionized manufacturing plants.

In the case of South Africa, the devastations wreaked by neoliberal retrenchment combined with AIDS may have stretched women's traditional protections beyond the breaking point. A similar situation of the loss of women's autonomy has been documented in a detailed historical and ethnographic study of the Nuer, a cattle-herding population of the Sudan (Hutchinson and Jok 2002). As Hutchinson (1996) points out, although the Nuer were a patrilineal society centered on cattle inherited through the male line, the system had protected women's rights. Historically, when the Nuer went to war with their neighbors, such as the Dinka, women were not assaulted. In the 1980s, the Nuer peoples had managed a strategic and flexible approach to modern times and many of the Nuer norms and values based on cattle exchange were still in place. However, from the 1990s, the long and brutal war between North and South in the Sudan, a reflection of global politics rather than Nuer territorial interests, finally undermined Nuer society. By 1992, the war had destroyed the protections of women and children that were ingrained in the cattle symbolism. In recent years in the Sudan, women have been targeted, raped, and murdered (Hutchinson and Jok 2002).

As noted earlier, drawing on mounting evidence of increased sexual conflict, Posel (2005) argues that much of the political struggle within the new South African government over the recognition of HIV might be understood as part of a broader effort to limit the new sexual freedoms expressed by both men and women in the post-apartheid era. From this perspective, these "new" freedoms are causing the conflict. But, "new" here is a political or perhaps situational category. As we have seen, there is much documentation to suggest some older patterns of sexual permissiveness for both men and women. What is remembered or allocated authority as "traditional," as discussed in Chapter 11, is itself politically contested.

If we understand that new policies have made daily survival even more difficult for women than for men, we can understand how the increasing vulnerability of women, seeking multiple supports from men, combines with the increasing rage of many unemployed men whose masculinity is undermined because they can no longer support women. Poor women seek more partners as their situation worsens. As a consequence, men find many women forced to accept dominating and violent behavior in exchange for extremely limited financial and other support. This situation intersects tragically with the AIDS epidemic.

As we saw in Chapter 3, sexuality, femininity, masculinity, and reproductive rights have become contested in the emergence of a new African nationalism (Morrell 2001). The construction of AIDS prevention, protection, treatment, and care in terms of "traditional values" and even the resort to traditional healing are central to that project. A careful revisiting of the ethnographic record suggests that historical views of sexuality and reproduction may have been more flexible than the representation of "tradition" in the nationalist image. In addition, our on-the-ground observations of discussions of sexuality suggest that many women, even in the rural areas, still see their options in practical terms rather than according to principles of abstinence or virginity. The contradictions inherent in the necessary flexibility of women's roles as they strategize to support their households in poverty combined with the construction of a patriarchal militant masculinity in the new nation may be contributing to the turmoil over women's sexual and reproductive autonomy in the contemporary era.

# 7

# Public Spaces of Women's Autonomy: Health Activism

In this chapter, I describe women's participation in the public sphere: public speaking, working as volunteer community health educators, and – in a more "transformative" mode – working with the Treatment Action Campaign. I explore the role of organic intellectuals in framing practical issues in terms of transformative action. I then look at some of the challenges such as structural problems of transportation and water supply, which particularly affect people with AIDS. Activist organizations protesting these issues are widespread in South Africa but have not generally connected with transformative activism with respect to AIDS (Desai 2002). Finally, I look at the ways in which the questioning of the HIV virus and suspicions of the toxicity of Western medicine associated with the highest levels of the South African government intersect with the reinforcement of ideas of nutrition and herbal supplements as the appropriate treatment. I review ways in which women suggest that the ensuing confusion, death, and loss in the local communities fosters underlying explanations of witchcraft.

Although much contested, the gender barriers in the face of need, sickness, and death are certainly not pervasive. Women's roles may be more flexible in the public arena of leadership. In 2003, in Durban, among the Bead Workers and the Hope Workers, most of the participants were women and the chairperson was also a woman. As can be clearly traced in the patterns of private violence against women, the division of labor seemed to be much more intransigent in the more hidden areas of caring and sexuality (Albertyn and Hassim 2003; Park et al. 2000). As one woman said to us at a women's community meeting in the informal settlements in 1995, "I can speak out here, but who will defend me when I am alone with my husband in the bedroom?"

In public, women were certainly not confined to silence and submission; they could take forceful and articulate roles. Interestingly, some men we observed also crossed gendered boundaries to take on caring roles in public. In 2003, one of the most active and articulate volunteer care providers I met was a man who later died of AIDS.

Among the Hope Workers, a mission hospital support group, I observed a memorial for a woman (we shall call her Pumzile), who had died of AIDS. Set in a beautiful colonial house, in a large well-proportioned room with stained glass sky-lights, the memorial was attended by her mother and brother and her six-year-old son. Thirty women and about eight men were present. Interestingly, most of the men wandered in late, suggesting a certain reluctance to appear, or else meaning to indicate that they had important tasks to complete elsewhere. While the man who was introduced as the brother of the deceased remained silent, the little boy's grandmother made a moving speech in Zulu. She implored people to talk openly and everywhere about HIV and described her daughter's open and militant stance.

To show Pumzile's courage and straightforwardness, Pumzile's mother told a story about an instance when a stranger flirtatiously propositioned her daughter in a bar. Pumzile replied, "You may think I look pretty but do you know I have AIDS?" The grandmother then described another occasion in which Pumzile clearly refused to hide her diagnosis, but rather insisted on teaching members of the family about her illness. At a family Christmas celebration, noticing Pumzile was resting on a couch, her teenage nephew asked what was the matter. One of Pumzile's relatives, in an attempt to protect her privacy, said something about her being tired. Pumzile refused to allow this obfuscation. She insisted on explicitly stating that she was sick because she had AIDS. She explained that she wanted the young man to understand about AIDS and the risks that he might face. The grandmother told both these stories with pride at her daughter's memorial in the presence of Pumzile's six-year-old son. In this way, he too was encouraged to understand his mother's courage and to see the respect for his mother in the room.

Like Pumzile and her mother, men, too, crossed customary boundaries in public. They could adopt caring roles in public, while they might not take care of women in their own household. Thus, many men have taken leadership roles in organizing for effective treatment. As described in Chapter 3, the Treatment Action Campaign (TAC) was committed to bringing universal access to treatment in South Africa. The TAC is one organization in which men take part in the provision of care. As we shall see below, when we visited the TAC regional office in Durban, a young African man explained the treatment workshops the unit was organizing. He went into great detail about the medications available and his experience as a patient advocate, insisting on the correct medications for opportunistic diseases.

Activists in a rights-based group such as the TAC, involved in community-based support activities, are able to enroll more men than other groups that provide care and support. Possibly, the active political role allows men new or more effective venues to express masculinity in the face of the unemployment and decline in their abilities to maintain responsible household positions.

## Unearthing the Roots of Health Activism

As noted earlier, nearly all of the people trained as volunteer carers were women. They were frequently recruited and minimally trained in religious settings. Such carers also began to participate as health activists or at least to organize what I have labeled adaptive activist groups, meaning the emphasis lay clearly on assisting those in need, rather than transforming the situation.[1] However, such distinctions were not as firmly bounded as they seem at first sight. In each of the groups I have described, the roots of transformative health activism could also be observed.

### Adaptive activism

One common route I observed, which was widespread and might be viewed as adaptive activism rather than transformative, was the development of income-generating activities in relation to support groups. A choir organized by more educated urbanites made a CD to sell. Through its CDs, performances, and connections with wealthy donors, the choir managed to fund treatment for some of its members.

Besides the Bead Workers linked to a hospital, I also observed women involved in small income-generating projects of beading or sewing with no immediate connection to missionaries or health providers. In a few rooms above a grocery store and a fish stand in the center of Durban, I visited women sewing and embroidering clothes to local orders and making bead egg cups, pen holders, and ostriches for the tourist market. Although crafts may not provide an adequate or stable income for a household, they are an important bastion for women in the domestic economy (Nash 1993). And, although the vulnerability of such minimal income-generation projects has been widely documented, the women traveled far in the pursuit of such activities and clearly sought whatever small funds were generated. Such income-generating efforts may not transform the situation for women or for people with AIDS but they are evidence of effective, pro-active strategies that allow women to collectively create spaces of autonomy and possibly even to move towards more sources of collective knowledge, practical sense, and transformative activism.

### Zanele's dreams: transformative activism

Zanele's efforts and insights illustrate the ways in which urban activist women such as she were developing important practical understandings with respect to the epidemic. I would regard Zanele's work around the organization of a children's support group as potentially transformative. It might also be reasonable to regard a leader such as Zanele as an organic intellectual. Through her own practical experience she had generated insights into the perspectives of children of HIV-positive women. She was attempting to put these insights into practice by redefining the stigma and humiliation felt by parents and channeling their concerns into an active solution. She wanted to enlist children in a group that helped them to act in support of themselves and their parents in a straightforward and open way.

Zanele was an active member of the Hope Workers, a group that had been formed by a hospital social worker for people who knew they were HIV positive. She was a bright, talkative, competent woman. As a petite woman, in her Black fashionable clothes, Zanele reminded me of a New York City artist. She was clearly respected among the other women who came to the support group as well as by the hospital administrators.

My research associate and I talked with Zanele over a period of a week about her ideas and I also conducted a long biographical interview with her. She lived in an informal settlement about an hour away. She had received some training as a volunteer carer and, initially, had been given a small amount of supplies in order to voluntarily visit sick people in her neighborhood. She said she always brought food, purchased with her own money, and helped people to wash and take their medications. She shopped for necessities or simply stopped by when no one else did. Although unpaid, Zanele regarded this as her job. She was very proud of her work and described it as a daily obligation.

In spite of what I had interpreted as respect from the local nurses, Zanele mentioned that she did not feel supported in her tasks. Due to budget exigencies, she was no longer even given the little package of supplies that the hospital generally provided for carers. Nevertheless, Zanele seemed committed to continue with her responsibilities and talked of women left alone whom she had visited in the last few days.

It was Zanele who had organized a visit to a woman from the support group when she was not well enough to come to the meetings. A bus had been arranged but it broke down so the support group members had to go by public transportation, which meant that they were two-and-a-half hours late. It was also Zanele who arranged that all the visitors donate some food for the woman they were going to see.

The implications of this visit had been carefully thought about by the support group members. The women pointed out that a visit might create its own contradictions. Support group members might not be welcome if a person had not told their family or neighbors about their status.

Members of the support group also raised and discussed questions of funding for funerals for members as well as their wish that other members attend their funerals. Rituals of death were of major concern to the group and memorials to members, such as the one described earlier in this chapter, were a key feature of meetings.

Zanele and other Hope Workers had thought through and discussed many of the implications of the epidemic and practical strategies to alleviate the tragedy. One of the most painful and crucial issues for the Hope Workers appeared to be telling children about their parent's positive diagnosis and helping the children to plan for the future. This seemed in fact to be one of the most upsetting aspects of their illness for the HIV-positive women. Whenever women talked about their children, their efforts to keep the secret of their illness, and then, often, the maturity and caring their children demonstrated when they found out, the room would fall silent and tears could be seen on many faces.

Zanele was concerned that women who knew they were positive had difficulty telling their children. They were not sure what was the best way to proceed and many believed that the children might be better off if they did not know their mother's diagnosis. Zanele told me that her teenage daughter and other children were often angry at their parents. They could see the symptoms and see other people "pointing fingers" at their mothers. In addition, their friends at school often knew and mocked them. Zanele had kept her secret from her daughter for several years. In fact, it was her daughter who eventually told Zanele that she knew Zanele had AIDS. She was angry that her mother had not told her. Zanele said they had talked about it and she was now feeling better because her daughter knew her status.

As Zanele herself and many others in the group had found through personal experience, the children, as well as other relatives and friends, usually heard about a woman's diagnosis through other sources. In a number of personal accounts women talk about keeping the diagnosis secret and then finding that everyone knew. One woman told a story about waiting a long time for her results in the mail and then discovering that others in her family had opened the letter but not wished to pass it on to her. Another woman hid the letter under the carpet, but later could see that her family knew that she was HIV positive. One woman told a story about her husband who was enraged because she had locked him out when he was drunk. Banging on the front door, he shouted loudly that she had AIDS. This is how her children, age 7, 13, and 17, learned that she had AIDS. She was surprised and happy when she found the children very understanding and she realized that it was the best outcome. In each of these cases, although the relatives had the information, they did not turn against the woman with an HIV diagnosis.

Zanele told me that she wanted to start a child support group for HIV-positive women. This seemed a practical and thoughtful response to something that troubled many of the Hope Workers. As we shall see later, "what children knew" was also a crucial issue for the Bead Workers. However, they did not have the same resources or the same social context to generate a similar practical sense.

Taking into consideration the multiple dilemmas of knowing and not knowing among the children of HIV-positive mothers, Zanele wanted to arrange a group where mothers could discuss how to talk with their children and also bring their children to join a support group. She envisioned this as a safe place where the children of the affected could meet and work out a way to cope with their situations.

A few days after this interview, at a celebratory dinner for some visiting dignitaries, Zanele sat next to me, laughing and joking. She left early saying she had a headache. The next day I heard she was in intensive care with pneumonia.

Although Zanele was a patient at a hospital where treatment was available and where some members of some support groups were on treatment, she could not afford treatment. At this time, early August 2003, the South African government was still disputing the efficacy of anti-retroviral treatment and stressing the risk of toxicity.

It was a shock to me, even though I had been working with people with AIDS for 17 years, that someone who was so knowledgeable, energetic, and helpful to other women in need, and who worked in a hospital on a daily basis, should have no access to treatment. She was not receiving anti-retroviral treatment but only medications for opportunistic diseases. Zanele was still in the hospital when I left South Africa a few weeks later and her plans to set up a children's support group were not yet in effect. However, by 2005, when I returned to the area, a children's support group was in place.

As a young teenager, Zanele's daughter had been a founding member of this children's group. However, over time she had become angry and defiant and eventually became pregnant and left. In 2007, she was raising her child alone and Zanele was back in hospital. I learned that Zanele was finally receiving treatment but, at this point, it seemed that she was in dire condition. Either she had received the treatment too late to be effective, as has frequently been the sad situation in South Africa, or she was not taking her medications regularly. I am not sure of the reasons, but in either case, it was not clear that she was going to recover.

In practical and strategic ways the Hope Workers continually worked to mediate the epidemic in the face of limited resources and little access to known treatments. As an insightful and charismatic grassroots leader, Zanele was able to transform the situation for parents and children even though it probably came too late for both her and her daughter.

## Hope Workers and Bead Workers: Contrasting Perspectives and the Significance of Habitus

The caring efforts, understanding of treatment, and activism among the predominantly urban Hope Workers differed from the predominantly rural-based Bead Workers in a number of significant ways. It is here that I would like to suggest that the surrounding environment, the levels of poverty, the availability of treatment, contact with organic intellectuals and the ideas in circulation shaped the strategies chosen by rural-based versus urban-based women. In contrast to the Bead Workers, among the Hope Workers, treatment was highly sought after and the ability to access free diagnostic tests and medications by joining research projects was widely discussed.

People from the Hope Workers, many of whom were unemployed, worked as volunteers around the hospital where treatment was available to paying patients. I heard women discussing the latest diagnostic tests that were available through a particular research project centered in a hospital building. They were considering the best way to be recruited to the project and receive a free evaluation. Although Hope Workers were not exactly sure what the test was for, it was free and they were under the, possibly mistaken, impression that it might lead to further assistance from the health care providers.

Some of the Hope Workers were actually on anti-retroviral treatment, paid for through foreign donations. A few educated Hope Workers, unemployed but not yet destitute, had formed a choir. Significantly, although the majority of the Hope Workers and most of the singers were women, the main organizers of the choir were men, as was the treasurer. The choir sang in churches and other venues where they collected cash donations. They also sold CDs of their singing to make money. After this choir was invited to the United States, through a combination of missionary zeal and the efforts of medical researchers, they managed to collect enough donations to pay for treatment for about four of the 30 choir members. Hope Workers seemed to be in little doubt that such treatments were effective. In fact, the main source of tension appeared to be around who had actually been selected to receive treatment and why others had not.

Hope Workers were generally well informed about the tests available, the costs for procedures, and the research projects that were looking for subjects and would subsidize certain aspects of AIDS treatment and diagnosis. This knowledge of the science of AIDS among the Hope Workers was in marked contrast to the Bead Workers. While at the hospital, the Bead Workers seemed sharply focused on bead-making as income generation and did not seem to have the time or the connections to be hospital volunteers. In their own communities, many of the Bead Workers worked as volunteer community health educators. However, as we shall see, their knowledge was garnered from missions and government health services; they did not have the same access to ongoing research or to learning about the latest treatments that the Hope Workers enjoyed through their participation in the clinics.

In 2003, none of the Bead Workers had access to anti-retroviral treatment. In fact, treatment did not seem to come into the Bead Workers' conversations or efforts at health education. Of interest here is a quote from a Bead Worker trained as a volunteer carer:

> We train young people how to look after themselves if they are positive – we talk to them about medications – "immune boosters."

In 2003, this is significant because "immune boosters" are not treatment such as anti-retrovirals but rather are substitutions that the South African government was advocating and teaching people about, even as the rollout of anti-retrovirals was being disputed. Another woman talked about the instructions she had received to eat garlic and how she was afraid this change in her diet might have alerted her relatives to the fact that she had AIDS.

Eating well is often cited by people as the advice they get from community health educators. Doubtless everyone should be careful to eat nutritiously and, in the early 1980s, vitamins and nutrition supplements were among the few available suggestions. However, two decades later, after millions of dollars of medical research and the generation of many effective drugs that actually reduce the manifestation of the virus, the stress on multivitamins, garlic, and African potatoes, rather than access to treatment and effective medications, is a particular result of government campaigning to substitute diet for treatment.

For example, on June 30, 2005, the Minister of Health stated:

> Nutrition is the basis of good health and it can stop the progression from HIV to full-blown AIDS, and eating garlic, olive oil, beetroot, and the African potato boosts the immune system to ensure the body is able to defend itself against the virus and live with it.[2]

Thus, bead-meaking women were strategizing with the information they were receiving as community health educators from both the government and the missions. Condoms were not discussed and treatment was not mentioned while nutritional remedies promoted by the Health Minister were recommended and widely practiced.

The Bead Workers seemed to have an even greater and more desperate need for money, and less education than the Hope Workers. As we shall see later, differences between the two groups were also manifest in their accounts of the significance of witchcraft or sorcery in their communities. Understandably, considering their lack of familiarity with treatment, the Bead Workers differed in their understanding or interest with respect to the TAC. I would suggest that it was more difficult, though not impossible, for the framing of transformative action by such organic intellectuals as the TAC to intersect with the strategic perspectives of the rural-based women.

## Transformative Activism

As noted in Chapter 6, transformative activism is used here to describe collective action that aims to change the overall structural constraints people confront. Transformative activism might involve fighting for public access to treatment, sex education, and barrier methods, or adequate education, transportation, and employment. The Treatment Action Campaign is one clear example of such transformative action. Members of the TAC came to talk to the missionary support group in 2003. Many people listened with interest and a few followed through and joined the TAC. One energetic woman became an effective TAC organizer and came back to the support group several times, maintaining contact with many members there.

At the TAC offices in 2003, I met a young man who had started out in that support group, and was now working in the TAC office. He enthusiastically described their current campaign for treatment literacy.[3] The aim was to educate HIV-positive people about the medications they might need and also work with the health care providers to explain what was necessary and help them to find a way to furnish the clinic. He talked in great detail about a campaign to help a local clinic to procure diflucane, a generic medication for thrush (candidiasis). He told me that originally when TAC representatives heard that patients at the clinic had been denied diflucane, they visited the clinic and discovered that the nurses at the clinic not only did not have the medication available but they did not know what it was for. The young man told me that they had developed good relations with the health providers at the clinic, educating them about what was needed. The TAC also campaigned to have diflucane and to advocate for patients who came to the clinic to have access to the drug.

In August, 2003, at a TAC national meeting in Durban, there were representatives from many sectors on the podium: from the unions, from each province, and also from the church. Over 500 people crowded the hall in the center of Durban. Delegates had traveled to the national meeting from all over the country and as hundreds of people filed into the main lobby and down the stairs to the assembly hall, a high level of excitement and enthusiasm was already building.

As with the support groups, rituals of death and paying respect to those who had passed away were a significant aspect of the meeting. Delegates from each province came to the podium and listed the names of TAC members who had died since the last meeting. Such listings gave those present the understanding that they were important as individuals and that the stigma of AIDS had not destroyed their significance as humans deserving of love and respect. In addition, the lists implicitly carried the wounding reminder that, had treatment been available, the people on the lists might still be alive.

I sat next to an African pastor from the Eastern Cape, one of the poorest areas in South Africa. He told me that there was a TAC branch in his rural parish and they had brought in Médecins Sans Frontières, who were distributing AIDS treatment. This branch of MSF, opened in January 2003 at Lusikisiki in the Eastern Cape (see Steinberg 2008), was actually the only branch of MSF outside the urban informal settlements at this time and had only been operating for about six months. Before MSF arrived, this pastor believed that treatments were toxic and killed people, which was, at the time, the government rhetoric (Epstein 2000; Mail & Guardian 2000).

This proper-looking, middle-aged pastor with graying hair and a seriously lined face, wearing a worn black suit, was sitting among the noisy and boisterous young people dressed in "I am Positive" T-shirts and sneakers who made up the majority of people at the TAC meeting. He said to me quietly and with dignity:

> I saw that the people that went for treatment were getting better. I saw that people in our village whom I thought had been on their deathbed came back strong and healthy – that is why I came to this TAC meeting.

The pastor's remarks and his analysis clearly demonstrated the power of practical reason, even in the church. He had traveled hundreds of miles by train to the meeting and would take his message back to the village. Clearly, the symbols and resources of the church can sometimes be powerfully employed in support of "practical sense" and not simply hegemonic "common sense." In effect, this pastor would be returning to his parish as an organic intellectual with transformative potential.

In the rural areas of KwaZulu-Natal, I met a young woman with some education who was training carers for a religious organization. On a part-time salary herself, she was training 100 volunteer carers to visit people through the scattered mountain homesteads. As we drove around the region, she told me that she had attended a TAC meeting in Durban and been amazed. She was going to tell the carers about it at her next monthly training session. She talked of the possibilities for treatment that she had not realized were there and was committed to bringing the message of possible survival to the volunteer care-providers in the mountains. Thus, even in the most remote areas, participating in "caring" training and activities can come to be quickly associated with the search for more politically transformative approaches.

Nevertheless, the Treatment Action Campaign was not always so easily accepted, especially among groups with little experience of treatment. Among the Bead Workers, where almost no one was on treatment, there seemed little support for the TAC. When TAC representatives came to talk to them, they barely looked up from their work and voiced resentment that they were losing money by paying attention to the speakers.

As noted earlier, in a world of destitution in both the rural and the urban areas, where most work, including caring for the sick, was done for no pay, such small income as was generated from selling beads or sewing clothes was highly prized. However, perhaps the resentment toward the TAC among the Bead Workers was fueled by their disbelief or doubts in the effectiveness of treatment. As described above, the Hope Workers, in constant interaction with hospital administrators, health care personnel, and researchers, and through their own observations, under-stood that treatment worked. Bead Workers, without this counteracting dynamic, were more susceptible to the doubts widely promulgated by the South African government and many of the popular media that it was actually the Western drugs and not the AIDS virus that was killing people (McGregor 2007; Specter 2007).

## Questions of Criminality, Sorcery, and Youth:
## Red versus School

Lack of knowledge about treatment not only opened the way to a resentment or disbelief about the TAC but also widened the scope for accusations of witchcraft. Accusations of sorcery and witchcraft are often associated in common parlance with "tradition." However, as noted earlier, the Comaroffs have convincingly found associations between notions of witchcraft and millennial capitalism (Comaroff and Comaroff 2001a). Discussions of witchcraft were not absent among the Bead Workers or Hope Workers, but they were not spoken about with credibility, at least in these public meetings. Nevertheless, women talked of witchcraft accompanied by fear of sorcery. Reliance on traditional healers was also common.

In one case, a Bead Worker, Promise, talked about young boys whose parents had died of AIDS:

> There are lots of children whose parents have died. The problem is that the children think that their parents have been killed by neighbors (by witchcraft) and we don't know how to help them. In one family, both the husband and wife and their son and daughter-in-law died and there are children (boys) who are left and are involved in criminal activities. They believe their parents were killed and are wild. The community views them as criminals and do not like them.

Promise tied this account directly to the need for adequate information about AIDS in the rural areas.

In another family, a beading woman said: "One brother was sick and the other used to take him to traditional healers. The community thinks he got infected through the ritual of cutting and putting medicine on each other. They both died." Among the Hope Workers, a woman told a story about her husband who collapsed on his way home and attributed it to sorcery against him. Later, when he was diagnosed with AIDS, he believed the witchcraft made him vulnerable to AIDS.

Clearly, narratives of witchcraft carry some weight. They rise to the forefront for explanation in the saddest and most destitute situations, such as when children find themselves all alone with no source of parental support or economic resources, or when, in the absence of adequate local clinics or any form of treatment, desperate people seek traditional healers. However, these explanations are not widely accepted as people begin to understand that there are alternatives. As one of the Bead women said with asperity in response to a narrative of witchcraft:

> Why is treatment not available to people? I think that people from the rural areas still need education and to be given the opportunity to speak for themselves.

Perhaps participating with the Bead Workers had given this woman a sense of possibility. She clearly perceived a link between lack of realistic choices and the pervasive power of "traditional" approaches. We see here the beginnings of an opening for appreciation of the transformative demands of the Treatment Action Coalition.

## Civic Issues: Women's Burdens of Transportation and Water

Much of the labor and cost of caring, predominantly assigned to the women, is compounded also by policy decisions about infrastructure with respect to such needs as transportation and water. Since 1996, as noted in earlier chapters, sufficient funding for primary care or medications is not yet available and hospital care has also been receiving less funding. As a consequence, in the search for treatment and care for AIDS, people have to travel long distances. Thus the need for public services such as transportation has become greater in the face of the epidemic and the costs of caring and replacing services have increased (Thomas 2003).

While the new South African government has invested heavily in the trans-Kalahari highway and in other new motorways and bridges, there has not been a corresponding investment in affordable public transportation, municipal buses, and local trains. The cost of local transportation falls dramatically on the backs of women care-providers. In fact, it has been estimated that transportation expenses account for 40 percent of the cost of home-based care (Abdool Karim and Frolich 2000). Both transportation issues and water have been the focus of public activists in the new South Africa, but although, as we see below, the issues are crucial for people with AIDS, the women whom we observed were not directly involved in the widespread activism about these issues. In fact, in spite of the widespread protests with respect to such infrastructural issues common in South Africa (Desai 2002), there has been little coordination. Possibly for politically strategic reasons, including different relations with the African National Congress, the demands of the leaders of the TAC and the leaders of such organizations of the "poors" (Desai 2002) have not been linked. While the TAC continues to claim and demonstrate a strong allegiance to its early roots in the ANC, the movements of the "poors" are much more direct and unyielding in their attacks on government policy. Thus the clear connections between general infrastructural needs and the problems of AIDS are seldom linked in public discourse.

## Transportation

Transportation issues hamper both rural and urban poor and were raised by both Bead Workers and Hope Workers. One Bead Worker who was trained by a government program as a volunteer "community health educator" in the rural midlands (outside Durban) commented: "transport is usually a problem for me to reach out to a lot of people. I don't work and therefore cannot reach out to a big area . . . houses in the area are scattered." Similarly, Hope Workers faced transportation problems in visiting their own members when they were not well enough to travel to meetings.

On one occasion, I observed a woman with AIDS, a member of a clinic support group, who had walked five miles up and down hills, carrying a hefty five-month-old boy, in search of cheaper infant formula. Although she managed to get two cans of formula, it turned out that the warehouse was low on formula and awaiting a new delivery and she had to return a month later to pick up the rest of her allowance.

Group taxis are available all over South African cities. If a person is well enough, they can walk to one of the recognized stops and wait for a usually crowded van to stop. If the rider can squeeze into a corner of a seat and pay a few rand (maybe 50 US cents), the group taxi will take them to other designated stops along the route. However, the vans follow prescribed routes and tend to bypass the informal settlements or poorer townships. If a person is too sick to walk to one of the main stopping places or to sit upright in a crowded van, individual rides have to be arranged. It is here that the cost of transportation adds dramatically to the labor of caring. Taxis almost never drive past individual homes in the informal settlements and certainly not in the rural areas. Home care-providers, especially in the rural areas, walk many miles each day to visit the sick. However, if the sick person needs medical attention, the cost of transportation can be extraordinary.

In July 2003, in interviews in a rural area in the Drakensberg Mountains, I met a woman who was trained as a care volunteer by a church organization. She talked about visiting many incapacitated people in the surrounding area. She pointed to the small houses below her homestead on the slopes of a hill and enumerated people whom she visited and people who had died. She, too, worked for no pay. Transportation to visit other homesteads was difficult and time consuming and people who worked as carers might walk around for many miles. Just as in the rural areas and informal settlements around Durban, one of her great expenses and problems was traveling to a municipal center in order to help people to register for assistance grants. She said, sometimes these were not forthcoming from the bureaucracy until after the grantee had passed away.

Over and over again, we heard descriptions of the cost of taxis or rides to bring sick people to hospital. From the townships just outside Durban to the hospitals that provide treatment, one round trip might cost 300 rand (about $50). This is before any costs are incurred for testing, visits, medications for opportunistic diseases, or, in 2003, the practically unattainable treatment. On one occasion the family of a woman with AIDS finally collected the funds for a taxi to pick her up at home. The patient was not seen by a doctor that day, but was asked to come back for further tests. The next visit, a few days later, she was so sick, she died en route, in the taxi. The family then had to find money to bury her. Most of the costs and the labor of transportation are borne by the sick person and the women care-providers.

## Water

Ironically, as a consequence of important changes in access to clean water, caring also costs money in new ways today. As a result of a government initiative to provide clean water to the rural areas and the informal settlements, water is in the process of being privatized. The old communal faucets provide free water. The more convenient water, piped to or near the houses is rationed and any use above a minimum (estimated by Patrick Bond (2006) as two toilet flushes) must be paid for. Carers must choose between using up the ration of pre-paid water and the extra labor of going to the village faucet and collecting the water. Once the pre-paid ration is used

**Figure 7.1**   Women and children in the Drakensberg Mountains fetch water from a free faucet, 2003 (© Ida Susser)

up, there is no alternative to the long walk for water and sometimes no alternative but the polluted river water of pre-improvement days.

In 2003 in the rural areas, I spoke with three young men washing their van in a shallow inlet. They explained that they did not want to use the water at home because of the rationing and this seemed entirely environmentally appropriate. However, I also saw many women collecting water, sometimes pushing wheel barrows full of plastic bottles up the hot dusty hills, and children, sent to collect water, playing with their containers around a public faucet.

So, as the state privatizes water and does not invest sufficiently in public transportation, the costs fall disproportionately on the sick and the care-providers, whether related women or community volunteers. In 1992, the same women who came to meetings about AIDS had also organized to demand community water taps in the informal settlements. Over the past decade, poor people have mobilized to demand both water and transportation facilities. However, women still have to struggle with many of these structural barriers in order to work as urban or rural carers or health activists.

## Conclusions

Today, women have the space to speak out in public. Some women are gaining access to schools, to employment, and even to political and religious leadership. In 1999, Gugli Dlameini announced that she was HIV positive and was stoned to death in her Durban township (Albertyn and Hassim 2003). But she did not die in vain. Since that tragic event, many women have joined People With AIDS groups and the Treatment Action Campaign and become open about their HIV status.

But, as noted in previous chapters, women are still subject to violence in private and sometimes in public as well. As a reflection of growing gendered hostility, lesbian women have become a particular target of public violence in recent years. For example, on Sunday July 8, 2007, Sizakele Sigasa, an outreach coordinator for the Positive Women's Network and a lesbian and gay rights activist, and her friend Salome Masooa were tortured and murdered. The Positive Women's Network arranged a memorial, supported by the TAC and many organizations around the world.[4]

There is much to suggest that as poor men have lost their early foothold in wage labor and women have not found such work, the division of labor and, specifically, gendered patterns of caring have hardened (Hunter 2005). This gendered division of labor in the household, policed and exacerbated by violence, has emerged from long-term practices and beliefs combined with problematic characteristics of the current era. The increase in private brutality, from rape in the streets to violence in the home, has narrowed the strategies available to women for negotiating around burdens of care in the household or for sexual protection.

As we saw in Chapter 6, it would be mistaken to assume that customary law restricted and constrained women while the new constitution liberated them. As might be expected, the picture is murkier. Women did find spaces of autonomy and political influence under customary law. In some ways, perhaps in the domestic and even sexual arena, customary law may have offered autonomous women a limited form of shelter. Nevertheless, at this point, emphasizing customary law, which has become deeply enmeshed with the patriarchal assumptions of Western colonialism, only weakens women's position. As land reform and rights are hotly contested and customary law continues to find its way to Constitutional Courts, the potential impact on women is shrouded in uncertainty. The 2005 *Bhe* decision, which ruled in favor of two girls who were denied inheritance of their father's estate at his death because of customary law, marked a significant victory for women's inheritance rights.[5] But, as other patriarchal customs are contested, the outcome may very well push women back under the domination of colonially shaped "traditional" authorities.

Unfortunately, laws establishing women's new constitutional rights have proved easier to implement in the public sphere and slow to be enforced in the domestic or extended family environment. Thus, we get the difficult situation where women may have little autonomy with respect to important HIV related rights such as sexuality. In the light of their new constitutional visibility, they are well represented in government, they are able to look for work and speak out in public more easily than before, but they may be subject to greater violence in their own homes.

In fact, the history of Western law involves a focus mainly on contract law for private property and the market. Constitutional law in most parts of the world has not been very successful in protecting women in the domestic sphere. Such issues are currently much contested in the battle for negotiation of household tasks, caring, and safe sex for women (Jewkes et al. 2002; Park et al. 2000). In this respect, shifts in global decisions and funding for women's reproductive and sexual rights, discussed in Chapters 1 and 2, become particularly significant for the negotiation of AIDS prevention, treatment, and care.

In terms of care for AIDS, the domestic burden on women remains heavy, but, as in the history of HIV in general, the most optimistic picture can be found in the health activism that has resulted in the possibility of universal access to treatment and in the implementation of government programs which take the burden of care into account.

As we have seen, in comparing the Bead Workers and the Hope Workers, the South African government's focus on the toxicity of anti-retroviral treatment and the centrality of nutrition has been accepted much more widely in the rural areas and among women without direct experience of the success of treatment. This campaign of misinformation may have discouraged Bead Workers from listening to the possibilities outlined by health activists. In addition, engendering as it did a hopelessness about the disease and a fear of treatment, the government's stand may also have contributed to images of witchcraft and sorcery among those affected.

Nevertheless, since 1992, women's demands for jobs as community health workers, protection from violence, inheritance rights, and AIDS treatment represent battles for democracy in the face of governmental participation in neoliberal global processes. Women's and men's demands for practical interventions have been echoed by organic intellectuals such as Zanele and the Lusikisiki pastor as well as by the TAC in general and the organizers of the "poors." However, the battle for treatment in its strategic success has also not yet addressed the myriad issues affecting the women at the grass roots. A transformative movement that took into account the overall impact of the neoliberal policies whose most tragic consequence has been the exacerbation of a disastrous epidemic has not yet emerged. The gendered conflict precipitated by neoliberal policies discussed in Chapter 6 may in fact undermine the success of the treatment action, as more women and men will become infected with the virus, unless a reframing of the broader issues emerges.

# 8

# "Where Are Our Condoms?" –
# Namibia

This chapter examines the interaction between the ongoing practical evaluations by local women and the significant voicing of counter-hegemonic good sense by organic leadership. In this instance, the leadership that supported the female condom emerged from cooperation between a women's development organization and a rainbow coalition of lesbian, gay, bisexual, and transgender groups, which counteracted the subordination of women as well as moral condemnation of the disease and the stigma attached to sexual orientation.

We turn to Namibia, where the AIDS epidemic has had a similar trajectory to South Africa. Since 1996, AIDS rates in the country have approached the highest in the world. By the end of 2003, 21.3 percent of adults in Namibia were estimated to be living with HIV, on par with South Africa's 21.5 percent (UNAIDS 2004:191). In Namibia, we find again, women, including active churchgoers, manifesting practical sense about condoms and AIDS. We see women's efforts to give their children practical advice in the face of contradictory messages sometimes promoted by institutionalized religion. Next, we see the emergence of a concerted demand for the female condom. I trace the efforts of NGOs and grassroots women in mobilizing the media and other groups to insist that government agencies make the female condom available and affordable. Finally, I analyze the results of these demands and consider both the partial successes and the unmet challenges.

In 1996, when I first went to Namibia with Richard Lee to initiate an AIDS training and research project, both the knowledge and the wish to implement preventive strategies were evident.[1] Just as in South Africa in the early 1990s, women from many walks of life appeared articulate, informed, and worried about AIDS. However, in spite of their knowledge and concern, there were many barriers to women's efforts at prevention. Therefore, we must consider and document the multiple other problems that women face in combating the epidemic. I proceed somewhat chronologically in this discussion in order to dispel any myths about local women's misunderstanding and complicate a simple emphasis on the need for education.

The first most striking point to me on rereading our notes from my first trip to Namibia, in July 1996, is the disjuncture between what the local women knew about AIDS and what the religious and administrative authorities were doing about AIDS. The second striking point, which emerges over the ten-year period in which I returned to Namibia for some weeks nearly every year, is the disjuncture between the strategies for which women were asking, such as the female condom, and the resources provided.


## Mapping Namibia


In reviewing the following narrative, we need to stress that Namibia represents a large landmass but a much smaller population than South Africa. Namibia is home to less than two million people while more than 45 million people live in South Africa. Windhoek, the capital, is the only large city, and the economy still relies largely on extractive industries in tin and diamonds, established under colonialism. After World War I, previously German territory became the British protectorate of South West Africa. Later, the region was occupied by the apartheid South African regime that used South West Africa as a military buffer from the rest of Africa. The South African army was eventually forced out by the guerilla army of the South West Africa People's Organization (SWAPO). In 1988, Namibia became independent, governed by SWAPO.

As in South Africa, war was a major factor in the spread and understanding of AIDS in Namibia as many young guerilla recruits had spent the 1980s in Angola. In fact, as in South Africa, we found returning SWAPO fighters were more aware and knowledgeable about AIDS than the resident population. As in South Africa, AIDS appeared just as the new African nation was establishing itself. Although denialism was not prevalent in public discussion in Namibia, treatment was hardly available until 2003. Nevirapine was rarely administered to women in childbirth until about the same time. In the 1990s, although the health department was conducting research on condom use and other such factors, there was not yet an active prevention program.

In discussions with people close to the administration in 2002, I frequently heard doubts expressed about the existence of the HIV virus. Although many local health professionals were highly informed about the disease, in informal conversations, some people wondered whether African AIDS might be different than the Western disease. There was also some speculation that perhaps health professionals from the US might be stressing problems that were not relevant to Namibia. However, as we shall see, the public discourse around AIDS and women's issues did not take on the same combative tones about African masculinity as in South Africa. Other issues, such as unemployment among men who had migrated in search of work, seemed more politically significant in the stigmatization of groups with the disease.

Nevertheless, as in South Africa and in the United States, in understanding AIDS in Namibia, the contrasts between "common" and "practical" sense in the discussions of the disease become crucial. We see women at the grass roots and community organizations concerned with the rights of women and sexual orientation fighting against a hegemonic construction of morality and sin with respect to the disease. We see these groups take up this struggle to implement the practical preventive options such as the female condom for which local women were asking.

The Ovambo and the Kavango peoples discussed in this chapter had been largely horticultural societies and many residents of their homesteads were still involved in collective cultivation of cash crops. The Herero, also historical residents of South West Africa, were massacred and forced into neighboring territories by the Germans in the early twentieth century. We will meet the Herero, a cattle-complex society similar to the Zulu and the Xhosa of South Africa, and still intimately involved in cattle raising, in the next two chapters. Many Herero returned from Botswana to Namibia in 1996 to live with their cattle in the Kalahari alongside the San, historically a hunting-and-gathering society.

## Religious Controversy, Condoms, and AIDS in Ovamboland

The largest concentration of population in Namibia is in the northern Ovambo region. Here, increasing density of settlement, paralleling the government's investment in many miles of water pipeline along the straight road north, has combined with goat and cattle grazing to render the area arid, dusty, and devoid of grass.

Buses bring migrant workers home weekly to this region of dirt roads, crowded, lively markets, and Kuka shops (makeshift bars). Isolated Ovambo homesteads were constructed some distance off the main roads, made up of small huts of clay, corrugated iron or other materials, enclosed by mud walls, and surrounded by fields. Most cultivated cassava, a crop with arguably the lowest level of useful nutrients of all staples. Such homesteads usually housed an extended family including grown children, teenagers, infants, and boarders who might be staying there to help with the fields.

In 1996, Richard Lee, a pre-eminent researcher of the Kalahari San, fluent in the Ju language, and I began a long-term project of AIDS research and training in affiliation with the University of Namibia and the University of Botswana in Garborone, funded through Columbia University's HIV Center and the Fogarty Foundation.[2] We were accompanied in the initial research by two Ovambo research assistants, Pombili Ipinge and Karen Nashaya, undergraduates whom we recruited from the sociology department at the University of Namibia. In our first research endeavor, we drove up north to Ovamboland to interview nurses, doctors, community outreach workers, church officials, and local people about AIDS.

In the course of this first investigation, we visited many people in their home-steads and talked with the women at home. The women we interviewed in some of the relatively prosperous homesteads were all churchgoing and sent their children to the mission school. One of them even had a son at the university. We also talked with the grandmother of a college student, who sold fruit at a vibrant, populous roadside market. She sat all day among stalls selling bananas, mangoes, dried meat, cloth, and nuts. Later, we talked with men and women who lived in the poorer area composed of many single shacks, whom we found refreshingly out-spoken and less connected to institutional religion than the more established homesteads.

Karen and I visited two friendly and concerned women in their extended family homestead. As we talked, they prepared food and homemade beer in the open area that served as a kitchen. They offered us two different kinds of beer, one non-alco-holic for the children, in large gourds, extracting the thick white bubbly liquid with large wooden spoons. The two women were sisters, both graceful, dressed in long straight skirts. Kerchiefs covered their hair as they knelt at work on the mud floor of the kitchen.

The younger sister seemed in her thirties and the older was probably in her forties. The older sister was married to a man who lived most of the year in a dif-ferent town where he worked in the civil service. They had three sons and two daughters, aged between 14 and 28. The other sister had three lively younger chil-dren, who played around our feet and climbed on the small tree in the compound as we conversed in the hot sun.

They said they had heard about AIDS in 1992–93. One sister said that at that time, "Everyone started talking about AIDS. Two people started dying and they started suspecting they might have it. Now everyone knows about it – and you can tell who has it in the hospital."

They were churchgoing women and worked with the disabled as church volun-teers. The other sister said, "We started working with disabled people, and later there were some nurses and they brought up the issue of AIDS. Just this Sunday, some nurses were telling us how AIDS is spread and how to protect ourselves." The older sister remarked anxiously, "We are really scared and really sure AIDS is a deadly disease."

I then told the women that the local pastor, who we had interviewed extensively the day before, doubted if people believed that AIDS was a disease. The older woman answered, "People really know that there is AIDS . . . Men say 'the thing that will take me out of this world is AIDS.' Men keep mistresses but they know." She continued, "No, people don't say it's witchcraft. They prefer to go to the hos-pital when it gets worse. They feel better. They are served all their meals and nobody says they won't cook for you."

At this time, however, with no treatment available in the public clinics in Namibia, the overburdened hospitals were not keeping people very long, but rather sending them home to die. The younger sister told a story about a local man who found out that he was HIV positive.

He told his girlfriend and then when he got sick he wrote a letter to the whole church that he was dying, and they should pray for him. Everyone knew he had AIDS. He also told another girlfriend he had.

She added, approvingly:

After he got the test, he told his girlfriend and went back to the hospital. He did not spread AIDS further. He's dead now.

She went on:

Girlfriends usually disappear when they find they were with men who have AIDS. This girlfriend had one miscarriage and her second baby only lived 11 or 12 months. When his girlfriend got pregnant and had a baby, the man was getting weak. That might have been the reason he went for the test. He went for the test and while he was waiting for the results, the baby died . . . There was another girlfriend and people thought he was bewitched by a jealous girlfriend. Maybe he also thought he was bewitched, but after counseling he sent the letter to the church . . . When he sent the letter he didn't mention AIDS, he said he had the "disease that has got no cure." He asked people to forgive him his sins and he wanted to warn people.

I was told that four people in the little village had already died of AIDS, "older people with houses," and also a fifth, a young teenage girl. The young girl had one child who was still healthy. The women noted that all the families were good to the young people with AIDS. The whole extended household knew and everybody talked about it. They mentioned that older people who died had already nursed their young people until they passed away.

Later, the younger sister remarked:

Older people can't trust each other . . . When the husband goes away to work, the wife stays home waiting. But the husband has 20 to 50 mistresses when he's away. If he has a car, he goes to Kuka shops . . . There he might find 20 mistresses and he goes to town – another 20 women. When he comes back, he gives the wife AIDS.

On a later trip to Namibia in 2003, I heard that the younger sister who told this story had died of AIDS. I thought of all the things she had told me and wondered if she had known. I looked over my notes and found she had said:

People are scared, maybe they think they should go for the test . . . They don't want to know how many days they have left, maybe a week, a month. [She also said,] When the disease comes, they don't hate the person. The person is sick and they just have to care for the person. They are frightened, thinking, what stage might I be at; it might happen to me.

As I was leaving the homestead of the two sisters, I looked inside a small corrugated tin hut, the bedroom of one of the teenage sons. I saw a roll of condoms on

**Figure 8.1**   Ovambo-speaking women, in the kitchen area of their homestead prepare a meal with local produce and homemade wooden utensils. In homesteads like these, with many different clay huts, we observed condoms at the bedsides of teenage boys, 1996 (© Ida Susser)

the little table at his bedside. His older brother told me that his mother had recommended them to her sons.

The obvious point here is that, although they might have become infected before they knew about AIDS, by 1996 people were not dying in ignorance. If people in the rural areas were this well-informed more than ten years ago, then it is hard to believe that anyone today, except perhaps the youth, become infected because of lack of understanding of the modes of transmission of AIDS.

In 1996, the week we arrived in Windhoek, *The Namibian*, the main national newspaper, announced that an executive secretary of the president was sick with AIDS. At a hospital in northern Namibia, it was said that the prime minister's son, his daughter-in-law, and other relatives of prominent members of the administration were being tended for AIDS. If AIDS was a secret, everyone knew about it.

However, interviews with the pastors and hospital counselors began to give us a better sense of the secrecy surrounding the disease. The day before we met with the women interviewed above, we had met with their Lutheran pastor, who was responsible for the Lutheran school and also linked to the main hospital, also Lutheran. While the main funding for the mission at this time appeared to come from Finland, this African pastor was trained in a more fundamentalist tradition in Utah.

Our constrained and opaque conversation with Pastor L. contrasted sharply with the direct and straightforward discussion we had later with the two sisters and other conversations with neighboring women. I was accompanied in the interview with the pastor by Richard Lee and our Ovambo-speaking student assistants Karen Nashaya and Pombili Ipinge.

The pastor was clearly informed about AIDS. At first one might get the impression that he was concerned to educate his parishioners. He told us that the church had started an AIDS counseling program:

> There are many cases all through Northern Namibia. It is related to suicide cases. [We were told about suicide by many people.]

However, he then went on to say:

> AIDS is not public. Statistics are only known by medical personnel. They are not known by anyone else. People say they died of diarrhea, TB, and other things. That is why people are on the one hand not scared about it . . . It's hard to tell or say that a person died of AIDS. The church makes no public announcements . . . You'll never know if someone died of AIDS. Maybe there will be a rumor after they die . . . One will never find out what the person died of.

The pastor followed up by saying: "We don't discuss AIDS in the church because there is no evidence that anyone died of AIDS." In terms of prevention and condoms, the pastor said: "Our church does not support the case that condoms can be used, especially by unmarried people."

In fact, as we shall see below, the Finnish Lutherans who funded the Namibian Lutheran Church require no such restrictions. But, this pastor had been back two years from his training in Utah. He continued:

> Our rules are based on the issue of a woman and a man getting married. If you give people a condom, it's as if you get rid of the principle and . . . give freedom for people to run around.

He then proceeded to list a number of practical problems he perceived about the condom:

> Condoms are not easily available . . . Namibia is a very hot place. People don't have proper houses and condoms are exposed to the sun and destroyed.

Finally, the pastor quoted the common saying:

> A condom is like eating a sweet with the paper on, tasteless . . . It's very difficult to use condoms . . . Condoms are too expensive. Most people dying of AIDS are illiterate, poor, and less fortunate ones who have no means of acquiring condoms.

Male condoms were actually available at subsidized prices at every supermarket. In addition, AIDS in Namibia, as we have seen, was certainly not confined to the poor and destitute, and, as the reader is probably aware, the claim that condoms might disintegrate in the sun has not prevented their effective use in most parts of the world.

Although these particular arguments may appear a little scattershot, the outcome of these views and church policies was that the main regional hospital, which happened to be Lutheran, did not educate people about AIDS or provide condoms. In addition, when we talked with the AIDS counselors at the public hospital, they told us that the government program to distribute condoms had been delayed on both the local and national level in response to such religious institutional objections.

After we had this interview with the pastor, we all drove to a hot, dust-swept homestead at the periphery of the mission school. Three women invited us in to a cool mud shelter in the back to talk with them, their teenage daughters, carrying babies, and a number of younger children.

Again, I was impressed at their openness about sex and AIDS and the general information the women discussed. We were happy the women were willing to talk to us and I noticed with interest that they did not censor their conversation in front of the younger children, who were running in and out. As the conversation progressed, the women enthusiastically called in several neighbors to meet us and eventually five adult women and a number of teenagers and infants were talking with us. People seemed to welcome the opportunity to discuss AIDS and sexuality. In spite of our vigorous disclaimers, they probably hoped that we might have some way to help them to stem the epidemic.

We began the discussion by simply asking what the major public health problems and diseases in the area were. The first woman answered, without hesitation:

> AIDS is a major health problem, and TB . . . People are very open that there is AIDS and they talk about it. They are not hiding it anymore because they know people are getting it . . . We know people who have AIDS and we talk to them.

The women then proceeded to discuss numerous issues, including how to take care of someone with AIDS, and concerns about their daughters becoming sexually active or raped at school and contracting AIDS. Later the women told us, "Although it was not acceptable in the past for people to talk about sex-related issues, now we have seen people who have died of AIDS. It is visible now and people are open about it."

One woman even said, "Men are more open now about having a mistress. At meetings or when people are drinking they talk about funerals and 'this modern disease.'" Like the two sisters described earlier, and clearly contradicting the perceptions of the pastor, the women said, "Now people believe there really is a disease."

In terms of the church, the women at this neighboring homestead, whose children attended the mission school, said explicitly, and with resentment:

> Women's organizations are influenced by churches because the heads there are mostly pastors' wives. They are opposed to condoms and have the notion of "no sex before marriage." . . . Pastors and church leaders like protecting their children and giving them condoms and birth control while for the others they tell them not to use condoms. They have to say that to keep their status as church leaders.

At the end of our lively discussions with the five women at the homestead, Pombili, our Ovambo research assistant, suggested that I bring out the female condom and the large picture book I carried that described how the female condom could be used. Pombili handed the female condom around for the women to examine and proceeded to use the book to explain how to use it. Pombili, who was from the area, had no compunction in talking about these issues with the women, and the women did not seem the least bit embarrassed by this conversation.

The women were extremely enthusiastic about the idea of a condom women could use and called their friends over to show them the pictures. Then, as had happened in South Africa in 1995, they said to us, "Women here in Namibia are too vulnerable . . . Go to the ministry and tell them to order female condoms. The ministry has to see for itself. Maybe it's better if you have a report and write them a letter." They explained: "The president talks about condoms. Most of the leaders have been in exile and local people say they have brought immorality."

Then, proceeding to demonstrate a public shift to practical sense in the face of the epidemic, the women said, "People who were outspoken [about sex] were regarded as immoral. Now, it's openly talked about because of AIDS."

A few days later, at an interview at the Rehabilitation Center of the Lutheran Hospital, we met a visiting Finnish woman doctor sent to Namibia by the Finnish Lutheran Church that funded the hospital. We were told that there were two Finnish doctors who were conducting an AIDS education program at the hospital. The doctors had organized several workshops on AIDS to teach pastors how to care for people with AIDS as well as how to use condoms. The counselor in the Rehabilitation Center told us: "People around this area understand that pastors don't like condoms." However, she said that, "the hospital can get free condoms to distribute along with pamphlets," but that this was not much available to the public. In addition, she said, there was supposed to be 15 minutes devoted to AIDS education at Sunday services. Finally, the rehabilitation counselor said: "The church leaders have to understand reality. The condom does not give people a green light for sex."

As this brief outline demonstrates, the resources and training provided by institutional religion wield major influence in poor settings in southern Africa. This is particularly the case in rural areas where scarce alternative sources of care and information may be many miles away. Again, as we have seen in South Africa, the influence of religious resources was not solely in one direction. The Finnish Lutheran Foundation was going to some effort to provide AIDS education. However, the pastor we interviewed, trained in a fundamentalist environment in the US, reflected some of the significant constraining influences of religion in Namibia. In 1996, in spite of the efforts of Finnish doctors, condoms were not available at the Lutheran hospitals.

Many of the barriers to local women's efforts to protect their communities from AIDS were clear in the limits set by the lack of investment in treatment or even male and female condoms on the part of the government, the multiple strictures of the church, and, finally, their men partners.

**Figure 8.2**   In a sewing cooperative in Rundu, Namibia, women examine a publication explaining the use of the female condom, 1997 (© Ida Susser)

## Rundu 1997: Bring Us the Female Condom!

In 1997, we visited Rundu, a small town along the Okavango River, which forms the border between Namibia and Angola. On the banks of the river we saw hippopotami and crocodiles and we were so close to Angola that we could see the thatched wooden huts and people sitting around open fires across the river. At the time, the region was peaceful and the town was geared to attract ecotourism, although we saw few people in the enormous wooden lodges tastefully constructed for this purpose. A few years later, we were warned that the war in the Congo had spread to this area and that it was not safe to travel along these same border roads.

I went with Karen Brodkin, an anthropology colleague from the US, to seek out a women's sewing cooperative about which we had heard. We found a large shop with colorful clothes of all sorts displayed in the window and about 20 women sitting at sewing machines in the back. When we brought up the topic of AIDS the women seemed informed but uninterested. They had heard much about the disease and did not ask us any questions. However, when we mentioned the female condom, the women's faces lit up. They asked us to bring some to the shop and show them how to use them. Suddenly, it seemed to them, there might be a way out of the endless dilemmas of AIDS prevention that had worn them down. As in South Africa in 1992 and 1995, and the Ovambo homesteads we visited in 1996, the Kavango women were so enthusiastic about the prospect of women-controlled barrier methods that they wanted to write to the Minister of Health.

## "Where Are Our Condoms?" – Changing the Public Discourse

In light of the high level of interest and desperate need for preventive strategies in the face of AIDS, one might have expected that the governments of southern Africa or the United Nations agencies or the World Health Organization would immediately introduce female condoms, just as they had male condoms at the start of the epidemic. However, in line with the contested reactions to AIDS prevention discussed here, responses were far less clear.

In July 1999, I organized a small shipment of female condoms to be mailed to Windhoek for use as demonstration materials in our AIDS Research Training Course at the University of Namibia. The package was stopped by customs at the airport. In the process of trying to get the package released, I met with a woman doctor from the World Health Organization and a woman representative of UNAIDS in Namibia. Both women told me that they had tried to introduce the female condom in Namibia but that the Ministry of Health had not been interested. The understanding I gleaned from these conversations and the failed efforts to get the package released from the airport was that the Ministry of Health did not want to supply female condoms. Although UNAIDS at that time was in a position to supply 10,000 female condoms without cost, these female representatives explained that the government was concerned about the expense that might be incurred if women in Namibia were to demand female condoms more generally.

However, later in the same month, July 1999, but not directly related to our course, women associated with two non-governmental organizations in Namibia began to publicly demand the female condom. As we shall see, as a result of the outcry that was generated over the next year, the female condom became available to people throughout the country.

At a meeting in Mahenene in the Omusati region of northern Namibia on July 20, 1999, Veronica de Klerk, the leader of Women's Action for Development (WAD), began to demand publicly that the female condom be made available to Namibian women. According to de Klerk:

> ... in the presence of health authorities, decision-makers, community leaders, traditional authorities etc. ... [WAD] boldly pioneered the introduction of the female condom and opened the debate on the free distribution of free female condoms by the Ministry of Health (de Klerk 2001).

WAD, a Namibian NGO focused on women's social and economic self-help, was funded by the Konrad-Adenauer-Stiftung Foundation in Germany. This foundation had funded similar projects in Zimbabwe and other parts of the world and formed WAD in Namibia in 1994. Veronica de Klerk was born in Namibia and had worked through WAD to develop economic status and political voices for rural Namibian women. WAD had initiated a number of successful sewing cooperatives and agrarian training projects and was particularly committed to helping women form savings clubs to finance their future activities. Relevant to this case study was the emphasis in WAD on training women to lobby for political influence. WAD elected women as "Women's Voices" in each region to lobby for the needs of women in that area. When the cause of the female condom was adopted by WAD, these "Women's Voices" led the public outcry in each region.

Also significant were the close links between WAD and the Namibian government. President Sam Nujoma contributed a preface to the 1999 edition of the WAD booklet and, as will be discussed below, when the female condom was finally launched by the Namibian government, Veronica de Klerk was invited to speak.

In August 1999, a few days before an official "National Condom Use Day" scheduled by the Ministry of Health, de Klerk was quoted in *The Namibian* under the headline, "'Where are our condoms?' asks women's group: Women's Action for Development says the National Condom Use Day declared by the Ministry of Health and Social Services violates women's rights by making only male condoms available" (Maletsky 1999).

According to de Klerk, WAD, using its regional links in the northern rural areas, followed its announcements with a march and demonstrations among its member groups. WAD demanded the government make "female condoms available to women, free of charge, as was the case with male condoms" (de Klerk 2001).

On September 15, 1999, the Permanent Secretary of Health and Social Services Dr. Kalumbi Shangula announced that a second National Condom Use Day was being planned and that it would include the woman's condom. The Ministry of Health then assigned the problem of the woman's condom to the Ministry of Women Affairs and Child Welfare. By July 2000, the Namibian government had formed a Technical Working Group, under the administration of the Ministry of Women Affairs and Child Welfare, and the female condom had been placed under its jurisdiction. The Technical Working Group included representatives of the Ministries of Health as well as Women Affairs, UNAIDS, WAD, the Okutumbatumba Hawkers and Shebeen Associations, the AIDS Care Trust, the Namibia Planned Parenthood Association, National Social Marketing (NaSoMa), and others, a number of whom had been participants in our training program at the University of Namibia. The group conducted a pilot study, funded by UNAIDS, to see if couples would use the woman's condom and to document their reactions. They held public meetings to educate people in general about HIV/AIDS, to demonstrate the use of the female condom, to answer questions from the audience, and to recruit volunteers, both men and women, to try the condoms and to train others to use them.

The report on the trials is informative and useful in understanding the significant role for the female condom in Namibia (MWACW 2001). Although there is no claim that the respondents necessarily formed a random or representative sample, the volunteers did come from a number of different regions and the findings give important insight into people's concerns. The majority of people who volunteered to try the condom were women, although about a third were men. The volunteers ranged in age from 18 to 52 and came from a variety of occupations, including a policeman, several clerks, house cleaners, and two women construction workers. At training sessions, following the initial public demonstrations, volunteers were given female condoms. A major complaint at this point was that there were too few samples for the large number of people willing to volunteer. Eight female condoms were distributed to each volunteer: two for demonstration, three for use, and three to give away.

Each person who volunteered to try the female condom was asked to fill out an initial questionnaire and then contacted a few weeks later to ask how they fared. Many of those who received the female condoms did not respond to the follow-up questions. Some responded that they had given the condoms away to a friend or neighbor, or had not used them because they had no partner, or their partner refused to try them. One volunteer even said, "lost all condoms or may be stolen!" However, the comments of the 88 volunteers who actually completed the training process and answered questions about their use of the free condoms were on the whole positive.

Frequently, people simply said, "no difficulties experienced" or "fine, no problems." Some were negative, such as the following: "My partner complained all the way through, saying he was having sex in plastic," "My partner's attitude puts me off; he was complaining too much," and "My partner was talking too much." Some were positive after some difficulty. One woman noted, "Partner objected at first but said it was fine after sex." Other comments included, "difficult to insert at first" and "first insertion was painful." One woman who was later successful said, "I tried to insert the condom the first time with no success, maybe because I was under the influence of alcohol." One man reiterated a common problem among partners when he said about the first use, "It was very difficult explaining to the girlfriend how to insert the condom." Yet on the third use he reported, "easy to insert and comfortable." In fact, in spite of numerous complaints, including the slipperiness of the condom, the noise it made, and difficulty with the initial insertion, of the 88 volunteers who reported back on their use of three free female condoms each, 65 said that by the third try, the female condom was easy to insert and even comfortable. This was an encouraging and surprising result, partly because, as the report on the trials notes, the training sessions were much criticized for the lack of training provided and the unevenness of the educational programs.

Following the female condom meetings and trials, the Ministry of Women Affairs began to receive letters and petitions requesting that the government provide the woman's condom as one of the options for HIV prevention in Namibia. In addition, the internationally funded NGO Sister Namibia (which, like WAD, receives much funding from Germany, a significant contemporary manifestation or perhaps reversal of colonial history since Namibia was a German colony prior to World War I), which focuses specifically on sexual rights and has championed the rights of lesbian and gay people in Namibia, published articles describing the female condom both in English and in Oshiwambo, the language of the Ovambo people of northern Namibia, and joined the general outcry calling for free female condoms. In fact, Sister Namibia is quoted in the opening pages of the Ministry of Women Affairs and Child Welfare Report on the female condom:

> Many of us have heard about the female condom. Some lucky ones might have seen it and even luckier ones might have used it once or twice. Despite widespread curiosity about the female condom, as it is also known, most of us are, to say the least, still in the dark about it. Are there any plans to introduce the female condom in Namibia? (MWACW 2001).

Interestingly enough, just to complete the analysis of global–local links, the researcher for Sister Namibia was a student in our training program in Windhoek in July 2000 and had even e-mailed me in New York City asking for information about the shipment of approximately 100 female condoms that I had tried to bring to Namibia the previous July. At that time, as noted above, the shipment was, for some mysterious reason, stopped by customs and, in spite of assistance from UNAIDS and other groups, we were not able to get them released in time for a demonstration seminar at the training program.

In April 2001, the female condom was approved for widespread distribution by the Namibian government. In fact, the female condom was "launched" at a much publicized event organized with UNAIDS by the Ministry of Women Affairs and Child Welfare, and attended by a number of other cabinet ministers and government officials. Veronica de Klerk was invited to give the keynote speech.

Throughout the process, the female condoms had been supplied and paid for by a number of donors, coordinated by UNAIDS in cooperation with the Female Health Company. In 1999, the Female Health Company worked with UNAIDS to develop a subsidized rate for the female condom in poor countries such as Namibia. Initially, during the pilot project and the launch, more than 20,000 female condoms were distributed by the Ministry of Women Affairs and Child Welfare. A further 100,000 were expected to be distributed through the regional centers, possibly at youth centers. Since the launch, female condoms have been on sale at subsidized rates in most of the local pharmacies. NaSoMa (National Social Marketing) sold female condoms to pharmacies and other outlets for N$5.22 (about US$0.75) and they were sold by the stores for N$8.00 (approximately US$1.00) for three. Male condoms, also subsidized by NaSoMa, were cheaper: the man's Cool Ryder condom costs N$0.87 for six wholesale, while the store price was N$1.50 (approximately US$0.25) for six.

Thus, women's condoms, even at subsidized prices, were selling for ten times as much as men's. Nevertheless, after the public launch, NaSoMa estimated that they would sell 1,000 female condoms per month. In fact, in the first three months 18,000 female condoms were sold in Namibian stores. Certainly, female condoms were finally available at an affordable price and people were buying them in unprecedented numbers.

In July 2001, we saw female condoms for sale for the first time at the truck stop on the new trans-Kalahari highway on the Namibian side of the border with Botswana. This was a particularly significant location. The long, straight two-lane highway – which connects three countries as it stretches from Johannesburg to Gaborone in Botswana and then to Windhoek and points north – was opened in 1998 as part of the much-awaited economic development of southern Africa. Clearly, as the trucks race by, they open the door to both new trade and new infection, and the question is whether the development will cancel the increased availability of the woman's condom.

Nevertheless, although female condoms are now available for a reasonable price in stores in Namibia, this case also illustrates the unevenness of access for all methods. They are not yet available free for all Namibian women. Most Namibian women are, in fact, too poor to buy such protection consistently, even at subsidized prices, and would not have access to them unless the female condoms were distributed free by the Namibian government. There was much hope that the Ministry of Women Affairs would distribute the free female condoms as they were shipped from the international donors. One shipment of 100,000 may save many lives, but to stem the epidemic, a consistent predictable process of free distribution to poor women in both the urban and rural areas needed to be worked out.

In 2003, we visited public clinics among the San peoples in northern Namibia and found that a few hundred female condoms had been given out by the nurses there to women who had requested them. We also visited the woman doctor responsible for the district hospital, Dr. Malita, and asked her whether she had female condoms available. It was a little disheartening to find that she had received free female condoms from WAD but no new supply from the government had been forthcoming.

It developed that the Ministry for Women Affairs, which had launched the female condom campaign, had few regional outlets and was not in constant communication with local clinics. In light of their meager resources and lack of ongoing district connections, they had not implemented any systematic distribution program. Thus, the campaign succeeded initially, as it was sponsored outside the Ministry of Health, but the long-term goals were undermined by, among other issues, the lack of power and resources of the Ministry for Women Affairs.

Like the women of Durban, the women of Namibia clearly understood the modes of transmission of AIDS and the needs for prevention. They were even willing to use such awkward barrier methods as the female condom. However, multiple factors, such as institutionalized religion and the marginalization of women's issues on the local and national levels, contributed to their inability to protect themselves or their families from the disease. Nevertheless, this example from Namibia demonstrates the ways in which organic leadership combated moral condemnation and voiced political demands that connected with the local practical sense of many men and women, who were able to partially realize a transformative vision.

I returned to Namibia early in June 2008, when, in fact, the rollout of AIDS treatment was finally well under way. I specifically wanted to see Jennifer Gatsi Mallet who had founded a branch of ICW in Windhoek and whom I had met through ATHENA and the IAS Mexico City planning meetings. In Jeni's office I found two young women from Katatura (the area which had been the African township adjacent to Windhoek) helping to staff the office of an active organization that trained young people to speak out about HIV and connected them with parliamentary representatives. Jeni introduced me to the Honorable Elma Dienda, a Member of Parliament for the opposition party, who was now chair of a committee on HIV. The Honorable Dienda immediately arranged a meeting for us at the parliamentary buildings to plan for further programs and proposals with respect to women and AIDS in Namibia. This was the first time in my many visits to Namibia and meetings with government officials that such an active interest was expressed in these issues. The energy and commitment of both women were illustrated one night when a patient had called Jeni at ICW to say that she had been forced to deliver her infant alone in a hospital room. The nurses had refused to touch her because they heard she was HIV positive. I went with Jeni and the Honorable Dienda as they rushed to the hospital that evening after work to look for the new mother. We never met the woman while I was there, but such efforts to check on the situation of an HIV-positive patient, far beyond the normal routines, are a significant reminder of the ongoing resilience of grassroots women as well as the importance of committed elected representatives. Such events bode well for the revitalization of reproductive rights for AIDS patients that may be possible in Namibia today.

# 9

# Ju/'hoansi Women in the Age of HIV: An Exceptional Case

"Give us some and we will teach our husbands how to use them," was the reply in 2001 when I asked a group of young married women in Dobe, a Ju/'hoansi village in Botswana on the Namibian border, if they would be able to use a box of male condoms.[1] Although this was by no means a measure of actual practice, these remarks of Ju/'hoansi women expressed a sense of entitlement and straight-forwardness with respect to sexual decisions, which was not evident among the Ovambo women with whom we spoke in Namibia or among the women in KwaZulu-Natal.

Women from other populations frequently mentioned the fear of battering by their men partners if they should bring up the question of condoms. As we shall see later in this chapter, Ju women were also subject to gendered violence and even murder by their partners, particularly under the influence of alcohol. Nevertheless, while the Ju women clearly evidence practical sense like women in other situations, the terms in which they spoke did not assume the gendered deference frequent elsewhere. For example, Ju/'hoansi women greeted enthusiastically the opportunity to "teach" their husbands about condoms, suggesting a different kind of interaction with their partners and a different level of autonomy.

The following two chapters describe interactions among the Ju/'hoansi, a language group amongst the San peoples, who live in the Kalahari Desert that crosses the borders of what are now Namibia and Botswana. The chapters discuss women living in villages on both sides of the border and the ways in which people have come to understand and address the AIDS epidemic. This chapter examines the ways in which AIDS has been understood in the population with respect to gender, and the different risks men and women face. It describes the effects of development and ecotourism on the social context of AIDS prevention.

## Ju/'Hoan Women's Autonomy

Eleanor Leacock and feminist anthropologists since the 1970s (Gailey 1987; Leacock 1981) have documented that in hunting-and-gathering societies, often classified as egalitarian, women are accustomed to autonomy in relation to men. Providing a famous example with respect to the Montagnais-Naskapi of North America, Leacock records Father Paul Le Jeune, head of the Jesuit mission in Quebec in the 1630s, rebuffing a man for allowing his wife too much sexual freedom:

> I told him that it was not honorable for a woman to love any one else except her husband, and that this evil being among them, he himself was not sure that his son, who was there present, was his son. He replied, "Thou hast no sense. You French people love only your own children; but we all love all the children of our tribe." I began to laugh, seeing that he philosophized in horse and mule fashion (Leacock 1981:50).

Egalitarian societies, usually composed of small bands of 12 to 30 wandering people, were organized around a gendered division of labor in which women gathered and men usually hunted. Women controlled their own work, when and where they gathered, with whom they chose to go, and the way in which the products of their labor were distributed among their small band. Women shared childrearing with men and among themselves, even to the extent of breastfeeding each other's children when a mother's tasks separated her from her child. Although couples might stay together for a lifetime, divorce, in terms of a woman or man simply leaving a partner, was relatively easy. Generally, children were reared with a high level of autonomy, helping women gather and men hunt. "Do it yourself, old man!" was the response of a child when his father shouted loudly at him to bring his tobacco pouch. This sharp retort was received without rancor as the father simply stood up and fetched the pouch himself (Draper 1975:92). Children's precocious autonomy, combined with support and access to the common resources of a band, allowed women more freedom than in most other societies.

Based on fieldwork in the 1960s among the Ju/'hoansi of Dobe, Richard Lee's ethnography *The !Kung San* stands as a classic benchmark in providing systematic contemporary evidence for women's autonomy in a foraging society (Lee 1984). Later ethnographic fieldwork in the 1970s also documented women's high status and freedom of action among the Ju/'hoansi. Young women could and did veto marriage plans. Women's voices were heard in the village councils. They provided 70 percent of the food and this economic autonomy was an important source of their strength. Accounts of women's experiences of sex, work, and family provide us with a rich history on which to base our current understandings of Ju/'hoan response to the threat of HIV (Draper 1975; Marshall 1976; Rosenberg 1997; Shostak 1983).

Significant to the current situation, Leacock argued that while women maintained autonomy in hunting-and-gathering societies, such autonomy was undermined as people in such societies came into contact with missionaries, traders, and other mercantile influences. She showed that, at least in North America, as the relations of production shifted towards capitalism, women lost their previous independence (Leacock 1972).

The San peoples of southern Africa, of whom the Ju are but one language group among many, have a long history of interactions with cattle-herding groups as well as ongoing battles and skirmishes with soldiers and cattle ranchers (Gordon 2000). Over the past 150 years some have become part of the general population as they were forced out of the Drakensberg mountain range of South Africa. Other small, scattered groups wandered through the Kalahari Desert and elsewhere. As noted above, the Dobe Ju/'hoansi were, in fact, living a nomadic foraging life in the early 1960s (Lee 2003; Marshall 1976).

Over the past 40 years, much has changed among the Ju/'hoansi (Lee 2003; Lee and Hurlich 1982; Lee and Susser 2006). As a result of colonialism, wars, and agricultural incursions by both German settlers and African farmers, much of the Ju way of life has disappeared and some aspects have been retained or recreated. However, when we started HIV research there in 1996, we met many of the same people who were described as youth in the early ethnographies. Lee was able to trace their children, grandchildren, and great-grandchildren throughout the villages we visited.

Nevertheless, many Ju/'hoansi have left the villages and now live on the margins of cattle farms, working intermittently at a number of jobs (Sylvain 2001). They are paid little and often sleep in groups along the side of the road or in vacant lots or schoolyards. In 1997, when we visited Rundu in the Okavango Region of Namibia, the community health director for the area took us to the back of a deep sandy public school yard where a group of San people had set up shelters, made from branches and blankets. The ash from their fires and cooking pots were still in evidence, although the children she was looking for were nowhere in sight. In this setting, the Ju were regarded as destitute and in need of public health intervention although in their own villages such wandering behavior was interpreted differently.

In addressing the HIV/AIDS epidemic, we need to understand the extent to which Ju/'hoansi women of the villages, in contrast to those who wander the cattle farms, may be able to maintain their autonomy and in what ways they are able to control their sexuality and their life choices. Our ethnographic research sheds some light on contemporary Ju/'hoansi women's autonomy and sexual authority and the particular ways in which their history and current forms of subsistence may protect them from HIV as well as their current imminent vulnerabilities.

## Baraka, 1996: What the Ju Knew About AIDS

In 1996, we introduced our research on HIV/AIDS at a civic council meeting at Baraka, a Ju/'hoansi village in Namibia, near the border with Botswana. The rondavels at this site were specifically constructed to create a center for the elected representatives of the Nyae Nyae Farmers Cooperative, now known as the Nyae Nyae Conservancy, a local group organized among the Ju/'hoansi for self-government. In 1996, at the meeting that the representatives called at Baraka, all the participants were men.

**Figure 9.1**    It was largely the responsibility of Ju/'hoansi women to build the homes in their villages. Many families preferred to move out to these more remote areas where they lived in small groups. They might travel frequently to other settlements, such as Dobe or Tsumkwe, 1999 (© Ida Susser)

When we asked about their knowledge of HIV/AIDS, the representatives told us that they knew about AIDS. Cal,[2] one of the representatives, noted, "We have heard that three people died of AIDS here and that there are three more infected. But we don't know who they are. The clinic takes the blood for testing but they don't give us the results."

They also knew about sexual transmission and condoms, as is evident from Benji's remark: "Sex could be better if you add condoms, then you won't get the disease, like raw versus cooked food." Later Bo teased Benji and said he had gone for an AIDS test. Benji replied, "I went for the test three times here in Tsumkwe, and I had to pay for the results."

Tsau noted, "The mother can give AIDS to the baby. First, they call it TB; then, after the mother dies, they call it AIDS. But the husband and children are still there."

This group of leading men, several young and educated, others older and illiterate, clearly understood the sexual transmission of AIDS and knew in theory that the condom could protect someone from infection. They showed us a typed manuscript about AIDS, written in Ju/'hoansi. Patrick J. Dickens (1953–1992), a South African linguist who had published a dictionary of the Ju/'hoan language, had, in fact, translated a handbook on AIDS into Ju/'hoansi before he, himself, died of the disease.

## Women's Autonomy and HIV/AIDS

As the opening quote above suggests, Ju/'hoansi women differed in their sense of autonomy from other women we interviewed in Namibia. Our conversations with women and young girls among the Ju/'hoansi generally revealed a greater degree of

**Figure 9.2**  Ju/'hoansi children study instructions on use of the female condom. The solar panels behind the children were set up by the Nyae Nyae Farmers Cooperative when Baraka was built as a central meeting place. It featured small rondavels for meetings and a guest-house. Baraka, 1996 (© Ida Susser)

confidence in sexual negotiation with men than Ovambo women in the rural home-steads of northern Namibia.

In 1996, we asked young Ju/'hoansi women at Baraka whether they would ask their husbands or boyfriends to use a condom. "Yes, why not – they will listen because they are also scared of the disease," was one response. Later on, a woman said, "Everyone makes their own decision. Yes, women can say they won't sleep with a man without a condom – it's not the way, but many will [ask a man to use a condom]."

After some discussion among the leading men and women of the village, one of the men said, "If we can tell people here, some people will listen and tell others. It's better for men and women to be together and hear about AIDS in front of every-body. We can have a meeting any time. Women can tell the men to use a condom, and if they want to have children, go for a test."

Richard Lee and I did proceed to talk at a small educational meeting organized by the council representatives at Baraka. I talked about AIDS and condoms, as a member of the council translated. People examined with some fascination a picture book about anatomy and the female condom, which I had brought with me.

A few years later, in 1999 in Dobe, after much discussion of condoms and my demonstration of a female condom, we asked an 18-year-old woman named Nisa, "Would you ask a boy to use a condom?" She replied with assurance, "If he did not have one and I had one, I would put on a female condom."

The women insisted, without apparent doubt, that, if the men did not do as the women and young girls asked, the women would not hesitate to refuse sex. In 1996, very few men or women were using condoms or doing anything practical about

AIDS. Nevertheless, the way both men and women talked about the issue assumed a certain autonomy in sexual relations.

At that time, Ju/'hoansi women who we interviewed saw no particular advantage to the female condom. They said if they wanted a man to use a male condom they would ask him. In contrast, Ovambo and Kavango women, as we have seen, were extremely enthusiastic about the possibilities of the female condom, as they saw it as an alternative strategy which would be under the woman's control and acceptable to men (Susser and Stein 2000).

When Lee interviewed young men in Dobe in 1999, their responses seemed to corroborate the women's views. They talked as if women had the power to turn down sexual advances and they said that if a young woman were to accept such advances, they would see that as representing the opportunity to marry her.

The following indicative and amusing exchange is extracted from a conversation that took place in the evening among a group of soccer players with Richard Lee, after a game with two visiting young North Americans, Philip Kreniske (17, my son), David Lee (28, Lee's son) and five young men from Dobe, ages 20 to 25:

| | |
|---|---|
| TSAU, a young Ju man: | "I was just given a wife by her parents." |
| RICHARD: | "How many girls did you approach before marrying her?" |
| TSAU (without hesitation): | "Five. The first four refused. The fifth agreed." |
| RICHARD: | "What exactly did you ask for?" |
| TSAU: | "I asked that we should lie down together, then make love, then cook food." |

Several other young men told similar stories:

| | |
|---|---|
| KASHE: | "I approached four and they refused. The fifth agreed." |
| RICHARD: | "Why do girls refuse? What are they after?" |
| KUMSA: | "They want Goba [not Ju, but other African] boys, because they say Ju boys have no money." |

Ethnographic findings by one of our research associates, Pombili Ipinge, suggested that, in contrast, Ovambo men expected to have sexual relations with more than one woman and did not say they expected to marry a woman if she agreed to a sexual relationship (Ipinge et al. 2000).

In Dobe, also in 1999, we can hear a certain assurance about her boyfriend's commitment in Nisa's reply when we asked her about marriage:

Kao's family asked my father, but my father refused, but not outright. My father said he'd have to ask his father first. He hasn't gone yet because he's working on drought relief but he's going to go to Namibia to talk to his father, in a village near Tsumkwe. [She explained] If I got pregnant I would be happy . . . I don't want a child now but in another year I would like to have children.

In another general example of autonomy, she did not seem to feel any great pressure to get married quickly under these conditions.

We had been told by several women that they had their first child before they got married and that this was acceptable and common practice. This was confirmed from the men's point of view. When Richard asked if Kashe, a father in his thirties, had slept with his wife before they were married, Kashe said: "Sure we did. Our first child was born before we were married." And Cao, who was standing next to Kashe, said it was the same for him.

We talked further with three unmarried young women who stopped by our camp to visit. Each of these young girls told us the names of their relatives and Richard was able to trace their heritage to parents and grandparents he had known among the Ju/'hoansi of Dobe many years ago. Karu, the oldest, dressed in a stylish turquoise Western dress, was 20; the next young girl in a pretty pink top and skirt was about 18; the youngest said she was 16 years old.

Karu was the daughter of a man who had recently carved a wooden drum we had admired as we walked by his home. He had offered to sell it to us but for quite a high price. Later that month, we heard chanting in the night and Richard and I and our sons walked along the dusty paths lit by the stars toward the sound. After following a winding trail through the dried desert bush for about twenty minutes, we found a healing ceremony taking place. Karu's mother, descended from a long line of women healers, was going into trance and her father was drumming on the newly crafted instrument. Karu and her sister were also standing chanting by the fire, and a few other people emerged from the dark to participate in the long night's ritual.

When Karu and her two friends stopped by our camp to talk the next day, our conversations with the three young women indicated a marked difference from conversations we had had before. By 1999, these young unmarried women not only knew about condoms, but also were explicit that they used them without a problem. Confirming the complaints of the young soccer players, two out of three of these women had Herero boyfriends. The Herero, as noted in Chapter 7, were a traditionally cattle-raising population centered in Namibia and Botswana.

Karu said she had been together for five years with her Herero boyfriend who had a Herero wife and many children in a nearby village. Karu told us that she and her partner used a condom: "We got them from the doctors and nurses and now we have a pile of them . . . I have the condoms and when he goes, they stay with me." Each of the young women told us they had condoms at their house. They claimed to have their own, not relying on their partners. Karu stated unequivocally, "If a man says he doesn't have a condom, I will give him one."

Karu did not mention marriage with her Herero boyfriend, but expressed her main dilemma straightforwardly: "I want to have a baby. I use the condoms because I'm worried about sickness, so I really don't know what to do. If you have a child, sickness could also get in." She continued, "My boyfriend really likes me, he divides his time between his village and here – he spends weeks at a time with me. We use a condom every time . . . My boyfriend gives me shoes, blankets, and food."

**Figure 9.3**    Women discuss the female condom. Dobe, 2001 (© Ida Susser)

Later, she commented on a previous conversation I had with a few Ju women when she was present: "The married women with children said they didn't know anything about condoms. We were quiet because, after all, they are our elders." Thus, by 1999 women of different generations had different perspectives on sexuality. The three young Ju women who came to talk to us at our campsite were direct and straightforward in their discussions of their lives and familiar with AIDS and condoms. The married women were not reticent but appeared less familiar with condoms, perhaps because their partners were Ju men, who themselves had less exposure to AIDS education than the surrounding populations or perhaps because married women wanted and expected to have children.

The men from surrounding populations, primarily the Herero and the Tswana, have more money and resources in general than the Ju/'hoansi. Ju/'hoansi women have long had relationships with Herero and Tswana men, although in Tsumkwe, as we shall see, the number of new migrants to the area has risen precipitously. Unfortunately, Ju/'hoansi women seem to have less leeway in their relationships with their Tswana or Herero boyfriends, who might give them presents but were, in fact, married to other women.

A conversation with Hwanla, who was visiting Dobe with her grandchild, illustrates the glaring difference in the situation between the reasonably stable and autonomous lives of women in the Ju villages and those on the margins of settlements. Hwanla's son had married a woman from Dobe and this may have been why she was at Dobe with her grandson. She lived far from the Ju/'hoansi villages, near the road to Sehitwa, Botswana, a rural town at a crossroads near Lake Ngami (now dry). When we had driven through this town, we had seen two or three closed huts advertising liquor for sale. Symbolizing the destitution and barrenness of this area, a dead donkey lay under the unrelenting sun on the wide dusty plain that stretched into the distance from the asphalt road.

Hwanla had three children whose father was San although not Ju. He had left her many years ago and she had built mud houses for a living, for the men who worked at road construction sites. This may sound unusual, but, in fact, Ju women customarily make the small houses using patties of mud and clay for the walls. She said she also cooked for the workers and was paid in cash.

Hwanla made an interesting distinction between the lives of her sons and daughter. About her sons, she said, "They took wives." She defined them as married, because they helped raise the children. However, Hwanla was afraid her daughter might be at risk for HIV: "No, she is not married. She has three children, each with different fathers. Two of the fathers were Goba (African but not Ju) and one was from a different group of San." Later Hwanla said explicitly, "The Goba do not marry us. They 'fool around' and then they leave. Then, the Ju men ask for the girls' hands in marriage."

There was no question that Hwanla knew about AIDS and that it was transmitted through sex. "We still have not seen it, we just hear on the radio. I fear it because it's not curable. If you get it, no one will save you," she said. Then, she expressed concern about her daughter, clearly indicating that her daughter was involved in what has been called "survival sex":

> She is taking terrible chances. She has a child with this man and he leaves and then she is with another man. She could be getting sick . . . I tell her about the risk she's taking going with men like this and she says, "Don't talk to me! You are not giving me anything. What can I do? I have to support myself."

Hwanla elaborated, "They do not give her cash – just soap, food and sugar." In answer to a question, she answers, "No, the men do not live with her. They have their own village and would stay a night where she lives with me, then come back in a week." Hwanla explained to us that she did get general rations from government assistance: "mealie meal [corn], beans, cooking oil and sorghum [cassava], but no sugar."

Hwanla said she knew about condoms, but reiterated the generational difference remarked upon by the young girls in Dobe: "People my age [probably in her forties] don't use them, but people in their twenties and thirties do use them. Both Goba and Ju carry condoms with them in their pockets. I have not seen women carrying them, but I have seen many men with them."

Like some other people with whom we spoke at Dobe, Hwanla knew that AIDS was transmitted through sex, but she did not know it could be transmitted from the mother to the child.

## The Women Bring AIDS

"We are thinking it can be transmitted through sex from outsiders with local women and from women to men," said a leading political representative of the Ju, a man, at Baraka in 1996. According to another male political leader, Bo:

> There are lots of outside people staying in Tsumke from places where the problem existed already. At the shebeens [shelters where home-brew liquor is sold] the outsiders will make friends with the local women, drink together, and then propose sex to them.

Later on in the discussion, Bo says again:

> We think it's women. . . . [Y]ou can see some of the women have children with people from outside, but men don't have many children from outside.

Pombile, our research assistant, asks: "Do men have children in two villages?" Bo responds: "Yes, men can have wives in different villages."

As in the conversation with Hwanla, men are said to have "wives" even when they have two partners among the Ju. Women are seen as having "boyfriends," perhaps because, in these cases, their partners are not Ju. The Ju women may have been more autonomous than women from other populations but, as this interchange amply demonstrates, they were still seen as the source of AIDS. Ju political representatives were convinced that women would bring AIDS to Tsumkwe. As we have seen above, they were right that women were finding boyfriends among outside groups. This was translated by the male leadership as a way to see women as the source of AIDS, even though they were willing to admit that men might also have more than one partner.

As the quotes above indicate, the men at the meeting insisted that AIDS was brought among the Ju/'hoansi by Ju/'hoansi women who had sexual relations with men from other groups and they disapproved of this. We were told that in Tsumkwe there were many men who were not Ju/'hoansi who came to buy beer from the numerous temporary grass shelters set up as bars – shebeens – where they met with the Ju/'hoansi women. Drinking was widely discussed and seemed a major problem to the local people. From our first visit to Tsumkwe in 1996, Richard and I saw many people drinking at the shebeens. Shebeens were generally frequented by Ju but not owned or organized by Ju men and women.

Thus, from our first meeting at Nyae Nyae in 1996, the male leadership claimed that women were the carriers of AIDS. In blaming women, they were echoing a perception common to men in New York City and to populations elsewhere in Africa (Susser and Gonzalez 1992; Treichler 1999). However, it may also be the case among the Ju that the women have broader outside contacts and may be the first to come into contact with HIV/AIDS and also more likely to be the first to die from the disease.

We were told in 2001 that three women were known to have died from HIV/AIDS at Tsumkwe. Another woman, whose family had just returned to Dobe, had died from an unknown cause. Her husband, who had been taken from Dobe as a young boy and spent decades in farm labor, had stayed on in Dobe with the rest of his family after she died. No deaths among Ju men were reported to us although we were told of the death of a Goba boyfriend of a Ju woman.

## Tsumkwe: Den of Iniquity

"At Tsumkwe there were boys but I refused them. Many boys were chasing me but I refused," said Nisa, in a 1999 interview with Richard and I in Dobe.

| | |
|---|---|
| RICHARD and I: | "Why?" |
| NISA: | "I refused sickness." |
| RICHARD and I: | "Which sickness did you fear?" |
| NISA: | "AIDS." |
| RICHARD and I: | "Did someone teach you about it?" |
| NISA: | "I've seen people at Tsumkwe – girls like me – who were sick. Hwantla was sick." |
| RICHARD and I: | "Is she alive?" |
| NISA: | "She's still alive, but she's sick with that illness." |

Nisa went on to tell us that she was still living with her mother and father in Dobe, but had traveled to Tsumkwe, about 50 kilometers away on the Namibian side of the border with Botswana, to visit her grandfather. Her comments clearly reflected the general perception among the Ju that Tsumkwe was the center of the AIDS epidemic in the area.

Tsumkwe was once a Ju/'hoansi village centered around an ancient baobab tree, which is still standing. In 1960, Tsumkwe was made a central administrative site by the occupying South African government. Before Namibia won its independence in 1989, Tsumkwe was a military recruitment area and the South African government built a clinic, a store, and a few other administrative buildings along a short stretch of gravel road. In the surrounding area, rows of cement houses were constructed, similar to those that were built under the disreputable Bantustan policy in South Africa (Lee 2003). The village is now the administrative center for the Tsumkwe District, a Ju/'hoansi region in Namibia. There is also a co-ed boarding school in Tsumkwe where the young boy students played soccer on Sundays.

Tsumkwe is where the film *The Gods Must Be Crazy* (Uys 1981) was filmed and where the star of that film, Xau, still lived in one of the few small brick houses next to the store when we first visited. His wife died in the early 1990s of a long illness said to be tuberculosis. Xau died in 2003 while we were in Tsumkwe. Again, this was said to be from drug-resistant tuberculosis. In 1997, a Safari Lodge opened in Tsumkwe to provide a base from which tourists could visit the Ju/'hoansi villages and witness Ju/'hoansi dancing and healing rituals staged for their consumption.

In 1996, in Tsumkwe, we interviewed two health workers employed by Health Unlimited, a British NGO. They visited the Ju/'hoansi villages monthly to provide some medical assistance and health education. These two health workers were aware of HIV and beginning to discuss it on their monthly rounds to the villages. Testing and diagnosis were not yet readily available and treatment at that time was not even considered.

Although tuberculosis had long been epidemic in the Kalahari, the fact that it was sometimes resistant to treatment suggested that AIDS might have been present, if not recognized. By 2001, AIDS had been diagnosed by doctors who served the Ju/'hoansi region. Health Unlimited had initiated a program to train Ju/'hoansi grade school teachers, who worked in the villages, about AIDS prevention.

In 2001, we met one of the AIDS prevention teacher trainees, who spoke excellent English, visiting his relatives in Dobe, on the Botswana side of the border. He was extremely well informed and helpful in discussing AIDS with his kin in the community, suggesting that such training had important implications for knowledge and prevention beyond the confines of the school.

Throughout our research since 1996, Tsumkwe emerged as a main center for the spread of HIV for a variety of overlapping reasons. Firstly, the South African army was based there in the 1980s and the local soldiers, from many populations, may have introduced new diseases among the Ju/'hoansi. Secondly, the border guards and other administrative personnel spent many lonely nights in the region and some frequented the local nightlife. Thirdly, nowadays there are passable gravel roads from Namibian towns into Tsumkwe – although the nearest non-Ju/'hoansi village is about 200 kilometers away – as well as a nearby airstrip.

As Richard Lee's work has shown, the influx of South African soldiers defending the apartheid regime into the Ju area of Namibia in the 1980s was accompanied by an increase in homicide and violence among the Ju. A Ju elder says in a documentary about Tsumkwe, "the soldiers bring the killing" (Marshall 1980). This violence included assaults by men on their wives, especially under the influence of alcohol. We were told about several women who had been murdered by their husbands over the past decades.

As the quotes from Nisa suggest, the Ju themselves see Tsumkwe as a vortex for AIDS. Both the Ju/'hoansi who live in Tsumkwe and those who live elsewhere, but have visited the area, talk about the incidence of drinking and sexual exchange as different from the surrounding villages. On one occasion in 1996, we drove a little beyond Tsumkwe in our four-wheel drive and were met by drunken men and women clustering outside clay rondavels.

In 2001, a discussion with an older couple and two younger men in a village at Dobe led to their naming the three women who they believed had died of AIDS. All of them lived in Tsumkwe, although they were near kin to the people at Dobe. We were told that one young woman died, unmarried, at age 20. The ages of the other two were estimated at 35 and 40. The two older women had young children, but there was no knowledge of children's deaths. No sense of shame or stigma seemed to be expressed in this conversation.

Thus, both Ju in the villages of the Kalahari Desert and those who had migrated south to the cattle farms and towns of Namibia and Botswana understood about the sexual transmission of AIDS. Several of the more knowledgeable and articulate young men told us they had been tested for AIDS two or three times. "Survival sex" seemed to be a feature of the lives of some Ju women who had left the Ju villages and looked for work in the rural towns.

Among the Ju women in the Ju villages, we found a certain sense of autonomy with respect to Ju men and questions of sex. However, under the influence of alcohol, women no longer seemed to be able to protect themselves and were particularly vulnerable to exploitation and violence by men from other groups as well as the Ju. Nevertheless, like the Ovambo and Durban women, Ju women had generated their own practical sense without introducing outside moral precepts about pregnancy before marriage or about their sexual partners. Although vulnerable to violence and disease, the women were quite aware of and articulate about their situation.

# 10

# Changing Times, Changing Strategies: Women Leaders Among the Ju

One early morning in July 2003, Richard Lee and I walked around to the Ju homes surrounding Tsumkwe. It was still a little chilly after the cold of the desert night and people were beginning to wake up. Many of the Ju children were still sleeping under blankets and often mosquito netting, usually curled comfortably against other members of their family. Other people were crouched around fires, warming their hands and holding mugs of coffee and tea as they talked or simply sat in silence. People greeted Lee from many sites and some people we knew invited us to sit with them on the ground near a small fire. We had been invited to a meeting here in the village with some of the women to talk about AIDS and other issues.

Within half an hour, the sun was high in the sky, beating down on the hot sand, and we were removing our sweaters and walking away from the small fires. One of the leading women began to call people together and we gathered in the deep sand of a fenced-in back yard. There were about eight women, some children running around, and three or four men leaning on the posts surrounding the yard. In the next yard, a young slender woman lay on a mattress and we were told that she was sick from tuberculosis. Another woman was sitting with her on the mattress, brushing a comb through her long hair. The meeting was organized by Francina Simon, a woman in her thirties, the daughter of a respected San elder. Francina had emerged over the past few years as a leader in the area.

This chapter follows the emergence of Francina as a leader within the complex interactions faced by the Ju in a changing political arena. We have seen in the previous chapter the outspoken and autonomous practical perspectives of many Ju women, but also noted their lack of representation in the new leadership. In this chapter, we see Ju women even more vulnerable to the ravages of economic and political interests as neoliberal policies draw the Ju territory into national plans, with little apparent advantage to the Ju themselves. As these changes take place, we see the Ju women finding their own voices in the new political arena.

**Figure 10.1**   With men standing listening nearby, women talk and laugh about relationships with their partners. Tsumkwe, 2003 (© Ida Susser)

In 2003, Francina, with the support of the predominantly male Ju Traditional Authority and other Ju women, initiated strategies for pragmatic change. They were attempting to enforce a law banning the sale of kashipembe, a new form of particularly powerful distilled liquor, in order to limit the damage caused by alcohol, particularly on the lives of Ju women. Only home brew was legal in the region but, in 2003, kashipembe was widespread and sold in small shot bottles at most shebeens.

In this endeavor, the Ju were working with the help of the "fire and brimstone" of the pastor of the Dutch Reformed Church. As noted in previous chapters, this church was notorious for its nationalist, moralistic, and patriarchal teachings in its association with the apartheid regime in South Africa. However, in this instance, I would suggest that even the pastor himself was taking a practical step in a difficult situation. He did not broach the subject of home brew but launched his assault simply on the hard liquor that was newly imported into the area by private businesses with the help of what many Ju believed were political connections and protection.

In the context of the threats to Ju autonomy from the interconnected problems of alcohol and AIDS, this movement, supported by the church, provides an interesting challenge to the idea of the counter-hegemonic intellectuals I have been developing in this book. However, as we follow the women and men of Tsumkwe through their current experiences, I explore the idea that Francina and the other participants in the movement to limit hard liquor were adopting a pragmatic strategy for survival in difficult circumstances. In this instance, I would suggest neither the pastor nor the women involved were taking a stand on ideas of sin and moral condemnation. Paradoxically, perhaps, the protest initiated by the Ju and the pastor could be characterized as a counter-hegemonic movement.

## Changes at Tsumkwe

The early morning meeting began by discussing the somewhat repetitive topics of AIDS and condoms. Soon, however, a man raised the issue of alcohol and the she-beens. We asked if men and women went alone to the shebeens. As we had already observed in our stay at Tsumkwe, both men and women answered that women usually went with their husbands.

One of the young women at the meeting told an illuminating story. She said her husband had given her his money, saying that he did not want to spend it all at the shebeen and that she should guard it for him. Later in the evening, when he had spent all he had, he asked her for the 20 Namibian rand he had given her. She refused to give him the cash and, drunk now, he threatened to beat her if she did not produce the money. She then handed the money over to him.

Such accounts were tragically corroborated by the story of two infant orphans who were being cared for by the doctor at the regional hospital. When we visited the hospital we met about nine children who were living there in newly built rooms. Among these children was a baby of five months and a two-year-old boy who had been brought to the doctor by their grandmother. The doctor and a number of Ju told us that these two infants were the children of a woman who had recently been murdered by her husband. Their father had killed their mother one night at a shebeen when she refused to give him money for alcohol. The grandmother had brought the children to the hospital for their protection from their drunken, angry father.

Such stories may sound extreme, and we were not sure how common they were, but they certainly illustrated the tragedy caused by alcohol at Tsumkwe. They also explained why Francina, influential on the Traditional Authority, chose to focus her attention on tackling the increasing sale and consumption of hard liquor in the area, which seemed to be directly associated with recent demographic changes.

Since our last visits in 1996 and 1997, much had changed, both in the lives of the Ju women and in the strategies available to them. Between 1996 and 2003, a complex dynamic between development, inclusion, and politics has pushed the Ju into greater interaction with cash, profits, and alcohol. As the Ju had lost land rights to migrant workers and ecotourism had brought safari travelers, the population in the area had more than doubled, mostly with the influx of migrant workers from other groups.

In 2003, we were told of at least 17 Ju from Tsumkwe who were known to have died of AIDS over the previous seven years. Many of them were women whose partners were among a new population of migrant workers. In fact, the regional doctor told us that, in 2003 alone, she knew of seven AIDS deaths among the non-Ju itinerant workers surrounding the Ju/'hoansi villages (Lee and Susser 2006).

We also found contradictory trends in terms of Ju women's autonomy. While there was an under-representation of women in the leadership, women made artic-ulate demands to be heard. Such contradictions were also evident in the ability of women to negotiate for AIDS prevention. In 2003, in contrast to our visit seven years earlier, when only men were present at the meetings of the Nyae Nyae Conservancy, we found Francina elected to the Traditional Authority. At the same time, however, we found women increasingly vulnerable to sexual exploitation at the numerous shebeens.

The shebeens at Tsumkwe represented an important social meeting place for people from many groups, and making and selling home brew has historically provided women in southern Africa with a crucial foothold in the informal economy (Bonner 1990). As we wandered through the shebeens, we saw several that were run by migrant women, who prepared the home brew and sold it to migrant men and Ju men and women alike. At some shebeens, however, silent very young migrant women could also be seen, standing near the door, apparently available for cash.

Thus, at the same time as we began to understand the profound level of subjugation of some women, both Ju and others, at the shebeens, we found Francina, a strong and articulate San woman, had emerged as a legitimate, respected, and informed leader, leading the movement against the sale of hard liquor.

## Migration, Construction and Development

By 2003, Tsumkwe was certainly on the map of Namibian politics (for a full discussion of the changes in Tsumkwe, see Lee 2007). Much new construction was being planned by government agencies, church organizations, and international NGOs. Many workers from all over Namibia, including particularly veterans from the war of independence, were recruited to Tsumkwe for development and construction. New government workers constructed their own homes around Tsumkwe, along with many unemployed men seeking work and women finding work in brewing beer and other informal activities.

One afternoon in 2003, we walked behind the main road where new housing was to be built and where the rows of shebeens were to be found. We entered one of the more elaborate set-ups. In the dark cool interior of a clay shelter, music was playing from a boom box and a ping-pong table was placed near the bar. A young woman was sitting silently next to the bar owner. On the shaded benches outside, a Ju couple were drinking little bottles of the newly produced kashipembe.

Again in 2003, early one morning, we walked through the outskirts of Tsumkwe where the shebeens proliferated. In the grey light of a weekday morning, we talked with a woman who seemed to be in her thirties. A few non-Ju men had stopped by in the cold, misty dawn to sit around the fire and she was serving home brew from a large barrel. People sat with mugs in their hands on the wooden logs strewn around. This shebeen was one of the many located on the barren dusty strip of land that stretched for about a mile behind the main street corner of Tsumkwe. The hostess explained that her husband worked for the government and this provided her with some of the funds to buy the hard liquor as well as ingredients for the home brew. Although she had a rondavel constructed nearby, she mentioned to us that her husband had a government house.

Thus, a new wave of government employees, their families, and people desperate for work has begun to migrate to Tsumkwe. Lee estimates that about one half of the Tsumkwe population are now Ju and the other half Ovambo, Kavango, Herero, and Damara (Lee 2007:161). In 2003, government officials pointed out to us the new construction planned for housing and government buildings. Presumably, many of the recent migrants were hoping for work from these ventures.

## Commercialization of Tsumkwe

In the 1990s, government pensions were distributed to the Ju in their villages. The agent responsible for the pensions delivered them to the Ju elders every month. The truck from the local store followed the delivery of the pensions, which the villagers used to pay for the provisions. There was at that time practically nothing for sale in the one open store in Tsumkwe.

This local store was owned by the man who was in the process of developing a safari lodge. In 1996 the lodge was not yet open and we did not see or hear of any safari tours in the villages.

Also in 1996, when we tried to buy crafts very little was available. After much inquiry at Baraka, I managed to find my way to the back of the meetinghouse and purchase a necklace of ostrich shells and a bow and arrow. These were the only objects to be seen in the dusty, dark room and the only objects even offered for sale. No Ju came up to us offering crafts for sale. Ju approached us, just as they did in the following years, asking for tobacco, but they did not try to sell us crafts. Whatever crafts were made at this time were collected by the pastor or the Nyae Nyae Conservancy and taken to Windhoek and elsewhere for sale.

At this time, although Ju came to Tsumkwe, and many lived in surrounding houses built by the South African government in the infamous style of South African Bantustans, most Ju did not have to travel to Tsumkwe for pensions, goods or health care, or to sell their crafts for cash. Even the Ju who lived in Tsumkwe did not proffer beads and purses for sale to passing visitors and hardly seemed to rely on the store. There were a few shebeens selling home-brewed beer on the outskirts of Tsumkwe.

Even in these early years, the Ju would visit Tsumkwe from time to time. In fact, in 1997, N!ai and Gunte, made famous by the 1980 documentary *N!ai* by John Marshall, and by then a married couple in their fifties, asked us to drive them to Tsumkwe from the border – about 50 kilometers – to stay with members of their family. N!ai and her friend gave us some small beaded necklaces and a decorated tortoise shell with powder in it. Nevertheless, little was bought and sold for cash in the area. By 1997, the new Safari hotel was nearly open – we slept in the unoccupied wooden huts – although there were no obvious customers as yet. Still the Ju were not approaching strangers or offering to sell crafts.

In 2003, when we returned to Tsumkwe for more extended fieldwork, all of these small details had changed and the overall effect was marked. Firstly, and perhaps most importantly, the pension distribution system had been reorganized and the new company in charge of distribution had established pension automated telling machines (ATMs) only in Tsumkwe. Elderly people from all over the area had to travel to Tsumkwe to get their entitlements in cash from the machines. As Ju had to come to Tsumkwe for the machines, the truck from the store no longer went out to the villages. Purchases of food and goods took place at Tsumkwe.

Also by 2003, the pastor was no longer circling the villages to buy crafts. He said his small warehouse was too full and he could not sell the materials any more. The market was flooded with small bead necklaces, bags, and tortoiseshell make-up holders. In addition, the officers of an NGO who used to drive around in an SUV picking up crafts from the villages had stopped this routine. Instead, international volunteers had been recruited to build a craft shop at the main road junction across from the school, the Baby Smile shebeen, the second local store, and the SWAPO meetinghouse.

Elderly Ju who now had to travel to Tsumkwe for their pensions did not come alone but rather were accompanied by several members of their family. The group together hitch-hiked in from the outlying villages and collected the money. As a group, they needed food and drink when they arrived. According to reports from a local NGO worker, the pension collected would just about cover the costs of the few days spent at Tsumkwe, frequently around the shebeens, before people embarked on the long and unpredictable hitchhike home. While waiting at Tsumkwe, women from the villages would attempt to sell beads to passing tourists, generating cash for further expenses.

By 2003, Tsumkwe's two open stores sold chewing gum, soda, bread (if it had been baked), cans of food, rice, toothpaste and other products. The SUVs of safari tours would park momentarily outside the stores. Well-heeled travelers in hiking boots and khakis would jump out to buy cold soda, potato chips and other immediate provisions. Outside the stores, Ju women would again try to sell crafts for a dollar or two, as in some of the poorest situations in the world where begging is the norm.

As the pension system was centralized, the water was privatized and its distribution centralized. The contract for providing water had been sold to a corporation that was in the process of placing rationed water pipes around the village of Tsumkwe. The man in charge of water drove his white SUV up and down the main street and became one of the principal customers at the store, as also did the young volunteers building the new craft shop. Presumably, it was not the Ju who would provide the cash to buy the water, any more than they would frequent the new craft shop. The new water arrangements seemed to be geared to the planned housing that we were told was to be built on the cleared land behind the main buildings, now a trail of clay shelters and shebeens inhabited by migrant workers.

The new water rations seemed to have a centrifugal rather than centripetal effect on the Ju. One woman told us that her household had moved into the bush just outside Tsumkwe because they did not want to be responsible for paying for rationed water for their cattle.

As a consequence of shifts towards the privatization of pension distribution, water, and craft sales, in 2003, Tsumkwe had become a village with the dynamics of begging and exploitation, particularly of women, in place.

## Ecotourism

Most of the schemes bringing tourists to the Ju were originally organized in terms of "ecotourism," geared to cooperative crafts and other strategies, in the effort not to disrupt the Ju way of life but to allow Ju to benefit from tourism financially.

Among the Ju villages in the 1980s in Botswana and Namibia a number of trusts had been created. The Nyae Nyae Conservancy represented one such trust in Namibia. In Botswana, a trust had been created around the Ju village of /Xai/Xai (Hitchcock 2006; WIMSA 2004). Despite variations, the idea behind each was to organize economic development at the community level. In this way, money from the sale of crafts, village visits, and the leasing of hunting rights to safari companies at /Xai/Xai was collected for the village as a whole and invested in paying for a school building, teachers, and a clinic.

As noted in Chapter 9, the Nyae Nyae Conservancy had created their headquarters at the new village of Baraka. Small rondavels were built, meetings were held, a kindergarten program was established, and training and work in mechanical repairs and maintenance, and other activities were available for a number of years.

Neither the Nyae Nyae Conservancy nor the /Xai/Xai trust functioned effectively or without problems. Cooperatives might function extremely well for a while and then feuding or lack of interest by the board or the population often led to decline if not complete disintegration.

Nevertheless, the proceeds to the cooperatives paid for such essential services as education, and programs for children and youth, public health outreach and employment training, water pipes and bore holes. They provided the groundwork for the emergence of an effective new generation of educated and healthy San. For each of the cooperatives mentioned above, ecotourism generated some, if not most, of the resources.

In 2003, at a meeting of the Nyae Nyae Conservancy at Baraka, still only Ju men were sitting at the leadership table when the Ju met with their national political representatives to help hammer out a national platform for indigenous peoples. Male leaders of national indigenous rights groups reported to the Ju with respect to ongoing decisions, national elections, and relevant meetings. Several hundred people from the Namibian Ju villages gathered to sit in the hot sand at the center

**Figure 10.2**   In a meeting with national San representatives at the Nyae Nyae Conservancy, women, who may appear subordinate sitting at the feet of their men, nonetheless sharply criticized the lack of mosquito netting to sew and sell. Baraka, 2003 (© Ida Susser)

of the village and listen to the presentations. Later, everyone shared in the roasting goat meat from nearby fires.

The Ju women, although relegated to the margins of the meeting and huddled in little groups in the dust with their children on their knees, still spoke up vociferously concerning issues that related to them. They wanted to know, for example, why they were no longer being given mosquito netting to sew for sale and why they had no mosquito nets to distribute in their villages.

The villages of Baraka and /Xai/Xai, which generated income as a product of ecotourism, contrasted sharply with Tsumkwe in 2003, where welfare payments were the main source of cash and begging women tried to sell crafts in the streets and in the worst situations families spent their money at shebeens.

## Neoliberal Policies and the Privatization of Risk

Clearly ecotourism can have a different effect when organized according to neoliberal privatizing policies as opposed to cooperative trusts. Under these conditions, rather than leading to the generation of funds for the construction of a modern, educated community, a village could degenerate into a population of street sellers, mostly women, hawking cheap crafts, home brew, hard liquor, and, ultimately, sex. In 2003 in Tsumkwe, these possibilities were evident.

Within the concept of the neoliberal is the privatization of risk. Neoliberal policies, the privatization of pensions, water, and the individual sale of crafts, combined with the lack of investment in public transportation, pushed local Ju people to travel long distances individually or in groups to collect cash and sell goods.

The Ju have always moved around and flexibly re-created their homes in pleasant forest clearings, looking for shade and hidden springs. Such delightful settlements can still be found. Sometimes, instructed by Ju who wished to visit relatives or who had hitched a ride home with us, we turned our SUV off the main road, down practically invisible dirt tracks, and several miles later found ourselves next to a group of clay huts and grass shelters. On several occasions, we spent an afternoon seated on a fallen log in shady clearings talking with the families who had collected there to live. In the evening, men and women gathered round the fire to dance and sing evocative songs with complex rhythms.

However, in 2003, many people gathered along the side of the road waiting for rides to or from Tsumkwe. While waiting in Tsumkwe, they visited the Welcoming shebeens and much cash was spent long before they returned to their villages. This is a relatively recent development, not simply a product of a cash economy or of the clash of capitalism with a foraging society but, more precisely, the immediate result of newly implemented neoliberal policies.

## Public Transportation/Public Education

The Tsumkwe Junior Secondary school in the village of Tsumkwe has long served a mixed population of children from approximately age seven through eighteen. Although established in Tsumkwe, a Ju region, in 2003, less than half of the 452 students were Ju and in the higher grades, only a small proportion per class were Ju. In recent years, possibly seeking to protect their adolescents from what they see as the temptations of city life, families from all over northern Namibia have sent their children to this school in Tsumkwe in spite of the fact that over 300 kilometers of desert, bush, and treacherous sandy roads separate the school from the nearest town.

In 2003, in spite of what appeared to us as meager meals of thin soup, the students appeared lively and animated. Necessities such as soap and toothpaste or other amenities were not available. When we asked the young girls what they needed, they said soap. When we talked with some of the adults working nearby, we were told that the young girls might barter sex for soap.

Problems at the school were also generated by the lack of investment in public transportation. On at least one occasion, at vacation time, no transportation was provided for the children to return to their homes in other parts of Namibia. The girls and boys camped on the side of the road waiting for rides from passing trucks. While they waited, they became hungry and cold. They wandered around the various evening fires of the Ju, looking for heat and food. But they also wandered over to Baby Smile shebeen, right next to the school, on the very corner where they were waiting for rides. It might take several days for a ride to appear. Obviously, these conditions left teens, girls in particular, vulnerable to exploitation. When a girl became pregnant, school policy was to expel her from the school. This was certainly a frequent issue with which the school administration had to deal.

Ju children were luckier than others in that their families and general community were much closer to the school. However, in 2003, the Ju children were also surrounded by the local shebeens and with limited access to amenities or financial resources to pay for soap, clothes, shoes, or other necessities.

## Namibian Politics

Tsumkwe had in fact become a political symbol for Namibia. On two occasions in 2003, Tsumkwe appeared on national and international news. On one occasion President Sam Nujoma came to speak, accompanied from the concrete airstrip in the bush near Tsumke by a long cavalcade of SUVs. Several hundred people, including at least one hundred school children in their sky-blue uniforms waited outside the hall to be inspected before entry. In anticipation, cars and people crowded the main intersection of the gravel road, opposite the school, the store, the small building with the flag in front that represented SWAPO headquarters, and Baby Smile shebeen. After a couple of hours, the President and his entourage returned to Windhoek.

Later, the star of *The Gods Must be Crazy*, Xau, died. He used to live in a small house on that same strip of road. About one hundred people arrived, including about 25 from beyond Namibia, to attend his funeral in the church hall on the other side of the main road. The same children from the school, in their blue skirts and tops, sang in the church choir. A large group of tourists from an eastern European safari trip were present. The Ju were mostly standing in the corners at the back of the crowded hall. The memorial, with eulogies by international personages, was broadcast globally by TV stations including CNN. This time a hearse was trailed by a snaking line of white SUVs with children hanging out the windows and sitting on the roofs, back past the school and Baby Smile, to an area of bush newly designated as a cemetery where a grave had been dug to bury the coffin. Lee commented that the ceremony at the burial site, replete with crowds of people, cameras, tripods, and bullhorns, had little resemblance to any funerary ritual he had observed among the Ju.

On the edge of Tsumkwe, we visited the new young wife of the star after the funeral, driving through the bush in a different direction. Sitting in front of a grass shelter, a number of men and women were scattered in the pleasant evening shade of the trees. They told us they had moved away from Tsumkwe so that they would not have to pay for the water they needed for the cattle. As noted in Chapter 9, Xau's previous wife had died in the early 1990s from tuberculosis. According to the nurse practitioners in Tsumkwe, Xau, too, a man in his late forties, had finally succumbed to tuberculosis after he refused to take his medications any longer.

**Figure 10.3**   The burial of Xau, the star of *The Gods Must Be Crazy*, brings together news media, movie company representatives, tourists, and government workers at a newly created cemetery a few miles outside of Tsumkwe, July 2003 (© Ida Susser)

The nationally televised visit by the President was clearly associated with the new building plans and the investment of government funds in the region. The audience for the speech was from the local African population, children from the school, and media representatives, as well as Ju.

During his visit, the president also met with Ju representatives and the newly appointed Ju member of parliament, indicating that the Ju did have some political leverage. The Ju asked for restrictions on the sale of liquor and some constraints on the migration of Herero cattle herders and others over their land.

## Politics, Liquor, and Religion

The politics of gender have often been tied to liquor and religion. The history of the US temperance movement and the Pentecostal movement studied by Mintz in Puerto Rico in the 1950s – and clearly reflected in my own research in Puerto Rico with respect to HIV/AIDS prevention in a rural barrio in the 1990s – provided many examples of women finding strength in the organization of the church to combat the transfer of their husband's earnings directly to the liquor industry (Mintz 1974; Susser 1992). In this respect, Ju women appear to be following a well-trodden path (Brasher 1997; Griffith 1997; Robbins 2004).

As noted earlier, by 2003, Francina, an articulate, English-speaking !Kung woman, probably in her thirties, had been elected to the Traditional Authority, which, at the time, was otherwise composed of Ju men. In village meetings we observed, she was the main spokesperson. The Traditional Authority council voted to ban the sale of kashipembe at Tsumkwe. Hard liquor was, in any case, illegal in the area. They asked the local police to enforce the ban. The police did not take any active role in approaching the shebeens.

The local pastor wrote a letter to the police asking that they address the kashipembe problem. The police claimed they had no spare automobile to carry out inspections and enforce the regulations. Eventually the pastor loaned his vehicle and drove it around the shebeens with the police publicly confiscating barrels of kashipembe. Following this, the pastor was publicly rebuked by local non-Ju politicians and the event received top billing on the front pages of the national newspapers.

We visited a number of shebeens in the following weeks and kashipembe was again much on offer. It was generally believed that kashipembe sales were supported by the local allies of the ruling party, as one of the major sellers was influential in regional party politics.

## Conclusions from 2003

Ju women have a history of autonomy, which still appears significant among Ju of today. Ecotourism as we encountered it in the 1990s did not seem to necessarily be destroying or undermining the social relations between Ju men and women. However, the ecotourism combined with the neoliberal policies that we observed in 2003 seemed to be precipitating rapid and disintegrative changes in the lives of the Ju. One of the consequences appeared to be the concentration of Ju women selling cheap beaded and leather crafts at the main intersection and in front of the now active stores. Another consequence of these shifts, combined with the influx of migrant workers, employed and unemployed, the lack of funds for children in the boarding school, and the lack of investment in any form of public transportation seemed to be the congregation of many Ju and many schoolchildren around the shebeens.

Ju women and other women were much subjugated and exploited around the shebeens when they drank or when their men drank. Francina, as the first woman elected to the Ju council, had been central in trying to address this issue and called on both the church and the local police for assistance. However, in 2003, the new centrality of Tsumkwe to party politics seems to have prevented the Ju men and women from addressing the problem for the moment. As Tsumkwe had been drawn into the neoliberal era and party politics had been linked to the sale of water concessions, tourist and safari concessions, pension concessions, and liquor concessions, the Ju of the Kalahari, up till then somewhat protected by their village networks, had not yet been able to shape or reform the new markets in water, alcohol or women and sex that seem to be emerging.

Remarkably, by 2008, the trend seemed to be reversed. The efforts of the Nyae Nyae Conservancy, the San women in leadership, the Deputy Prime Minister as well as the Minister for Gender Equity and Child Protection, the Namibian Association of Norway, several NGOs, and the engaged anthropologists who formed the

Kalahari People's Fund had redirected development towards capacity building and communal interests.

## Positive Signs in June 2008

Thus, by 2008, by dint of the ongoing efforts of Francina and the other women and men in leadership positions, as well as financing from NGOs and government agencies, many of the trends described in 2003 had been reversed. A San leader was elected to district office for the whole region and there were more women representatives on the Traditional Authority. The newly built housing had been allocated to the Traditional Authority and the San leadership were living there.

Francina had become a major figure and vice chairman of an all-Namibia organization on plant use. While we were in Tsumkwe, she went to Cape Town to meet with indigenous groups to discuss controls on the commoditization of Hoodia.

In 2007, the San had managed to convince the Deputy Prime Minister, Honorable Dr. Libertina Amathila, to come to Tsumkwe and close down the shebeens, which according to most people whom we interviewed has dramatically reduced drinking in the area. Although illicit alcohol was probably available in a few places, when we walked and drove around the edge of town at various times of the day and night, we were surprised to see no openly functioning shebeens and no women sentinels waiting outside.

Ju women sat comfortably outside the new Conservancy G!unku Crafts Store that had been built across from the school, staffed by Ju women and displaying their own new designs of ostrich egg and leather jewellery for reasonable prices. Even when women sold crafts to passing cars, the prices often approximated those in the store.

In spite of the small proportion of San children in the Tsumkwe school, by 2008, we found more young men and women than before who could speak English. For the first time, we found two young San women who could translate for us. Baby Smile shebeen, notoriously operating right next to the school, had been closed down and other shebeens had been pushed far from the school, if they had not completely disappeared. In addition, we saw donkey carts drive waiting children home each Friday and bring them back on Sunday afternoons.

We were extremely impressed with the government and NGO developments which had taken place in Tsumkwe over the previous five years. We found a new clinic, well-developed plans for a forestry conservancy to protect the plant life (such as Hoodia) in the same way as the Nyae Nyae Conservancy protected the wild life. Meetings were taking place to discuss the new conservancy with the Traditional Authority. San were attending training sessions as eco-guides and youth were learning hunting and tracking techniques from those who remembered the old skills.

Along with the other changes Lee and I noticed in Tsumkwe in 2008 was what appeared to be an increase in settlement and intermarriage in the area of the !Kung (a different language group from the Ju but also among the San peoples) as well as Ovambo and other groups. For example, Ju teenagers met and sometimes married students from other groups in school. In addition, as the Ju were now entitled to the land and farming subsidies available in the area, it seemed that more established and respectful marital and economic relationships between groups from the outside and local women were developing. The incomers, following historical patterns, seemed to be easily incorporated into the flexible kin networks and farm outposts of the Ju.

We visited new San outposts with names such as Apelbos, Dospos, and others where the San, some with Ovambo relatives, have planted maize and kept goats and other animals.

San have also found ways to benefit from their exotic representation. At one new outpost we visited, the farm of !Nai and Gunte, !Nai's daughter led us with a group of San women and children to a specially reconstructed grass village a few hundred meters from the outpost. Dressed in elaborate beadwork and a leather skirt over her regular clothes (which we heard had been bought from the pastor's collection of San crafts), !Nai's daughter showed us, and particularly her old friend Richard Lee, how they would dance the traditional dances for tourists to earn money for the village. The dancers, a few women and many young children, were clearly enjoying the performance. It was evident that the San were experimenting with ways to benefit communally from their international reputation.

AIDS has not skyrocketed in the way we feared, and that seemed to vindicate our argument about women, gender equity and the San, as the surrounding groups (who also live right there, walk the same streets, use the same clinic) have the extremely high rates, similar to the rest of southern Africa.

Unfortunately, while AIDS is not as widespread as might have been predicted, drug resistant tuberculosis has become a lethal epidemic particularly among the San. In 2008, according to the nurse at the new Tsumkwe clinic, among approximately 70 people with tuberculosis who were tested, only two were found positive for HIV. However, we heard a number of reports of entire families living on the new farms surrounding Tsumkwe who had succumbed to tuberculosis. We attended a funeral of a 17-year-old boy who had died of drug-resistant tuberculosis, as had his father and other siblings before him. However, Francina told us that the San have asked the government for help and are planning to develop gardens so that they can grow food for people who need to eat something when they come to the clinic to take their medications. We can perhaps be hopeful that this problem too will be effectively addressed by the San leadership with the help of the many new resources.

In 2008 we visited a newly opened Community Learning and Development Center, the latest result of many years of work by Megan Biesele, director of the Kalahari People's Fund and others. The new center provided Internet connections (from which I was able to e-mail the publisher!), national newspapers, and books about the San, some being translated into Ju/'hoansi by Ju speakers at the center. We observed residents at Tsumkwe, both Ju and others, using the center like a local library, stopping to read the newspapers and access computer training. Afternoons, after school, young people watched television together. Meanwhile, AIDS training was also evident, with male and female condoms available and much other important information.

Such findings show that the emerging problems of privatization can, in fact, be reversed by long-term cooperative investment by the San themselves. This has been encouraged by the San women and men in leadership and many different activists, researchers, and government agencies. The widespread sale of alcohol and the shebeens, along with the street competition for the sale of crafts to tourists, which seemed to be undermining the autonomy of the San women and setting the scene for the spread of AIDS in 2003 has been halted. Instead, remarkably, the gender equity that, we argued, protects the village San from AIDS has been supported by the Conservancy G!unku Crafts Store, the plans for the forestry conservancy to protect the plants for the benefit of the local residents, and the expansion of the number of women in the Traditional Authority.

# 11

# "The Power of Practical Thinking" – The Role of Organic Intellectuals

This book began with a discussion of globalization and the anti-global movements with the aim of placing the social movements around AIDS in this context. AIDS is a worldwide epidemic but, as we have seen, it bears most brutally on the global South and within that sphere affects women more than men and young women most of all. However, AIDS has also been the cause of some of the most effective anti-global initiatives. I use the term "anti-global" not in the sense of opposing globalization, but in the sense of challenging global regulation to take account of the need for medicines at affordable prices in the global South. Over the past decade, anti-global movements for the treatment and prevention of AIDS, operating in global forums, such as International AIDS Society conferences, the World Trade Organization meetings at Davos, Qatar and elsewhere, G8 annual summits as well as the counter-hegemonic World Social Forum, have transformed the discourse on AIDS.

Clearly the movements around AIDS have changed the rules of global capital in ways many did not believe possible. Pharmaceutical companies have had to permit lower pricing for poor countries and allow the manufacture of some drugs outside of world patent laws. Obviously, capital has regrouped, defending prices and profits in wealthy countries while introducing new ways to patent second-stage drugs.[1] However, even here, many of the changes that were won required corporations to negotiate with the global South and recognize the needs of the poor in previously unforeseen ways (Parker 2003; Petchesky 2003).

South African AIDS policy has also been challenged and forced into concessions as a result of a powerful combination of local and international protests (Marais 2000; Petchesky 2003; Robins 2006; Schneider 2002; Schneider and Stein 2002). At the 2006 Toronto International AIDS Society Conference, the South African Minister of Health, Manto Tshabalala-Msimang, was rebuked on the international stage for her promotion of lemon and wild garlic as AIDS treatment. Following this event, she was temporarily replaced in negotiations around AIDS by her deputy, Nozizwe Madlala-Routledge, herself an important activist with respect to women's historical conditions in South Africa. Later, Quarraisha Abdool Karim and other health activists were brought back into the monitoring and evaluation of the AIDS rollout and, in December 2007, Thabo Mbeki was replaced as President of the ANC by Jacob Zuma. New openings for AIDS treatment and prevention became possible. Even in South Africa, a treatment plan is slowly being implemented.

Nevertheless, AIDS prevention has faced major setbacks. As noted in the opening chapters here, scientific research around women's issues has been slow. The very funding successes, and particularly the $15 billion earmarked by President Bush in 2003, have undermined preventive messages, limited the distribution of condoms, both male and female, and promoted moralistic, punitive, and marginalizing perspectives. Additional funding authorized by the US Senate in July 2008 may involve the same limitations to a greater or lesser extent.[2]

Worldwide, more people are contracting AIDS than are being treated. Even as treatment is being distributed around the world, it cannot keep up with the spread of the epidemic (AIDS Vaccine Advocacy Coalition 2007). And, as we have known for a decade, sexual subordination of women is a major engine of new infection (Piot 2001). Although the predominance of AIDS in women of the global South can certainly be attributed the structural violence of the world economy (Barnett and Whiteside 2002; Farmer et al. 1996), I have been trying to show that this is only half the story. Indeed, the failure to develop an in-depth analysis of difference leaves political economy open to "cultural" critiques that ignore the class nature of the problem and focus only on "identity." I have argued that to interrogate gendered difference, racial ideologies and religious traditions must be critiqued within an analysis of changing political and economic process. In particular, only through modes of prevention that actually consider carefully and address women's different bodily, social, and sexual experiences within historical contexts can we hope to fight the AIDS epidemic effectively. In other words, we must take history seriously and examine the particular ways in which difference has been constructed over time and in different situations.

For some researchers, the concept of "inclusive citizenship" illuminates civil society demands around civil rights, welfare rights, and health care (Chanock 2000; Leach 1998; Petryna 2002). In the current era of welfare state restructuring, when poverty or childrearing are no longer recognized as legitimate reasons for dependency (Susser 1996b; Susser 1997), people can demand assistance due to disease diagnosis and this too can be viewed as a demand for inclusive citizenship (Petryna 2002). For example, in the 1980s in New York City, homeless people were entitled to permanent housing if they had an AIDS diagnosis but otherwise they were consigned for the night to large warehouses with beds. Since at that time the diagnosis for AIDS did not include the common symptoms found in women, many women died homeless and penniless before they ever met the criteria for diagnosis for AIDS. As we saw in Chapter 1, women had to fight in order to change the description of symptoms of AIDS by researchers – and government – since they needed the diagnostic label in order to access services.[3] Such women might be seen as excluded from biological citizenship and demanding that recognition.

However, the concept of "citizenship demands" accepts the redefinition of the welfare state and defines the sick narrowly as an interest group that is able to make legitimate demands on the state. The history of social movements around AIDS has a much stronger component of resistance to capital, such as the demands on the pharmaceutical companies for free and cheaper medicines, and critiques of global inequality. Such wider perspectives on the restructuring of the state and capital are not adequately recognized by defining social movements simply as struggles for citizenship among a variety of different identities.

In the effort to contribute to a politically engaged anthropology (Brodkin 1988; Singer 1995; Smith 1999; Susser 1982; Susser 1985), I have analyzed people's active contribution to political change within the cultural and historical processes which led them there. I have drawn for my analysis on Gramsci's understanding of the role of intellectuals and also on his concepts of common and practical sense in the interpretation of culture. Although I have mentioned these concepts schematically along the way, in this chapter we turn to these ideas in order to explore the relations between people's on-the-ground experiences and the broader political challenges of AIDS.

In terms of the power of practical thinking, the findings of this research are surprisingly hopeful. In spite of the remorseless depredations of AIDS, with its ever-increasing rate of infection among both married women and girls, we have seen critical perspectives prevail and social movements transform public culture. Through the darkest hours of misinformation, profiteering, and nationalist rhetoric, we have seen poor women communicating about their collective situation in practical, non-judgmental ways, as they address the collective prevention of AIDS. In the face of government mystification, misinformation, and inaction, we have seen women recognize both preventive measures such as the female condom and the effectiveness of AIDS treatment.

In terms of the question of transformative action, in each setting described in this volume, whether South Africa, Namibia, or among the San of the Kalahari, we have seen the emergence of organic intellectuals who sharpen the recognition of possible solutions and frame dreams as realistic demands. We have seen such leaders work with the support of the local people to generate social movements and change the public discourse around AIDS. In South Africa, we saw plans for treatment taking shape and accelerating. In Namibia, we saw the female condom finally appear in the truck stops and the supermarkets at heavily subsidized prices. In each case, major barriers had to be overcome in order to win government support and constant struggles are required to maintain any successes.

To recognize the seeds of progressive social transformations we need to begin to identify which groups promote social justice for all, including women and people of color. In contrast, we need to be able to see which groups promote moralistic perspectives, stereotyping sexual mores of subordinate populations and using such negative stereotypes to assign blame and punishment for society's ills. Moral judgments and commentaries on sexuality provide a canvas to interpret protest movements fighting for AIDS treatment and prevention. The pervasive or hegemonic construction of AIDS "risk groups" early on, in terms of gay sexuality, "Haitian" identity, drug using or prostitution, went far beyond the issue of sexual identities in constructing stigmatized groups (Baer et al. 2003). The first organized social movements with respect to gay identity such as Gay Men's Health Crisis (GMHC) and ACT UP, countered the moralistic and stigmatizing labeling of men who have sex with men (Padgug and Oppenheimer 1992; Shilts 1987). The racial and subaltern stigmas associated with the labeling of Haitian identity as a risk were also countered by protest (Baer et al. 2003). In 1990 thousands of Haitian doctors, other professionals, and local residents marched over the Brooklyn Bridge in protest against the classification by the US government of "Haitians" as a risk group for AIDS.[4]

The success of harm-reduction approaches highlights the importance of counteracting the stigmatization and criminalization of drug users. At the Toronto 2006 International AIDS Society Conference, harm-reduction perspectives finally attained international recognition in the face of objections from the Bush regime and other governments, as a plenary speaker presented a wealth of incontrovertible evidence showing the success of such programs (Wodak 2006).[5] For the past two decades, sex workers have mobilized for union recognition and legal status in many parts of the world, as exemplified by the Sex Workers Advocacy Network (SWAN) and Sonagachi (the path-breaking Calcutta sex workers collective mentioned in Chapter 1). They have transformed the image of "prostitutes" perpetrated in the early risk categories (Cornish and Ghosh 2007; Jana et al. 2004). However, all such initiatives continue to be marginalized by President Bush's PEPFAR initiative, and are still struggling for international implementation.

In its very nature, collective organizing around AIDS has had to address the hegemonic moral judgments embedded in ideas of class status, religious respectability, and national (including post-colonial) pride. As Pierre Bourdieu explored in his concept of *habitus*, "style" and manners are crucial in the making of class difference and marking elite status (Bourdieu 1993). Following this insight, post-colonial literature has shown the ways in which purveyors of moralism help to differentiate by style and manners, even matters of sexual conduct, the colonized from the colonizers, and the middle class from the poor (Comaroff 1997; Stoler 2002). Such differentiation is frequently based on the manners and presentation of women and their sexuality.

The control of women's sexuality has been tied to the history of state power, to the perpetuation of lineage alliances, the differentiation of class in the capitalist state, and the differentiation of the colonizers from the colonized. Whether we are reading about the Irish working class in the England of the nineteenth century, the Inca women after the Spanish conquest of the Andes (Silverblatt 1980; Silverblatt 1987) or the black population in South Africa under apartheid, we encounter the derogatory moralizing comments about the sexual morals of the subaltern population. In fact, interestingly, among the Inca, we find women who break the rules under Spanish colonial settlement referred to as wild women or witches (Silverblatt 1980), recalling the classification of women as witches by the Inquisition in early modern Europe (Schneider 1991).[6] The richness of the research in South Africa allows an examination of these issues in historical context.

As noted in Chapter 6, in order to capture the counter-hegemonic mobilization with respect to morals so essential to AIDS discourse, I have adopted the Gramscian distinctions between "common" sense and "practical" or "good" sense to describe grassroots views. Building on these distinctions, we can also begin to understand the role of intellectuals in concentrating the murmurs and possibly silenced critique of a disenfranchised or subordinated population. Intellectuals who promote common sense moralisms of sin and condemnation that bear heavily on the disenfranchised without attention to the practical struggles of daily life contribute to the ruling hegemony. In contrast, the ideas of the organic intellectual can be seen as drawing on the roots of practical sense of the subaltern population as it struggles to improve conditions.

With respect to grassroots movements around AIDS, movements may be organized either in terms of hegemonic "common sense" or counter-hegemonic "practical sense." (See Linger 1993 for a similar discussion about Italian social movements.) For example, virginity movements represent a grassroots social movement that adopts hegemonic moralistic categories of sin and redemption. In contrast, the Treatment Action Campaign, in its practical non-judgmental approach to AIDS, represents a counter-hegemonic grassroots movement.

In South Africa, the making of masculinity, femininity, and sexuality have clearly reflected changing moral pressures. Hunter (2005) calls on "common sense" to discuss the fragmented cultural roots of the making of masculinity among Zulu-speaking men. He finds that in the early twentieth century, both single men and women were allowed a certain amount of sexual freedom, as long as no pregnancy resulted. By the 1950s such expectations had diverged: men's sexual license grew to include married men, while women became more restricted. In the later period, those women who had more than one lover were often referred to in derogatory terms.

Just as researchers have begun to look at the historical making of masculinity and femininity, we can trace over time the making of good sense and organic intellectuals in the historical documentation of political consciousness (Bonner 1990; Bozzoli and Nkotsoe 1991; Walker 1991). In their study *Women of Phokeng*, Bozzoli and Nkotsoe use the terms "derived" and "inherent" ideas to distinguish the emergence of women's consciousness. Their research focused on women who, between 1945 and 1960, were subject to the oppressive measures of apartheid, an era that included both the eviction of women from Sophiatown and the much-resisted effort by the apartheid government to impose passes on women. Bozzoli and Nkotsoe define "derived" in terms of the ideologies of popular organizations and "inherent" as the ideas the women derived from their own experiences. In some sense, these distinctions correspond to the "derived" ideas of organic intellectuals and the "inherent" ideas that women generate, which I have labeled "practical sense." They see these two sets of ideas intersecting in the protests over the evictions and the pass laws. They note that the reactions of the women were varied and changed over time. However, they do classify many as "conservative" (i.e. following the common-sense explanations of the government). For example, Bozzoli and Nkotsoe quote one conservative woman in describing the unrest over the imposition of the pass laws on women:

If there is a group of people which has accepted the law, there is no alternative for the others to accept it also. We don't own the land; it is theirs [Whites]. . . . One has to obey authority and do according to its bidding (Bozzoli and Nkotsoe 1991:170).

Although Bozzoli and Nkotsoe note that few women were political activists, a number manifest what they term "political consciousness" – or what I have called here a practical counter-hegemonic view – and some participated in protest movements at particular historical moments. Of significance is the fragility and changeability of such approaches. Following the heavy repression of the apartheid era, they show the breaking of women's resolve and their retreat to conservatism and common sense hegemonic echoes.

In her collection of oral histories of the gendered and spatialized violence in Mpumulanga District in the 1980s, Debby Bonnin (2000) documents women adopting the symbolic role of "mother." She describes women taking stands to defend young men and women in the midst of the brutal murders associated with the battle for control of territory between the youth of the United Democratic Front (which was at that time the public anti-apartheid coalition) and those of Inkatha. While Bonnin is explicit that such women were not "feminists" and they were fighting with their men for freedom from apartheid and not specifically for women's rights, she nevertheless notes that such practical experience changed both women's use of space in the township and their relations to their men partners. Women became more assertive in fighting for their own autonomy and took over many of the household decisions. In addition, where feminists did echo women's practical sense, they served in the role of organic intellectuals, framing the demands of the community.

This case is particularly relevant today, as Bonnin describes Nozizwe Madlala-Routledge, as we have seen, a pivotal figure in the battle for treatment in South Africa today. During the violent confrontations of the late 1980s, Madlala-Routledge was one of the leading members of the South African National Organization of Women, which organized a prayer vigil of women for peace. In this case, in responding to a call by Nelson Mandela for women to stand up for peaceful negotiation, such women could be understood as organic intellectuals who combined their demands for national unity among working-class Africans against apartheid with the women's movement. As mentioned earlier, in 2006, Madlala-Routledge was involved in the implementation of the national AIDS plan[7] in the months-long absence of the Minister of Health, Manto Tshabalala-Msimang. Madlala-Routledge was deputy Minister of Health until fired by Mbeki in 2007 in a decision which aroused national and worldwide criticism (New York Times 2007).

Recent studies have examined the moralisms inherent in the AIDS movement and its association with virginity testing, which was started in the 1990s by two teachers who trace their ideas to Zulu tradition. As we saw in Chapter 6, although there were and still are a variety of coming-of-age ceremonies for young girls and potential brides, the origins and form of virginity testing in pre-colonial times are open to much discussion (Gluckman 1965; Hunter 2005; Krige and Comaroff 1981;

Leclerc-Madlala 2001; Scorgie 2002). However, virginity testing has now converged with fragments of Christianity to develop a moral code of abstinence for girls before marriage. Current rituals involve new ideas of secondary virginity, which are now common in South Africa and other regions such as Uganda as well as the United States. In addition, while such virginity testing is ostensibly based on an observation of a broken hymen, it has become merged with images of youthfulness, a lithe body and other manifestations of the desirable young woman (Scorgie 2002). Thus, the women teachers who started the virginity testing campaign and those who promote such rites, are in fact adopting hegemonic ideas of sin and morality melded with the use of fragmented images of Zulu "culture."

Many have noted how young girls have given birth within months of being declared virgins (Scorgie 2002). In fact, some people seem to be developing a practical critique of the rituals as they argue that the maintenance of abstinence among youth requires education and lifestyle changes more than such a one-time test. Some young girls also see the virginity testing rite as a festival and a status maintaining label. Rather than relying on the abstinence such rituals are supposed to represent, some participants talk candidly and practically about the need for condoms so that they will not find themselves pregnant. Such conversations do not seem to carry images of sin and condemnation but rather emerge in the discussion of practical matters (Scorgie 2002).

Thus, as we have seen with virginity testing, Christian ideas of sin and virginity have merged with Zulu images of the healthy, marriageable girl and the control of fertility. Such hegemonic ideas fit well with the historical gendering of space and power. In rural areas in most of southern Africa, customary law has favored patrilineal inheritance and the national land reform projects are leaving women furthest behind. Even in urban areas under apartheid, housing was frequently assigned to the male head of household. If a woman in need of housing for herself or her family had no husband, she had to ask the oldest son to sign her lease.[8]

As we have seen, inequality by gender was historically entrenched in both the rural and urban areas. However, recently, under the impact of restructuring, more men have become unemployed. The increasing loss of jobs among men in the past decade has greatly exacerbated men's search for status through multiple partners as well as rape and brutality against women (Hunter 2005; Niehaus 2003). Women, meanwhile, subject to invisible unemployment[9] and consistently poorer, remain in need of men's financial support (Bentley 2004). Clearly, when the increasing joblessness of men is combined with their patrilineal rights to land and housing, in both the urban and rural areas, we can understand how gendered conflict was inflamed.

## Public Intellectuals

Through formulating and articulating the narrative of class, organic intellectuals help to transform a working-class which fits an abstract sociological category into a class that is self-conscious and can act in its own interests. Further developing the distinction between organic intellectuals and traditional intellectuals, we might see the organic intellectual as one who combined active engagement with the rethinking of society from the point of view of working-class people. Manning Marable places Frantz Fanon and Malcolm X in this context, quoting Gramsci saying that, "The new intellectual can no longer consist in eloquence, which is an exterior and momentary mover of feelings and passions, but in active participation in practical life, as constructor, organizer, 'permanent persuader' and not just a simple orator" (Marable 2005:6). Terry Eagleton's analysis of the nineteenth-century Anglo–Irish intellectuals, *Scholars and Rebels* (1999), is also of interest here. He defines these intellectuals as marginal to the colonial center and, as a result, espousing the nationalist cause in Ireland with a sense of practical engagement. Eagleton contrasts the practical engagement and vibrant intellectual community of the colonized and marginalized Irish scholars with the scholarly disengagement of the English intellectuals of the same period.

As the Anglo–Irish situation demonstrates, the historical moment in which scholars emerge may produce a more or less engaged community of organic intellectuals. I would suggest that the long struggle against apartheid in South Africa generated its own small but vibrant community of organic intellectuals among the Black, Indian and White population (to use the inevitable apartheid categories). In their discussions of land rights, education, and health for a democratic state, they articulated a vision of a non-racial society as represented in the Freedom Charter developed in the early twentieth century by the ANC and restated in 1943 and 1955.

Many of the anti-apartheid leaders who helped promote the Freedom Charter and their younger followers have been involved in framing the debate around AIDS in the current era. In recent years, Nelson Mandela has been a powerful, outspoken advocate and we might see Zackie Achmat as one of the younger followers, whose politics and emotional allegiances were carved out in the apartheid battles. However, in the current era, intellectuals such as Thabo Mbeki and Jacob Zuma, who might have represented the next generation of organic intellectuals leading the anti-apartheid struggle, have come to represent a new elite, with new traditions and newly imposed sexual moralities in relation to the contemporary social condition.

In a sense, adopting dissident views, Mbeki on AIDS was fighting the moral messages of colonialism as he understood them. In a 2001 memorial to Z. K. Matthews, a former professor at Fort Hare (attended by Mbeki's father, Govan Mbeki) and a revered ANC leader from the 1940s, President Thabo Mbeki lamented the view "that we are but natural-born, promiscuous carriers of germs, unique in the world; they proclaim that our continent is doomed to an inevitable mortal end because of our unconquerable devotion to the sin of lust."[10] His argument was made to counteract the "shameful" image of the black man that the West has created. Jacob Zuma has been more open to AIDS research and has not actively joined AIDS denialists. However, he became famous for his remark that he took a shower after sex with an HIV-positive women because it "would minimize the risk of contracting the disease [HIV]" (BBC News 2006; Motsei 2007). Zuma's argument, which was accepted by a jury when he was charged with rape, was basically that he was an African man and that rape was not only acceptable, but expected customary behavior (Motsei 2007). In his court testimony, he explained that he was prepared to marry the accuser and "if we had reached an agreement with that, I would have had my cows ready" (BBC News 2006). Thus, he framed his actions in a "traditionalist" patriarchal moralism (Mthathi 2006). As Sipho Mthathi, then General Secretary of the TAC, wrote "Zuma's statements about what 'culture' says about women, sexual relationships and men's entitlements, and how HIV is transmitted shocked all of us" (Mthathi 2006:2). For both Mbeki and Zuma, we might understand their defense of African masculinity as resistance to Western tropes.

Where poor African men find themselves with less and less access to work, they are reminded of the Zulu or Xhosa, or many other groups', militant male identity (a warrior identity exacerbated in the wars over colonial settlement) and patrilineal inheritance patterns, as well as the "*inhoxale*" expectations of respect for men by women (Hunter 2005; Morrell 2001). From a common-sense perspective, they might turn to gendered conflict to ameliorate their situation. In this explosive setting, the images of masculinity, which have been widely promoted in different ways by both Thabo Mbeki and Jacob Zuma, resonate with such gendered conflict. Such images, representative of a hegemonic ideology of masculinity, tap into the resentment and loss of poor African men.

Ironically, as Martin Chanock has pointed out in his review of culture and human rights in Africa, opposition to what are perceived by many as Western tropes such as women's rights and sexual rights provide the language for the hegemonies of post-colonial power today. Orientalizing and occidentalizing are parts of the narrative paradigms of today:

> ... those rights discourses in which culture is invoked as an argument against universalism now largely belong to rulers, not to those who may need rights protected, who talk in terms of wrongs and needs, not rights and culture (Chanock 2000:15).

Unfortunately, as noted earlier, the loss of poor men's employment, which many argue has precipitated brutal gendered conflict, may in fact have been exacerbated by the policies of neoliberalism implemented by the ANC government. In addition, the worsening of women's condition through neoliberal restructuring, including lack of investment in smaller manufacturing as well as social services, where women are both employed and seek assistance, has increased women's dependence on men's resources and the necessary resort to multiple partners.

As the increasing unemployment and insufficient investment in social programs precipitated the worsening patterns of gendered violence, it also opened the way for men seeking political support to promote cultural claims of patriarchal traditions. As mentioned in Chapters 3 and 4, in South Africa, such patriarchal values resonated well with the fundamentalist Christian values of the former apartheid members of the far right, some of whom were still among the wealthy white elite.

Thus the cultural claims of an elite came to fit well with economic restructuring, as Chanock notes for other parts of Africa:

> As the foreign-inspired structural adjustment programmes cut into popular areas of patronage it was easier for elites to organize support for their own version of rights against a "foreign" version which had little basis of internal support to begin with. It was not difficult for the challenged elites to present different versions of rights in terms of cultural struggle because in the first place the demand for first-generation civil rights was "foreign"-supported, and, in the second place, second-generation collective rights, which could be portrayed in culturally collective terms, were compatible with and, indeed, strengthened the elites' control of the state (Chanock 2000:30).

## Rites, Rituals, and Resistance

Ideas alone do not mobilize people, as anthropologists have long pointed out. From a conservative point of view, involvement in mass rituals and collective emotional experiences help to generate loyalty and action in relation to the state or hegemonic "common sense." In *Making the Fascist Self*, the participation in mass rallies in Verona and elsewhere helped to create a committed fascist youth movement in Italy (Berezin 1997). In southern Africa, we might see a punitive moral in the virginity rituals previously described.

Similarly, people with emerging practical sense may hear their ideas framed or sharpened by organic intellectuals but it is in the ritual process of protests, demonstrations, prayer vigils, and, for AIDS, near-death experiences that the emotions and commitments are built among activists (Robins 2006). Thus, collective participation is a crucial component of counter-hegemonic mobilization and the transformation of the moral and economic order, whether it be the Durban 2000 International AIDS Society Conference and the protests by the South African Treatment Action Campaign, the Women and Girls' March at the Toronto 2006 International AIDS Society Conference or the march for the female condom in Namibia.

The South African Treatment Action Campaign (TAC) has had an enormous impact, not only in inspiring people with respect to treatment but also in redefining AIDS away from sexual shame. In Soweto, when Mandela put on the TAC "HIV Positive" T-shirt, he was joining in the efforts to redefine public culture around AIDS and shame (BBC News 2006). The TAC has also educated people about what they might need and how to organize to get it. The location of clinics by Médecins Sans Frontières, dispensing treatment in Soweto and the Eastern Cape, had crucial roles in counteracting the myth of the toxicity of Western medicine. Beyond the progressive humanitarian organizations, the missions that provided treatment and the universities, foundations, and the Global Fund to Fight AIDS, Tuberculosis and Malaria (itself the product of a worldwide treatment action campaign) which paid for demonstration treatment programs all contributed to transforming public culture in South Africa. As treatment was seen to work, local people joined the TAC to demand that it be made accessible.

In her story, Sibongile Mkhize talks about the lack of knowledge that treatment existed or how to find it at all. Clearly, Sibongile's sister was the kind of woman with practical sense who would have benefited from the TAC. She was spirited enough that she might even have joined such a social movement, had she lived long enough to find out that treatment was possible. The movement provided the impetus to challenge the discourse on AIDS treatment and the vision to bring about the changes. Sibongile's sister and her openness and outspokenness about AIDS represent the grass roots from which such a movement could grow.

Similarly, the dying man who wrote to the church congregation in Namibia and the pastors who came for training in Windhoek were working towards a practical-sense perspective on AIDS (see Chapter 8). In their participation in our seminar, the pastors made clear that they were not concerned about sin, but simply wanted to know how to help youth protect themselves from this disease. In spite of the fact that we heard another local pastor extolling the hegemonic views of sin and refusing to advocate condoms, mothers simply did not follow the teachings. Namibian mothers devoted to the church provided their young sons with condoms, as they told us and as we saw by one son's bed in the hut that he occupied.

On a smaller scale, international and national non-governmental organizations succeeded in changing the public discourse about the female condom in Namibia based on overwhelming grassroots support. When women and men learned about the female condom, they were keen to try it and none of the local women invoked religious disapproval. In Namibia and South Africa, as well as Zimbabwe, women wrote petitions asking their governments to provide the female condom. In Namibia, these demands were crystallized in the campaign initiated by Veronica de Klerk, the president of Women's Action for Development, supported by international funds. In August 1999, on National Condom Day, de Klerk announced to the national newspapers with much outrage, that there was not a female condom to be found in the stores of Namibia. She demanded that the government include the female condom in its campaigns. From that beginning, WAD together with the Rainbow Coalition (an internationally funded non-governmental organization focused on sexual rights), and the local representatives of UNAIDS and WHO worked to make the female condom available in Namibia.

It is significant here that the Rainbow Coalition was an organization working for gay and lesbian rights. The organization had led marches to protest the denial of citizenship to a lesbian woman whose partner was Namibian. In this respect, the Rainbow Coalition and the demands for the female condom each emerged from a counter-hegemonic challenge to moralistic images of human sexuality. Such moralisms, here, as in South Africa, can be traced back to missionary influences and post-colonial religious organizations (Comaroff and Comaroff 1997; Hunter 2005).

As we examined the gendered cultural barriers to science and prevention (in Chapters 1 and 2), it became evident that social movements were key to changes in the representation of women in science and politics as well as in public culture in general. It also became clear in later chapters that poor African women, given the opportunity to see and hear for themselves what was possible, demonstrated a practical-, good-sense approach as a product of the thoughtful analyzing of experience. They counteracted the moralistic and inflexible "common sense" which can be understood as a repetition of long-worn familiar and unexamined ideas.

But some women, relying on government and mission misinformation about nutrition and herbal remedies, had no practical knowledge of broader options of either treatment or prevention. We hear the "common sense" unexamined approach when people are afraid or uninformed about practical possibilities. However, overwhelmingly, the women in these case studies adopted a thoughtful practical perspective to their problems. Thus, notwithstanding the continuing shocking rates of infection among young women in South Africa, we can hope that the nexus of popular practical sense and protest movements, focused by organic intellectuals and seeking treatment, correct scientific information, and comprehensive reproductive resources, can begin to stem the tide.

## The Past in the Present

To me, one of the most revealing aspects of this research has been the significance of historical experience in shaping people's reactions to contemporary situations. The ethnographic findings suggest that sexual decisions are framed by gendered perspectives etched by such expectations as the payment of *lobola* among the people of KwaZulu or the autonomy of Ju/'hoansi women. Just like the vestiges of a church marriage in Europe, defined in a legal system long after many of the wedded no longer practice religious rituals, such expectations are the building blocks or possibly markers upon which contemporary strategies can be created and adjusted.

For example, we know that political economic shifts have placed poor men in a difficult position. Ironically, as men lose their jobs, poor women, largely excluded from the formal labor market, have little choice but to depend on men even more. However, now that many men have fewer jobs, women must multiply the number they depend upon to make ends meet, precipitating jealousy and violence.

To address these exigencies and the increasingly contradictory demands on both men and women, in some parts of KwaZulu, women talk about men paying only the initial *lobola*, which used to indicate the first step of marriage. According to traditional rules, after the initial payment the couple has legitimate rights to have sexual relations. However, many men do not have the resources or full expectations of completing the full *lobola* payments over time. In this new situation, they can initiate such payments with several women. Thus, the payment of *lobola*, which used to protect women and constitute a form of engagement and security, is still salient in urban communities but no longer assures the woman that her husband will stay with her or take care of the children. This may also reflect the decreasing importance of children, who were previously crucial to agricultural labor, in an urban setting. In addition, of course, this new pattern greatly increases the vulnerability of women to AIDS.

As we saw in Chapters 9 and 10, among the Ju, women's autonomy is still clearly evident in their reactions to everyday events. Women speak up in front of powerful men at important national organizing meetings and demand mosquito netting materials or criticize political decisions. Women see themselves as able to teach their husbands about condoms and, if necessary, provide them in a sexual encounter. However, the autonomy of the women also allows them to go to bars where they become vulnerable to beating, rape, and exploitation from Ju men and especially men from other groups among whom they have less respect.

In terms of the breadth of knowledge, government and religious institutions seemed to have much influence. In South Africa, we found that government discourse about the toxicity of treatment led women with limited exposure to alternative sources of information to reject the calls to mobilize and support the Treatment Action Campaign. Government and religious institutions also had a major impact on the availability of preventive technology. In northern Namibia, some international religious representatives and many women members of congregations advocated AIDS education and the use of condoms. Nevertheless, in spite of the fact that even devout mothers were providing such life-saving resources to their sons, condoms were not available on the premises of major hospitals.

Overall, people's strategies reflected a practical understanding of their relationships shaped by a historical experience of cultural difference. Here, to more precisely situate the role of culture, I would like to consider the issues of "culture" and the argument initiated by Ferguson (1999) with respect to Zambia. Ferguson maintains that the emphasis on class and the emergence of capitalism led urban anthropologists to look for family forms in southern Africa similar to those they had observed in Western societies. The nuclear family was expected to appear as industrial capitalism developed. Ferguson argues instead that culture reasserted itself and that kinship relations of today resemble many of the patterns first described in the African tribal situations. I would make a similar argument but emphasize instead the flexibility of culture. As many have phrased the issue, it would be more accurate to point to the way in which historic cultural tropes have been reinvented by local people or by political leaders to address historically specific situations (Ranger 1997).

Certainly, we cannot overemphasize the impact of global capital. Clearly we are dealing with a society today in which class is salient, and the national and global economy are crucial forces. Since the 1930s in southern Africa, workers have indeed contested power in the mines and elsewhere in similar ways to the nineteenth-century Welsh mineworkers of Great Britain (Burawoy 1998; Gluckman 1961). Since the waves of crippling strikes in South Africa during the 1980s, the power of the South African trade union movement (COSATU) has been recognized as a crucial force in the successful battle against apartheid. Researchers as diverse as A. L. Epstein (1958) and Mayer (1971) were cognizant of the differences between changes in the workplace, associated with wages, employer–employee relations, and unions, and changes in the household associated with patterns of marriage, inheritance, and responsibility for children.

However, clearly, one of the more glaring gaps in the early urban analyses had to do with kinship and gender. In overlooking the politics of gender in relation to kinship, the Manchester School anthropologists reflected 1950s Marxism, the American sociology of Talcott Parsons and Robert Merton, and the anthropology of George Murdock. The idea that kinship under capitalism could be characterized in terms of a "nuclear family" based on the man's wage and the woman's domestic labor was, as we now know, a particularly mistaken assumption that described aspirations toward a specific bourgeois class experience in a particular era (Coontz 1988; Sennett 1970). Residence in a "nuclear household" is only one aspect of family. Political systems that regulate resource sharing, food distribution, and inheritance patterns serve to consolidate wealth, poverty, and class in capitalist societies in many different ways.

However, in criticizing the notion that a nuclear family was necessarily the result of capitalism, we need not neglect the insights of A. L. Epstein and others among the urban anthropologists of the Zambian Copperbelt, who understood that cultural constraints operated differently in different situations and particularly with respect to waged labor as opposed to family. In his classic study of urban Lusaka, *The Kalela Dance*, Clyde Mitchell (1956) described how mineworkers sang tribal songs in competitive dances during their day off from the mines. Mitchell analyzed these displays in class terms and suggested that even tribal identifications in Lusaka were structured by the new urban environment. Nevertheless, he described marriages still established and adjudicated according to custom. Epstein also suggests that the historical processes that generate cultural difference were more salient in relation to kinship and gender than they were in the workplace. His research demonstrated that mineworkers looked to unions, not customary law, to address their grievances, while they structured their home lives according to customary procedures that allowed them the privileges of masculinity.

While both Mitchell and Epstein described marriage and kinship as intimately intertwined with customary law, neither of them assume that this is an unchanging category. In their view, people strategized with respect to customary law (Van Velsen 1967). It was never one static set of rules. People implemented customs and acknowledged kinship according to the situation and in this way influenced the gendered distribution of income, property, and security in both urban and rural settings (Gluckman 1965; Turner 1957; Watson 1971).

Abner Cohen talked of tribalization and detribalization being significant at different historical moments (Cohen 1974). His theoretical framework did not take into account the ways in which tribal and customary identification may shift in one direction in the public realm of trade and urban politics but may shift in a different direction in the equally public discourse with respect to women. Nevertheless, in his 1960s ethnography of Hausa cattle trading in Nigeria, Cohen described the situational nature of customary restrictions on women who observed purdah in marriage but were perfectly capable of traveling and trading unprotected when single or divorced.

Customary law remains vital to this day in defining the obligations of family and particularly in framing women's situations (Nhlapo 2000). As Gwendolyn Mikell has shown so well, the underlying contradiction for women today in many African societies is the relationship between customary law and Western constitutional formulations (see this argument with respect to AIDS in Bassett and Mhloyi 1991). However, as Chanock argues in his review of debates in Africa around customary rights, the maintenance of customary law is frequently in the interests of the maintenance of patriarchal status quo:

> The areas of family law and land law are most often invoked as falling within the realm of the cultural, and are both often linked also to religion . . . it is by no means obvious why some areas of law have retained seemingly secure places in the realm of culture while others relating to basic matters of rights, entitlements, powers and duties (say . . . contract, labor law . . .) have not (Chanock 2000:34).

Chanock also points out the centrality of rights to land in conflicts over customary law and recognizes the relationship of such conflicts to labor migration and insecurity:

> It was, and is, the threatened loss of land which produces the most vigorous claims about its cultural embeddedness and inalienability. And it was, and is, the strains on family organization produced by the cash economy, migration and urbanization and the feared collapse of reciprocal obligations between generations, that make emphasis on the cultural nature of family authority and roles so necessary (Chanock 2000:35).

As the government demands greater sacrifice from workers and poor people lack social services, customary law becomes even more important as a point of security and stability. We can clearly see this process in Ferguson's (1999) description of the return to custom following Zambia's disastrous economic decline. Clearly, as AIDS wreaks death and destruction across southern Africa, such rights and obligations become areas of extreme conflict, which often break down, as noted earlier, along gender lines. These lines of insecurity and conflict leave the situation wide open for hegemonic intellectuals to explain in their own terms. As Chanock points out:

> The experience of difference depends on the power to create culture, on the labor of elites in essentializing, displaying, and institutionalizing elements of the myriad of practices in any community (Chanock 2000:20–21).

## Contemporary Notions of Witchcraft

A related area in which anthropological insights are particularly illuminating is the debate around witchcraft and sorcery. Modernization arguments see witchcraft disappearing as modernity and industry lead to more rational scientific perspectives. In contrast, during the 1960s, Shirley Lindenbaum showed that among the Fore of New Guinea, ideas of sorcery were exacerbated by the expansion of colonial control and the loss of land. Since then, many contemporary anthropologists have documented the continuing salience of such ideas (Comaroff and Comaroff 2001b; Geschiere 1997b) and this has been fully borne out in the world of AIDS (Ashforth 2000; Ashforth 2005; McGregor 2007).

There are, however, divergences in the explanations for the continuity of witchcraft. As noted above, Ferguson argues that "culture" survives in the form of witchcraft and sorcery and that arguments that capitalism would transform culture were mistaken. Jean and John Comaroff (2001a) argue that in South Africa and elsewhere, millennial capitalism itself, or what many have seen as the neoliberal turn bringing cutbacks in services and income for the poor, precipitated an increase in mystical thinking as people tried to imagine ways to get rich or simply survive in an unpredictable economic world.

Geschiere (1997b) makes a more grounded and nuanced argument which helps to illuminate some of the cultural categories that confuse the AIDS public health debate. He points to the increasing significance of markets and cash in rituals as diverse as those related to marriage or death. He argues that many folk concepts have been re-invented to suit the contemporary context or, in his words, "the creative hybridization of endogenous concepts" (Geschiere 1997a:343). Here, we can begin to see the interplay of AIDS and sorcery. As noted earlier, marriage, reproduction, and fertility are central to the survival of the lineage and also the society in general (see Meyer Fortes' preface in Ngubane 1977). As a result, central facets of conflict and ritual tension in Zulu and other narratives concern women who, as outsiders, must marry into a patrilineage and bear its children (Ngubane 1977). Sites of danger and tension are also the sites of sorcery accusations, where folk healing and *sangomas* (witch doctors) are crucially involved. Even more centrally, funeral rituals reflect or express the conflicts between the affines or relatives of the in-married wife and the husband's lineage (Geschiere 1997a). At the funeral and in the event of a husband's death, in terms of customary law, the daughter-in-law is in the position to lose all rights to stay in the husband's house or inherit his property. Many accusations of sorcery circulate around such circumstances. In the 1950s, one widow noted: "To be a widow in the country . . . is to be made responsible for all the misfortunes of the neighbourhood. A widow is always suspected" (Mayer 1971:242). Similar sentiments were replicated among rural migrants in Zambia in the 1990s although, since for many groups in Zambia, the children belong to the matrilineal relatives, the same stresses may work out differently on the ground (Ferguson 1999). Such tensions clearly play a part even in the urban biography of Khabzela, the South African popular radio disc jockey who died of AIDS in Soweto. In the narrative researched by the journalist Liz McGregor, Khabzela's mother and sister accuse his wife of sorcery. She is evicted from his house and from caring for him after they move in. Witchcraft concerns are still very powerful today in urban Soweto (Ashforth 2000).

In addition, conflict over the amassing of bride wealth reflects generational issues over the spending of cash (Geschiere 1997a). As Chanock argues: "Much of the essentializing of the notion of culture, in the past few decades of rapid change in Africa, has been done in the context of the confrontational dialogues between generation and gender . . . It has also been employed as a metaphor around which generations and genders, otherwise sharply divided, could be encouraged to unite in opposition to outsiders" (Chanock 2000:20). Thus, any disruption of the survival of the middle-aged kin members and the loss of bride wealth for the next generation might precipitate accusations of sorcery, as we heard reported among the orphans in the rural village in Chapter 7.

As mentioned in Chapter 6, research on contemporary rituals suggests that women's protections in customary norms are undermined by war (Hutchinson 1996; Hutchinson 1997; Hutchinson and Jok 2002). Among the Nuer, historically a cattle-herding population of the Sudan, women were still central to the symbolic realm in the 1980s. Even as Nuer men energetically entered the politics of the modern state, women's lives were intimately tied to the exchange of cattle (Hutchinson 1996). However, by the 1990s, the protection that these rituals and practices historically afforded women had been destroyed by the decades of warfare in that region (Hutchinson and Jok 2002). As noted earlier, if war has this effect, it is quite possible the destruction wreaked by AIDS in southern Africa could undermine women's ritual protections and leave them open to levels of violence never before countenanced. For example, practices, such as that described above, in which the security of women was assured by the payment of *lobola*, are no longer working. While terms of marriage appear to be following ancient tradition, in fact, only the initial symbolic trappings remain, undermining the actual security and alliances they originally cemented.

Where AIDS destroys patterns of marriage and childbirth, and where deaths are too soon and too many for ritual conflicts to be assuaged, it would be surprising if witchcraft and sorcery were not intertwined in the contemporary moment. Nor should we expect such ideas to be limited to the "traditional healing practices" of the past but, rather, they might be viewed as an opening for "alternative healing," including the "denialist" ideas of the West. As the government has promoted confusing messages and Western medicine has been portrayed as toxic, "alternative" healing in South Africa has becomes, not a complementary alternative as described in many ethnographic instances, but instead, a rationale for rejecting treatment. In fact, "alternative healers" are claiming that Western medicine is killing people and requiring that Western treatment be rejected in order for the alternative method to succeed (McGregor 2007; Nattrass 2007).

As in many parts of the world, the market can be heavily implicated in contemporary ritual (Geschiere 1997a). In fact, the healing solutions currently being sold in South Africa cost money and are making some people rich (McGregor 2007; Nattrass 2007). Such solutions are not being invented only by African "traditional" healers. The medicine "Africa's Solution" was bottled and sold to Khabzela by Tine van de Maas, who was born in Holland (McGregor 2007). Multivitamins have been invented and marketed by a corporation led by Matthias Rath, a European entrepreneur (Specter 2007).[11] Rath, promoted by Minister of Health Tshabalala-Msimang, has drawn the Treatment Action Campaign into ongoing and costly litigation, using resources and energy that would have been much more constructively spent in educating people about AIDS treatment.

Thus, with respect to AIDS and "denialism" in South Africa, I would be less inclined to accept a general explanation of millennial capital or the perpetuation of "culture" as the explanations for the adoption of a mixture of "alternate" treatments. As I have argued throughout, women who saw Western treatment working took *practical*-sense perspectives and often even enthusiastically joined the Treatment Action Campaign. However, people with no such immediate models, rejected the TAC. Surrounded by doubt and mystery, they were much more likely to be drawn into the whirlpool of alternate beliefs, traditional or newly invented. They were much more vulnerable to the market forces of unproven concoctions brewed up by non-scientific entrepreneurs, small and corporate. The government, in the form of Minister of Health Tshabalala-Msimang, weighed in with both promotional and financial support for such unproven non-scientific ventures, and not only delayed the distribution of anti-retroviral treatment backed by proven health results but labeled the medically proven drugs toxic. In addition, as noted in Chapter 4, Herbert Vilakazi, a US-trained sociologist and Chairman of the Presidential Council on Traditional Medicine, contended that such treatments were poison sent by the West to kill Africans (Nattrass 2007; Specter 2007). He testified in front of parliament on behalf of uBhejane, a "traditional" medicine, and assured *New Yorker* journalist Michael Specter that "I have personally seen hundreds of people who have taken uBhejane and they have gotten relief." Vilakazi continued: "Who benefits from ARVs? . . . Pharmaceutical companies . . ." (Specter 2007:36). Under these circumstances, the manifestation of critical "good sense" among poor African women is extraordinary. One example of this extraordinary display of "good sense" occurred in 2005 in Queenstown in the Eastern Cape, an extremely poor area. Several hundred women braved police firing rubber bullets to march into the local hospital, demanding that the hospital speed up the provision of HAART.

Examining community experiences with AIDS in historical perspective, it is clear that women's views of the family and expectations of marriage continue to differ from those outlined in Western social science. This is not a simple argument for "cultural difference." "Culture" as a concept has to be used very gingerly in South Africa and in describing subaltern populations or class differences. Much of what is labeled "culture" falls into Gramsci's unexamined fragmented hegemonic "common sense" – an amalgam of religious constructs and folk beliefs that seem to be used to outline an unexamined but highly judgmental moral universe. As we have seen, many women described in these pages were adapting in pragmatic and creative ways to the epidemic but their "good sense" (in Gramscian terms) was framed by their historical experience, which included a history of customary marriage patterns as well as their everyday interactions. However, the signature feature of such "good sense" is that it did not take on a moralistic dimension but rather opened a path to a constructive and creative transformation of daily life.

# 12

# Conclusions: Neoliberalism, Gender, and Resistance

In its largest outlines, the purpose of this book has been to examine the varied ways in which neoliberalism facilitates, fosters, and exploits particular ideologies of gendered subordination and in the process increases the transmission of AIDS. A grim picture – fortunately complicated by people on the ground whose practical initiatives often critically address the inequalities of gender and the distortions of gendered ideologies. Drawn from historical experience, such critiques counteract the static, patriarchal images of "culture" that have been widely promulgated by those in leadership positions in the United States and southern Africa. In that sense, this book argues that, to the extent that the practical sense of the local is echoed in the critiques of health activists and others, social movements around AIDS may be understood as part of a wider battle for local, national, and global democracy.

In the course of fighting the AIDS epidemic, even as women are counted, monitored, and tested, their life cycles, social experiences, and agency continue to be erased. They are categorized in "vulnerable groups" or discussed in terms of cultural barriers. Meanwhile, women, whatever their work – sex workers or doctors, drug users or not, married or not – nurse, care for, and support their children. All the while women, although certainly to different degrees, live under the threat of sexual or physical violence, episodic or chronic, at home and in public. From this perspective, in every group "vulnerable" to AIDS from an epidemiological point of view, an entire clearly identifiable set of biological and social needs remain specific to women. Although women are certainly included extensively in our research, the implications of the whole experience of women, with and indeed without children, have not been conceived in their broader social framework either in the treatment or prevention of AIDS. Women are invisible in plain sight.

Regarding the science of AIDS, this lack of a social framework for understanding the range of women's experiences arguably blocks the usefulness of scientific solutions. New technologies alone have not and will not prevent AIDS. Nearly all the new technologies, even the vaccines that are still but imaginary, require social change for their distribution and negotiations between genders in their implementation. While the epidemiology of AIDS led to the positing of risk groups or vulnerable groups, the need for social change forces our understandings toward social categories. In other words, women are not simply a "vulnerable group" but are in fact an important bulwark of social structure.

For example, we have models for the demographic impact of male circumcision, but the models assume social behavior that may not hold true in any particular situation. If we do not comprehend what circumcision might mean in the social interactions of men and women, then we cannot rely on the demographic arguments that male circumcision would reduce AIDS in the population as a whole. Since men frequently refuse condom use with their wives or women with whom they wish to have children, male circumcision could conceivably increase the deaths of mothers and concomitantly increase mortality in orphans and children. Medical male circumcision is a new and hopeful technology for the scaling up of prevention. As with other technologies, such as the condom, the female condom, and the diaphragm, its effective impact depends on the social context in which it is introduced, including issues of class, race and ethnicity and the changing relations between men and women.

A second major erasure occurs with the invisibility of the mother in the presence of a fetus or infant. For 15 years, women were excluded from drug trials for AIDS treatment because pharmaceutical companies feared that harm to a fetus could result in legal claims. All women were excluded from possibly life-saving options in order to protect even an unconceived fetus. Equating all women with pregnant women and giving unquestioned priority to saving the fetus meant in effect that it was acceptable for women to die for lack of treatment. Of course, as it turned out, treatment during pregnancy was the very thing that would protect the child to come. This lesson has not yet been learned well enough, nor the lesson that treating the mother protects, even saves, the child. A healthy mother fosters healthy children. Breastfeeding provides one of the clearest illustrations of the equation of healthy mother = healthy child but, in fact, the importance of this principle extends beyond infancy into the teenage years, if not adulthood. An HIV-positive mother on treatment for AIDS which has lowered her viral count is unlikely to transmit the virus to her newborn at birth, and, in addition, highly unlikely to transmit the virus through breast milk. We also know that breast milk saves infants' lives throughout the global South. Thus, unquestionably, the best way to save the baby of an HIV-positive mother is to treat the mother. A healthy mother can care for, educate, and support her family. A mother who falls sick and dies leaves daughters who will have to take on the women's burden of care and drop out of school or other activities, while all her children suffer emotionally and economically.

Absurd as it sounds to enunciate these truisms, the repeated disappearance of women's experience from research and public discussion makes it necessary.

To be sure, men need treatment too, and fathers can be central to the domestic economy, but not with such intensive biological and social bonds. So, I contend the mother–child dyad has yet to take its rightful place in conceptualizations of AIDS.

**Figure 12.1** Colleen Madamombe has won the award for the Best Female Artist of Zimbabwe three years in a row and has toured the world with her art. "Growing Well" (1997) represents the importance of the mother–child dyad

We find women excluded from treatment trials in favor of the fetus and then, in later years, drawn into nevirapine trials and other pregnancy treatments simply to save the baby. Then, rather than emphasizing their treatment and health, women are given formula, supposedly to save the baby, but in fact often increasing infant mortality in the second year. In all these cases, a healthy mother, in this case an HIV-positive mother on treatment, could save the fetus, the infant, and provide stability for the growing child.

Once we have established that women must be seen holistically on their own terms, and that a healthy mother leads to a healthy child, we can begin to explore the national policies or global regulation that help to make these simple findings so difficult to address in daily life. Here we confront persistent patterns of gendered inequality, manifested, as we have seen, in different ways in different historical moments and, with globalization, increasingly in country-specific ways. The ANC government in South Africa has devoted itself to developing the formal economy, reducing debt so as to play a leading role in the global arena. This has led the government to limit expenditures on capacity building. While this may be understood as prudent long-term economic policy, with stringent regulation initially lightening the burden of debt later on, the short-term decisions to limit health care and job-creating social programs cost lives in the era of AIDS.

In the last few years, as highly active anti-retroviral treatment (HAART) has begun to be made available, we could be hopeful that the present policies will save lives. However, as I have argued throughout this book, preventing the spread of the HIV virus requires a robust investment in human resources, including education, housing and health, work for men and women beyond the formal economy, and a reduction in income inequality. No matter how many people finally receive treatment, if the patterns of gender subordination and unemployment for both men and women continue, new infections will continue to outpace the rollout of treatment.

In South Africa, as the formal economy grows, the few formal sector jobs that pay well go predominantly to men while women are largely confined to the lower paid, non-unionized work and to the informal sector in situations of extreme poverty. Income grants, disability grants, and pensions, while they help, do little to offset fundamental income inequality. They also maintain the burden of care on women and the gendered differential access to housing, land, work, and a living wage. Thus, there is the need for women to depend on men's resources to support them and their children, and the power of men over women in sexual negotiations may be exacerbated, increasing the risk of violence and the spread of AIDS.

The description of the situation among the Ju/'hoansi demonstrated a different but parallel impact of privatization and neoliberal policies on gendered inequality and AIDS. Patterns of privatization associated with new forms of ecotourism and land development were encroaching on the lives of these former foragers, whose history permitted considerable women's autonomy. Women were still relatively less subordinate in their domestic relations but were becoming susceptible to AIDS, gendered violence, and new subordination as alcohol, the sale of cheap tourist commodities, and migrant workers with more cash than local men penetrated previously remote villages, in which formerly most resources had been shared. We saw the ways in which new women leaders in the Traditional Authority, along with the men already in leadership and others, spearheaded the struggle against these emerging forms of subordination. In fact, by 2008, the Ju seemed to be rebuilding communal structures fostered by the Conservancy and even ecotourism.

The third point that emerges from the analysis here is that beyond gendered patterns of inequality, we find gendered ideologies that have become particularly powerfully intertwined with the cumulative dispossessions of neoliberalism. As I discuss in the first chapter, the fact that most women who were HIV positive in the US were black or Latina contributed to the erasure of the idea of heterosexual transmission. Next we find that, as inequality widens and poverty increases in the US, religious ideologies of morality and blame, with particular stress on the righteousness of patriarchy and women's role in reproduction, are promoted by the Republican Party and President George W. Bush. Thus, while the Bush administration sends women to war with the claim that they are freeing women in Afghanistan and elsewhere for education and democracy, we find the funding of abstinence-only policies and the punitive withdrawal of international funding even for agencies that only advise clients on women's reproductive choice.

In South Africa, as the exigencies of neoliberal inequality are amplified by the post-apartheid regime, we find parallel trends towards the fostering of patriarchal ideologies and their concrete manifestation in land rights and gendered violence.

Thus, while the US literally funds and exports a patriarchal religious fundamentalism through its immense international funding for faith-based groups, particular national trends, as we saw in Uganda and South Africa, complement and further such gendered ideologies according to their own historical traditions. Any effort to address the spread of AIDS in southern Africa, or indeed sub-Saharan Africa, has to take seriously the far-ranging impact of fundamentalist religious groups as well as global and national neoliberal pressures which may facilitate the dispossession of women and children through the exacerbation of gendered inequalities and revitalized gendered ideologies.

Finally, we have seen the critical acuity of some women on the ground expressed in terms of social movements and practical sense. Women in a sewing cooperative in Rundu, Namibia, and in an informal settlement in Durban, South Africa, demanded and eventually won the female condom. Devout churchgoing mothers in Namibia faced down religious disapproval to provide their sons with condoms. Lutheran pastors set aside moral condemnation to bring their parishioners comprehensive messages of sex education and prevention. A pastor at a Durban TAC meeting said he would go back to his parishioners with reassurances that Western AIDS treatments are not poisonous. The South African TAC educates nurses and volunteer care-givers about HAART and treatments for opportunistic diseases. We need to take full stock of such agency and ingenuity. However we must not romanticize it either.

Social movements around AIDS have not yet fully acknowledged, not to say resolved, the contradictions of gender ideologies and the intertwining of politics, traditionalism, and Western fundamentalist religions. Meanwhile, women, in their roles as mothers, care-givers and "first responders" to the AIDS epidemic, are undermined by the lack of day care, education, transportation, and adequate water supply. Thus, a broader coalition – southern African and global – is needed that would unite demands for treatment and gender equity with the campaigning of the "poors" for government investment in basic human needs. The fight for treatment and prevention of AIDS cannot be disentangled from the continuing struggle for social justice.

# Notes

## Preface

1. Early work on the themes in this book previously appeared in: 2007, Confounding Conventional Wisdom: The Ju/'hoansi and HIV/AIDS, with Richard Lee, in the edited volume *Updating the San: Image and Reality of an African People in the 21st Century*, R. Hitchcock, et al. (eds), Senri Ethnological Series no. 70, National Museum of Ethnology, Osaka, Japan, pp.45–46; 2006, The other side of development: HIV/AIDS among men and women in Ju/'hoansi villages, in *The Politics of Egalitarianism: Theory and Practice*, Jacqueline Solway (ed.), Berghahn Books; 2004, From the Cosmopolitan to the Personal: Women's mobilization with respect to HIV/AIDS, in *Social Movements*, June Nash (ed.), Blackwell Publishing; 2001, Sexual Negotiations in Relation to Political Mobilization: The prevention of HIV in comparative context, in *The Journal of AIDS and Behavior* June 5(2): 163–172; 2000, Culture, Sexuality and Women's Agency in the Prevention of HIV/AIDS in Southern Africa, with Zena Stein, in *American Journal of Public Health* July 90(7):1042–1049.
2. Michael Burawoy, currently on the sociology faculty of UC Berkeley and a strong advocate and theorist for ethnographic methods in sociology, was also from Manchester, where I grew up, and became a student of Van Velsen at the Zambian Institute.
3. An anthropologist who, early on, explicitly argued for humanism to be combined with a materialist analysis was Thomas Belmonte (1979, third edition, 2005) who died of AIDS in 1995.

## Introduction

1. See the recent reports presented at the 2008 International AIDS Society Conference Symposia on the rapid increase in sexual violence that accompanied crises in Kenya and Zimbabwe, as well as the ongoing sexual violence in the Eastern Congo: Panel "Political Crises, Sexual Violence and HIV/AIDS," the satellite, Sunday, August 3,

organized by Anne-Christine d'Adesky; "Mujeres Adelante – Moving Forward: New Visions and Actions to Address HIV and Gender-based Violence"; as well as a speech delivered by Stephen Lewis, Co-Director, AIDS-Free World, at the TIDES Foundation "Momentum" Conference San Francisco, California, USA ,Sexual Violence: An Issue of Health, Monday, July 21, 2008. For cautions regarding the association of AIDS and the military, see Barnett and Prins 2005.

2. "According to the European AIDS Treatment Group, seven nations – Brunei, Oman, Qatar, Sudan, South Korea, United Arab Emirates and Yemen – deny entry for people living with HIV and 30 countries deport foreigners reported to have HIV. In addition, more than 65 nations enforce some degree of travel restriction for HIV-positive individuals." Kaiser Daily HIV/AIDS Report, AIDS 2008, Advocates Discuss Travel Restrictions Around the World for People Living With HIV/AIDS (August 6, 2008).

3. In 2006, 4.3 million people became newly infected with HIV (UNAIDS 2006b:1). In sub-Saharan Africa, over 24 million people were living with HIV and over 2 million people died in 2006 alone (UNAIDS 2006b, specifically table 1, "Regional HIV and AIDS statistics and features 2004–2006").

4. Marrakesh Agreement Establishing the World Trade Organization, Annex 1c signed in Marrakesh, Morocco, April 15, 1994.

# Chapter 1

1. Other researchers did also call for collective interventions to address gender and family issues (among others, Bond and Vincent 1997, Farmer et al. 1994, Gupta and Weiss 1993, Mann and Tarantola 1996, Schoepf 1988, Susser and Kreniske 1997). In Puerto Rico, beginning in the late 1980s, John Kreniske and I worked with local health activists to develop a collective approach to prevention of HIV infection among heterosexual couples as well as among high-school youth (Susser and Kreniske 1997). In 1992, Peter Davis, Villon Films, made *Side by Side: Women against AIDS in Zimbabwe*, focusing on women in Zimbabwe working collectively to address HIV/AIDS in rural villages. As we shall see in Chapter 3, doctors and activists in South Africa were also concerned about the structuring of gender (Dlamini-Zuma 1988).

2. See Dworkin and Ehrhardt 2007.

3. For instance, in 1990, Chicago's Cook County Hospital refused to admit women into the city's only hospital AIDS ward on the basis that they had no women's AIDS ward. Two days after gay and lesbian activists set up a women's ward in the street in front of the hospital, Cook County Hospital began admitting HIV-positive women for the first time.

4. This research was the result of the efforts led by Louise Binder and Blueprint for Action on Women and HIV with ATHENA and became a model for gathering further data on gender balance and women's issues at such conferences.

5. On June 27, 2001, Executive Director of UNIFEM Noleen Heyzer continued further at the United Nations General Assembly Special Session on HIV AIDS with these comments: "I would like to very briefly summarize the outcome for women and girls of this historic meeting in four overall points. First, the greater threat that HIV/AIDS

poses for women and girls – especially the young – and the effects of the pandemic on women's lives and futures are now undisputed. Second, there is a fast-growing understanding that gender inequality and power imbalances between women and men in every society heighten women's vulnerability to infection and leave them with heavier burdens when HIV/AIDS enters households and communities. At the same time, the world is gradually acknowledging that because of their sex, women and girls have more limited access to HIV/AIDS-related information, prevention, treatment, care, support, commodities, and services. Third, there is a new level of awareness. We have recognized that we need to deepen our understanding of the gender dimensions of HIV/AIDS. In that way, we will be able to translate the declaration into targeted plans and programs, into equal access to information, services, protections, and resources. Finally, there is a sense of urgency."

6.  Isolation of a T-Lymphotropic Retrovirus from a Patient at Risk for Acquired Immune Deficiency Syndrome (AIDS), Science, 220, 868–871 (1983) F. Barré-Sinoussi1, J. C. Chermann1, F. Rey1, M. T. Nugeyre1, S. Chamaret1, J. Gruest1, C. Dauguet1, C. Axler-Blin1, F. Vézinet-Brun2, C. Rouzioux2, W. Rozenbaum3, L. Montagnier1.

7.  Hemophilia is genetically transmitted through mothers to their sons. Women do not manifest the disease.

8.  In the United States, among MSMs infected with HIV, atypical forms of tuberculosis came to be recognized as opportunistic infections (bovine or avian tuberculosis). Among middle-class men, such unusual forms of tuberculosis were an immediate flag that AIDS might be present. Later, among migrants, poorer residents, and especially those in prisons and homeless shelters, a mini-epidemic of tuberculosis occurred among both men and women. Many of these men and women were HIV positive but not all. Many of these cases turned out to be multiply resistant to drugs and again this was mainly but not exclusively among patients who were HIV positive. Nowadays it is thought that some of these early TB cases with multiple drug resistance might actually have been the XDR TB, a particularly virulent form of TB identified in South Africa. However, TB was a much less reliable indicator of HIV infection among the poor, both men and women, than among middle-class gay men.

9.  These issues are regularly discussed in the ICW's newsletter, *ICW News*.

10. According to estimates, the International Center for AIDS Care and Treatment Programs at the Mailman School of Public Health, Columbia University. This is one of the programs that has been on the leading edge in focusing on the needs of men, women, and children in HIV care.

11. In spite of the unstinting global efforts by health activists, the rollout of treatment worldwide has not moved as quickly as originally envisioned by the United Nations in 2000. The Millennial Development Goals set the task of treating 3 million people in 5 years – known as the 3by5 MDGs. In fact, in 2005, less than 2 million people had received treatment and among poorer populations access to treatment was still remote. In addition, the global treatment rollout was nowhere near as fast as the new infections. See the Toronto 2006 International AIDS Society Conference proceedings and the works of the AIDS Vaccine Advocacy Coalition (AVAC). However, by 2007, the 3 by 5 goal had been met and was widely celebrated at the 2008 Mexico City International AIDS Society Conference.

12. *The Hindu, News Update Service*, Sunday July 30, 2006. www.hinduonnet.com/holnus/001200607301110.htm.

13. For example, the International Center for AIDS Care and Treatment Programs, Columbia University and Partners in Health, Harvard University.
14. Dr. Cicely Williams, born in 1893, pioneered maternal and child care in developing countries by utilizing local traditions and resources rather than depending on Western drugs and systems. Also, she was the first head of the Maternal and Child Health Section of the World Health Organization. Her life's works are archived in the Wellcome Library in London.
15. Informative pamphlets included In Our Own Hands: SWAA-Ghana Champions the Female Condom 2006, SWAA-Ghana Quality Issue #17, published by the Population Council, and Female Condom: a Powerful Tool for Protection, PATH, funded by UNFPA 2006.
16. A study of the US newspaper reactions to the original launching of the female condom in the 1990s found similar ridicule and misrepresentation across the media (Susser 2002).
17. The researchers were still working with the figures about women partners to see whether the results from such a small population could be useful when this book went to press.
18. For example, see Dr Lydia Mungherera's "Mama's Club" for HIV-positive mothers: www.womensenews.org/article.cfm/dyn/aid/2835/context/archive.
19. Kaiser Daily HIV/AIDS Report, AIDS 2008, Advocates discuss Travel Restrictions Around the World for People Living with HIV/AIDS (August 6, 2008) (see quote in note 2, Introduction).
20. I am indebted to Maria De Bruyn for this account. She is an anthropologist and was a member of the Community Liaison Committee for the 1992 Amsterdam IAS and was also one of the organizers of this pre-conference. According to Maria De Bruyn: "The women who were key drivers of the initiative . . . included: Anita Bolderheij, Esther Nederhoed, Jeannine van Woerkum and Hannah Jansen. They asked a few HIV-negative women to help them in the preparations; they included Jeannette Slootbeek (now a consultant on HIV/AIDS and youth programs) and myself. Sadly, Anita, Esther and Jeannine are no longer with us; Hannah is still going strong. She is the . . . mother of two . . . children and still supports other women living with HIV in The Netherlands." ICW was established at that meeting by a group of about 40 women. "They chose women to lead the effort – including Jo Manchester and Kate Thomson (UK), Beverly Greet (Australia), Patricia Pérez (Argentina – currently ICW LA contact person) and Cindy Robins (USA). . . . Some women volunteered to be regional contact persons (e.g., Dorothy Onyango from Kenya). All the women . . . mounted the stage during the closing ceremony and called out the country they were from. Many of these women had not yet come out publicly in their own countries – and there they were being filmed on TV! It was a very emotional moment and the start of a unique organization/network." Dorothy Onyango, Patricia Pérez, and Kate Thomson, among others, were key speakers at XVII International AIDS Society Conference in Mexico City, August 3–8, 2008.
21. www.athenanetwork.org.
22. A thorough discussion of the UN's Millennial Goals can be found in Barton and Prendergast 2004. See specifically essays by Carol Barton, Mary Robinson, and Lynn Freedman.

# Chapter 2

1. In 2006, PEPFAR funds were approximately US$1,320 million and constituted 32 percent of all funding from major donors. The Global Fund for HIV/AIDS, Tuberculosis and Malaria is made up of contributions from the US as well as from other countries and distributed $712 million, 17 percent of global funds. The World Bank was the third largest global funding source for AIDS and distributed $286 million, 7 percent of global funds (Oomman et al. 2007:3). Since the US is a major donor to both the Global Fund and the World Bank, US policies and politics are clearly crucial to the framing of programs worldwide. However, in this chapter, I concentrate on PEPFAR regulations in order to outline some of the priorities framed by the US and their impact on women's options. Since, in August 2008, the US Senate approved just under $50 billion more for PEPFAR and, in spite of much political controversy, retained requirements for a large proportion of the funds to be earmarked for Abstinence-only and Be Faithful programs and the requirement for an anti-prostitution pledge discussed in this chapter, the issues outlined here become even more significant.

2. A "prostitution pledge," which was removed from the United States' versions of these strategy papers, was left in for international distribution and implementation.

3. According to the Committee on the Rights of the Child (a UN body which monitors the Convention on the Rights of the Child): "Effective HIV/AIDS prevention requires States to refrain from censoring, withholding or intentionally misrepresenting health-related information, including sexual education and information, and that, consistent with their obligations to ensure the right to life, survival and development of the child, (art. 6) States' parties must ensure that children have the ability to acquire the knowledge and skills to protect themselves and others as they begin to express their sexuality." (Committee on the Rights of the Child, General Comment No. 3 (2003) HIV/AIDS and the rights of the child, 32nd Sess. (2003), para. 16, quoted in Human Rights Watch, Uganda, vol. 17, no. 4 (A) p. 17.)

4. Most plenary speakers submit a paper to the IAS beforehand, which is embargoed until the actual presentation. The prepared speech then becomes available in hard copy and online for journalists and others. Frequently the actual presentation varies in some details from the published report (Y. Museveni: Plenary Report: XIV International AIDS Symposium, Bangkok).

5. "PEPFAR has been providing an unusually high share of total AIDS funding to the country." Zambia and Mozambique, in comparison, were receiving aid from multiple donors and the PEPFAR support was proportionately less (Oomman et al. 2007:5).

6. From an interview with Bill Moyers for PBS, 2004.

7. This is the abstract for Edward Green's presentation entitled "ABC: an old or a new paradigm of AIDS prevention?" on CNN vs. ABC panel at XIV International AIDS Society Conference 2004, Bangkok, delivered on Monday afternoon, July 12, 2004.

   *Issues:* the global AIDS prevention paradigm was originally developed in the United States for an epidemic concentrated in high-risk groups. This model, comprised of a standard package of risk-reduction interventions, was then exported to developing countries, including those with generalized epidemics, with little modification of the paradigm to accommodate cultural or epidemiological realities.

*Description:* a review and analysis was conducted with special focus on successful prevention programs in Africa and the Caribbean, to test the adequacy of the risk reduction model in these areas and to better answer the central question of prevention: What works?

*Lessons learned:* HIV infection rates in general populations cannot be reduced by risk-reduction interventions or behaviors alone; there must be changes in risk-avoidance behavior (reduction in casual sex, delay of sexual debut, abstinence) as well.

*Recommendations:* major donors must rethink the practice of allocating most or all resources to risk reduction (condom and drug) interventions. Prevention programs should resemble Uganda's original ABC program. There should be more AIDS education in primary schools, more involvement of religious organizations and leaders, and more empowerment of women and girls. Governments of developing countries should have more say in how prevention funds are spent; they should not be dictated to by foreign donors. VCT can help prevent AIDS if prevention counseling embraces a broader ABC approach and not a narrower risk-reduction only approach.

8.  Green has worked on ethnographic projects related to AIDS in Africa since the early 1980s. His 1994 book specifically focused on collaborations between traditional healers and Western medicine (Green 1994). Green has criticized the engaged anthropology of others such as Paul Farmer, claiming that the work neglects traditional healers. Green rejects analyses, such as Farmers', that point out global responsibility for the AIDS epidemic. Green has a PhD in anthropology from the Catholic University of America and for most of his career, rather than a full-time appointment in an anthropology department, he has worked in Africa and Washington DC as a medical anthropologist on government projects. He is a member of the President's Advisory Council on AIDS. His résumé describes him as a "professional applied anthropologist" And he is listed at Bangkok as being affiliated with the Harvard Center for Population and Development Studies. Green has long criticized the emphasis on condoms in AIDS prevention and on his curriculum vitae he is credited with "AIDS policy reform (getting the United States to adopt the Ugandan model of prevention)."

9.  These issues have been explored by Jane Collins (2009) and, in terms of race, by Leith Mullings (2005).

10. Women received entitlements, such as pensions, only in relation to their legally certified association with husbands or to replace the loss of such support. If women had no such legitimized male supports, they were not entitled to benefits but, if they could prove need, they did receive charity from the initially small program "Aid to Dependent Children."

11. Ever since the Republican President Lincoln and the Civil War, the Democratic Party had been associated with racial segregation in the South. It was the Southern Democrats who limited President Franklyn D. Roosevelt and perpetuated the racial discrimination of the New Deal. In 1964, Barry Goldwater began the long path to re-invigorate the Republican Party on a platform of coded racism, which came to fruition in the elections of President Ronald Reagan and both Herbert Walker Bush and George W. Bush. For a recent recapitulation of this history, see Krugman 2007, *The Conscience of a Liberal.*

12. In tracing the current surge of neoconservative rhetoric, it is significant that at the same time as the Hyde Amendment was passed, 30 years ago, we first see leading neoconservatives, Donald Rumsfeld (Secretary of Defense under President Ford and President

George W. Bush, 1973–74, 2000–2007) and Richard (Dick) Cheney (President Ford's Chief of Staff 1973–74, Vice President 2000–2008) cutting their teeth in the Nixon administration. They worked together to dismantle programs such as Mobilization for Youth, which had been part of the 1960s War on Poverty initiated by the Democratic President Lyndon B. Johnson.

13. "The Act de-linked federal financial assistance from Medicaid, the federal health care safety net program for the poor, ending federal guarantees of income support to families with children. PRWORA also eliminated the long-standing requirement that welfare recipients be given access to family planning services" (McGovern 2007).

14. Which might be understood as consistent with the efforts of Rumsfeld and Cheney in the 1970s, now again powerful in the Republican pantheon, to close down the neighborhood work programs instigated by Mobilization for Youth.

15. A meeting of the eight countries regarded as the world's most wealthy and powerful.

16. To briefly outline the continuing restrictions in the renewed PEPFAR funding, I have quoted in full the press release from CHANGE which addresses the Senate authorization of the renewal of the Global AIDS Relief Package, July 18, 2008.

**Thursday, July 18**

Today, CHANGE, in partnership with Advocates for Youth, the International Women's Health Coalition, American Jewish World Service, the Sexuality Information and Education Council of the United States, and the National Council of Jewish Women issued the following press statement in response to the recently passed Senate bill (S. 2731) to reauthorize the President's Emergency Plan for AIDS Relief (PEPFAR).
*Coordinated by Serra Sippel, Center for Health and Gender Equity*

It's Broke, But They Won't Fix It: The Senate Authorizes a Global AIDS Relief Package that Comes Up Short Washington, DC – On Wednesday, the Senate voted 80 to 16 to reauthorize the President's Emergency Plan for AIDS Relief (PEPFAR), a five-year, $48 billion global initiative to combat HIV/AIDS, tuberculosis and malaria.

The Senate missed a golden opportunity to epitomize the generosity of the American people by making US global HIV/AIDS relief more effective, compassionate and fiscally responsible. As a result, millions of people are at greater risk of HIV infection.

Under pressure to act quickly, policymakers failed to address critical shortfalls in the bill that would have ensured effective use of scarce public funds and a sustainable response to the pandemic. Much has been learned since PEPFAR was enacted in 2003. However, rather than heeding to the evidence collected by our own government agencies, the bill passed by the Senate compromises sound public health practice for ideology and political expediency.

- One key change that should have been made in the PEPFAR bill was the abolishment of arbitrary funding guidelines that determine how money can be distributed on the ground. The Senate bill calls for spending at least fifty percent of prevention funds designed to halt the sexual transmission of HIV, in countries with generalized epidemics, only on abstinence and faithfulness programs. PEPFAR recipients that do not meet this requirement must justify their programmatic decisions through an onerous reporting requirement to Congress, potentially facing defunding.

This provision was left in the bill despite a 2007 report from The Institute of Medicine, which recommended the removal of PEPFAR's then-requirement that one-third of prevention funds be spent on abstinence-only-until-marriage programs. The Senate's decision to leave these de facto restrictions in the bill means that those fighting the HIV epidemic on the front lines will be deprived of the vital discretion they need in determining how funds are best spent.

- The PEPFAR bill passed by the Senate also failed to fully increase protection for women and young people, two groups increasingly vulnerable to new infections in nearly every region of the world. Women and young people are most likely to use family planning and other reproductive health services, and would benefit greatly from a strategy that integrated HIV prevention and treatment with family planning. Recent studies suggest that upwards of 90 percent of HIV-positive pregnant women in countries such as Uganda and South Africa have unmet need for integrated family planning and HIV services. However, the bill passed by the Senate fails to call for, or even acknowledge, the need to strengthen critical linkages between family planning and reproductive health services and HIV prevention efforts.

- The 2003 PEPFAR legislation contains a provision that enables organizations receiving US funding to pick and choose the prevention and treatment services they wish to provide. Millions of dollars go to organizations to provide prevention services, even though they refuse to discuss the potential of condoms or other contraceptives in preventing the spread of HIV. As abstinence and partner reduction programs have outpaced programs that enable individuals to have all the information they need to prevent HIV, the law stands in the way of the effective use of resources.

  The Senate has taken this bad policy and made it worse by extending the so-called "conscience clause," or refusal clause, to organizations that provide care and support to people living with HIV/AIDS, their families and their communities. This provision paves the way for taxpayer-fund on based on "moral" and religious grounds, allowing PEPFAR funding recipients to refuse to provide care for someone based on their religion, how they got infected or any other basis. The refusal clause is yet another damaging provision that flies in the face of good public health practice.

- Lastly, the Senate upheld the requirement that groups fighting HIV/AIDS overseas publicly pledge their opposition to prostitution and sex trafficking before receiving US money.

  Prevention programs that have reached sex workers, a group that is marginalized and exceedingly vulnerable to HIV infection, have yielded dramatic reductions in HIV transmission. According to numerous reports, the pledge has led to further alienation and discrimination of already stigmatised groups. This policy drives sex workers underground and away from the nongovernmental organizations and health workers best poised to provide them with services they need to protect themselves from infection.

  It is our moral obligation and fiscal responsibility to use PEPFAR funding to prevent as many infections as possible. However, large sums of money, spent unwisely, will not save lives and will require an ever-growing need for increased resources in the future. The bill fell short exactly where more was needed: full and flexible funding of prevention programs that would enable us to make a difference in the lives of millions.

# Chapter 3

1. The Immorality Amendment Act, Act no. 21, was amended in 1957 to Act no. 23. This act prohibited adultery, attempted adultery or related immoral acts (extramarital sex) between White and Black people.
2. For a more detailed discussion of the history of the many ethnic and tribal groups and languages to be found in South Africa see Vail 1989, Krige and Comaroff 1981.
3. In the 1960s, Makeba went to the United States, married Stokely Carmichael of the Student Non Violent Coordinating Committee, an early spokesperson for the idea of Black Power, and went to live in Ghana. When the ANC came to power she returned to South Africa.
4. Changes in education can also be interpreted in terms of the pressing needs of an industrial capitalist state, but, again, reflected the distortions of the politics of apartheid. In this context, education was expanded and funded by the state, while at the same time the quality was undermined. Under colonial rule, mission education, which generally involved a humiliating silencing of local knowledge, had established a small, educated African middle class. Later, in the White settler society of the early twentieth century, such mission education and a few avenues to teachers' colleges, universities and even nursing schools for women had been minimally available for Black leadership. Women were educated as teachers and nurses, which became crucial professions for the emergence of an African middle class (Marks 1993).
5. This policy of apartheid has to be clearly differentiated from arguments about the importance of native languages and emphasis on the recognition of local knowledges in the post-apartheid era (Alexander 2007; Alexander and Heugh 2001). As stated in the Bantu Education Act of 1953, a simplified, bare bones curriculum was what the government thought useful for Africans. The Bantu Education Act precipitated an early student boycott of schools, which pre-dated the Soweto student uprisings of the 1970s. The boycott was extremely effective in some townships that had not already been decimated by relocation policies, for example the mining community of Brackman (Sapire 1989), but not in others (Hyslop 2001). The expansion of state-funded primary schools was welcomed by many African families while the fact that teacher training became segregated and atrophied and the educational curriculum reduced to the study of local crafts and language was less clearly recognized (Hyslop 2001).
6. See Oppenheimer and Bayer (2007) for a description of this epidemic.
7. Now an MD/PhD in anthropology who became Vice Chancellor of Cape Town University after apartheid and later worked at the World Bank. Her most recent book, *Laying Ghosts to Rest: Dilemmas of the transformation of South Africa* (Ramphele 2008), addresses many of the same issues discussed in this work.
8. Thabo Mbeki's father, Govan Mbeki, was a communist and a leading member of the ANC who was imprisoned with Mandela after the Rivonia Trial in 1963. He had spearheaded early demands for rural land rights.
9. In 1976, the school children of Soweto were gunned down by government police and army tanks as they took to the streets in peaceful demonstrations. They were protesting the newly implemented provisions of apartheid which required that they study Afrikaans in school. In their thousands, African schoolchildren ran out of their classrooms into the streets. Many were killed by the South African military, rolling towards them in massive

armored tanks. Some of those who survived could not see the point of going back to such schools and left home altogether to join the revolutionary wing of the ANC.

10. In New York City, in 1987 and 1988, NAMDA and the Committee on Health in Southern Africa (CHISA) organized conferences on health in South Africa co-sponsored by the School of Public Health and by the Institute for African Studies at Columbia University, whose director was the African historian Marcia Wright. CHISA was a US organization originally formed in the early 1980s by South African exiles, including Mervyn Susser and Zena Stein, in support of the ANC and NAMDA in their fight against apartheid. The 1987 conference focused on the health of workers in Africa, and the 1988 conference on the health of women and children and the future of progressive primary health care in South Africa. I was present at both these conferences although I did not go to Maputo.

11. Based at the time at Whittington Hospital in London and chairperson of the Regional Committee of the ANC in Britain.

12. At the 1988 conference, there was a final section on progressive primary health care, modeled on the pioneering 1950s community health care of South African Sidney Kark with the addition of political activism. Quarraisha Khan, later Abdool Karim, who was to be the first national director on AIDS in the new South Africa, spoke on health care workers. Salim Karim and Jerry Coovadia, later AIDS researchers, discussed the importance of progressive primary health care.

13. Dr. Liz Floyd later became the Director for AIDS for the new province of Gauteng, which includes the major urban center of Johannesburg.

14. "It is useful to look at the example of the National Union of Mineworkers. The impetus for working on AIDS did not come from the membership but from the leadership . . . However, other priorities compete with these tasks, and the union finds it difficult to identify the resources necessary . . . Youth organizations tend to say that they are directly involved in a political struggle that demands all their energy . . . Experience shows that if health is a separate agenda and AIDS is just one item on that agenda, then organizations are unlikely to get around to doing anything active on AIDS . . . If we aim to set up separate structures and education for HIV and AIDS, it is likely to remain a very small program reaching small numbers of people who are probably not those who need it most" (Floyd 1990:91–92).

15. One of the principles stated by Ramaphosa is: "No worker who is HIV positive should suffer any adverse consequence. Dismissal on the basis merely of HIV infection is not defensible policy" (NUM 1990:108). Later on, under principle "7. Public responsibility," the letter clearly states: "The mining industry is in a unique position. It is the major employer of the country's (and southern Africa's) economy. It is also a large employer which has shaped the labor market to meet its needs. There should be a commitment on its part in regard to the AIDS crisis to the creation of appropriate lifestyles, to the protection of HIV-infected persons from discrimination, to the creation of appropriate treatment centers, and to the implementation of effective and duly negotiated measures to assist the containment of the disease" (109).

16. The Bond et al. volume (1997) is based on a 1991 conference on AIDS in Africa and the Caribbean held in New York City.

17. Outrage in the news focused on the high cost of the play. Dlamini-Zuma used funds for AIDS education from the European Union and was criticized in parliament for not fully following accounting procedures.

18. This research was funded by the International Committee for Research on Women. The principal investigator was Quarraisha Abdool Karim and I was an anthropologist on the team.
19. Besides Nkosazana Dlamini-Zuma and the women from the community, present at this meeting were Ellen Weiss, the International Committee for Research on Women, Eleanor Preston-Whyte, Zena Stein, and myself.
20. Deborah Posel suggests that much of the government reaction against AIDS treatment can be understood in terms of a defense against new sexual mores (Posel 2005).
21. For a review of the varied role of Zionism as a combination of Christian beliefs and pre-colonial rituals which served partially as resistance and specifically in the Zulu Zionist Church in the strengthening of patriarchy (see Comaroff 1985:22).

# Chapter 4

1. For a detailed analysis of the debates and impact of GEAR, see Hein Marais's *South Africa Limits to Change* (2001). As noted in later chapters, since 2004, there has been an effort to increase social grants and alleviate some of the hardships created by the economic policies adopted in 1998. In 2008 a much more comprehensive rollout of treatment is in progress.
2. According to the South African economist Jeremy Seekings, there is a "broad academic consensus that income poverty worsened in the late 1990s, although precise findings vary according to the specific data used and assumptions made in the analysis" (Seekings 2007:4).
3. Although I briefly outline these changes in this chapter, for detailed descriptions of Thabo Mbeki's relations with AIDS denialists and the civil society battles in South Africa from the 1990s through 2006, see Nattrass 2007.
4. However, even in Brazil "the failure to even begin to develop an . . . integrated strategy for responding to AIDS as a key part of women's reproductive health care, seemed almost guaranteed to assure that levels of both heterosexual and vertical transmission would continue to rise dramatically . . ." (Parker 2003:174).
5. Health GAP was newly formed to address the treatment gap between the global North and South.
6. From 1992, Edwin Cameron, who later became a Supreme Court Judge and an international advocate for AIDS and human rights, chaired the AIDS Consortium which, organized by a full-time advocate Morna Cornell, held monthly meetings and brought together political activists such as Zackie Achmat and Mark Heywood with researchers such as Mary Crewe as well as the National Association of People Living With AIDS (NAPWA).
7. Marais points out a similar contradiction in his discussion of the ideological function of Mbeki's notions of African Renaissance "lodged in a distinctive compilation of Afrocentric histories, identities, practices and realities, the discourse at the same time is explicitly welcoming to white domestic capital" (Marais 2001:249).

8. I have drawn on Nicoli Nattrass's latest work as the most recent and comprehensive recounting of the politics of AIDS denialism at the government level and the battle of the South African TAC over that period.

9. For an example of contemporary discussions in anthropology with respect to this issue, see the debates about Caldwell's early review of AIDS in Africa (Ahlberg 1994; Caldwell et al. 1994; Le Blanc et al. 1991).

10. As Marais points out, the post-apartheid state had to come to terms both with "traditional" chiefly power and with the right wing values of the Nationalist Party (Marais 2001:92).

11. See also Edwin Cameron's memoir (Cameron 2000).

12. The community voices were organized by Joyce Hunter and others from the Women's Caucus of the International AIDS Society, in conjunction with community women's activists from South Africa, led by Mercy Makhalemele, the first woman in SA to disclose her HIV status and a leading women's activist, Lungi Mazibuko, representing National Association of People With AIDS, Betsi Pendry, from the Living Together Project in South Africa, and Anne Christine D'Adesky, an HIV/AIDS journalist and treatment activist based in New York City. Women who helped to set up the community engagement in Durban 2000 went on to meet with the International Council of AIDS Organizations and the International Community of Women Living with AIDS (ICW) at the Barcelona International AIDS Society Conference 2002. Again, they hosted an independent, free parallel conference for women and drafted the Barcelona Bill of Rights. In Bangkok, 2004, the cumulative effects of this organizing led to a further panel of women's groups, including ICW, ICASO, and others, and a session sponsored by the Canadian Government on the Barcelona Bill of Rights. By Toronto, 2006, many human rights and feminist groups had joined to form the ATHENA Network and, together with Canadian Positive Women, arranged for a Women's Networking Zone in the, now fully established, Global Village. (Personal communication with Betsi Pendry, 2007.)

13. Initial grants to KwaZulu-Natal from the Global Fund for AIDS were blocked by the South African government (Nattrass 2007).

14. Manto Tshabalala-Msimang singled out Dr. Jerry Coovadia, a renowned researcher and organizer of the 2000 Durban International AIDS Society Conference, for public insult and accused him of "elitism" (Nattrass 2007:69), as well as calling Mark Heywood the "white man" from the TAC (Nattrass 2007:117).

# Chapter 6

1. I borrow the notion of "transformative action" developed in Mullings 1995 and Mullings 1997 as everyday actions that challenge rather than simply adapt to the status quo.

2. Delius (1996) describes rural–urban relations among people of the Pedi kingdom, a cattle-raising group with a strong history of resistance. Although there are variations in practice, beliefs, and language between the many groups – such as Zulu, Xhosa, and Pedi – from a broader point of view, today, there are also many similarities.

3. Women frequently spoke of the Khomanani "Caring Together" Campaign, which is an HIV/AIDS education campaign supported by the government from 2002–2007. For more information, see www.info.gov.za/speeches/2003/03041514011002.htm.

4. Pum is a pseudonym, as are all the names used for grassroots women in this chapter and those that follow.

5. For reviews of the history of gender, customary law, and constitutional law in South Africa, see Murray 1994 and Leibenberg 1995.

6. For an important discussion of the diverse formations of tribal authorities among different South African ethnic groups, see Vail 1989.

7. These foundational ideas are reviewed in contemporary literature. See Baer et al. 2003, specifically the Reproduction chapter. An excellent review and contemporary examples of the strategies remembered and reworked by young people today can be found in Steinberg 2008.

8. The recent Constitutional Court decision in the *Bhe v. Magistrates* (2005) case marks a notable shift from this system of inheritance and a victory for South African women under customary law. The question the court was prompted to answer was if African women and girls are entitled to inherit property from their father in the absence of a will. Under customary law and Section 23 of the Black Administration Act, the property would belong to the eldest male relative. On October 15, 2004, the Constitutional Court ruled in favor of two girls who were denied inheritance of their father's estate at his death because of the customary law of primogeniture, and asserted that primogeniture, as writ in the Black Administration Act, is unconstitutional. See *Bhe and Others v. Magistrate, Khayelitsha and Others*, case #CCT 49/03 as well as Yanou 2006.

9. See the Landless People's Movement, the Programme for Land and Agrarian Studies (PLAAS), the Rural Women's Movement, the Transkei Land Service Organization (TRALSO), and the Association for Rural Advancement (AFRA) for examples of this work.

10. The Communal Land Rights Act referred to another Act that passed through Parliament just weeks before, the Traditional Leadership and Governance Framework Act. For an explanation of the relationship between these "sister acts," see Cousins and Claassens 2005.

11. Drawn from Mayer's 1970 unpublished research report "Wives of Migrant Workers," pp. 74–5, quoted in Delius and Glazer 2003.

12. Ferguson (1999) discusses similar accounts in relation to structural adjustment in Zambia.

# Chapter 7

1. As with Chapter 6's notion of "transformative action" that I borrow from Mullings 1995 and Mullings 1997, I draw from her development of "adaptive activist groups" in this chapter.

2. See the online news bulletin *ANC Today*, vol. 7, no. 34, August 31–September 6: www.anc.org.za/ancdocs/anctoday/2007/text/at34.txt.

3. Former TAC General Secretary Sipho Mthathi explained in an interview in June 2008 how she had conceptualized the Treatment Literacy Campaign in 2002 and worked to put it

into operation. Treatment Literacy work has now been replicated by AIDS activists world-wide. For an informed approach to treatment literacy that highlights women's needs as well as the biographies of positive women and their experiences, see the TAC Newsletter, Equal Treatment, specifically June 2006 and November 2006 (TAC 2006a; TAC 2006b).

4. One such international organization, Liberation 4 All Africans – a committee of lesbian, gay, bisexual and transgender African immigrants residing in the US – promoted a vigil in New York for the two women with the following statement: "This is not the first time that African lesbians and HIV positive women have been raped and/or mur-dered simply for being who they are. In June, Simangele Nhlapho, a member of a support group for women living with HIV, coordinated by the South Africa-based Positive Women's Network (PWN), and her two-year-old were raped and murdered. Sixteen-year-old Madoe Mafubedu was also attacked and killed in April of this year. In all these cases the perpetrators have not been called to answer for their crimes. In a country where more women then men are living with HIV, we are seeing an escalation of violence against women. South Africa has the world's highest rate of reported rape and women are usually targeted for rape because of their actual or presumed sexual orientation. Stigma associated with both rape and homosexuality dictates that many of these attacks are not reported. We are tired of seeing women, who served as the voices of their community, raped and/or murdered simply for fighting for the rights of their communities to survive and thrive. If these role models, who dared to be out about their sexual orientation and HIV status, are killed, how then can we expect others to live their lives publicly, without shame and fear? How do communities eradicate misogyny, homophobia, transphobia and HIV-based stigma when it appears that the state apparatus condones violence against Lesbian, Gay, Bisexual, Transgender (LGBT), and HIV-positive individuals?"

5. See note 8, Chapter 6.

# Chapter 8

1. Richard Lee and I conducted research together in Namibia and Botswana in all the sites described in Chapters 8, 9, and 10.

2. The Fogarty Foundation was a US-funded training program in AIDS research based at US universities to train researchers and to operate in less developed countries. Our pro-posal for an ethnographic training program in "The Social Context of AIDS Research" became the only Fogarty program that funded anthropological research and training, at least at that time, and was funded through the HIV Center at Columbia University.

# Chapter 9

1. At the time, I was speaking with a group of Ju women, translated for me by the local village pre-school teacher whose mother was Ju and her father Herero.

2. Again, the names used here are pseudonyms. Today, Ju/'hoansi often use Western as well as Ju names.

# Chapter 11

1.  For a discussion of these international issues, such as second-generation drug prices, see www.healthgap.org/camp/trade.html and, specifically, Asia Russell's position papers on TRIPS and intellectual property rights.
2.  For further details, see note 16, Chapter 2. In general, Pepfarwatch.org provided a wealth of materials on this topic.
3.  In 2008, I received an e-mail from AIDS activists in the Ukraine saying that women were choosing to become pregnant as a way to access drug rehabilitation services.
4.  For Haitian march, see Dunkel 2007. Also, see Baer et al. 2003, Farmer 1992, Oppenheimer 1988, and Shilts 1987 for histories of AIDS and representation in the US.
5.  The issue of syringe exchange programs was still hotly contested in Canada during the Toronto 2006 International AIDS Society Conference.
6.  For an insightful examination of Aztec women in colonial times, see Nash 1980.
7.  The plan is called the HIV and AIDS and STI Strategic Plan for South Africa, 2007–2011.
8.  For similar discussions of property rights, inheritance, and gender in Kenya, see Human Rights Watch 2003.
9.  Women, as the long-term unemployed in both rural and urban areas, are seldom counted or even considered unemployed in many analyses.
10. The Inaugural Z. K. Matthews Memorial Lecture entitled "He Wakened to His Responsibilities" was delivered by President Thabo Mbeki on October 12, 2001. For the full speech, visit www.anc.org.za/ancdocs/history/mbeki/2001/tm1012.html.
11. The Treatment Action Campaign (TAC) resisted Matthias Rath's multivitamin campaign. For example, see the following briefing from the TAC: www.tac.org.za/newsletter/2005/ns19_04_2005.htm.

# Bibliography

Abdool Karim, Quarraisha, and Janet Frohlich, 2000 Women Trying to Protect Themselves from HIV/AIDS in KwaZulu-Natal, South Africa. *In* African Women's Health. M. Turshen, ed., pp. 69–82. Trenton, NJ: Africa World Press.

Abdool Karim, Quarraisha, and Neetha Morar, 1994 Women and AIDS in Natal/KwaZulu: Determinants to the Adoption of HIV Protective Behavior. Washington, DC: International Center for Research on Women.

Abdool Karim, Quarraisha, and Salim Abdool Karim, 2002 The Evolving HIV Epidemic in South Africa, International Journal of Epidemiology 31:37–40.

Abdool Karim, Salim S., and Quarraisha Abdool Karim, eds, 2005 HIV/AIDS in South Africa. New York: Cambridge University Press.

Abdool Karim, Salim S., T. T. Zigubu-Page, and R. Arendse, 1994 Bridging the Gap: Potential for a Health Care Partnership Between African Traditional Healers and Biomedical Personnel in South Africa. South African Medical Journal (Supplement) 84:1–16.

Abramovitz, Miriam, 1996 Regulating The Lives of Women: Social Welfare Policy From Colonial Times to the Present. Boston: South End Press.

Abu-Lughod, Lila, 2004 Dramas of Nationhood: The Politics of Television in Egypt. Chicago: University of Chicago Press.

ACT UP, 2004 Bush's Global AIDS "Coordinator" Denigrates Condoms: http://www.actup. org.

Adler, Glenn, and Eddie Webster, eds, 2000 Trade Unions and Democratization in South Africa, 1985–97. Johannesburg: Witwatersrand University Press.

Aggleton, Peter, K. Rivers, and S. Scott, 1999 Use of the Female Condom: Gender Relations and Sexual Negotiations. *In* Sex and Youth: Contextual Factors Affecting Risk for HIV/AIDS. UNAIDS, ed. UNAIDS Best Practice Collection. Geneva: UNAIDS.

Ahlberg, B. M., 1994 Is There a Distinct African sexuality? A Critical Response to Caldwell. Africa 64(2):220–242.

AIDS Vaccine Advocacy Coalition, 2007 Resetting the Clock: 2007 AVAC Report. New York: AIDS Vaccine Advocacy Coalition.

Ain-Davis, Dana, 2006 Battered Black Women and Welfare Reform: Between a Rock and a Hard Place. New York: State University of New York Press.

Albertyn, Catherine, and Shireen Hassim, 2003 The Boundaries of Democracy: Gender, HIV/AIDS and Culture. *In* The Real State of the Nation: South Africa since 1990. D. Everatt and V. Maphai, eds. Johannesburg: INTERFUND.

Alexander, Neville, 2007 After Apartheid: The Language Question. *In* After Apartheid Conference. New Haven: Yale University Press.

Alexander, Neville, and Kathleen Heugh, 2001 Language policy in the New South Africa. *In* After Apartheid. R. Kriger and A. Zegeye, eds, vol. 2, pp. 15–40. Cape Town: Kwela Books.

Allen, Anita, 2000 Shovelling Out the AIDS Controversy: Conference revealed a great deal of hypocrisy. *In* The Citizen, July 21. Johannesburg, South Africa.

Altman, Dennis, 2001 Global Sex. Chicago: University of Chicago Press.

American Medical Student Association, 2005 AIDS Has a Woman's Face. Accessed January 10, 2008. www.amsa.org/global/aids/WomenAndHIV2.ppt#256,1.

Annan, Kofi, 2002 In Africa, AIDS Has a Woman's Face. *In* New York Times, Health Section, December 29.

Appadurai, Arjun, 1998 Modernity at Large: Cultural Dimensions of Globalization. Minneapolis: University of Minnesota Press.

Aretxaga, Begona, 1997 Shattering Silence. Princeton, NJ: Princeton University Press.

Asad, Talal, 2000 What Do Human Rights Do? An Anthropological Enquiry. Theory & Event 4(4).

Ashforth, Adam, 2000 Madumo: A Man Bewitched. Chicago: University of Chicago Press.

Ashforth, Adam, 2005 Witchcraft, Violence, and Democracy in South Africa. Chicago: University of Chicago Press.

Baer, Hans, Merrill Singer, and Ida Susser, 2003 Medical Anthropology in the World System, 2nd edition. Westport, CT: Praeger Publishers.

Baker, Lee, 2001 The Color-Blind Bind. *In* Cultural Diversity in the United States. Ida Susser and T. Patterson, eds, pp. 103–119. Malden, MA/Oxford: Blackwell.

Baldo, Mariella, and Antonio Jorge Cabral, 1990 Low Intensity Wars and Social Determination of the HIV Transmission: The Search for a New Paradigm to Guide Research and Control of the HIV-AIDS Pandemic. *In* Action on AIDS in Southern Africa: Proceedings of Maputo Conference on Health in Transition in Southern Africa, April 9–16. Zena Stein and Anthony Zwi, eds. Published by Committee for Health in Southern Africa (CHISA), HIV Center for Clinical and Behavioral Studies, New York State Psychiatric Institute, and Colombia University in the City of New York.

Bank, Leslie, and Gary Minkley, 2005 Going Nowhere Slowly? Land, Livelihoods and Rural Development in the Eastern Cape. Social Dynamics 31(1):1–39.

Bank, Leslie, William Beinart, Patrick McAllister, and Gary Minkley, eds, 2005 Land Reform and Rural Development in South Africa's Eastern Cape. Social Dynamics, Special Issue 31(1).

Barbosa, Regina Maria, Suzana Kalckmann, Elza Berquó, and Zena Stein, 2007 Notes on the Female Condom: Experiences in Brazil. International Journal of STD & AIDS 18(4):261–266.

Barnard, David, 2002 In the High Court of South Africa, Case No. 4138/98: The Global Politics of Access to Low-Cost AIDS Drugs in Poor Countries. Kennedy Institute of Ethics Journal 12(2):159–174.

Barnett, Tony, and Gwyn Prins, 2005 HIV/AIDS and Security: Fact, Fiction and Evidence: A Report to UNAIDS. London: LSEAIDS.

Barnett, Tony, and Alan Whiteside, 2002 AIDS in the Twenty-First Century: Disease and Globalization. New York: Palgrave.

Barton, Carol, and Laurie Prendergast, 2004 Seeking Accountability on Women's Human Rights: Women Debate the UN Millennium Development Goals. New York: Women's International Coalition for Economic Justice.

Bassett, Mary Travis, 2000 The Pursuit of Equity in Health: Reflections on Race and Public Health Data in Southern Africa. American Journal of Public Health 90(11):4.

Bassett, Mary Travis, 2001 Keeping the M in MTCT: Women, Mothers and HIV Prevention. American Journal of Public Health 91:701–703.

Bassett, Mary Travis, and M. Mhloyi, 1991 Women and AIDS in Zimbabwe: The Making of an Epidemic. International Journal of Health Services 21(1):143–156.

BBC News, 2004 Mbeki slammed in rape race row. BBC News, October 5. London. http://news.bbc.co.uk/2/hi/africa/3716004.stm.

BBC News, 2006 SA's Zuma "Showered to Avoid HIV." BBC News Online. April 5. London. http://news.bbc.co.uk/2/hi/africa/4879822.stm. Accessed January 10, 2008.

Beall, Jo, 1990 Women Under Indentured Labor in Colonial Natal, 1860–1911. *In* Women and Gender in Southern Africa to 1945. C. Walker, ed. Cape Town/London: David Philip/James Currey.

Beck, Ulrich, 1992 Risk Society: Towards a New Modernity. London and Newbury Park, CA: Sage Publications.

Bello, Walden, 2001, Dispatch from Doha. The Nation, 14 November.

Bello, Walden, 2002 De-Globalization: Ideas for a New World Economy. London: Zed Books.

Belmonte, Thomas, 1979 (3rd edn 2005) The Broken Fountain. New York: Columbia University Press.

Benatar, Solomon R., 2001 South Africa's Transition in a Globalizing World: HIV/AIDS as a Window and a Mirror. International Affairs 77(2):347–375.

Bennett, Jane, 2001 "Enough lip service!" Hearing post-colonial experience of heterosexual abuse, conflict and sex wars as a state concern. Agenda: Empowering women for gender equality African Feminisms(50):88–96.

Bentley, Kristina, 2004 Women's Human Rights and the Feminisation of Poverty in South Africa. Review of African Political Economy (100):247–261.

Berer, Marge, 2006 Condoms, Yes! "Abstinence," No. Reproductive Health Matters 14(28):6–16.

Berer, Marge, 2007 Male Circumcision for HIV Prevention: Perspectives on Gender and Sex. Reproductive Health Matters 15(29):45–48.

Berer, Marge, 2008 Male Circumcision: The Implications for Women and for Men who have Sex with Men. Presented at XVII International AIDS Society Conference, Mexico City, August 3–8.

Berezin, Mabel, 1997 Making the Fascist Self: The Political Culture of Interwar Italy. Ithaca: Cornell University Press.

Berkman, Alan, 2003 Personal interview, New York City.

Beyrer, Chris, 2006 Epidemiology Update and Transmission Factors. XVI International AIDS Society Conference, Toronto, 2006.

Black AIDS Institute, 2008, Left Behind: Black America: A Neglected Priority in the Global AIDS Epidemic.

Bluestone, Barry, and Bennett Harrison, 1982 The Deindustrialization of America: Plant Closings, Community Abandonment, and the Dismantling of Basic Industry. Basic Books.

Bond, George C., and Joan Vincent, 1997 AIDS in Uganda: The First Decade. *In* AIDS in Africa and the Caribbean. George Bond, John Kreniske, Ida Susser, and Joan Vincent, eds. Boulder, CO: Westview Press.

Bond, George C., John Kreniske, Ida Susser, and Joan Vincent, eds, 1997 AIDS in Africa and the Caribbean. Boulder, CO: Westview Press.

Bond, Patrick, 2006 Talk Left, Walk Right: South Africa's Frustrated Global Reforms, 2nd edn. Pietermaritzburg: University of KwaZulu-Natal Press.

Bonner, Philip, 1990 "Desirable or Undesirable Basotho Women?" Liquor, Prostitution and the Migration of Basotho Women to the Rand, 1920–1945. *In* Women and Gender in Southern Africa to 1945. Cherryl Walker, ed. Cape Town/London: David Philip/James Currey.

Bonner, Philip, Peter Delius, and Deborah Posel, eds, 1993 Apartheid's Genesis, 1935–1962. Braamfontein, SA: Ravan Press.

Bonnin, Debby, 2000 Claiming Spaces, Changing Places: Political Violence and Women's Protests in KwaZulu-Natal. Journal of South African Studies 26(2):301–316.

Borosage, Robert L., 1999 The Battle in Seattle. *In* The Nation (December):20.

Bosmans, M., M. Cikuru, P. Claeys, and M. Temmerman, 2006 Where Have All the Condoms Gone in Adolescent Programmes in the Democratic Republic of Congo? Reproductive Health Matters 14(28):80–89.

Botswana, UNDP/Government of, 2000 Towards an AIDS-Free Generation. Botswana Human Development Report: UNDP/Government of Botswana.

Bourdieu, Pierre, 1993 The Field of Cultural Production. New York: Columbia University Press.

Bozzoli, Belinda, and Mmantho Nkotsoe, 1991 Women of Phokeng: Consciousness, Life Strategy, and Migrancy in South Africa, 1900–1983. Johannesburg: Ravan Press.

Bradshaw, Debbie, and Rob Dorrington, 2005 AIDS-related Mortality in South Africa. *In* HIV/AIDS in South Africa. Salim S. Abdool Karim and Quarraisha Abdool Karim, eds, pp. 419–432. New York: Cambridge University Press.

Bradshaw, Debbie, Pam Groenewald, Ria Laubscher, Nadine Nannan, Beatrice Nojilana, Rosana Norman, Desirée Pieterse and Michelle Schneider, 2003 Initial Burden of Disease: Estimates for South Africa 2000. Cape Town: South African Medical Research Council, March.

Brasher, Brenda, 1997 Godly Women: Fundamentalism and Female Power. New Brunswick: Rutgers University Press.

Brecher, Jeremy, 2000 Globalization from Below: The Power of Solidarity. Cambridge: South End Press.

Brenner, Neil, and Nik Theodore, eds, 2002 Spaces of Neoliberalism: Urban Restructuring in North America and Western Europe. Oxford: Blackwell.

Brier, Jenny, forthcoming Infectious Ideas: AIDS and US Politics, 1980–2000. Chapel Hill: University of North Carolina Press.

Brocado, Vanessa, 2005 Focusing in on Prevention and Youth. *In* SIECUS–PEPFAR Country Profiles. New York: SIECUS, The Sexuality Information and Education Council of the United States.

Brodkin, Karen, 1988 Caring by the Hour: Women, Work and Organizing at Duke Medical Center. Champaign: University of Illinois Press.

Burawoy, Michael, 1972 The Colour of Class on the Copper Mines: From African Advancement to Zambianization. Manchester: University of Manchester Press.

Burawoy, Michael, 1998 The Extended Case Method. Sociological Theory 16(1):4–33.

Burawoy, Michael, et al., eds, 2000 Global Ethnography: Forces, Connections, and Imaginations in a Postmodern World. Berkeley: University of California Press.

Butler, Anthony, 2005 South Africa's HIV/AIDS Policy, 1994–2004: How Can it Be Explained? African Affairs 104(417):591–614.

Caldwell, John C., Pat Caldwell, and Pat Quiggin, 1991 The African Sexual System: Reply to Le Blanc et al. Population and Development Review 17(3):506–515.

Cameron, Edwin, 2000 The Deafening Silence of AIDS. The First Jonathan Mann Memorial Lecture. July 10, 2000. XIII International AIDS Society Conference, Durban, South Africa.

Cameron, Edwin, 2005 Witness to AIDS. Cape Town: Tafelberg, NB.

Campbell, Catherine, 2003 Letting Them Die: How HIV/AIDS Prevention Programmes Often Fail. Oxford/Cape Town: The International African Institute/James Currey.

Carroll, Rory, 2004 Mbeki Says Crime Reports Are Racist. The Guardian, October 5. London.

Castells, Manuel, 1996 The Information Age: Economy, Society and Culture. 3 vols. Oxford: Blackwell.

Center for Health and Gender Equity, 2004 Debunking the Myths in the U.S. Global AIDS Strategy: An Evidence-Based Analysis. Tacoma Park, MD: Center for Health and Gender Equity.

Center for Reproductive Rights, 2003 The Bush Global Gag Rule: Endangering Women's Health, Free Speech and Democracy. Center for Reproductive Rights.

Centers for Disease Control, 1981 Kaposi's Sarcoma and Pneumocystis Pneumonia Among Homosexual Men – New York City and California. Morbidity and Mortality Weekly Report (MMWR) 30:305–308.

Centers for Disease Control (CDC): K. A. Fenton and R. O. Valdiserri, 2006 Twenty-Five Years of HIV/AIDS – United States, 1981–2006. Morbidity and Mortality Weekly Report (MMWR) 55(21):585–589.

Centre for Development and Enterprise, 2005 Land Reform in South Africa: A 21st Century Perspective. Research Report 14. Johannesburg: CDE (Centre for Development and Enterprise).

Chae, Suhong, 2003 Contemporary Ho Chi Minh City in Numerous Contradictions: Reform Policy, Foreign Capital and the Working Class. *In* Wounded Cities. Jane Schneider and Ida Susser, eds, pp. 227–251. New York: Berg.

Chanock, Martin, 2000 "Culture" and Human Rights: Orientalising, Occidentalising and Authenticity. *In* Beyond Rights Talk and Culture Talk: Comparative Essays on the Politics of Rights and Culture. M. Mamdani, ed. pp. 15–36. New York: St. Martin's Press.

Chapman, Michael, ed., 2001 The Drum Decade: Stories from the 1950s. Pietermaritzburg: University of Natal Press.

Clarke, John, 2004 Changing Welfare, Changing States: New Directions in Social Policy. London: Sage Publications.

Cleland, John, Mohamed M. Ali, and Iqbal Shah, 2006 Trends in Protective Behaviour Among Single vs. Married Young Women in Sub-Saharan Africa: The Big Picture. Reproductive Health Matters 14(28):17–22.

Cohen, Abner, 1974 Urban Ethnicity. New York: Tavistock Publications.

Cohen, Myron, 2008 Plenary: Prevention of the Sexual Transmission of HIV-1: A View from the 21st Century. Presented at XVII International AIDS Society Conference, Mexico City, August 4.

Cohen, Susan, 2004 Beyond Slogans: Lessons From Uganda's Experience With ABC and HIV/AIDS. Reproductive Health Matters 12(23):132–135.

Collins, Evans, 2008 Research on Women, Are We Doing Enough?: An Analysis of Abstracts from the IAS Conference on HIV Pathogenesis, Treatment and Prevention, 2007. International AIDS Society Conference. Mexico City.

Collins, Jane, 2009 *In* Rethinking America. Ida Susser and J. Maskovsky, eds. Boulder, CO: Paradigm Press.

Comaroff, Jean, 1985 Body of Power, Spirit of Resistance: The Culture and History of a South African People. Chicago: University of Chicago Press.

Comaroff, Jean, 1997 The Empire's Old Clothes: Fashioning the Colonial Subject. *In* Situated Lives: Gender and Culture in Everyday Life. Louise Lamphere, Helena Ragone, and Patricia Zavella, eds. New York: Routledge.

Comaroff, Jean, and John L. Comaroff, eds, 2001a Millennial Capitalism and the Culture of Neoliberalism. Durham and London: Duke University Press.

Comaroff, Jean, and John L. Comaroff, 2001b First Thoughts on a Second Coming. *In* Millennial Capitalism and the Culture of Neoliberalism. Jean Comaroff and John L. Comaroff, eds, pp. 1–56. Durham, NC and London: Duke University Press.

Comaroff, John L., 1997 Contests of Conscience: Models of Colonial Domination in South Africa. *In* Tensions of Empire: Colonial Cultures in a Bourgeois World. F. Cooper and A. L. Stoler, eds. Berkeley: University of California Press.

Comaroff, John L., and Jean Comaroff, 2004 Criminal Justice, Cultural Justice: The Limits of Liberalism and the Pragmatics of Difference in the New South Africa. American Ethnologist 31(2):188–204.

Constitutional Court of South Africa, 1996 New South African Constitution. Braamfontein.

Coontz, Stephanie, 1988 The Social Origins of Private Life: A History of American Families, 1600–1900. London and New York: Verso.

Coovadia, Hoosen M., Nigel C. Rollins, Ruth Bland, Kirsty Little, Anna Coutsoudis, Michael Bennish, and Marie-Louise Newell, 2007 Mother-to-child Transmission of HIV-1 Infection During Exclusive Breastfeeding in the First 6 Months of Life: An Intervention Cohort Study. The Lancet 368(9567):1107–1116.

Corea, Gena, 1992 The Invisible Epidemic: The Story of Women and AIDS. New York: HarperCollins.

Cornish, Flora, and Riddhi Ghosh, 2007 The Necessary Contradictions of "Community-Led" Health Promotion: A Case Study of HIV Prevention in an Indian Red Light District. Social Science & Medicine 64(2):496–507.

Cousins, Ben, and Aninka Claassens, 2005 Communal Land Rights and Democracy in Post-Apartheid South Africa. *In* Democratizing Development: The Politics of Socio-Economic Rights in South Africa. P. Jones and K. Stokke, eds, pp. 245–270. Boston: Martinus Nijhoff Publishers.

Coutsoudis, A., 2008 Mother and Child Dyad Issues: Breastfeeding and Child Survival. Presented at XVII International AIDS Society Conference, Mexico City, August 3–8.

Craddock, Susan, 2005 AIDS and Ethics: Clinical Trials, Pharmaceuticals, and Global Scientific Practice. *In* HIV and AIDS in Africa: Beyond Epidemiology. Ezekiel Kalipeni, S. Craddock, J. Oppong, and J. Ghosh, eds, pp. 240–252. Malden, MA: Blackwell.

Crapanzano, Vincent, 1986 Waiting: The Whites of South Africa. New York: Vintage Books.

Crehan, Kate, 2002 Gramsci, Culture and Anthropology. Sterling, VA: Pluto Press.

Crewdson, John, 2002 Science Fictions: A Scientific Mystery, a Massive Cover-up and the Dark Legacy of Robert Gallo. Boston: Little, Brown.

Cunningham, Ineke, 1994 Prevalent Sexual Practices and HIV-Related Risk Behaviors Among University Students: Gender Differences. *In* HIV Center on Clinical and Behavioral Studies. New York: New York State Psychiatric Institute.

Das, Veena, 1995 National Honor and Practical Kinship: Unwanted Women and Children. *In* Conceiving the New World Order: The Global Politics of Reproduction. R. Rapp and F. Ginsberg, eds. Berkeley: University of California Press.

de Klerk, Veronica, 2001 Speech to Launch the Female Condom. *In* Women in Development Report, Vol. 12.

De Sousa, Cesar Palha, et al., 1990 The Scale of HIV Infection in Mozambique: Its Relation to Primary Health Care and Prevention. *In* Action on AIDS in Southern Africa: Proceedings of Maputo Conference on Health in Transition in Southern Africa, April 9–16. Zena Stein and Anthony Zwi, eds. Published by Committee for Health in Southern Africa (CHISA), HIV Center for Clinical and Behavioral Studies, New York State Psychiatric Institute, and Colombia University in the City of New York.

Delius, Peter, 1996 A Lion Amongst the Cattle: Reconstruction and Resistance in the Northern Transvaal. Portsmouth, NH/Oxford: Heinemann/James Currey.

Delius, Peter, and Clive Glaser, 2003 The Myth of Polygamy: A History of Extra-Marital and Multipartnership Sex in South Africa. Presented at the Sex and Secrecy Conference. University of Witwatersrand: International Association for the Study of Sexuality, Culture and Society.

Des Jarlais, Don, Samuel Freidman, and Jo Sotheran, 1992 The First City: HIV Among Intravenous Drug Users in New York City. *In* AIDS: the Making of a Chronic Disease. Elizabeth Fee and Daniel Fox, eds, pp. 279–298. Berkeley: University of California Press.

Desai, Ashwin, 2002 We are the Poors: Community Struggles in Post-Apartheid South Africa. New York: Monthly Review Press.

Di Leonardo, Micaela, 2000 Exotics at Home: Anthropologies, Others, and American Modernity. Chicago: University of Chicago Press.

Dlamini-Zuma, Nkosazana 1988a Women and Health. 1988 CHISA Conference, NYC. Committee for Health in Southern Africa.

Dlamini-Zuma, Nkosazana 1988b Women in South Africa. *In* Women's Health and Apartheid: The Health of Women and Children and the Future of Progressive Primary Health Care in Southern Africa. Marcia Wright, Zena Stein, and Jean Scandlyn, eds. New York: Columbia University Press.

Dlamini-Zuma, Nkosazana, 1996 A response to the report of the Public Protector on his investigation into HIV/AIDS play Sarafina II. *In* South African Parliament. Issued by: SA Communication Service, www.doh.gov.za/docs/pr/1996/pr0605.html.

Doane, Molly, 2007 The Political Economy of the Ecological Native. American Anthropologist 109(3):452–462.

Dolny, Helena, 1995 Slovo – The Unfinished Autobiography. Randburg: Ravan Press.

Draper, Patricia, 1975 !Kung Women: Contrasts in Sexual Egalitarianism in Foraging and Sedentary Contexts. *In* Toward an Anthropology of Women. R. Rapp Reiter, ed., pp. 77–109. New York: Monthly Review Press.

Du Pisani, Kobus, 2001 Puritanism Transformed: Afrikaner Masculinities in the Apartheid and Post-Apartheid Period. *In* Changing Men in Southern Africa. R. Morrell, ed. London and New York: Zed Books.

Dunkel, Greg, 2007 Tenth Department Haitians Massively Mobilize In Haiti: A Slave Revolution, 200 years after 1804. International Action Center, ed. www.iacenter.org/haiti/index.htm.

Dworkin, Shari L., and Anke A. Ehrhardt, 2007 Going Beyond "ABC" to Include "GEM": Critical Reflections on Progress in the HIV/AIDS Epidemic. American Journal of Public Health 97(1):13–18.

Eagleton, Terry, 1999 Scholars and Rebels in Nineteenth-Century Ireland. Oxford and Malden, MA: Blackwell.

Ebrahim, Noor, 2001 Noor's Story: My Life in District Six. District Six Museum.

Edelman, Marc, 1999 Peasants Against Globalization: Rural Social Movements in Costa Rica. Stanford, CA: Stanford University Press.

Ehrenreich, Barbara, 2004 The Faith Factor. The Nation, November 29. Washington, DC.

Ehrhardt, Anke, and Theresa Exner, 1987 The Impact of HIV Infection on Women's Sexuality and Gender Role. *In* Women and AIDS: Promoting Healthy Behaviors. Susan E. Blumenthal, Anita Eichler, and Glena Weissman, eds, pp. 35–39. Rockville, MD: US Department of Health and Human Services.

Epstein, A. L., 1958 Politics in an Urban African Community. Manchester: Manchester University Press.

Epstein, Helen, 2000 The Mystery of AIDS in South Africa. *In* The New York Review of Books, Vol. 47. July 20.

Epstein, Helen, 2007 The Invisible Cure: Africa, the West, and the Fight Against AIDS. New York: Farrar, Straus and Giroux.

Escobar, Arturo, 1998 Whose Knowledge, Whose Nature? Biodiversity, Conservation, and the Political Ecology of Social Movements. Journal of Political Ecology 5:53–82.

Etienne, Mona, 1997 Women and Men, Cloth and Colonization: the Transformation of Production-Distribution Relations Among the Baule (Ivory Coast). *In* Perspectives on Africa: A Reader in Culture, History, and Representation. Roy Grinker and Chris Steiner, eds, pp. 518–535. Cambridge, MA: Blackwell.

Evans-Pritchard, E. E., 1951 Kinship and Marriage Among the Nuer. Oxford: Clarendon Press.

Exner, Theresa M., Shari L. Dworkin, Susie Hoffman, and Anke Ehrhardt, 2003 Beyond the Male Condom. Annual Review of Sex Research, 14:114–136.

Exner, Theresa M., et al., 2008 Women's Anal Sex Practices: Implications for Formulation and Promotion of a Rectal Microbicide. AIDS Education and Prevention: An Interdisciplinary Journal, 20(2):148–159.

Fadul, Elisabet, 2008 Plenary: State of the Epidemic and Young People. Presented at XVII International AIDS Society Conference, Mexico City, August 4.

Farmer, Paul, 1992 AIDS and Accusation: Haiti and the Geography of Blame. Berkeley: University of California Press.

Farmer, Paul, M. Connors, and J. Simmons, eds, 1996 Women, Poverty, and AIDS: Sex, Drugs, and Structural Violence. Monroe, ME: Common Courage Press.

Farmer, Paul, M., J. Good, and Shirley Lindenbaum, 1993 Women, Poverty and AIDS: An Introduction. Culture, Medicine, and Psychiatry 17(4):387–398.

Fassin, Didier, 2007 When Bodies Remember: Experiences and Politics of AIDS in South Africa. Berkeley: University of California Press.

Fassin, Didier, and Helen Schneider, 2003 The Politics of AIDS in South Africa: Beyond the Controversies. British Medical Journal 326:495–497.

Fee, Elizabeth, and Daniel Fox, eds, 1988 AIDS: The Burdens of History. Berkeley: University of California Press.

Feinstein, Andrew, 2007 After the Party: A Personal and Political Journey Inside the ANC. Cape Town: Jonathan Ball Publishers.

Female Health Company, The, 2007 Press Release: The Female Health Company Reports Record Profit for Both 4th Quarter and Fiscal Year '07. November 26. Chicago.

Ferguson, James, 1999 Expectations of Modernity: Myths and Meanings of Urban Life on the Zambian Copperbelt. Berkeley: University of California Press.

First, Ruth, 1965 117 Days. New York: Stein and Day.

First, Ruth, Ann Scott, and Nadine Gordimer, 1980 Olive Schreiner: A Biography. New York: André Deutsch/Schoken Books.

Flint, Karen Elizabeth, 2001 Negotiating a Hybrid Medical Culture: African Healers in Southeastern Africa from the 1820s to the 1940s. Dissertation: University of California, Los Angeles.

Floyd, Liz, 1990 HIV and AIDS in South Africa Today. *In* Action on AIDS in Southern Africa: Proceedings of Maputo Conference on Health in Transition in Southern Africa, April 9–16. Zena Stein and Anthony Zwi, eds. Published by Committee for Health in Southern Africa (CHISA), HIV Center for Clinical and Behavioral Studies, New York State Psychiatric Institute, and Colombia University in the City of New York.

Fortes, Meyer, 1977 Introduction. *In* Body and Mind in Zulu Medicine: An Ethnography of Health and Disease in Nyuswa-Zulu Thought and Practice. Harriet Ngubane, ed. Academic Press.

Foucault, Michel, 2003 The Birth of the Clinic. London: Routledge.

Fraser, Nancy, and Linda Gordon, 1994 A Genealogy of Dependency: Tracing a Keyword of the US Welfare State. Journal of Women in Culture and Society 19(2):1–28.

Freedman, Lynn P., 1999 Censorship and Manipulation of Reproductive Health Information: An Issue of Human Rights and Women's Health. *In* Health and Human Rights: A Reader. J. Mann, ed. London: Routledge.

Friedman, Samuel R., and Douglas Lipton, eds, 1991 Cocaine, AIDS, and Intravenous Drug Use. New York: Haworth Press.

Freidman, Sam, Maryl Sufian, and Don Des Jarlais, 1990 The AIDS Epidemic Among Latino Intravenous Drug Users. *In* Drugs in Hispanic Communities. R. M. Glick and Joan Moore, eds, pp. 45–54. New Brunswick, NJ: Rutgers University Press.

Friedman, Samuel R. et al., 2007 Harm Reduction Theory: Users' Culture, Micro-Social Indigenous Harm Reduction, and the Self-organization and Outside-organizing of Users' Groups. The International Journal on Drug Policy 18(2):107–117.

Friedman, Steven, and Shauna Mottier, 2004 Rewarding Engagement? The Treatment Action Campaign and the Politics of HIV/AIDS: Globalisation, Marginalisation and New Social Movements in Post-Apartheid South Africa. Durban: UKZN.

Friedman, Thomas L., 2005 The World Is Flat: A Brief History of the Twenty-first Century. New York: Farrar, Straus and Giroux.

Frohlich, Janet, 2005 The Impact of AIDS on the Community. *In* HIV/AIDS in South Africa. Salim S. Abdool Karim and Quarraisha Abdool Karim, eds. New York: Cambridge University Press.

Fumento, Michael, 1993 The Myth of Heterosexual AIDS: How a Tragedy Has Been Distorted by the Media and Partisan Politics. Washington, DC: Regnery Publishing.

Gailey, Christine Ward, 1987 Evolutionary Perspectives on Gender Hierarchy, Analyzing Gender. *In* Analyzing Gender. F. B. Hess, ed., pp. 32–67. Beverly Hills: Sage.

Gailey, Christine Ward, 1998 Feminist Methods. *In* Handbook of Methods in Cultural Anthropology. H. R. Bernard, ed., pp. 203–234. Walnut Creek, CA: Altamira Press.

Gailey, Christine Ward, and T. C. Patterson, eds, 1987 Power Relations and State Formation. Washington: American Anthropological Association.

Geschiere, Peter, 1997a Kinship, Witchcraft and the Market. *In* Perspectives on Africa: A Reader in Culture, History, and Representation. R. R. Grinker and C. B. Steiner, eds, pp. 340–358. Cambridge, MA: Blackwell.

Geschiere, Peter, 1997b The Modernity of Witchcraft: Politics and the Occult in Postcolonial Africa. Charlottesville, VA: University Press of Virginia.

Gevisser, Mark, 2007 Thabo Mbeki: The Dream Deferred. Cape Town: Jonathan Ball Publishers.

Gill, Lesley, 2004 The School of the Americas: Military Training and Political Violence in the Americas. Durham, NC: Duke University Press.

Gilson, Lucy, and Di McIntyre, 2007 Post-apartheid Challenges: Household Access and Use of Health Care in South Africa. International Journal of Health Services 37(4):673–691.

Girard, Françoise, 2004 Global Implications of U.S. Domestic and International Policies on Sexuality. R. Parker, ed., Working Paper #1. New York: International Working Group on Sexuality and Social Policy.

Gluckman, Max, 1961 Anthropological Problems Arising from the African Industrial Revolution. *In* Social Change in Modern Africa: Studies Presented and Discussed. A. W. Southall, ed., pp. xi, 337. Oxford: Oxford University Press.

Gluckman, Max, 1965 Politics, Law and Ritual in Tribal Society. Oxford: Blackwell.

Gluckman, Max, 2002 "The Bridge": Analysis of a Social Situation in Zululand. *In* The Anthropology of Politics: A Reader in Ethnography, Theory, and Critique. Joan Vincent, ed., p. 476. Malden, MA: Blackwell.

Gollub, Erica, 2000 The Female Condom: Tool for Women's Empowerment. American Journal of Public Health 90:1377–1381.

Gollub, Erica, 2008 A Neglected Population: Drug-Using Women and Women's Methods of HIV/STI Prevention. AIDS Education and Prevention: An Interdisciplinary Journal (20)2:107–120.

Gordon, Linda, 1998 Pitied But Not Entitled: Single Mothers and the History of Welfare. Cambridge, MA: Harvard University Press.

Gordon, Robert, 2000 The Bushman Myth: The Making of a Namibian Underclass (Conflict and Social Change Series). Boulder, CO: Westview Press.

Gouws, Eleanor, and Quarraisha Abdool Karim, 2005 HIV Infection in South Africa: The Evolving Epidemic. *In* HIV/AIDS in South Africa. Salim S. Abdool Karim and Quarraisha Abdool Karim, eds. Cambridge: Cambridge University Press.

Govender, Pregs, 2007 Love and Courage: A Story of Insubordination. Auckland Park: Jacana Media (Pty) Ltd.

Gramsci, Antonio, 1971 Selections from the Prison Notebooks. London: Lawrence & Wishart.

Green, Edward C., 1994 AIDS and STDs in Africa. Pietermaritzburg: University of Natal Press.

Griffith, Marie R., 1997 God's Daughters: Evangelical Women and the Power of Submission. Berkeley: University of California Press.

Gupta, Akhil, 1998 Postcolonial Developments: Agriculture in the Making of Modern India. Durham, NC: Duke University Press.

Gupta, Geeta R., 2000 Plenary Presentation: Women and AIDS. 13th International AIDS Society Conference, Breaking the Silence, Durban, SA.

Gupta, Geeta R., and Ellen Weiss, 1993 Women's Lives and Sex: Implications for AIDS Prevention. Culture, Medicine and Psychiatry 17:399–412.

Guttmacher, Sally, and Ida Susser, 1985 Destructive Engagement: The Impact of Apartheid on Health Care in South Africa. Health PAC Bulletin 16(2):9–15.

Hall, Ruth, 2004 Land Agrarian Reform in South Africa: A Status Report 2004. Research Report No. 20 Cape Town: Programme for Land and Agrarian Studies, University of the Western Cape.

Halliburton, Murphy, 2004 Finding a Fit: Psychiatric Pluralism in South India and its Implications for WHO Studies of Mental Disorder. Transcultural Psychiatry (41)1:80–98.

Harris, T. G. et al., 2005 Incidence of Cervical Squamous Intraepithelial Lesions Associated with HIV Serostatus, CD4 Cell Counts, and Human Papillomavirus Test Results. JAMA 293(12):1471–1476.

Harrison, Faye, 1995 The Persistent Power of "Race" in the Cultural and Political Economy of Racism. Annual Review of Anthropology 24:47–74.

Hart, Gillian, 2002 Disabling Globalization: Places of Power in Post-Apartheid South Africa. Berkeley: University of California Press.

Harvey, David, 1990 The Condition of Postmodernity: An Enquiry Into the Origins of Cultural Change. Cambridge, MA: Blackwell.

Harvey, David, 2005 A Brief History of Neoliberalism. New York: Oxford University Press.

Hassim, Shireen, 2006 Women's Organizations and Democracy in South Africa: Contesting Authority. Madison: University of Wisconsin Press.

Health Systems Trust, 2006 South African Health Review. Durban: Health Systems Trust.

Heise, L. L., and C. Elias, 1995 Transforming AIDS Prevention to Meet Women's Needs: A Focus on Developing Countries. Social Science and Medicine 40:931–943.

Herdt, G., ed., 1997 Sexual Cultures and Migration in the Era of AIDS: Anthropological and Demographic Approaches. Oxford: Clarendon.

Heywood, Mark, 2006 The Price of Political Inaction and What Needs To Be Done To End It. Presentation to the plenary session of the Toronto 2006 XVI International AIDS Society Conference.

Hirsch, Jennifer S. et al., 2007 The Inevitability of Infidelity: Sexual Reputation, Social Geographies, and Marital HIV Risk in Rural Mexico. American Journal of Public Health 97(6):986–996.

Hitchcock, Robert, 2006 "We Are the Owners of the Land": The San Struggle for the Kalahari and Its Resources. *In* Updating the San: Image and Reality of an African People in the Twenty-First Century. Robert Hitchcock, Kanzunobo Ikeya, Megan Biesele, and Richard Lee, eds, pp. 229–256. Senri Ethnological Studies. Osaka: National Museum of Ethnology.

Hitchcock, Robert, Kazunobu Ikeya, Megan Biesele, and Richard Lee, eds, 2006 Updating the San: Image and Reality of an African People in the Twenty-First Century. Osaka: National Museum of Ethnology.

Hlongwana K., and Sibongile Mkhize, 2007 HIV/AIDS Through the Lens of Christianity: Perspectives From a South African Urban Support Group. Journal of Social Aspects of HIV/AIDS 4(2):556–563.

Human Rights Watch, 2003 Double Standards: Women's Property Rights Violations in Kenya. *In* Sub-Saharan Africa, Vol. 15. Washington, DC: Human Rights Watch.

Human Rights Watch, 2005 Uganda: The Less They Know, the Better. *In* Sub-Saharan Africa, Vol. 17. Washington DC: Human Rights Watch.

Hunter, Monica, 1936 Reaction to Conquest: Effects of Contact with Europeans on the Pondo of South Africa. London: Oxford University Press.

Hunter, Mark, 2005 Cultural Politics and Masculinities: Multiple-partners in Historical Perspective in KwaZulu-Natal. *In* Men Behaving Differently: South African Men since 1994. G. Reid and L. Walker, eds. Cape Town: Double Storey.

Hunter, Susan S., 2003 Black Death: AIDS in Africa. New York: Palgrave Macmillan.

Hunter, Susan, and John Williamson, 1997 Children on the Brink: Strategies to Support Children Isolated by HIV/AIDS. *In* Health Technical Services Project, p. 56: USAID.

Hutchinson, Sharon Elaine, 1996 Nuer Dilemmas: Coping With Money, War, and the State. Berkeley: University of California Press.

Hutchinson, Sharon Elaine, 1997 The Cattle of Money and the Cattle of Girls Among the Nuer. *In* Perspectives on Africa: A Reader in Culture, History, and Representation. Roy R. Grinker and Chris B. Steiner, eds, pp. 190–210. Malden, MA: Blackwell.

Hutchinson, Sharon Elaine, and Jok Madut Jok, 2002 Gendered Violence and the Militarisation of Ethnicity: A Case Study from South Sudan. *In* Postcolonial Subjectivities in Africa. Richard P. Werbner, ed., pp. 84–108. London and New York: Zed Books.

Hyslop, Jonathan, 2001 A Ragged Trousered Philanthropist and the Empire: Robert Tressell in South Africa. History Workshop Journal 51:64–86.

ICAP, 2007 ICAP Overview: ICAP South Africa. New York: Mailman School of Public Health, Columbia University.

Iipinge, S., Ntau C., Ipinge P., Katjire M., Hofnie K., Susser I., and Lee R. B., 2000 Capacity Building in Social Research on AIDS Case Studies in Namibia. Breaking the Silence: XIII International AIDS Society Conference, Durban, 2000.

Iliffe, John, 2006 The African AIDS Epidemic: A History. Athens: Ohio University Press.

Jana, Smarajit, Ishika Basu, Mary Jane Rotheram-Borus, and Peter A. Newman, 2004 The Sonagachi Project: A Sustainable Community Intervention Program. AIDS Education and Prevention: An Interdisciplinary Journal 16(5):405–414.

Jewkes, Rachel, 2002 Intimate Partner Violence: Causes and Prevention. The Lancet 359(9315):1423–1429.

Jewkes, Rachel, Jonathan Levin, and Loveday Penn-Kekana, 2002 Risk Factors for Domestic Violence: Findings from a South African Cross-Sectional Study. Social Science & Medicine 55(9):1603–1617.

Jewkes, Rachel, K. Dunkle, H. Brown, G. Gray, J. McIntryre, and S. Harlow, 2004 Gender-Based Violence, Relationship Power, and Risk of HIV Infection in Women Attending Antenatal Clinics in South Africa. The Lancet 363(9419):1415–1421.

Jochelson, K., M. Mothibeti, and J. P. Leger, 1991 Human Immunodeficiency Virus and Migrant Labor in South Africa. International Journal of Health Services 21(1):157–173.

Jones, Delmos, and Ida Susser, eds, 1993 Special Issue: The Widening Gap Between Rich and Poor. Critique of Anthropology 13(3):211–214.

Kabeer, Naila, 1997 Women, Wages and Intra-Household Power Relations in Urban Bangladesh. Development and Change 28(2):261–302.

Kalipeni, Ezekiel, S. Craddock, J. Oppong, and J. Ghosh, eds, 2004 HIV and AIDS in Africa: Beyond Epidemiology. Malden, MA: Blackwell.

Kaplan, Esther, 2004 With God on Their Side: How Christian Fundamentalists Trampled Science, Policy, and Democracy in George W. Bush's White House. New York: The New Press.

Kaufman, Stephen, 2005 Bush Seeks End to Agricultural Subsidies by 2010: State's Newman says move will greatly benefit African farmers. http://www.america.gov/st/washfile-english/2005/July/20050707091621avillusa8.381289e-02.html.

Kehler, Johanna, 2001 Women and Poverty: The South African Experience. Journal of International Women's Studies 3(1).

Klare, Carl, 2004 Blood and Oil: The Dangers and Consequences of America's Growing Dependency on Imported Petroleum. New York: Metropolitan Books.

Klein, Naomi, 2007 The Shock Doctrine: The Rise of Disaster Capitalism. New York: Metropolitan Books/Henry Holt.

Klein, Rick, 2006 Missionaries in Training. *In* The Boston Globe, October 11, 2006.

Kligman, Gail, 1995 Political Demography: The Banning of Abortion in Ceausescu's Romania. *In* Conceiving the New World Order: The Global Politics of Reproduction. R. Rapp and F. Ginsberg, eds. Berkeley: University of California Press.

Klugman, Barbara, 2000 Responding to Demands; Initiating Policy: the Story of the South African Women's Health Project. *In* African Women's Health. M. Turshen, ed., pp. 93–216. Trenton, NJ: Africa World Press.

Kranish, Michael, 2006 Part 2: Church Meets State: Exporting Faith – Religious Right Wields Clout: Secular Groups Losing Funding Amid Pressure. *In* The Boston Globe, October 9, 2006.

Kreniske, John, 1997 AIDS in the Dominican Republic: Anthropological Reflections on the Social Nature of Disease. *In* AIDS in Africa and the Caribbean. George Bond, John Kreniske, Ida Susser, and Joan Vincent, eds. Boulder, CO: Westview Press.

Krige, Eileen Jensen, and John L. Comaroff, 1981 Essays on African Marriage in Southern Africa. Cape Town: Juta.

Krugman, Paul, 2007 The Conscience of a Liberal. New York: W.W. Norton.

Kuhn, Louise, 2007 High Uptake of Exclusive Breastfeeding and Reduced Post-Natal HIV Transmission: Prospective Results from the Zambia Exclusive Breastfeeding Study. Fourth International AIDS Society Conference on HIV Pathogenesis, Treatment, and Prevention, Sydney, Australia.

Kwong, Peter, 2009 What's Wrong with America's Immigration Debate? *In* Rethinking America. I. Susser and J. Maskovsky, eds. Boulder, CO: Paradigm Press.

LaFraniere, Sharon, 2004 After Apartheid: Heated Words About Rape and Race. New York Times, November 24.

Lamptey, Peter, 2002 Reducing Heterosexual Transmission of HIV in Poor Countries. British Medical Journal 324:207–211.

Lancet, 2004 Is it churlish to criticise Bush over his spending on AIDS? The Lancet 364(9431):303–304.

Latif, Ahmed S., 1990 Clinical Aspects of AIDS in Africa. *In* Action on AIDS in Southern Africa: Proceedings of Maputo Conference on Health in Transition in Southern Africa, April 9–16. Zena Stein and Anthony Zwi, eds. Published by Committee for Health in Southern Africa (CHISA), HIV Center for Clinical and Behavioral Studies, New York State Psychiatric Institute, and Colombia University in the City of New York.

Lawinski, Terese, 2007 Welfare Restructuring in the Suburban US. The Graduate Center, CUNY.

Le Blanc, Marie-Nathalie, Deidre Meintel, and Victor Piche, 1991 The African Sexual System: Comment on Caldwell et al. Population and Development Review 17(3):497–505.

Leach, Belinda, 1998 Citizenship and the Politics of Exclusion in a "Post-Fordist" Industrial City. Critique of Anthropology 6(18):181–204.

Leacock, Eleanor, 1972 Introduction. *In* Origin of the Family, Private Property, and the State. F. Engels, ed. New York: Pathfinder Press.

Leacock, Eleanor Burke, 1981 Myths of Male Dominance: Collected Articles on Women Cross-culturally. New York: Monthly Review Press.

Leacock, Eleanor, and Mona Etienne, 1980 Women and Colonization. New York: Bergin & Garvey.

Leclerc-Madlala, Suzanne, 2001 Virginity Testing: Managing Sexuality in a Maturing HIV/AIDS Epidemic. Medical Anthropology Quarterly 15(4):533.

Lee, Richard B., 1984 The !Kung San: Men, Women and Work in a Foraging Society. Holt Rinehart and Winston.

Lee, Richard B., 2003 The Dobe Ju/'hoansi. Belmont, CA: Wadsworth Thompson Learning.

Lee, Richard B., 2007 The Ju/'Hoansi at the Crossroads: Continuity and Change in the Time of AIDS. *In* Globalization and Change in Fifteen Cultures: Born in One World, Living in Another. George Spindler and Janice E. Stockard, eds. pp. 144–170. Thomson Wadsworth.

Lee, Richard B., and Susan Hurlich, 1982 From Foragers to Fighters: South Africa's Militarization of the Namibian San Press. *In* Politics and History in Band Societies. Eleanor Leacock and Richard B. Lee, eds, pp. 327–346. Cambridge, UK: Cambridge University Press.

Lee, Richard, and Ida Susser, 2006 Confounding Conventional Wisdom: The Ju/'hoansi and HIV/AIDS. *In* Updating the San: Image and Reality of an African People in the Twenty-First Century. R. Hitchcock, Kazunobu Ikeya, Megan Biesele, and Richard Lee, eds, pp. 45–61. Osaka, Japan: National Museum of Ethnology.

Lewis, Herbert S., 1998 The Misrepresentation of Anthropology and Its Consequences. American Anthropologist 100(3):716–731.

Lewis, Stephen, 2006 Remarks. Closing Session of the Toronto 2006 XVI International AIDS Society Conference.

Liebenberg, Sandra, 1995 The Constitution of South Africa from a Gender Perspective. Cape Town: Community Law Centre at the University of the Western Cape in Association with David Philip.

Lieberman, Donna, 2008 Letter to the Editor, New York Times, January 22.

Lindenbaum, Shirley, 1997 AIDS: Body, Mind and History. *In* AIDS in Africa and the Caribbean. George C. Bond, John Kreniske, Ida Susser, and Jean Vincent, eds, pp. 191–195. Boulder, CO: Westview Press.

Linger, Daniel T., 1993 The Hegemony of Discontent. American Ethnologist 20(1):3–24.

Lloyd, John, 2000 Globalization's Arch Enemy: Since The Roquefort Hit The Fan, Farmers In Southern France Have Been Fighting Mad. *In* Toronto Globe & Mail, July 5:A13.

Lodge, Tom, 1981 The Destruction of Sophiatown. The Journal of Modern African Studies 19(1):107–132.

Long, Lynellyn, and E. M. Ankrah, 1996 Women's Experiences With HIV/AIDS: An International Perspective. New York: Columbia University Press.

Lurie, M. N., B. G. Williams, K. Zuma, et al., 2003 The Impact of Migration on HIV-1 Transmission in South Africa: A Study of Migrant and Nonmigrant Men and their Partners. Sexually Transmitted Diseases 30(2):149–156.

Lutz, Catherine, 2001 Homefront: A Military City and the American Twentieth Century. Boston: Beacon Press.

Lyons, Maryinez, 1997 The Point of View: Perspectives on AIDS in Uganda. *In* AIDS in Africa and the Caribbean. Goerge Bond, John Kreniske, Ida Susser, and Joan Vincent, eds, pp. 131–149. Boulder, CO: Westview.

Magubane, Bernard, 1971 A Critical Look at Indices Used in the Study of Social Change in Colonial Africa. Current Anthropology 12(4/5):419–445.

Magubane, Bernard, 1979 The Political Economy of Race and Class in South Africa. New York: Monthly Review Press.

Mail & Guardian, 2000 AIDS Exists. Let's Fight It Together. Mail & Guardian. February 11.

Maletsky, Christof, 1999 "Where Are Our Condoms?" Asks Women's Group, The Namibian, August 19.

Mamdani, Mahmood, 1996 Citizen and Subject: Contemporary Africa and the Legacy of Late Colonialism. Princeton, NJ: Princeton University Press.

Mamdani, Mahmood, 2004 Good Muslim, Bad Muslim: America, the Cold War, and the Roots of Terror. New York: Pantheon.

Mane, P., and Peter Aggleton, 2000 Cross-National Perspectives on Gender and Power. *In* Framing the Sexual Subject. Richard. G. Parker, Regina Maria Barbosa, and Peter Aggleton, eds, pp. 104–116. Berkeley: University of California Press.

Manjate, Rosa Marlene, Rachel Chapman, and Julie Cliff, 2000 Lovers, Hookers, and Wives: Unbraiding the Social Contradictions of Urban Mozambican Women's Sexual and Economic Lives. *In* African Women's Health. M. Turshen, ed., pp. 49–69. Trenton, NJ: Africa World Press, Inc.

Mann, Jonathan, and Daniel Tarantola, eds, 1996 AIDS and the World II: Global Dimensions, Social Roots, and Responses. New York: Oxford University Press.

Mantell, Joanne E., Shari Dworkin, Theresa Exner, Susie Hoffman, Jenni Smit, and Ida Susser, 2006 The Promises and Limitations of Female-Initiated Methods of HIV/STI Protection. Social Science & Medicine 63(8):1998–2009.

Mantell, Joanne, Zena Stein, and Ida Susser, 2008 Women in the Time of AIDS: Barriers, Bargains and Benefits. AIDS Education and Prevention: An Interdisciplinary Journal 20(2):91–106.

Marable, Manning, 2005 The New Black Renaissance: The Souls Anthology of Critical African-American Studies. Boulder, CO: Paradigm Publishers.

Marais, Hein, 2000 To the Edge: AIDS Review 2000. Pretoria: University of Pretoria.

Marais, Hein, 2001 South Africa Limits to Change: The Political Economy of Transformation. London and New York: Zed Books.

Marcus, George E., 1995 Ethnography of the World System: The Emergence of Multi-Sited Ethnography. Annual Review of Anthropology 24:95–117.

Marie Stopes International, 2002 Marie Stopes International Condemns "Absurd" Bush Decision to Refuse Funds to United Nations Population Fund. Marie Stopes International.

Marks, Shula, 1990 Natal, the Zulu Family and the Ideology of Segregation. Journal of Southern African Studies 16(3):431–451.

Marks, Shula, 1993 The Nursing Profession and the Making of Apartheid. In Apartheid's Genesis. Philip Bonner and Peter Delius, eds. Braamfontein, South Africa: Ravan Press.

Marks, Shula, 2002 An Epidemic Waiting to Happen? The Spread of HIV/AIDS in South Africa in Social and Historical Perspective. African Studies 61(1).

Marks, Shula, and Stanley Trapido, 1979 Lord Milner and the South African State. History Workshop Journal 8(1):50–81.

Marks, Shula, and Stanley Trapido, eds, 1987 The Politics of Race, Class and Nationalism in Twentieth-Century South Africa. Cape Town, London, and New York: Longman.

Marshall, John, 1980 N!ai: The Story of a !Kung Woman. In Odyssey Films. John Marshall, ed. United States: PBS.

Marshall, Lorna, 1976 !Kung of Nyae Nyae. Cambridge, MA: Harvard University Press.

Marte, Carola, 1996 Gynecological Disease Among Women with HIV/AIDS. In AIDS and the World II: Global Dimensions, Social Roots and Responses. Jonathan Mann and Daniel Tarantola, eds, pp. 230–233. New York: Oxford University Press.

Martin, Emily, 1996 The Society of Flows and the Flows of Culture: Reading Castells in the Light of Cultural Accounts of the Body, Health and Complex Systems. Critique of Anthropology 16(1):49–56.

Mascia-Lees, Frances, Patricia Sharpe, and Colleen Ballerino Cohen, 1989 The Postmodernist Turn in Anthropology: Cautions from a Feminist Perspective. Signs 15(1):7–33.

May, Julian, Chris Rogerson, and Ann Vaughan, 2000 Livelihoods and Assets. In Poverty and Inequality in South Africa: Meeting the Challenge. Julian May, ed. Cape Town: David Philips Publishers.

Mayer, Philip, 1971 Townsmen or Tribesmen: Conservatism and the Process of Urbanization in a South African City. Cape Town and London: Oxford University Press.

Mbali, Mandisa, 2003 HIV/AIDS Policy-Making in Post-Apartheid South Africa. In State of the Nation: South Africa 2003–2004. J. Daniel, A. Habib, and R. Southall, eds. Cape Town: HSRC Press.

Mbali, Mandisa, 2008 Gender, Sexuality and Global Linkages in the History of South African AIDS Activism, 1982–1994. In The Politics of AIDS: Globalization and Civil Society. Maj-Lis Follér and Håkan Thörn, eds. Palgrave Macmillan.

Mbeki, Moeletsi, 2008 The Curse of South Africa. New Statesman, January 17. London.

Mbeki, Thabo, 2000 Opening Ceremony, XIII International AIDS Society Conference, Durban.

Mbeki, Thabo, 2001 "He Wakened to his Responsibilities." Inaugural Z. K. Matthews Memorial Lecture, University of Fort Hare.

McClintock, Anne, 1990 Maidens, Maps, and Mines: *King Solomon's Mines* and the Reinvention of Patriarchy in Colonial South Africa. *In* Women and Gender in Southern Africa to 1945. Cherryl Walker, ed. Cape Town/London: David Philip/James Currey.

McGovern, Theresa, 2007 Building Coalitions to Support Women's Health and Rights in the United States: South Carolina and Florida. Reproductive Health Matters 15(29):119–129.

McGovern, Theresa, et al., 1999 Assessing the Effects of Welfare Reform Policies on Reproductive and Infant Health. American Journal of Public Health 89(10):1514–21.

McGregor, Liz, 2007 Khabzela: The Life and Times of a South African. Johannesburg: Jacana Media.

MCHTSA, 1990 Maputo Conference on Health in Transition in Southern Africa (MCHTSA): Maputo Statement on HIV and AIDS in Southern Africa. *In* Action on AIDS in Southern Africa: Proceedings of Maputo Conference on Health in Transition in Southern Africa, April 9–16. Zena Stein and Anthony Zwi, eds. Published by Committee for Health in Southern Africa (CHISA), HIV Center for Clinical and Behavioral Studies, New York State Psychiatric Institute, and Colombia University in the City of New York.

McIntyre, Di, and Michael Thiede, 2007 Health Care Financing and Expenditure. South African Health Review, pp. 35–47. Durban: Health Systems Trust.

McNeil, Donald D. J. Jr., 2007 Redesigning a Condom so Women Will Use It. New York Times, November 13:F5.

Mikell, Gwendolyn, 1997 African Feminism: The Politics of Survival in Sub-Saharan Africa. Philadelphia: University of Pennsylvania Press.

Milligan, Susan, 2006 The Muslim World: Exporting Faith. *In* The Boston Globe, October 10, 2006.

Mintz, Sidney Wilfred, 1960 Worker in the Cane: A Puerto Rican Life History. New Haven, CT: Yale University Press.

Mintz, Sidney Wilfred, 1974 Worker in the Cane: A Puerto Rican Life History. W.W. Norton & Company.

Mitchell, Don, 2003 The Right to the City: Social Justice and the Fight for Public Space. London: Guilford Press.

Mitchell, J. Clyde, 1956 The Kalela Dance: Aspects of Social Relationships Among Urban Africans in Northern Rhodesia. Manchester: Published on behalf of the Rhodes-Livingstone Institute by Manchester University Press.

Mollenkompf, John H., and Manuel Castells, eds, 1991 Dual City: Restructuring New York. New York: Russell Sage Foundation.

Morgen, Sandra, 1988 "It's the Whole Power of the City Against Us!": The Development of Political Consciousness in a Women's Health Care Coalition. *In* Women and the Politics of Empowerment. A. Bookman and S. Morgen, eds, pp. 97–115. Philadelphia: Temple University Press.

Morgen, Sandra, 2002 Into Our Own Hands: The Women's Health Movement in the United States, 1969–1990. New Brunswick: Rutgers University Press.

Morrell, Robert, 2001 Changing Men in Southern Africa. London and New York: Zed Books.

Mothapo, Moloto, 2003 Congress of South African Trade Unions (COSATU) Condemns Minister's Statement on Anti-retroviral Drugs. Cape Town, South Africa: Congress of South African Trade Unions.

Motsei, Mmatshilo, 2007 The Kanga and the Kangaroo Court: Reflections on the Rape Trial of Jacob Zuma. Cape Town: Jacana Media.

Mphahlele, Es'kia, 1959 Down Second Avenue. London: Faber & Faber.

Mthathi, Sipho, 2006 A Women's Movement to End Oppression. *In* Equal Treatment: Women and HIV. Newsletter of the Treatment Action Campaign. Cape Town: June, pp. 2–3.

Muller, Johan, Nico Cloete, and Shireen Badat, eds, 2001 Challenges of Globalisation: South African Debates with Manuel Castells. Cape Town: Longman.

Mullings, Leith, 1995 Households Headed by Women: The Politics of Race, Class and Gender. *In* Conceiving the New World Order: The Global Politics of Reproduction. F. D. Ginsburg and R. Rapp, eds, pp. 122–139. Berkeley: University of California Press.

Mullings, Leith, 1997 On Our Own Terms: Race, Class, and Gender in the Lives of African American Women. New York: Routledge.

Mullings, Leith, 2003 After Drugs and the "War on Drugs": Reclaiming the Power to Make History in Harlem, New York. *In* Wounded Cities: Destruction and Reconstruction in a Globalized World. Jane Schneider and Ida Susser, eds. New York: Berg.

Mullings, Leith, 2005 Interrogating Racism: Toward an Antiracist Anthropology. Annual Review of Anthropology 34:667–693.

Murphy, Elaine M., M. E. Greene, A. Mihailovic, and P. Olupot-Olupot, 2006 Was the "ABC" Approach (Abstinence, Being Faithful, Using Condoms) Responsible for Uganda's Decline in HIV? PLoS Medicine 3(9):e379.

Murray, Christina, 1994 Gender and the New South African Legal Order. Cape Town: Juta & Co., Ltd.

Museveni, H. E. Yoweri Kaguta, 2004 Report on Political Commitment and Accountability. XIV International Conference on AIDS and Sexually Transmitted Diseases (STDs), Bangkok, Thailand, 2004.

MWACW, 2001 The Female Condom. Republic of Namibia: Ministry of Women's Affairs and Child Welfare.

Nalugwa, Sarah, 2003 Indigenous Approaches to the HIV/AIDS Scourge in Uganda. *In* Social Science Research Report Series, Vol. 30. Addis Ababa, Ethiopia: Organization for Social Science Research in Eastern and Southern Africa.

Nash, June C., 1980 Aztec Women: The Transition from Status to Class in Empire and Colony. *In* Women and Colonization: Anthropological Perspectives. M. Etienne and E. Leacock, eds. New York: Praeger.

Nash, June C., 1983 Women, Men, and the International Division of Labor. State University of New York Press.

Nash, June C., 1993 Crafts in the World Market: The Impact of Global Exchange on Middle American Artisans. Albany, NY: State University of New York Press.

Nash, June C., 2001 Mayan Visions: The Quest for Autonomy in an Age of Globalization. New York: Routledge.

Nash, June C., ed., 2005 Social Movements: An Anthropological Reader. Malden, MA: Blackwell.

National Council of Research on Women, 2004 MISSING: Information About Women's Lives, pp. 1–24. New York: National Council for Research on Women.

Nattrass, Nicoli, 2007 Mortal Combat: AIDS Denialism and the Struggle for Antiretrovirals in South Africa. Scottsville, South Africa: University of KwaZulu-Natal Press.

Nattrass, Nicoli, and Jeremy Seekings, 2001 "Two Nations"? Race and Economic Inequality in South Africa Today. Daedalus: Journal of the American Academy of Arts and Sciences 130(1):45–70.

New York Times, 2007 Firing an AIDS Fighter, Editorial, New York Times, August 14.

New York Times, 2008 Editorial: H.I.V. Rises Among Young Gay Men, New York Times January 14.

News Hour with Jim Lehrer, 2000 Focus On Thabo Mbeki. News Hour with Jim Lehrer, May 23. PBS.

NEWVERN, 2008 NEWVERN is the information system for the Central Contraceptive Procurement (CCP) team of the GH/PRH/CSL Division of USAID. Arlington, VA: John Snow, Inc. http://portalprd1.jsi.com/portal/page/portal/DELIVERWEBSITE. Accessed 18 January 2008.

Ngubane, Harriet, 1977 Body and Mind in Zulu Medicine: An Ethnography of Health and Disease in Nyuswa-Zulu Thought and Practice. Academic Press.

Nhlapo, Thandabantu, 2000 The African Customary Law of Marriage and the Rights Conundrum. In Beyond Rights Talk and Culture Talk: Comparative Essays on the Politics of Rights and Culture. M. Mamdani, ed., pp. 136–148. New York: St. Martin's Press.

Niehaus, Isak, 2003 "Now everyone is doing it": Towards a Social History of Rape in the South African Lowveld. Presented at the Sex and Secrecy Conference. University of Witwatersrand: International Association for the Study of Sexuality, Culture and Society.

NUM, 1990 National Union of Mineworkers (NUM): Statement on AIDS. In Action on AIDS in Southern Africa: Proceedings of Maputo Conference on Health in Transition in Southern Africa, April 9–16. Zena Stein and Anthony Zwi, eds. Published by Committee for Health in Southern Africa (CHISA), HIV Center for Clinical and Behavioral Studies, New York State Psychiatric Institute, and Colombia University in the City of New York.

Nussbaum, Martha Craven, 1999 Professor of Parody. In The New Republic, December 22.

Nyamnjoh, Francis, 2002 "A Child is One Person's Only in the Womb": Domestication, Agency and Subjectivity in the Cameroonian Grassfields. In Postcolonial Subjectivities in Africa. Richard P. Werbner, ed., pp. x, 244. London and New York: Zed Books.

O'Connor, James, 1973 The Fiscal Crisis of the State. New York: St. Martin's Press.

Office of the Public Protector, 1996 Report No. 1 (Special Report ) Investigation of the Play Sarafina! South Africa: Office of the Public Protector.

Oomman, Nandini, Michael Bernstein, and Steven Rosenzweig, 2007 Following the Funding for HIV/AIDS: A Comparative Analysis of the Funding Practices of PEPFAR, the Global Fund and the World Bank MAP in Mozambique, Uganda, and Zambia: HIV/AIDS Monitor and the Center for Global Development.

Oppenheimer, Gerald, 1988 In the Eye of the Storm: The Epidemiological Construction of AIDS. In AIDS: The Burdens of History. Elizabeth Fee and Daniel Fox, eds, pp. 267–300. Los Angeles: University of California Press.

Oppenheimer, Gerald, and Ronald Bayer, 2007 Shattered Dreams? An Oral History of the South African AIDS Epidemic. New York: Oxford University Press.

Padgug, Robert, and Gerald Oppenheimer, 1992 Riding the Tiger: AIDS and the Gay Community. In AIDS: the Making of a Chronic Disease. Elizabeth Fee and Daniel Fox, eds, pp. 245–278. Berkeley: University of California Press.

Padian, Nancy, et al., 2007 Diaphragm and Lubricant Gel for Prevention of HIV Acquisition in Southern African Women: A Randomised Controlled Trial. The Lancet 370(9583):251–261.

Padilla, Mark, 2007 Caribbean Pleasure Industry: Tourism, Sexuality, and AIDS in the Dominican Republic. Chicago: University of Chicago Press.

Park, Yoon Jung, Joanne Fedler, and Zubeda Dangor, eds, 2000 Reclaiming Women's Spaces: New Perspectives on Violence Against Women and Sheltering in South Africa. Johannesburg: Nisaa Institute for Women's Development.

Parker, Richard, 2001 Sexuality, Culture, and Power in HIV/AIDS Research. Annual Review of Anthropology 30(1):163–179.

Parker, Richard, 2003 The Brazilian Response to HIV/AIDS: Assessing its Transferability. Rio de Janeiro. Divulgacao, Special Issue 27:143–184.

Parker, Richard G., Regina Maria Barbosa, and Peter Aggleton, eds, 2000 Framing the Sexual Subject: The Politics of Gender, Sexuality, and Power. Berkeley: University of California Press.

PATH and UNFPA, 2006 Female Condom: A Powerful Tool for Protection. Seattle: Program for Appropriate Technology in Health.

Patton, Cindy, 1990 Inventing AIDS. New York: Routledge.

Peck, Jamie, 2001 Workfare States. New York: The Guilford Press.

Peck, Jamie A., and Adam Tickell, 2002 Neoliberalizing Space: The Free Economy and the Penal State. *In* Spaces of Neoliberalism: Urban Restructuring in North America and Western Europe. Neil Brenner and Nik Theodore, eds, Antipode Book Series. Oxford: Blackwell.

Periasamy, Kousaliya, 2008 Widowhood. Presented at XVII International AIDS Society Conference, Mexico City, August 3–8.

Petchesky, Rosalind Pollack, 2003 Global Prescriptions: Gendering Health and Human Rights. London: Zed Books.

Petryna, Adriana, 2002 Life Exposed: Biological Citizens After Chernobyl. Princeton, NJ: Princeton University Press.

Phleta, Godfrey, 2007 Gender Scripts and Social Interactions of Young People in Burgersfort. *In* Post-Sexuality Leadership Development Fellowship Report Series No. 1: Africa Regional Sexuality Resource Centre. Accessed at: www.arsrc.org/downloads/sldf/Godfery_Gender_Scripts_SLDFPFP05.pdf.

Physicians for Human Rights (PHR), 2007 Epidemic of Inequality: Women's Rights and HIV/AIDS in Botswana and Swaziland, p. 203. Cambridge, MA: Physicians for Human Rights.

Piot, Peter, 2001 A Gendered Epidemic: Women and the Risks and Burdens of HIV. Journal of the American Medical Women's Association 56:90–91.

Piven, Frances Fox, 2004 The War at Home: The Domestic Costs of Bush's Militarism. New York: The New Press.

Piven, Frances Fox, Joan Acker, Margaret Hallock, and Sandra Morgan, eds, 2002 Work, Welfare and Politics: Confronting Poverty in the Wake of Welfare Reform. Eugene: University of Oregon Press.

Platzky, Laurine, Cherryl Walker, and Surplus People Project (South Africa), 1985 The Surplus People: Forced Removals in South Africa. Johannesburg: Ravan Press.

Posel, Deborah, 2005 Sex, Death and the Fate of the Nation: Reflections on the Politicization of Sexuality in Post-Apartheid South Africa. Africa 75(2):125–153.

Potash, Betty, 1989 Gender Relations in Sub-Saharan Africa. *In* Gender and Anthropology: Critical Reviews for Research and Teaching. S. Morgen, ed., pp. 189–227. Washington, DC: American Anthropological Association.

Pred, Allan, 2000 Even in Sweden: Racisms, Racialized Spaces, and the Popular Geographical Imagination. Berkeley: University of California Press.

Preston-Whyte, Eleanor, and C. M. Rogerson, 1991 South Africa's Informal Economy. Cape Town: Oxford University Press.

Preston-Whyte, Eleanor, Christine Varga, Herman Oosthuizen, Rachel Roberts, and Frederick Blose, 2000 Survival Sex and HIV/AIDS in an African City. *In* Framing the Sexual Subject: The Politics of Gender, Sexuality, and Power. Richard B. Parker, Maria Regina, and Peter Aggleton, eds. Berkeley: University of California Press.

Ramphele, Mamphela, 1993 A Bed Called Home: Life in the Migrant Labour Hostels of Cape Town. Cape Town: David Philip.

Ramphele, Mamphela, 2001 Citizenship Challenges for South Africa's Young Democracy. Daedalus: Journal of the American Academy of Arts and Sciences 130(1):1–18.

Ramphele, Mamphela, 2008 Laying Ghosts to Rest: Dilemmas of the Transformation in South Africa. Cape Town: Tafelberg Publishers.

Ranger, Terence, 1997 The Invention of Tradition in Colonial Africa. *In* Perspectives on Africa: A Reader in Culture, History, and Representation. R. R. Grinker and C. B. Steiner, eds, pp. 597–612. Cambridge, MA: Blackwell.

Reid, Elizabeth, 1997 Placing Women at the Center of Analysis. *In* AIDS in Africa and the Caribbean. George Bond, John Kreniske, Ida Susser, and Joan Vincent, eds, pp. 159–164. Boulder, CO: Westview Press.

Reproductive Health Matters, 2006 Round Up: Research. Reproductive Health Matters 14(28).

Reynaga, Elena, and A. L. Crago, 2008 Plenary: Sex Work and Human Rights. Presented at XVII International AIDS Society Conference, Mexico City, August 5.

Richter, Linda, 2008 Plenary: No Small Issue: Children and Families, Universal Action Now. Presented at XVII International AIDS Society Conference, Mexico City, August 5.

Robbins, Joel, 2004 The Globalization of Pentecostal and Charismatic Christianity. Annual Review of Anthropology 33:117–143.

Roberts, Dorothy E., 1995 Irrationality and Sacrifice in the Welfare Reform Consensus. Virginia Law Review 81(8):2607–2624.

Roberts, Dorothy E., 2002 Shattered Bonds: The Color of Child Welfare. New York: Basic Books.

Robins, Steven, 2006 From "Rights" to "Ritual": AIDS Activism in South Africa. American Anthropologist 108(2):312–323.

Robotham, Don, 2009 Liberal Social Democracy, Neo-Liberalism and Neo-Conservatism: Some Genealogies. *In* Rethinking America. Ida Susser and Jeff Maskovsky, eds. Boulder, CO: Paradigm.

Rosenberg, Harriet, 1997 Complaint Discourse, Aging, and Caregiving among the !Kung San of Botswana. *In* The Cultural Context of Aging: Worldwide Perspectives. Jay Sokolofsky, ed. New York: Bergin & Garvey.

Rosenfield, Allan, 2002 MTCT-PLUS: Linking Efforts to Prevent Mother-to-Child HIV Transmission. Global Health in Times of Crisis, Washington, DC, 2002.

Rosenfield, A., L. Myer, and M. Merson, 2001 The HIV/AIDS Pandemic: The Case for Prevention. Henry J. Kaiser Family Foundation.

Ross, G., 2008 Women, AIDS, Fertility and Desire. Presented at XVII International AIDS Society Conference, Mexico City, August 3–8.

Rothstein, Frances, 2007 Globalization in Rural Mexico: Three Decades of Change. Austin: University of Texas Press.

Sabatier, Renee, 1989 AIDS and the Third World. Philadelphia: The Panos Institute, in association with The Norwegian Red Cross.

Sampson, Anthony, 1999 Mandela: The Authorized Biography. New York: Knopff.

Sanjek, Roger, 1987 Anthropological Work at a Gray Panther Health Clinic: Academic, Applied, and Advocacy Goals. *In* Cities of the United States: Studies in Urban Anthropology. Leith Mullings, ed., pp. 148–175. New York: Columbia University Press.

Santelli, John, et al., 2006 Abstinence and Abstinence-Only Education: A Review of US Policies and Programs. Journal of Adolescent Health 38(1):72–87.

Sapire, Hilary, 1989 African Political Mobilisation in Brakpan in the 1950s. African Studies Seminar Paper: University of the Witwatersrand, African Studies Institute.

Sassen, Saskia, 1990 The Mobility of Labor and Capital: A Study in International Investment and Labor Flow. London: Cambridge University Press.

Saul, John, 2001 Cry for the Beloved Country: The Post-Apartheid Denouement. Monthly Review, Vol. 52. New York: Monthly Review Press.

Saul, John, 2005 The Next Liberation Struggle: Capitalism, Socialism, and Democracy in Southern Africa. New York: Monthly Review Press.

Sawalha, Aseel, 2003 "Healing the Wounds of the War": Placing the War-Displaced in Postwar Beirut. *In* Wounded Cities: Destruction and Reconstruction in a Globalized World. Jane Schneider and Ida Susser, eds. New York: Berg.

Schneider, Helen, 2002 On the Fault-Line: The Politics of AIDS Policy in Contemporary South Africa. African Studies 61(1):145–167.

Schneider, Helen, and Joan Stein, 2002 Implementing AIDS Policy in Post-Apartheid South Africa. Social Science and Medicine 52(5):723–731.

Schneider, Jane, 1991 Rumpelstiltskin's Bargain: Folklore and the Merchant Capitalist Intensification of Linen Manufacture in Early Modern Europe. *In* Cloth and the Human Experience. A. Weiner and J. Schneider, eds, pp. 179–207. Washington, DC: Smithsonian Institution Press.

Schneider, Jane, and Peter Schneider, 2003. Wounded Palermo. *In* Wounded Cities: Destruction and Reconstruction in a Globalized World. Jane Schneider and Ida Susser, eds. New York: Berg.

Schneider, Jane, and Ida Susser, eds, 2003 Wounded Cities: Destruction and Reconstruction in a Globalized World. New York: Berg.

Schoepf, Brooke G., 1988 Women, AIDS and Economic Crisis in Central Africa. Canadian Journal of African Studies 22(3):625–644.

Schoepf, Brooke G., 2001 International AIDS Research in Anthropology: Taking a Critical Perspective on the Crisis. Annual Review of Anthropology 30(1):335–361.

Schoepf, Brooke G., 2004 AIDS in Africa: Structure, Agency, and Risk in HIV and AIDS in Africa. *In* Beyond Epidemiology. E. Kalipeni, S. Craddock, J. Oppong, and J. Ghosh, eds, pp. 121–133. Malden, MA: Blackwell.

Schreiner, Olive, 1924 The Story of an African Farm. Boston: Little, Brown, and Company.

Scorgie, Fiona, 2002 Virginity Testing and the Politics of Sexual Responsibility: Implications for AIDS Intervention. African Studies 61(1):55–75.

Seekings, Jeremy, 2007 Poverty and Inequality after Apartheid. *In* After Apartheid Conference. New Haven: Yale University.

Seekings, Jeremy, and Nicoli Nattrass, 2005 Class, Race, and Inequality in South Africa. New Haven: Yale University Press.

Sennett, Richard, 1970 Families Against the City: Middle Class Homes of Industrial Chicago, 1872–1890. Cambridge, MA: Harvard University Press.

Seripe, Bafana, 1990 AIDS: Issues and Policies for Workers and Unions. *In* Action on AIDS in Southern Africa: Proceedings of Maputo Conference on Health in Transition in Southern Africa, April 9–16. Zena Stein and Anthony Zwi, eds. Published by Committee for Health in Southern Africa (CHISA), HIV Center for Clinical and Behavioral Studies, New York State Psychiatric Institute, and Colombia University in the City of New York.

Serwadda, David, 1990 Care of Those Infected: Theory and Practices. The Magnitude of the Problems in Africa. *In* Action on AIDS in Southern Africa: Proceedings of Maputo Conference on Health in Transition in Southern Africa, April 9–16. Zena Stein and Anthony Zwi, eds. Published by Committee for Health in Southern Africa (CHISA), HIV Center for Clinical and Behavioral Studies, New York State Psychiatric Institute, and Colombia University in the City of New York.

Shilts, Randy, 1987 And the Band Played On: Politics, People, and the AIDS Epidemic. New York: St. Martin's Press.

Shostak, Marjorie, 1983 Nisa: The Life and Words of a !Kung Woman. New York: Vintage Books.

Sidley, Pat, Nicola Jenvey, and Nirode Bramdaw, 2000 Mbeki Still Skeptical About Gravity of AIDS Epidemic: President Tells Conference Extreme Poverty Is the World's Biggest Killer, Business Day, July 10. Johannesburg, South Africa.

Silverblatt, Irene, 1980 "The Universe has turned inside out . . . There is no justice for us here": Andean Women Under Spanish Rule. *In* Women and Colonization: Anthropological Perspectives. M. Etienne and E. Leacock, eds, pp. 149–185. New York: Praeger.

Silverblatt, Irene, 1987 Moon, Sun, and Witches. Princeton, NJ: Princeton University Press.

Sinding, Steven W., 2005 Does "CNN" (Condoms, Needles and Negotiation) Work Better Than "ABC" (Abstinence, Being Faithful and Condom Use) in Attacking the AIDS Epidemic? International Family Planning Perspectives 31(1):38–40.

Singer, Merrill, 1995 Beyond the Ivory Tower: Critical Praxis in Medical Anthropology. Medical Anthropology Quarterly 9(1):80–106.

Small, Janet, and Ludia Kompe, 1992 Organising Rural Women: The Experience of TRAC. Agenda 12:9–19.

Smith, Charlene, 2001 Proud of Me: Speaking Out Against Sexual Violence and HIV. Johannesburg: Penguin Books.

Smith, Gavin A., 1999 Confronting the Present: Towards a Politically Engaged Anthropology. Oxford and New York: Berg.

Smith, Neil, 2003 American Empire: Roosevelt's Geographer and the Prelude to Globalization. Berkeley: University of California Press.

Society of Women Against AIDS in Africa, 2006 In Our Own Hands; SWAA-Ghana Champions the Female Condom, vol. 17. New York: The Population Council.

Solway, Jacqueline, ed., 2006 The Politics of Egalitarianism: Theory and Practice. New York: Berghahn Books.

South African Institute of Race Relations, and Frans Cronje, 2007 South African Survey. www.sairr.org.za.

Sparks, Allister, 2003 Beyond the Miracle: Inside the New South Africa. Cape Town: Jonathan Ball Publishers.

Specter, Michael, 2007 The Denialists. The New Yorker, March 12, pp. 32–38. New York.

Stein, Sylvester, 1958 Second Class Taxi. London: Faber & Faber.

Stein, Sylvester, 1999 Who Killed Mr. Drum? Bellville: Mayibuye Books.

Stein, Zena, 1990 HIV Prevention: The Need for Methods Women Can Use. American Journal of Public Health 80(4):460–462.

Stein, Zena, 1994 Methods Women Can Use. Presented at X International AIDS Society Conference, Yokohama, August 7–12.

Stein, Zena, and Robin Flam, 1986 Behavior, Infection and Immune Response: An Epidemiological Approach. *In* The Social Dimensions of AIDS: Method and Theory. D. Feldman and T. Johnson, eds, pp. 61–76. Westport, CT: Praeger Publishers.

Stein, Zena, Ida Susser, and Marion Stevens, 2008 The Diaphragm Lives! Mujeres Adelante: Daily Newsletter on women's rights and HIV – Mexico City, August 8, ATHENAnetwork/AIDS Legal Network, p. 5.

Stein, Zena, and Mervyn W. Susser, 2008 Cautionary Notes on Interpreting History from Additional First-Hand Observers of Poverty, Health and Policy in South Africa. Journal of Public Health Policy 29(2):187–191.

Steinberg, Jonny, 2008 Three-Letter Plague. Cape Town: Jonathan Ball Publishers.

Stevens, Marion, 2008 Prevention, Treatment and Reproductive Choices. Presented at XVII International AIDS Society Conference, Mexico City, August 3–8.

Stiglitz, Joseph, 2002 Globalization and its Discontents. New York: W.W. Norton.

Stockman, Farah, Michael Kranish, Peter S. Canellos, and Kevin Baron, 2006 Part 1: Changing the Rules: Exporting Faith – Bush Brings Faith to Foreign Aid: As Funding Rises, Christian Groups Deliver Help – With a Message. The Boston Globe, October 8.

Stoler, Ann Laura, 2002 Carnal Knowledge and Imperial Power: Race and the Intimate in Colonial Rule. Berkeley: University of California Press.

Susser, Ida, 1982 Norman Street: Poverty and Politics in an Urban Neighborhood. New York: Oxford University Press.

Susser, Ida, 1985 Union Carbide and the Community Surrounding it: The Case of a Community in Puerto Rico. International Journal of Health Services 15(4):561–583.

Susser, Ida, 1991 Women as Political Actors in Rural Puerto Rico: Continuity and Change. *In* Anthropology and the Global Factory. F. Rothstein and M. Blim, eds, pp. 206–219. New York: Bergin & Garvey.

Susser, Ida, 1993 Creating Family Forms: The Exclusion of Men and Teenage Boys From Families in the New York City Shelter System, 1987–91. Critique of Anthropology 13(3):267–285.

Susser, Ida, 1996a The Shaping of Conflict in the Space of Flows. Critique of Anthropology 16(1):39–47.

Susser, Ida, 1996b The Construction of Poverty and Homelessness in US Cities. Annual Review of Anthropology 25(1):411–435.

Susser, Ida, 1997 The Flexible Woman: Regendering Labor in the Informational Society. Critique of Anthropology 17(2):389–402.

Susser, Ida, 2001 Sexual Negotiations in Relation to Political Mobilization: The Prevention of HIV in Comparative Context. The Journal of AIDS and Behavior 5(2):163–172.

Susser, Ida, 2002 Health Rights for Women in the Age of AIDS. International Journal of Epidemiology 31(1):45–48.

Susser, Ida, 2004 From the Cosmopolitan to the Personal: Women's Mobilization With Respect to HIV/AIDS. *In* Social Movements. J. Nash, ed. Oxford and Malden, MA: Blackwell Publishing.

Susser, Ida, 2006 The Other Side of Development: HIV/AIDS Among Men and Women in Ju/'hoansi Villages. *In* The Politics of Egalitarianism: Theory and Practice. J. Solway, ed. New York: Berghahn Books.

Susser, Ida, 2007 Women and AIDS in the Second Millennium. Women Studies Quarterly 35(1,2):336–344.

Susser, Ida, and M. Alfredo Gonzalez, 1992 Sex, Drugs and Videotape: The Prevention of HIV in a Homeless Men's Shelter. Medical Anthropology 14:307–322.

Susser, Ida, and John Kreniske, 1997 Community Organizing Around HIV Prevention in Rural Puerto Rico. *In* AIDS in Africa and the Caribbean. George Bond, John Kreniske, Ida Susser, and Joan Vincent eds, pp. 51–65. Boulder, CO: Westview Press.

Susser, Ida, and Jane Schneider, 2003 Introduction. *In* Wounded Cities: Destruction and Reconstruction in a Globalized World. Jane Schneider and Ida Susser, eds. New York: Berg.

Susser, Ida, and Zena Stein, 2000 Culture, Sexuality and Women's Agency in the Prevention of HIV/AIDS in Southern Africa. American Journal of Public Health 90(7):1042–1049.

Susser, Mervyn, 1983 Apartheid and the Causes of Death: Disentangling Ideology and Laws from Class and Race. American Journal of Public Health 73(5):4.

Susser, Ida, Zena Stein, and Marion Stevens, 2008 Child survival and reproduction in social context. Mujeres Adelante: Daily Newsletter on women's rights and HIV – Mexico City, August 7, ATHENA Network/AIDS Legal Network, pp. 1–2.

Swartz, Marc J., Victor Turner, and Arthur Tuden, 1966 Political Anthropology. Chicago: Aldine Publishing Co.

Sylvain, Renee, 2001 Bushmen, Boers and Baasskap: Patriarchy and Paternalism on Afrikaner Farms in the Omaheke Region, Namibia. Journal of South African Studies 27(4):717–737.

TAC, 2006a Equal Treatment: Women and HIV, Newsletter of the Treatment Action Campaign. Cape Town: June.

TAC, 2006b Equal Treatment: Making HIV Prevention Work, Newsletter of the Treatment Action Campaign. Cape Town: November.

Thomas, Elizabeth, 2003 HIV/AIDS: Implications for Local Governance, Housing and Delivery of Services. *In* Emerging Johannesburg: Perspectives on the Postapartheid City. R. Tomlinson, R. Beauregard, L. Bremner, and X. Mangeu, eds, pp. 185–197. New York: Routledge.

Thompson, Edward Palmer, 1963 The Making of the English Working Class. New York: Pantheon.

TRC, 2003 Truth and Reconciliation Commission of South Africa (TRC) Report, Vol. 6. Truth and Reconciliation Commission.

Treichler, Paula A., 1992 AIDS and HIV Infection in the Third World: A First World Chronicle. *In* AIDS: The Making of a Chronic Disease. Elizabeth Fee and Daniel Fox, eds, pp. 377–413. Berkeley, CA: University of California.

Treichler, Paula A., 1999 How to Have a Theory in an Epidemic: Cultural Chronicles of AIDS. Chapel Hill: Duke University Press.

Trenholm, Christopher, Barbara Devaney, et al., 2007 Impacts of Four Title V, Section 510 Abstinence Education Programs (Final Report). Washington, DC: Department of Health and Human Services, US Government.

Trust for Community Outreach and Education, 2004 Land is Life: The History of Land Dispossession in South Africa. Cape Town: Trust for Community Outreach and Education (TCOE).

Turner, Victor W., 1957 Schism and Continuity in an African Society: A Study of Ndembu Village Life. Manchester: Manchester University Press, published on behalf of the Rhodes-Livingstone Institute, Northern Rhodesia.

Tyler, Patrick E., 1996 China Concedes Blood Serum Contained AIDS Virus, New York Times, October 25:A3.

UNAIDS, 2000 AIDS in Africa: Country by Country, p. 243. Geneva: UNAIDS.

UNAIDS, 2004 Report on the Global AIDS Epidemic. Geneva: Joint United Nations Programme on HIV/AIDS.

UNAIDS, 2006a 2006 Report on the Global AIDS Epidemic: Executive Summary. UNAIDS.

UNAIDS, 2006b AIDS Epidemic Update: December 2006. p. 90. UNAIDS.

UNAIDS, 2007 AIDS Epidemic Update: Latest Developments in the Global AIDS Epidemic. UNAIDS.

UNFPA, 2007 Donor Support for Contraceptives and Condoms for STI/HIV/AIDS Prevention. New York: United Nations Fund for Population Activities.

UNICEF, 2000 The State of the World's Children 2001: Early Childhood. C. Bellamy, ed., p. 119. New York: United Nations International Children's Emergency Fund.

UNIFEM, UNAIDS, and UNFPA, 2004 Women and HIV/AIDS: Confronting the Crisis. New York: United Nations.

Uys, Jamie, 1981 The Gods Must Be Crazy. Botswana: CAT Films.

Vail, Leroy, 1989 The Creation of Tribalism in Southern Africa. Berkeley: University of California Press.

van Onselen, Charles, 1996 The Seed Is Mine: The Life of Kas Maine, a South African Sharecropper 1894–1985. New York: Hill and Wang.

Van Velsen, Jaap, 1967 The Extended-Case Method and Situational Analysis. *In* The Craft of Social Anthropology. A. L. Epstein, ed., pp. 129–152. London: Tavistock.

Vaughan, Megan, 1990 Syphilis, AIDS, and the Representation of Sexuality: The Historical Legacy. *In* Action on AIDS in Southern Africa: Proceedings of Maputo Conference on Health in Transition in Southern Africa, April 9–16. Zena Stein and Anthony Zwi, eds. Published by Committee for Health in Southern Africa (CHISA), HIV Center for Clinical and Behavioral Studies, New York State Psychiatric Institute, and Colombia University in the City of New York.

Vestergaard, Mads, 2001 Who's Got the Map? The Negotiation of Afrikaner Identities in Post-Apartheid South Africa. Daedalus 130(1):19–44.

Vincent, Joan, 1978 Political Anthropology: Manipulative Strategies. Annual Review of Anthropology 7(1):175–194.

Vincent, Joan, 1986 System and Process, 1974–1985. Annual Review of Anthropology 15(1):99–119.

Walker, Cherryl, 1990a Gender and the Development of the Migrant Labor System c.1850–1930. *In* Women and Gender in Southern Africa to 1945. Cherryl Walker, ed. Cape Town/London: David Philip/James Currey.

Walker, Cherryl, ed., 1990b Women and Gender in Southern Africa to 1945. Cape Town/London: David Philip/James Currey.

Walker, Cherryl, 1991 Women and Resistance in South Africa. Claremont: David Philip Publishers.

Walker, Cherryl, 2002 Agrarian Change, Gender and Land Reform: A South African Case Study. *In* Social Policy and Development. Paper No. 10: UNRISD.

Walker, Kathy le Mons, 2006 "Gangster capitalism" and peasant protest in China: The Last Twenty Years. Journal of Peasant Studies 33(1):1–33.

Wallerstein, Immanuel Maurice, 1974 The Modern World-System, Vol. 1: Capitalist Agriculture and the Origins of the European World-Economy in the Sixteenth Century. New York: Academic Press.

Wallerstein, Immanuel Maurice, 1975 World Inequality: Origins and Perspectives on the World System. Montreal: Black Rose Books.

Watson, William, 1971 Tribal Cohesion in a Money Economy: A Study of the Mambwe People of Zambia. Manchester: Manchester University Press, published on behalf of the Institute for African Studies, University of Zambia.

Wellbourn, Alice, 2006 Sex, Life and the Female Condom: Some Views of HIV Positive Women. Reproductive Health Matters 14(28):32–41.

Welz, Tanya, Victoria Hosegood, et al., 2007 Continued Very High Prevalence of HIV Infection in Rural KwaZulu-Natal, South Africa: A Population-based Longitudinal Study. AIDS 21(11):1467–1472.

Werbner, Richard P. 1984 The Manchester School in South-Central Africa. Annual Review of Anthropology 13:157–185.

White House, 2005 Fact Sheet: United States and G8 Renew Strong Commitment to Africa.

Wiesen Cook, Blanche, 1999 Eleanor Roosevelt: Volume 2, The Defining Years, 1933–1938. Viking Penguin.

Wilson, Ara, 2004 The Intimate Economies of Bangkok: Tomboys, Tycoons, and Avon Ladies in the Global City. Berkeley: University of California Press.

Wilson, Godfrey, 1941 An Essay on the Economics of Detribalization in Northern Rhodesia. Livingstone, Northern Rhodesia: Rhodes-Livingstone Institute.

WIMSA, 2004 Report on Activities April 2003 to March 2004. Windhoek, Namibia: Working Group of Indigenous Minorities in Southern Africa.

Wines, Michael, 2007 Zuma is Chosen Leader to Lead Party. New York Times, December 19.

Wodak, A., S. Sarkar, and F. Mesquita, 2004 The Globalization of Drug Injecting. Addiction 99(7):799–801.

Wodak, Alex, 2006 Controlling HIV Among Injecting Drug Users: Current Status of Harm Reduction. Presented at the XVI International AIDS Society Conference, Toronto, Canada.

Wolpe, Harold, 1980 Capitalism and Cheap Labour Power in South Africa: From Segregation to Apartheid. *In* Articulation of Modes of Production: Essays from Economy and Society. Harold Wolpe, ed. London: Routledge Kegan and Paul.

Xinhua News Service, 2006 Moon Beads as FP Device in Uganda. *In* Xinhua News Service. Hong Kong.

Yanou, Mike A., 2006 Access to Land in Post-Apartheid South Africa: Implications for the South African Black Woman. CODESRIA Bulletin 1&2:61–62.

# Index

Note: "n." after a page reference indicates the number of a note on that page.